BLACKSTONE'S GUIDE TO

Consumer Sales and Associated Guarantees

BLACKSTONE'S GUIDE TO

Consumer Sales and Associated Guarantees

Professor Robert Bradgate

and

Doctor Christian Twigg-Flesner

OXFORD
UNIVERSITY PRESS

OXFORD
UNIVERSITY PRESS

Great Clarendon Street, Oxford OX2 6DP

Oxford University Press is a department of the University of Oxford.
It furthers the University's objective of excellence in research, scholarship,
and education by publishing worldwide in

Oxford New York

Auckland Bangkok Buenos Aires Cape Town Chennai
Dar es Salaam Delhi Hong Kong Istanbul Karachi Kolkata
Kuala Lumpur Madrid Melbourne Mexico City Mumbai Nairobi
São Paulo Shanghai Taipei Tokyo Toronto

with an associated company in Berlin

Oxford is a registered trade mark of Oxford University Press
in the UK and in certain other countries

Published in the United States
by Oxford University Press Inc., New York

British Library Cataloguing in Publication Data
Data available

Library of Congress Cataloging in Publication Data
Data available

ISBN 0–19–925594–6

1 3 5 7 9 10 8 6 4 2

Typeset by Hope Services (Abingdon) Ltd
Printed in Great Britain by
Antony Rowe Ltd, Chippenham

Contents—Summary

Contents

Contents

Preface

The focus of this book is on the Sale and Supply of Goods to Consumers Regulations 2002, which came into force on 31 March this year. The Regulations implement the 1999 EC Directive 1999/44/EC on certain aspects of the Sale of Consumer Goods and Associated Guarantees, and make a number of significant amendments to the Sale of Goods Act 1979 and related legislation concerned with the sale and supply of goods, including the Supply of Goods and Services Act 1982, Supply of Goods (Implied Terms) Act 1973 and Unfair Contract Terms Act 1977.

The new regulations will have a significant practical impact. In particular, they introduce a range of new remedies for consumer buyers of goods where the goods do not conform to the contract of sale. Cases concerned with consumer sales are rarely reported but the sale of goods is an everyday activity and the law of sale, and especially the rules on the seller's duties in relation to the goods and the buyer's remedies for breach thereof, provides the backdrop against which those sales take place and disputes arising therefrom are resolved. It is an area of law with which most consumers are at least vaguely familiar. The new regulations significantly shift the balance of power between seller and buyer in resolving such disputes. Ostensibly the regulations introduce new rights for consumers to insist on the repair or replacement of defective goods in respect of defects which manifest themselves up to six years from the date of sale. In practice, however, it remains to be seen whether the new regime will actually strengthen or weaken the position of consumers dealing with sellers over defective goods.

It may be, however, that the new regulations will have a symbolic significance even greater than their practical significance. The law of sale is the central area of the private law of consumer protection and, arguably, of the law of contract. The new regulations may therefore be seen as a key step in the 'Europeanisation' of domestic contract law. The regulations also mark a key step in the modernisation of the law of sale and the emergence of a separate consumer sales law. Until recently it was possible to say that the law of sale of goods as contained in the Sale of Goods Act 1979 was largely unchanged from that of the Victorian era, the 1979 Act largely reproducing the provisions of Sir Mackenzie Chalmers' 1893 Sale of Goods Act. The last decade, however, has seen a series of amendments to key areas of the Act, including those concerned with seller's duties and buyer's remedies (Sale and Supply of Goods Act 1994), the *nemo dat* rule (Sale of Goods (Amendment) Act 1994) and the passing of property (Sale of Goods (Amendment) Act 1995). Now the new regulations continue that process of modernisation, making further amendments to the area covered by the Sale and

Supply of Goods Act 1994 before the reforms made by that Act are fully bedded in. The Sale of Goods Act 1979 is now some way removed from its Victorian roots. The 1893 Act was a unitary Act applicable to all sales with more or less no regard to the status of buyer or seller. Modern reforms have tended to distinguish consumer from business sales, recognising the differing needs of the two groups. The reforms introduced by the 2002 regulations, applicable only to sales to consumers, continue and accelerate that process. The time is fast approaching when the law applicable to consumer sales will have diverged so far from that applicable to business sales that it will cease to be meaningful to speak of the law of sale in general terms. We wonder whether a separate consumer sales code is not now needed.

The DTI chose to implement the 1999 Directive by regulations amending the 1979 Act. We have both expressed doubts elsewhere about the desirability of this approach. Integration of the new law with the old has resulted in a legislative framework of great complexity in an area where we think that simplicity is greatly to be desired. The difficulty of integrating the two is indicated by the delay in production of implementing legislation. The 1999 Directive should have been implemented by 1 January 2002. In fact the UK implementing regulations were not published until December 2002 and as noted did not come into force until 31 March 2003, some fifteen months after the deadline for implementation. Moreover the regulations are, in our opinion, a far from perfect text. We have remarked above on the complexity of the amended legislation. We also doubt whether in a number of areas the regulations have fully and properly implemented the Directive. We doubt that the 2002 regulations are the last word on this subject.

This is an area in which both of us have long-standing interests and on which both of us have written previously. In producing this *Guide* we have, of course, drawn on our own previous discussions of some aspects of the law. This is, however, an entirely new text (and further indications of the complexity created by the new legislation are provided by the time it has taken to produce this guide notwithstanding our previous work on the subject, and the length of the resulting text). The guide has three main strands. The UK legislation can only be understood in the context of both the Directive and the pre-existing domestic law. It will, moreover, of course, have to be interpreted so far as possible consistently with the Directive. We have therefore throughout the book first examined the provisions of the Directive itself and then considered the corresponding rules of domestic law in order to set the implementing regulations in their context, before considering the regulations themselves. We have sought at the same time to take account of relevant recent developments in domestic sales law in important cases such as *Clegg v Anderson* and *Jewson v Kelly*. We have sought not only to provide a guide to the provisions of the new legislation but also to comment on it as appropriate, identifying deficiencies in the law where we perceive them to exist. We hope that the resulting text will provide useful to all those with an interest in consumer sales law, whether as academics or practitioners, and although the *Guide* has been written primarily for a legal audience we hope that it will also prove useful to retailers and consumers and their advisers.

We would like to thank our respective partners, families and friends for their patience and support during the preparation of this *Guide*, and the publishers for their support and assistance in converting the typescript into the finished book.

Robert Bradgate
Christian Twigg-Flesner
Sheffield, August 2003

Table of Cases

European Union

Table of Legislation

Statutory Instruments

Table of International Instruments

List of Abbreviations

AC/Appeal Cases, House of Lords Law Reports [1891]–
All ER/All England Law Reports
All ER Comm/All England Law Reports Commercial
App Cas/Appeal Cases (1875–90)
B & S/Best, William Mawdesley, and Smith, George James Philip, Queen's Bench
   Law Reports
BLR/Building Law Reports
C & P/Car & P
CA/Court of Appeal
Ch/Chancery Division Law Reports [1891]–
CISG/Vienna Convention on Contracts for the International Sale of Goods
CLC/Commercial Law Cases
CLR/Common Law Reports
CLY/Current Law Year Book
C(RTP)A/The Contracts (Rights of Third Parties) Act 1999
CT(RS)O/The Consumer Transactions (Restrictions on Statements) Order 1976
   (SI 1976/1813)
DGFT/Directorate General of Fair Trading
DTI/Department of Trade and Industry
ECA/European Communities Act 1972
ECR/European Court Reports
EWCA Civ/Court of Appeal, Civil Division (England & Wales)
FSR/Fleet Street Reports
HL/House of Lords
KB/King's Bench Reports
Lloyd's Rep/ Lloyd's Law Reports
LQR/Law Quarterly Review
LT/Law Times
NZCGA/New Zealand's Consumer Guarantees Act 1993
OFT/Office of Fair Trading
PC/Privy Council
QB/Queen's Bench Reports
SGSA 1982/Supply of Goods and Services Act 1982
SLT (Sh Ct)/Scots Law Times Sheriff Court Reports
SoG(IT)A 1973/Supply of Goods (Implied Terms) Act 1973
SoGA 1979/ Sale of Goods Act 1979

SSGCR 2002/Sale and Supply of Goods to Consumers Regulations 2002 (SI 2002/3045)
UCTA 1977/Unfair Contract Terms Act 1977
UKHL/House of Lords (United Kingdom)
UTCCR/Unfair Terms in Consumer Contracts Regulations 1999
WLR/Weekly Law Reports

1

INTRODUCTION

1.1 INTRODUCTION

In recent years the European Union has had a steadily growing influence on the contract and commercial laws of its Member States, driven by the perceived need to remove legal obstacles to cross-border trade, and in July 2001 the European Commission published a consultation document canvassing opinions on whether divergences between national contract laws hinder the proper operation of the Internal Market. Against this background it has become common for lawyers to talk of the development of a European Contract Law. From a UK perspective 31 March 2003 may in due course come to be seen as a particularly significant date in that development process. On that date the Sale and Supply of Goods to Consumers Regulations 2002 (SI 2002/3045, hereafter 'SSGCR') came into force, implementing EC Directive 1999/44/EC 'on certain aspects of the sale of consumer goods and associated guarantees' of 25 May 1999 (OJ L 171/12).

As their name suggests, the Regulations make amendments to the law governing the sale and supply of goods to consumers, amending the Sale of Goods Act 1979 and analogous legislation applying to other forms of supply contract (Supply of Goods (Implied Terms) Act 1973 (hire-purchase), Supply of Goods and Services Act, 1982 (other forms of supply including barter, exchange and supply of work and materials)). The Regulations amend the law relating to the buyer's rights to receive goods of the right description and quality and fit for the buyer's purpose, and therefore impact upon one of the core, and most familiar, areas of private law.

The Regulations may appear to be less radical than other EC-inspired reforms, such as the Commercial Agents (Council Directive) Regulations 1993 and Unfair Terms in Consumer Contracts Regulations 1994 and 1999, which introduced a good faith test into English contract law. The Regulations do make some important changes to UK law, including introducing for the first time legally enforceable rights for the buyer of unsatisfactory or defective goods to have them repaired or replaced and putting beyond doubt the enforceability of manufacturers' and retailers' product guarantees. However, the centrality and familiarity of the law of sale lends the SSGCR a significance over and above their immediate impact. Moreover, as will be demonstrated in later chapters, although some aspects of the Regulations and the underlying Directive may seem reassuringly familiar, others are derived from a legal culture very different to the common law heritage of the Sale of Goods Act. Europeanisation of this area of law thus has a symbolic significance over and above the practical impact of the new regulations.

1.1.1 The emergence of the Directive

The process which led to the Regulations began more than a quarter of a century ago. Recognising the practical and symbolic importance of the law of sale a resolution of the Council of Ministers of 1975 recognised the need for EC action 'with a view to improving guarantee arrangements and after sales service' (Resolution of 14.4.75 OJ C92 25.4.75 p 1). With the completion of the Single Market the need to remove perceived barriers to cross-border trade assumed greater significance whilst at the same time the EU began to place increased emphasis on consumer protection, seeing consumers as the potential drivers of economic development within the Single Market and seeking therefore to encourage them to participate in cross-border transactions. The European Commission's original proposal for a Directive on Unfair Terms in Consumer Contracts in 1990 therefore contained proposals for harmonisation of what were termed 'consumer guarantees' (OJ C243 28.9.1990 p 20) but ultimately those proposals were abandoned and the Commission was asked to produce separate proposals on the topic. The result was a Green Paper, published in 1993, which explored the need for harmonisation and contained substantive proposals for action.

The Green Paper contained a survey of the laws of Member States. That survey in fact identified a large degree of similarity between their laws on the topic, and recognised, too, the centrality of the subject in domestic systems. Thus the European Parliament noted:

in the field of the legal guarantee there are regulations in all Member States, based on many years, sometimes centuries of tradition and administration of justice. (Resolution A3-0284/94 of 6 May 1994)

Nevertheless the Green Paper concluded that the differences between different national laws on this subject could hinder the completion of the Single Market, creating difficulties for businesses trading in more than one Member State and deterring consumers from engaging in cross-border transactions. Harmonisation would remove that impediment whilst at the same time 'strengthening the confidence of consumers in the large market and encouraging them to take an active part in its functioning', thus encouraging the 'free movement of consumers'. At the time of the Green Paper's publication it was possible to doubt the scope of the potential for consumer involvement in cross-border trade. The subsequent development of the Internet and growth of e-commerce means that since 1993 that potential has grown considerably.

1.1.1.1 *The Green Paper proposals*
The Green Paper considered two options for EC action, involving reform of either (a) relevant conflict of laws rules to ensure that consumers would always be able to rely on their own domestic law in any cross-border transaction or (b) the relevant substantive law, and expressed a clear preference for the latter. Allowing consumers to carry their domestic law with them would do nothing to ease the problems of businesses; indeed it would exacerbate them.

The Green Paper then identified two areas for harmonisation, terming them respectively the 'legal guarantee' and the 'commercial guarantee'. The term 'legal guarantee' (later abandoned) referred to the seller's obligation to supply goods of the right description, quality and so on derived from the general law, whereas 'commercial guarantee' referred to the typical manufacturer's or supplier's 'guarantee' or 'warranty' given at the manufacturer's or supplier's option.

In relation to the so-called 'legal guarantee' the Green Paper proposed harmonisation on the basis of a general requirement that on the sale of new consumer durables, the goods should conform to the consumer's 'legitimate expectations'. No definition of 'consumer durables' was proposed, although it seems that it was anticipated that it would be limited to 'durable' goods of a type ordinarily supplied for private use or consumption, the emphasis of the proposals apparently being on items such as motor cars and household electrical goods. In the event of the goods failing to satisfy this broad requirement, the remedies available to the consumer would be repair or replacement of the goods, partial reimbursement of the price or repudiation of the contract and restitution of the price in full. However, the choice of remedy would be largely controlled by the supplier. Most significantly of all it was proposed that the 'guarantee' should run with the goods and be enforceable by a donee or second-hand purchaser of the goods, and that the manufacturer of the goods as well as the supplier should be liable on the 'guarantee'.

1.1.1.2 *'Commercial guarantees'*
The Green Paper noted that there were considerable differences in the scope of 'commercial guarantees' from Member State to Member State. Moreover, the degree of clarity of the terms and conditions of guarantees varied considerably. It

was therefore proposed to introduce disclosure-based rules which would make it mandatory to provide specified details about a guarantee in clear language. In addition, in order to reduce the variation on guarantees given on goods sold throughout the EC, the introduction of a 'Euroguarantee' was suggested. This would be a standardised guarantee, possibly introduced together with a 'quality label'. Finally, in view of the jurisprudence of the European Court of Justice in the field of competition law, it was proposed that members of selective and exclusive distribution networks should be legally required to honour guarantees given by the manufacturer.

1.1.2 From the Green Paper to Directive 99/44/EC

1.1.2.1 *The first draft Directive*
Following publication of the Green Paper the European Commission undertook extensive consultation and in 1995 published a draft directive (COM (95) 520) containing considerably modified and, in many ways, less radical proposals. The restriction of the proposals to new, durable goods was abandoned in favour of a general requirement applicable to all goods, not that they should conform to the consumer's 'legitimate expectations' but that they should 'conform with the contract', with a presumption of 'conformity', expressed in language based on the wording of the United Nations 1980 Vienna Convention on Contracts for the International Sale of Goods, if the goods complied with description and sample, were of the right quality and were fit for their normal purpose and for any particular purpose notified by the consumer to the seller. Perhaps most disappointing, the bold proposals in the Green Paper for a 'guarantee' enforceable beyond the immediate contractual nexus were abandoned. Neither the idea of extending liability to manufacturers nor that of a 'guarantee' running with the goods so as to be enforceable by third party transferees was pursued in the draft Directive.

Most of the proposals made in respect of 'commercial' guarantees had also been abandoned by the time of the first draft. The relevant provision (Article 5) would have ensured that guarantees be legally binding and provide protection at least equivalent to the level of protection provided by the statutory rights of consumers. In addition, a basic disclosure requirement was proposed. In the end, even the requirement that a guarantee should at least meet the statutory standard was abandoned, as well.

The main thrust of the final text which emerged in 1999 closely followed the pattern of the draft Directive, and was therefore a much less radical text than the Green Paper had envisaged.

1.1.2.2 *Progress of the draft Directive*
The Directive followed the co-decision procedure under the former Article 189b (replaced by the Treaty of Amsterdam with a streamlined procedure now con-

tained in Article 251). The hallmark of this procedure is the involvement of the European Parliament in deciding on the final text of any measure adopted under it. In respect of what became Directive 99/44/EC, the Parliament took its role very seriously. During the first and second reading, it proposed a number of significant amendments, many of which were rejected by the Commission or the Council of Ministers (representatives of all the Member States). However, a measure cannot become law under the Article 251 procedure unless both Parliament and the Council of Ministers agree. The Parliament rejected the final draft proposed by the Council of Ministers, and in order to save the Directive, it was necessary to invoke the conciliation procedure. This procedure requires a committee comprising members of the Council and the Parliament to negotiate a compromise text. Although there were few contentious issues, the fact that the Directive involved several last-minute compromises may explain some of the problems apparent in the text as adopted.

1.1.2.3 *Legal basis*
Directive 99/44/EC was adopted on the basis of former Article 100a (now Article 95), which provides the legal basis for the adoption of measures which have as their object the establishment and functioning of the internal market. Although the Directive seeks to raise the level of consumer protection throughout the EC, the dominant objective is to remove barriers to the operation of the internal market caused by the different rules on the sale of consumer goods that existed between the legal systems of the Member States. The consumer protection aspect of the Directive is therefore only secondary. The EC has competence to adopt consumer protection measures independent of any internal market objective in Article 153. However, its scope in that regard is limited to supporting the activities of the Member States. The main purpose of Article 153 is to emphasise that any measures adopted under Article 95 should contribute to the achievement of a high level of consumer protection.

Recitals 2–5 therefore explain that the objective of the Directive is to reduce the competitive distortions caused by the different national rules on the sale of consumer goods and that this will encourage consumers to take part in the opportunities provided by the internal market.

This is not the place to speculate whether the Directive will contribute to greater consumer participation in the internal market. It is nevertheless necessary to be aware of the objectives pursued by the Directive when analysing its provisions.

1.1.2.4 *After-sales service*
We should also note here that whilst most of the proposals in the Green Paper were diluted and modified, one disappeared altogether: regulation of after-sales services. The Green Paper proposed as a minimum the introduction of a requirement that sellers should inform consumers about after-sales services and spare parts availability. An unpublished provisional draft Directive drawn up by a

Committee of Experts included substantive provisions on after-sales services, imposing both an obligation to make available after-sales services and regulating their provision. At one stage, the European Parliament considered the inclusion of a provision that would have required a seller to inform a consumer if no after-sales services was provided (see annexes to the First Report on the Directive A4-0029/98), but this was not pursued. The view was taken that after-sales service was a matter better dealt with at national level, i.e., the subsidiarity principle was invoked (see COM (95) 520 final, p 7). Interestingly, the recent *Green Paper on EU Consumer Protection* (COM (2001) 531 final, Follow-up Communication (COM (2002) 289 final)) once again raised the prospect of EC action in the field of after-sales services, but no concrete proposals have yet been published.

1.2 THE RELEVANCE OF THE VIENNA CONVENTION ON THE INTERNATIONAL SALE OF GOODS 1980

As noted above, the Directive draws on the 1980 United Nations Vienna Convention on the International Sale of Goods (CISG) in a number of ways, both the test of conformity and the remedial scheme being adopted, more or less, from the CISG.

The CISG is an international convention designed to harmonise the law governing international sales. It is much wider in scope than the Directive, although not as wide as the domestic Sale of Goods Act 1979, covering the formation of the sale contract and the rights and duties of the parties thereto, and remedies for their breach. It was the result of twelve years' work by UNCITRAL, the United Nations Commission on International Trade Law, and itself drew on the earlier Hague Uniform Laws on Formation of Contracts and International Sale of Goods. Since its completion in 1980 the CISG has been ratified by 62 states including all the Member States of the EU other than the UK, Ireland and Portugal. Although different views have been expressed on the desirability of the UK ratifying the CISG, it is in many ways a superior instrument to the domestic SoGA, being specifically designed to deal with international commercial transactions. The main doubts about its suitability relate to its application to typical large-scale international commercial transactions, especially on CIF terms, such as those in the commodities trades. In its *Communication on European Contract Law* of July 2001 the European Commission floated the idea that the EU itself might adopt the CISG as a means of harmonising the law governing commercial sales within the EU.

However, whatever the merits or otherwise of the CISG one must ask whether it was entirely appropriate to adopt it as a model for a consumer protection measure. The CISG is intended to harmonise the law relating to international *commercial* transactions, and consumer transactions are expressly excluded from its ambit (Article 2(a) CISG). The concept of 'conformity' with the contract is a broad, flexible one but, as English law recognised in 1994, consumers have needs and expectations of goods which differ from those of commercial buyers. Notwithstanding the similarity of the two texts, therefore, any temptation to draw on decisions on the CISG—and there is now an extensive body of case law on the CISG in many jurisdictions—in interpreting the Directive, and especially the conformity requirement should be resisted. The two instruments have different objectives. The CISG is intended to balance the interests of commercial sellers and buyers, who are assumed to be of equal bargaining power. The Directive, on the other hand, is a consumer protection measure and must to some degree be intended to favour the buyer.

There are in fact several subtle but significant differences between the two texts, and in fact the CISG is in some respects superior to the Directive, not least because it recognises as aspects of conformity, and therefore of the seller's legal obligation, a number of factors not covered by the Directive. Thus the CISG also requires the seller to deliver goods of the quantity required by the contract (Article 35(1) CISG) and which are free from third party claims (Articles 41 and 42 CISG). This includes third party intellectual property claims. Given the commercial importance in the modern age of intellectual products such as computer software and audio and video recordings, and the prevalence of piracy, this is an issue of growing importance to consumers as well as to business.

1.3 IMPLEMENTATION OF THE DIRECTIVE INTO DOMESTIC LAW

The Directive required Member States to implement it not later than 1 January 2002 (Article 11(1)). Responsibility for implementing the Directive in the UK rested with the Department of Trade and Industry (DTI). Broadly speaking the UK government could have opted to implement the Directive in any of several ways: by primary legislation, or by regulations made under the European Communities Act 1972, in either case by amending existing legislation or by adopting the Directive, or requirements based on it, as free-standing legislative requirements alongside the existing law. This last was, of course, the approach adopted when implementing the Directive on Unfair Terms in Consumer Contracts (1993/13/EEC), an approach which has been widely criticised for creating a regime which is complex and confusing. In fact implementation was considerably delayed, a first consultation document not appearing until January 2001. A second consultation document, which included draft implementing regulations, was only published in February 2002, a month after the deadline for implementation had expired. Final regulations were published in early December 2002 (Sale and Supply of Goods to Consumers Regulations 2002, 'SSGCR 2002'), and came into force on 31 March 2003, some fifteen months after the deadline specified in the Directive. It will be of little comfort to the UK government that several other Member States had not implemented the Directive by the deadline, because in early 2003, the European Commission included the UK in a list of eight Member States who would be subject to infringement proceedings for having failed to implement the Directive on time (see press release IP/03/3, 6 January 2003).

Following notification of the SSGCR 2002 to the Commission, proceedings in respect of the UK (as well as three other Member States) have been discontinued for the time being (press release IP/03/1009, 14 July 2003). However, although the UK government has adopted legislation to implement the Directive, it will be seen in this *Guide* that there are several shortcomings in the SSGCR 2002 which may yet result in a decision that the UK has not correctly implemented the Directive.

1.3.1 First Consultation (2001)—Broad Proposals

In the first consultation, the DTI presented its broad policy proposals for implementing the Directive and raised a number of specific issues for consideration. It is not necessary to review all of these here, and a reader who wishes to find out more is referred to the consultation document itself, which may be obtained via the DTI's web site (http://www.dti.gov.uk). Importantly the DTI indicated its intention to maintain existing levels of consumer protection where the existing law provided a higher level of protection than does the Directive. This policy has significant implications, especially for the remedial regime, where it has involved maintaining the short-term absolute right to reject goods for breach of condition derived from the SoGA 1979 alongside the new remedial regime derived from the Directive. Although it was not explicitly stated, the consultation also made it clear that the DTI's preferred approach would be to implement the Directive by amending the existing legislation.

In some respects, the first consultation made more concrete proposals, such as amendments to section 12 UCTA on the definition of 'consumer' (see chapter 2), and not to do anything by way of implementation of Article 4 on the right of recourse given to a seller (see chapter 9). However, most of the questions in the consultation invited general comments on issues which clearly troubled the DTI.

The difficulty with most of the points raised in this first consultation was that the DTI was rather vague in its intentions, and seemed somewhat confused about several fundamental aspects both of the Directive and existing domestic law. It may therefore not be that surprising that it took almost a year to publish draft implementing legislation, which was included in the second consultation document.

1.3.2 Second consultation (2002)—draft regulations

A second consultation appeared in February 2002. It contained more concrete proposals and also included the text of draft implementing regulations. The complexity of these draft regulations was a cause of some concern. This served to underline concerns expressed by some consultees after the first consultation that it would be very difficult indeed to retain a simple statutory framework whilst introducing major new and conceptually different rules. To take one example, the draft regulations would have produced three different definitions of 'consumer', and potentially two different definitions of 'seller'.

Key policy decisions had, however, been taken. Amendments to the implied terms would be made in all measures, i.e., the Sale of Goods Act 1979, the Supply of Goods and Services Act 1982 and the Supply of Goods (Implied Terms) Act 1973. On the other hand, the new remedies would be restricted to those contracts in which property in goods is transferred, i.e., under the Sale of Goods Act 1979 and Part I of the Supply of Goods and Services Act 1982. However, a number of policy questions remained unresolved. It was still necessary to decide whether to extend the six-month presumption of non-conformity (see chapter 3) to the pre-existing remedies, or limit it to the new remedies. Moreover, there was also still uncertainty as to whether to restrict the new remedies to a period of two years after delivery or to make them available for the full domestic limitation period of six years from the date of delivery.

In the wake of this second consultation exercise, the DTI accepted the proposals put forward by a number of consultees that it was desirable to amend the rules on the passing of risk and on delivery of goods to a carrier in the Sale of Goods Act 1979 to make these more consumer-friendly. A 'mini' consultation after the main second consultation invited comments, and changes were made to sections 20 and 32 by the SSGCR 2002 (see further, chapter 3).

1.3.3 SSGCR 2002

1.3.3.1 *Scope*
Implementing regulations were finally published in December 2002. The final text was considerably simpler than the earlier drafts. Most of their provisions amend existing primary legislation and the SSGCR contain only two operative provisions—a section on definitions (see chapter 2) and one on guarantees (see chapter 7). Surprisingly, the DTI had decided not to proceed with a number of its earlier proposals, such as amendments to SoGA section 14(2) and to limit the existing section 14(3) to non-consumer transactions. In fact, changes to the implied terms were minimal. As anticipated, the main changes related to the introduction of the new remedial regime from the Directive. The pre-existing domestic law remedies of damages and rejection of goods/repudiation of contract were retained, with new remedies derived from the Directive added alongside by inserting new parts

into the SoGA and SGSA, with a provision for linking old and new remedies (see chapter 4). No change was made to the remedial schemes applicable to contracts of hire or hire-purchase. The DTI had also taken on board many of the criticisms made of the draftsmanship of the draft regulations, and the SSGCR are a comparatively plain text. However, many difficulties remain, and these will be considered throughout this *Guide*.

1.3.3.2 *A note on the constitutionality of the Regulations*

The SSGCR were adopted on the basis of section 2(2) of the European Communities Act 1972, as amended ('ECA'), which provides for the implementation of Community obligations. Crucially, this may be done by statutory instrument and does not require primary legislation, even where this results in amendment to or the replacement of existing national legislation, including Acts of Parliament. The fact that amendments were made by the SSGCR to a number of established Acts of Parliament is therefore not problematic in itself. However, section 2(2) only applies to amendments necessary to implement Community obligations, not to unrelated amendments or additions to existing legislation which go considerably beyond what is required in order to comply with the requirements of a particular measure.

We will see in this *Guide* that the SSGCR introduce several changes which go further than necessary to implement Directive 99/44/EC. Many of these are not going to be problematic as far as the ECA is concerned. The Directive deals with the sale of consumer goods and permits rules which provide for a higher degree of consumer protection, and to the extent that the SSGCR introduce such rules in the context of the *sale* of consumer goods, there is no problem. However, some changes are made to legislation dealing with other transactions, such as hire and hire-purchase (changes to the implied terms) and contracts other than sale involving the transfer of property (barter). Such transactions fall outside the scope of the Directive, confirmed by the Council of Ministers expressly rejecting a proposal by the European Parliament to include contracts of barter within the scope of the Directive (see COM (1998) 217 final). There can therefore have been no Community obligation on the UK to amend the legislation in these fields. Consequently, it may not have been constitutional to introduce these changes through Regulations adopted under section 2(2) ECA.

We raise this point as a matter of caution, rather than because of any disagreement with the DTI's general policy of treating similar transactions in the same way. In our view, and disregarding the point just made, it would have been preferable to extend the remedial regime in the same way as the implied terms. However, there is concern over the legality of some of the changes made by the SSGCR which may need to be addressed by the DTI as a matter of urgency.

1.4 CRITERIA FOR EVALUATING THE REGULATIONS

A final point to be addressed in this introductory chapter is to set out the criteria that are used in evaluating the SSGCR 2002 in the chapters that follow. There are two broad perspectives. The first can be described as the 'internal' perspective, and considers whether the new legislation works as such. In other words, the coherence and clarity of the new rules are examined, with a particular focus on the objective of promoting consumer protection. The second perspective is the 'external' one, and examines whether the Regulations comply with the requirements of EC Law and provide at least the level of protection required by the Directive.

Common to both perspectives is the need to provide a suitable level of consumer protection. The Directive establishes a minimum level of protection which must be provided by the substantive rules. We must however also bear in mind the DTI's stated policy of not reducing pre-existing levels of protection provided by domestic law.

1.4.1 The internal perspective: coherence and consumer protection

1.4.1.1 *Coherence*
An important consideration in analysing any piece of legislation is whether it is internally coherent, i.e., whether it makes sense within itself and contains no obvious gaps or contradictions. Legislation becomes very difficult to apply if important terms are not defined. Moreover, it is vital that different parts of any particular measure work together and that where there are overlaps, it is clear how the different parts relate to one another. Thus, the legislation needs to be clear and comprehensible, and, in so far as this is possible, should treat like transactions alike.

We have identified above the possible ways in which the Directive might have been implemented. We have argued elsewhere (see Twigg-Flesner and Bradgate, 2000) that rather than amending relevant primary legislation it would have been simpler, in order to comply with the implementation deadline set in the Directive, to adopt free-standing regulations based on the text of the Directive, with an immediate reference to the Law Commission to consider a new, integrated, regime for consumer sales (as is happening in the field of unfair contract terms: see Law Commission Consultation 166, 2002). The DTI did not share this view and pressed ahead with its plan to implement by amendment rather than through free-standing regulations. The subsequent chapters will demonstrate that, although at a technical level, it has been possible to insert relevant sections in to the Sale of Goods Act 1979 and related measures, the legislation is anything but coherent.

1.4.1.2 *The position of consumers*
A further consideration is that the law should grant consumers effective and practical rights and remedies. It is estimated that consumers annually encounter

around 10 million problems with goods they have bought (OFT, 2000). Not all of these will give rise to a recognised legal cause of action. However, in those cases where a legal claim is made, formal legal proceedings are rarely instituted, and even fewer cases proceed to judgment. In her extensive study, Professor Genn (1999) found that only 3% of all potential legal claims by consumers came to court, and less than 1% were actually dealt with in a hearing. (Genn's study focused on 'justiciable events', i.e., matters which gave rise to specific legal claims, rather than subjective dissatisfaction.) Instead, around two-thirds of consumers sought a remedy by contacting the seller or manufacturer directly to complain. A similar picture was presented by research by the Office of Fair Trading (OFT, 2000) and the Department of Trade and Industry (DTI, 2001a). The DTI discovered that 87% of consumers who had reason to complain did so directly to the supplier of faulty goods.

Genn further discovered that only about one-half of those consumers who complained directly and informally managed to get a satisfactory solution to their complaint. Forty per cent were unsuccessful and did not press the matter any further. Only a small percentage persevered, e.g. by contacting a Citizens' Advice Bureau or a Trading Standards Department.

It is therefore clear that most consumers try to deal with problems in respect of faulty goods informally by contacting the seller, or manufacturer, directly. A significant proportion of consumers who do so are unable to negotiate a satisfactory outcome and are therefore left without a remedy. Further improvements to access to the justice system would probably not encourage many more consumers to use the courts. A primary reason may be the initial cost involved in commencing legal action. This often bears little relation to the value of the claim itself. In fact, those cases which come to court have tended to involve expensive consumer goods (a recent example being *Clegg v Anderson* [2003] EWCA Civ 320, [2003] 1 All ER (Comm) 721, which involved a yacht worth £250,000). In any event, consumers are aware of dispute resolution procedures and sources of advice, but utilisation remains low (DTI, 2001b). This suggests that consumers focus on resolving disputes directly and informally.

The law must be accessible to consumers to enable them to rely on it, if necessary, when pressing their case with a supplier or manufacturer. It is therefore important that consumers are able to point to clearly defined rights in the relevant legislation. This entails two things. First, consumers need to be aware of these rights. At present it seems that consumers' knowledge of their rights is 'generally patchy' (DTI, 2001a, p 13). At a practical level, it is therefore necessary to increase consumers' knowledge of their rights. (A related point is that sellers and manufacturers are often genuinely equally unaware of their obligations, which increases the difficulties faced by consumers.) Second, consumers need to be able to understand their statutory rights, which must be sufficiently clear to enable consumers to identify their rights against a supplier of faulty goods. However, clear rules are often rigid rules, and the need for clarity needs to be balanced against the need to retain sufficient flexibility in the system to deal with the wide range of problems that may arise in consumer sales transactions (see Law Commission, 1987, paragraph 4.4).

In evaluating the implementation of the Consumer Guarantees Directive, we will consider how accessible the legislation is as a result of the implementation and whether consumers can identify their entitlements with relative ease by looking at the legislation itself, bearing in mind that in the case of the Sale of Goods Act the relevant legislation is effectively a late Victorian commercial statute onto which modern consumer-protection measures and now EC consumer-protection measures have been grafted. Without pre-empting the detailed analysis in subsequent chapters, it can be stated at the outset that in the opinion of the present writers, the legislation rates poorly by this measure.

1.4.2 The external perspective: EC law requirements

It is important to remember that the SSGCR are intended to implement a European directive. Consequently, several aspects of European Community law are relevant both in evaluating the changes made to existing law and in applying these. Although it is beyond the scope of this book to give a detailed account of the relevant law, a summary of the main principles will be provided in this section (see further Steiner, J., and Woods, L., *Textbook on EC Law*, 8th edition, 2003, chapter 12).

1.4.2.1 *Minimum harmonisation*
The Guarantees Directive is described as a minimum harmonisation measure. Article 8(2) of the Directive states that:

Member States may adopt or maintain in force more stringent provisions, compatible with the Treaty in the field covered by this Directive, to ensure a higher level of consumer protection.

This provision therefore permits Member States to deviate from the Directive and to introduce, or to maintain, provisions which would provide a higher standard of consumer protection—a process sometimes referred to, somewhat pejoratively, as 'gold plating'. The Directive is not intended to provide a complete set of rules on consumer sales law, but to provide a basic level of consumer protection applicable throughout the Member States. Member States are free to adopt a higher standard of protection, provided that this is not incompatible with the EC Treaty, in particular Article 28 EC on the free movement of goods. Minimum harmonisation has been common in EC consumer protection measures, and most measures fall within this category. However, DG Sanco, the Commission's Directorate-General responsible for competition, has recently proposed to move away from minimum harmonisation measures (see Consumer Policy Strategy 2002–2006). This is not of immediate concern, although future revisions to the Directive could result in the repeal of Article 8(2).

1.4.2.2. *Implementation of a harmonising measure*

By virtue of Article 249 EC, directives are only binding as to the result to be achieved, and Member States are, in principle, free to decide how to implement a particular directive. Where a directive deals with an issue on which there is no previous domestic measure, it may be simplest to copy the provisions of the directive, but where there is existing legislation, a Member State may prefer to review such legislation and amend it as and if necessary in order to transpose the requirements of the directive. This might mean that a wording is used that differs from that of the directive. This may be acceptable as long as it is ensured that domestic courts will interpret the implementing legislation in accordance with the directive. It seems unlikely that the ECJ will allow a Member State to rely on existing legislation and argue merely that it *could* be interpreted in line with the directive unless there is clear evidence of this. A number of judgments by the ECJ involving consumer protection directives have established this position.

In *Commission v United Kingdom* (case C-300/95), the Commission brought infringement proceedings against the United Kingdom for a failure correctly to implement the so-called 'development risks' defence in Article 4(1)(e) of the Product Liability Directive (85/374/EEC). The wording of the implementing provision, section 7(1)(e) of the Consumer Protection Act 1987, differed from that in the Directive. The ECJ noted that at the time of the proceedings there was no UK case-law applying the provision, and therefore no evidence that the implementing legislation would lead to results different from those envisaged in the Directive. On the other hand a crucial factor in the decision was that section 1 of the 1987 Act states that the purpose of the Act is to implement the Product Liability Directive and that the Act is to be interpreted accordingly, therefore requiring national courts to interpret the Act in accordance with the Directive. Consequently, UK courts have adopted an approach whereby cases under legislation implementing a directive are dealt with by applying the corresponding directive itself (see *A and others v The National Blood Authority* [2001] 3 All ER 289 (High Court)).

More recently, in *Commission v Italy* (C-372/99), it was argued that Italy had failed to ensure that terms recommended by a trade association for use in standard form contracts could be challenged without there being a specific consumer contract in which the term had been used, as required by the Unfair Contract Terms Directive (see Article 7(3) of the Unfair Contract Terms Directive 93/13/EEC). The Italian legislation was ambiguous and could have been interpreted in a way that would conflict with the Directive, and there was case-law supporting interpretations both in accordance and in conflict with the Directive. In this case, the ECJ adopted a stricter approach and held that the fact that legislation is capable of being interpreted in accordance with the directive it implements is insufficient to satisfy the Member State's obligation to implement the directive, even where there is case-law that does not contradict the directive, if the legislation itself is insufficiently clear or is contradictory. The court's main concern was that the ambiguities in the legislation and the fact that Italian case-law was neither unanimous nor sufficiently well established to ensure an interpretation in line with the directive meant that it was not possible to ascertain the legal position of consumers from the legislation. This violated the principle of legal certainty.

Subsequently, in *Commission v Netherlands* (C-144/99), the ECJ held that the Netherlands had failed correctly to implement Directive 93/13/EEC on Unfair Terms in Consumer Contracts, in particular Article 4(2) (the exception from the fairness requirement for core contract terms) and Article 5 (the 'plain and intelligible language' requirement). The Dutch government argued that there was no need expressly to implement particular parts of a directive if existing national rules already provided substantively the same rules. In any event, compliance with the directive would be ensured by the courts which would interpret existing legislation in accordance with the directive, as required by the EC case-law on indirect effect. The ECJ, however, held that the legal position under national law must be sufficiently precise and clear and that individuals must be made fully aware of their rights (paragraph 17). There was insufficient evidence that the Dutch courts consistently interpreted the legislation in line with the Directive (paragraph 20). However, even if it is settled in the case-law of a Member State that provisions of national law *are* interpreted in line with a directive, this does not ensure the clarity and precision to meet the requirement of legal certainty, which is particularly relevant in the context of consumer protection (paragraph 21). This case therefore further tightens the obligations imposed on Member States when implementing a directive.

Therefore, Member States seem to be under an obligation to reflect the detailed substance of a consumer protection measure in the implementing legislation. The legislation must clearly and unambiguously implement the Directive. Moreover, where existing national rules are deemed to fulfil all or some of the requirements of a directive, this must be clear from the wording of the national provision, or there must be established and unequivocal case-law to that effect. It will be seen in the chapters which follow that the implementation of the Guarantees Directive into English law does not appear to comply with this most recent approach taken by the European Court of Justice, and that the UK is in danger of being found liable for incorrect transposition of the Directive into English law. The UK could escape liability only where the relevant provision in the Directive is ambiguous and the interpretation adopted in the implementing legislation is one possible reading of that provision and has been adopted in good faith (see case C-392/93 *R v HM Treasury, ex parte British Telecommunications plc* [1996] ECR I-1631).

1.4.2.3 *Interpretation of the implementing provisions*
It may be tempting to ignore any implementing legislation and instead consider a relevant directive directly in order to ensure compliance with EC law. However, it must be borne in mind that the European Court of Justice has consistently held that directives cannot, of themselves, give rights which individuals may enforce against private parties ('horizontal direct effect'—see, in particular, C-91/92

Faccini Dori v Recreb Srl [1994] ECR I-3325 and C-192/94 *El Corte Ingles SA v Rivero* [1996] ECR I-1281). Thus, a court cannot ignore domestic legislation in favour of a relevant directive if this would give a person a right against a private party which does not exist in domestic law. For example, if Member State A has failed to implement the remedies of repair and replacement required by Article 3 of the Guarantees Directive (see chapter 4), a court in Member State A may not look to the Directive and force a seller to provide the remedies not provided for in domestic legislation. However, the ECJ has developed an alternative route by which compliance with EC law may be ensured. The Court has emphasised that domestic legislation must be interpreted in accordance with the requirements of EC law. This principle is known as the doctrine of indirect effect.

The doctrine of indirect effect was first established in *Marshall and von Colson v Land Nordrhein-Westfalen* (case 14/83 [1984] ECR 1891). The ECJ referred to what is now Article 10 EC which requires Member States to 'take all appropriate measures' to ensure that they comply with EC Law obligations. The ECJ held that this Article extends to *all* the authorities of a Member State, including its courts. Therefore, domestic courts are obliged to interpret national law in such a way as to ensure that the objectives of EC law are met. Subsequently, in *Marleasing SA v La Comercial International de Alimentacion SA* (C-106/89 [1990] ECR I-4135), the ECJ held that domestic courts must interpret national law in the light of the wording and purpose of the corresponding directive in order to achieve the result pursued by the directive *as far as possible*. Moreover, this obligation is not restricted to legislation introduced following the adoption of a directive, but applies to the interpretation of all domestic legislation, *whether adopted before or after* the directive. However, if domestic legislation is not capable of being interpreted in accordance with EC law, e.g., because it contradicts a directive, the doctrine cannot apply (*Wagner Miret v Fondo da Guarantia Salaria* (C-334/92 [1993] ECR I-6911)). In such circumstances, an individual who suffers loss as a result of the inability to enforce rights granted by the directive will be left with a claim against the Member State for any loss suffered as a result of the failure to comply with EC law (C-6&9/90 *Francovich v Italy* [1991] ECR I-5357; C-46&48/93 *Brasserie de Pêcheur and Factortame* [1996] ECR I-1029).

It is important to distinguish two situations: one arises where a directive (or particular provisions of a directive) have not been implemented at all, the other where a directive has been implemented but in a way which creates an ambiguity. In the latter case, it is assumed that the national legislation was intended to reflect the directive and should be interpreted accordingly. In the former, it may still be possible to interpret national law in order to ensure compliance with the directive. However, if an existing domestic provision cannot mean what the directive requires, then the doctrine is not applicable. For example, it will not be possible to apply the doctrine of indirect effect where an attempt to interpret domestic law in line with a directive produces a conflict with the clear words and intentions of domestic law, particularly with regard to obligations imposed on individuals. This was confirmed by the ECJ in *Arcaro* (C-168/95 [1996] ECR I-4705) where the ECJ held that the 'obligation of the national court to refer to the content of the directive when interpreting the relevant rules of its own national law reaches a limit where such an interpretation leads to the imposition on an individual of an obligation laid down by a directive which has not been transposed'. However, *Arcaro* involved a criminal penalty and it is arguable that a less strict view might be taken in the context of private law obligations. Indeed, in *Oceano Grupo Editorial v Rocio Murciano Quintero* (C-240/98 [2000] ECR I-4491), the ECJ held that a domestic court could decline of its own motion the jurisdiction conferred upon it by a term which is unfair within the meaning of Directive 93/13/EEC, on the basis that this is required by the Directive (although not expressly!) even though it was not required by domestic Spanish legislation. Consequently, the interpretation of domestic law in accordance with EC law meant that a seller was deprived of a right under the contract with a consumer.

In short, once there is an EC measure in a particular field, the national courts may have to take into account the requirements of EC law in interpreting domestic rules as far as possible, regardless of whether these existed before the directive or were adopted to comply.

1.4.2.4 *Relevance of the doctrine in the context of the Guarantees Directive*
This doctrine may now become relevant in applying the 'satisfactory quality' test (see chapter 3), because a number of aspects contained in the Directive have not been expressly transposed into domestic law. In particular, the Directive makes the performance of the goods a relevant factor for the purpose of determining conformity, but there is no direct equivalent of this requirement in English law. However, the satisfactory quality test is flexible enough to take these factors into account, and a court faced with a claim based on goods' substandard performance would have to treat it as a relevant factor in applying the satisfactory quality test. Similarly the doctrine may be relevant in interpreting the remedial provisions of the SSGCR, which depart in a number of respects from the language of the Directive.

1.5 CONCLUSIONS

The purpose of this chapter has been to provide the background for the discussion in the following chapters. We will next consider the scope of the Directive and the implementing regulations (chapter 2), followed in later chapers by examination of the main substantive provisions of the legislation and their effects. Throughout this book, we will examine the law with regard to its internal consistency, whether it provides consumer protection and whether it meets the requirements imposed by European law. We will also consider gaps in the current system, and how potential future developments might affect the current legal framework.

2

SCOPE AND DEFINITIONS

2.1 INTRODUCTION

In this chapter we propose to examine the key definitions in the Directive and implementing regulations and then to explore the scope of the two instruments.

Broadly speaking the Directive is limited to consumer transactions involving the supply of consumer goods. As noted in Chapter 1, the earlier proposal to limit the Directive to sales of new consumer durables was abandoned, so that the Directive applies to all consumer goods, new or second-hand, durable or otherwise. The definitions of key provisions such as 'consumer' and 'seller' are therefore essential in defining the scope of the legislation. One surprising feature is that the definitions of both in the Directive differ from those used in other related consumer protection instruments and, as will be seen, the corresponding definitions in the SSGCR in turn differ from those in the Directive.

2.2 DEFINITIONS

2.2.1 Definitions in the Directive

Article 1 of the Directive provides definitions of the Directive's key terms, 'consumer', 'seller', 'producer' and 'consumer goods', which will be considered in detail in this section. It also contains definitions of 'guarantee' and 'repair' which will be considered in subsequent chapters.

2.2.1.1 *Consumer*
A consumer is 'any natural person who, in the contracts covered by [the] Directive is acting for purposes which are not related to his trade, business or profession'

(Article 1(2)(a)). The original draft Directive defined a consumer as 'any natural person who, in the contracts covered by [the] Directive is acting for purposes which are not *directly* related to his trade, business or profession'. The draft would therefore have required a direct connection between the transaction in question and the buyer's business to prevent the buyer being a consumer. The omission of 'directly' from the final text must mean that a more remote connection between the transaction and the buyer's business etc. is now enough to prevent the buyer being a consumer.

We may note here that the definition used in the Directive differs from that used in the Unfair Terms Directive which defines a consumer as a person who 'is acting for purposes which are *outside* his trade, business or profession' (Article 2(b)). It is not easy to make an immediate comparison between the two definitions, but it is submitted that a closer connection between the contractor and his business is required to prevent the contractor being a consumer under the Unfair Terms Directive than under the Sales Directive. To put it another way, a person may be acting for purposes which are outside, but still related to, his business. The reason for the discrepancy is not clear. It is submitted that it is unfortunate.

A buyer that is a limited company would clearly not qualify as a consumer under the Directive because it is not a natural person. Nor, it seems, would a partnership or a sole trader buying goods for purposes related to their business. For example, a solicitor who buys a computer for the office would not be a consumer, because the purchase is related to his business. Under the Directive, therefore, it seems that a buyer who purchases goods for a purpose which has some kind of connection with his business activity will not be a consumer. It is not clear whether the buyer would be a consumer if he bought the goods for purposes related to both business and non-business activities. It is arguable that, because one of the purposes is related to the trade, business or profession the buyer would not be a consumer.

2.2.1.2 *Seller*

A 'seller' is 'any natural or legal person who, under a contract, sells consumer goods *in the course of his trade, business or profession*' (emphasis added) (Article 1(2)(c)). A private seller, such as an individual selling his private car on a one-off basis, is therefore clearly not subject to the Directive. What about a business selling a business asset of a type in which it does not normally deal, such as a solicitor selling off a surplus computer? Would this be a sale 'in the course of' the seller's trade, business or profession? It is not clear whether 'in the course of business' should be given a wide reading to encompass all transactions made by a business, or whether this should be interpreted narrowly to require some degree of regularity of similar transactions, or something else. Again the definition differs from that in the Unfair Terms Directive, which defines a seller as a person 'acting for purposes related to his trade, business or profession', thus adopting a similar approach to that adopted for the definition of 'consumer' in the Sales Directive, discussed above. Here it seems clear that the Sales Directive deliberately requires a closer connection between the seller's business and the particular transaction than does the Unfair Terms Directive, and it would therefore make some sense to construe the phrase 'in the course of his trade, business or profession' as requiring some close connection between the two, or some degree of regularity of similar transactions.

The Directive's reference to the seller selling 'in the course of *his* trade, business or profession' may also be contrasted with the text used in English law (see below, 2.3.1.3), which uses the phrase 'in the course of *a* business'. The example of the solicitor selling off a surplus computer once again helps to illustrate the problem. Although the solicitor may be selling in the course of *a* business, it will not be in the course of *his* business. *His* 'trade, business or profession' is the provision of legal services to his clients. A sale of a computer is not part of that activity, and it would therefore not attract the requirement that the goods be in conformity with the contract of sale under the Directive.

The combined effect of the definitions of 'consumer' and 'seller' is somewhat to narrow the scope of the Directive. Any connection between a particular transaction and the buyer's business will not prevent his being regarded as a consumer but, it seems, the transaction will only fall within the Directive if there is some degree of regularity of similar transactions so that it can be regarded as 'in the course' of the seller's business.

2.2.1.3 *Consumer goods*

'Consumer goods' are defined widely as 'any tangible movable item' with the exception of:

(i)   goods sold by execution or otherwise by authority of law, and

(ii) water and gas when not 'put up for sale' in a limited volume or quantity, and

(iii) electricity (Article 1(2)(b)).

Thus any type of goods can be 'consumer goods' provided that they are sold by a seller to a consumer, as defined. However, there are two restrictions. First of all, electricity is not goods, nor is gas or water which is supplied through the utility network. However, where water or gas is sold in a fixed quantity in a separate container, it will be treated as goods. A consumer who buys bottled water therefore buys consumer goods within the meaning of the Directive.

A further requirement is that goods must be tangible and movable. Sales of immovables, such as land and houses, are therefore outside the scope of the Directive. However, the position is less clear in relation to items such as garden sheds or greenhouses which a consumer may purchase in an unassembled state (flat-pack) and then assemble himself. Once completely assembled, the shed may no longer be movable, e.g., because it has been set into a concrete floor. It is submitted that this should not change the initial nature of the goods as movable, and that the Directive should apply.

2.2.1.4 *The problem of computer software*

The Directive contains no special provision for computer software and its status as goods or otherwise is problematic and has provoked some discussion (see Grundmann and Bianca, 2002, especially chapter 2). Its status is similarly unclear in domestic law and it is discussed further below.

2.2.2 Scope of the Directive

The scope of the Directive is set out in Article 1(1) which states that its objective is 'the approximation of the laws, regulations and administrative provisions of the Member States on certain aspects of the sale of consumer goods and associated guarantees in order to ensure a uniform minimum level of consumer protection in the context of the internal market'.

The Directive applies to contracts for the sale of consumer goods and excludes from its ambit certain other types of transaction for the supply of goods to consumers. References to 'seller' and 'contract of sale' suggest that arrangements such as hire-purchase and barter are excluded from its scope. If it had been intended to include contracts other than sale, the Directive would have used the neutral term 'supply', as does the Unfair Terms Directive (93/13/EEC), Article 2(b). Moreover, the legislative history of the Directive confirms that barter and hire-purchase have been deliberately excluded from its scope. A Commission amendment to include contracts of exchange or barter was rejected by the Council because it would have caused difficulties for some Member States, and a proposed new recital which would have made it clear that the Directive applied to both contracts of exchange and contracts for the supply of goods in exchange for instalment payments was not adopted. With regard to credit supply contracts, the Parliament supported a provision to give the consumer the right to suspend payments until a lack of conformity has been cured. The Council rejected this on the grounds that the issue was properly the subject of consumer credit law. This seems to adopt an overly rigid and compartmentalised approach which ignores commercial reality, at least from a UK perspective. A contract for the supply of goods on conditional sale terms is a sale; one for supply on hire-purchase terms is not. Commercially the two types of transaction achieve the same effect—a supply of goods on credit terms, the price payable by instalments, secured by a retention of ownership of the goods. The approach of English law for some years now has been, so far as possible, to assimilate sales and hire-purchase and, indeed, to assimilate different types of supply contract. It is submitted that this approach is preferable to the compartmentalised approach of the Directive. As we have already suggested, these conflicting approaches may affect the legal validity of some of the implementing provisions contained in the SSGCR (see chapter 1 at 1.3.3.2)

Despite this, and perhaps surprisingly (to English eyes at least), the Directive makes no attempt to define 'sale'. It would seem therefore that in the absence of any other guidance the definition of 'sale' must be drawn from domestic law. It is clear, however, that the Directive applies to certain classes of contract which might not be regarded as 'sales' by English law. Article 1(4) treats as sales 'contracts for the supply of consumer goods to be manufactured or produced', and Article 2(5) applies the Directive's key provisions to contracts for the supply and installation of goods 'if installation forms part of the contract of sale . . . and the goods were installed by the seller or under his responsibility'.

2.2.2.1 *Manufacture and supply*

Article 1(4) could be read narrowly as simply confirming that a contract for the sale of goods not yet in existence—which in domestic law would be classified as a contract for the sale of 'future goods'—is within the scope of the Directive. Its terms, referring to 'consumer goods to be manufactured or produced' is wide enough to cover both contracts for future manufactured items—such as a contract to build and supply a boat—and contracts to supply produce, such as fruit or vegetables, to be grown (although such arrangements are probably rare as consumer transactions).

It seems, however, that the aim of Article 1(4) is something rather more than the confirmation that a sale of future goods is covered by the Directive. It seems, reflecting the position adopted in many Member States, that a contract is one of sale whenever a finished product is transferred to the consumer. If so, contracts for a supplier to produce and supply a finished product are to be regarded for the purposes of the Directive as sales of the finished product, and the Directive will therefore cover some transactions which in domestic law have previously been regarded as contracts for work and materials. This is perhaps implicit in the choice of the word 'supply' rather than 'sale' in Article 1(4). This reading is confirmed by Article 2(3), which provides that the seller is not liable under Article 2 for a lack of conformity in goods 'if the lack of conformity has its origin in materials supplied by the consumer'. Article 2(3) therefore clearly anticipates that a contract under which a supplier works on materials supplied by a consumer to produce a finished item is within the scope of the Directive.

However, the full extent of Article 1(4) is not clear. It is submitted that it will apply where the supplier supplies both labour and materials to produce a finished item for supply to the consumer, as where a boat-builder builds a boat for the consumer, and Article 2(3) makes clear that it must also apply where at least some of the materials are initially provided by the consumer as, say, where the consumer supplies timber for a joiner to manufacture a table. There would seem however to be nothing to restrict the scope of Article 1(4) and it would seem to be capable of application where all of the materials are provided by the consumer and the supplier merely assembles them. So, for instance, if a consumer buys the parts for assembly of a computer or a kit car and then contracts with an engineer or mechanic to assemble them to produce a computer or car as the case may be, the contract could be said to be one for 'the supply of consumer goods to be manu-factured or produced' with the result that the engineer/mechanic would be strictly liable for the finished item, subject only to the restriction that he would not be liable for any lack of conformity which originates in the materials supplied by the consumer. This is significant because contracts such as those described would probably in the past not, in English law, have been categorised as sales at all but as contracts for work (and materials) under which the supplier would only be liable on a negligence basis for the quality of his work.

This reading of Article 1(4) does however create some problems of its own. A contract for goods to be manufactured or produced could take one of a number of forms:

(a) a contract for a manufacturer to manufacture and supply an item to a stan-dard design;

(b) a contract for a manufacturer to design, manufacture and supply a non-standard item;

(c) a contract for a manufacturer to make and supply an item to the consumer's design;

(d) a contract for a manufacturer to design, manufacture and supply an item using material supplied by the consumer;

(e) a contract for a manufacturer to manufacture an item to the consumer's design using materials supplied by the consumer.

Under the Directive, all of these are to be treated as contracts for the sale of the finished item, with the result that it is a requirement that the finished item should be in conformity with the contract. In cases (c)–(e), however, the consumer has some input into the production by supplying design, materials or both. What if the non-conformity results from the consumer's input? Article 2(3) states that 'there shall be deemed not to be a lack of conformity for the purposes of [the Directive] if . . . the lack of conformity has its origin in materials supplied by the consumer'. Thus, in cases (d) and (e) above the seller would not be not liable under the Directive for any lack of conformity originating in the materials supplied by the consumer. But what if the non-conformity is due to the consumer's design? Common sense suggests that the seller should not be liable. It may be arguable that the seller is, or should be, under a duty of care to warn the consumer if the design is defective, but not that he should be under a strict liability obligation for the con-sumer's design. However, the Directive does not contain a provision for this situa-tion. The inclusion of an express provision to cover defects arising from the consumer's *materials* makes it at least arguable that the seller is liable for non-conformity originating in the consumer's *design*. It might be possible to argue that 'materials' should be interpreted to include designs, plans and the like, but this would require the word to be given an extended meaning. The German text of the Directive uses the word 'Stoff' which would normally refer to physical materials and would not be interpreted as covering designs and the like. In consequence, there is some uncertainty about the Directive's scope in this respect.

If Article 1(4) does have the extended meaning suggested here, it opens up a further problem in relation to computer software. If computer software is 'goods' for the purposes of the Directive a contract for a software engineer to write and supply a program—which might otherwise be thought to be one purely for professional services—will be a contract for the supply of goods—the finished program (see Serrano, 2002). It will however probably be rare for a consumer to contract for the supply of bespoke software programs for purposes not related to the consumer's trade, business or profession.

2.2.2.2 *Installation of goods*

Where 'installation forms part of the contract of sale and the goods are installed by the seller or under his responsibility', Article 2(5) (sometimes referred to as the 'IKEA clause') applies and provides that 'any lack of conformity resulting from incorrect installation shall be deemed to be equivalent to a lack of conformity of the goods'. In such a case, therefore, the supplier will be strictly liable for the goods as installed, including for the installation work.

The reference to installation forming 'part of the contract of sale' could be read as requiring Article 2(5) to be given a narrow scope, restricted to cases where the contract is essentially one of sale but includes an ancillary installation element and excluding contracts essentially for the supply of a service where the supply of goods is ancillary. The more natural reading, however, would seem to be that Article 2(3) applies wherever the seller is contractually obliged to install the goods, either personally or by proxy ('under his responsibility'—e.g.: where the goods are installed by a sub-contractor employed by the supplier, as is often the case with, say, double-glazing).

It would seem therefore that Article 2(5) will widen the scope of the Directive considerably to include a number of contracts which would not be categorised as 'sales' in English law. Thus a contract for a joiner to supply and hang a door would seem to be a contract for the sale and installation of the door under the Directive, as would a contract to supply and fit a cooker and a contract to supply and fit double-glazing and a contract to supply and fit a car stereo or a new tyre. So too, perhaps, would a contract to supply and install on the consumer's computer a software program. On the other hand a contract for a joiner to re-hang an existing door would not be a contract of sale even though in the course of performing the contract the joiner supplies new hinge screws (or even new hinges). Similarly a contract for a mechanic to service a car, installing new components as required, would on this approach not be a contract of sale. Nor would a contract for a decorator to supply paint and decorate a house.

However, these propositions cannot be asserted with complete certainty. If the reason for having to re-hang the door is that the hinge is sprained, could it not be argued that the contract is one for the supply and installation of the new hinge, so that if as a result of incorrect installation the new hinge does not operate correctly there is deemed to be a lack of conformity in the hinge—with the result that the consumer would be entitled to require the joiner to come and make good the lack of conformity by repairing or replacing the hinge. Similarly it would be possible to read the Directive as applying to the contract to service a car so that if the parts supplied are wrongly installed the supplier would be liable.

2.2.2.3 *Auction sales*
Article 1(3) of the Directive allows Member States to exclude second-hand goods sold at public auction where consumers have the opportunity of attending the sale in person from the scope of the definition of 'consumer goods'. However, the restriction only applies to auctions which the buyer can attend in person. If the auction is conducted over the Internet or by telephone, then the buyer may still be regarded as dealing as a consumer. It is important, though, to note that in order to take the transaction outside the scope of consumer dealing it is only necessary that individuals have the opportunity of attending in person, not that they actually do attend. Thus, if a buyer chooses to participate in an auction by telephone where he could have attended, he will not be dealing as a consumer.

2.3 PRE-IMPLEMENTATION ENGLISH LAW

2.3.1 Definitions

The SoGA 1979 is a general statute, applicable to private sales and to business to business and business to consumer transactions. For most purposes it makes no distinction between different types of seller and buyer. However, the Unfair Contract Terms Act 1977, which augments the SoGA and regulates attempts to exclude or limit liability for breach of the SoGA implied terms does distinguish between business and consumer transactions. Moreover for some purposes the rights and liabilities of the parties differ according to whether seller is acting in the course of a business or buyer is dealing as a consumer. On the whole the Act imports definitions of these terms from the UCTA.

The SoGA applies only to contracts of sale, as defined. Other statutes apply to other types of contract under which goods are supplied. Thus the Supply of Goods (Implied Terms) Act 1973 (SoG(IT)A) applies to contracts of hire-purchase and the Supply of Goods and Services Act 1982 (SGSA) applies to most other types of contract for the transfer of property in goods, including barter, exchange and contracts for the supply of work and materials, and to contracts of hire. Broadly speaking the 1973 and 1982 Acts seek to assimilate the law applicable to the classes of contract they cover with that applicable to contracts of sale, at least for the purposes with which we are presently concerned, and, unless otherwise stated, the comments made in this chapter above apply to those Acts as they apply to the SoGA.

2.3.1.1 *'Seller'*

English sales law defines 'seller' simply as 'a person who sells or agrees to sell goods' (SoGA section 61(1)). Since the Sale of Goods Act applies generally to all sales, including private sales, it makes no general distinction between a business and a non-business sale. However, some provisions of the Act, and of the legislation applying to other forms of supply contract, apply only where the seller sells 'in the course of a business'. Most importantly of all, the statutory implied terms relating to the quality and fitness for purpose of the goods supplied, only apply where the seller sells in the course of a business. Similarly the UCTA 1977, which regulates attempts to exclude or restrict the statutory implied terms relating to the goods, only applies where the seller acts in the course of a business.

2.3.1.2 *'Consumer'*

In the same way the SoGA applies generally to all buyers regardless of status, and 'buyer' is defined as 'a person who buys or agrees to buy goods'. However, a buyer who 'deals as consumer' is afforded some additional rights under the Act and additional protection against exclusion and similar clauses under the UCTA. The expression 'deals as consumer' is defined in section 12 of the UCTA. Prior to the implementation of the Directive, it required that

(a) the buyer not make the contract in the course of a business, or hold himself out as so doing,

(b) the seller make the contract in the course of a business, and

(c) the goods be of a type ordinarily supplied for private use or consumption.

This definition is imported into the Sale of Goods Act by section 61(5A) and into the legislation governing other types of supply contract (Supply of Goods and Services Act 1982 (section 18(4)), SOGITA 1973 (section 11(4))).

2.3.1.3 *In the course of a business*

The changes made to this definition to implement the Directive will be considered below. It can, however, be seen that under both UCTA and SoGA it is crucial to determine when a person is acting 'in the course of a business'. The phrase has, unfortunately, been given different interpretations under the two Acts. In *R & B Customs Brokers Co Ltd v United Dominions Trust Ltd* ([1988] 1 WLR 321), the Court of Appeal, following earlier decisions on other legislation (notably the House of Lords' decision in *Davies v Sumner* [1984] 1 WLR 1301 on the Trade Descriptions Act 1968) held that a person *bought* goods 'in the course of a business' for the purposes of UCTA where either

(i) the purchase was an integral part of the business, or

(ii) although the purchase was incidental to the business, there was a sufficient degree of regularity of similar purchases.

In *Stevenson v Rogers* ([1999] 1 All ER 613), however, the Court of Appeal held
that for the purposes of SoGA section 14, *any sale* by a business is 'in the course
of a business'. The Court noted that prior to 1973 the implied terms in section 14
only applied where goods were bought from a seller who dealt in goods of that
description. The present formulation, referring to 'sale in the course of a business', was introduced in 1973 to widen the field of application of the implied
terms, and to interpret it as requiring regularity of similar transactions would
effectively re-introduce the old, pre-1973, restrictions. As we have noted above,
just such a restriction seems to be intended in the Directive, and English law
appears here to be more generous to consumers.

The effect of *Stevenson* is, e.g., that a solicitor selling off a computer no longer
needed in his office would, for the purposes of SoGA section 14, be selling the
computer in the course of a business, and it would have to be of satisfactory quality. However, the same solicitor buying a replacement computer would not be acting in the course of a business, and could therefore be dealing as a consumer, for
the purposes of the UCTA, if the other requirements of the definition of 'dealing
as consumer' are satisfied.

The Court in *Stevenson* had to distinguish *R&B Customs Brokers*, by treating it
as concerned with the interpretation of a different statute and with the status of
the buyer rather than the seller. Both cases are therefore currently good law. Both
decisions can be said to extend consumer protection. However, there are a number
of difficulties. For example, it is not clear which test should be used to determine
whether a seller is acting in the course of a business for the purposes of UCTA, or
a buyer for the purposes of the SoGA. The position is further complicated by the
fact that the UCTA definition of 'deals as consumer' is imported into the SoGA
for certain purposes, creating the possibility that a person could be 'buying in the
course of a business' for some purposes and not for others under the same piece of
legislation. Such uncertainties make it difficult to set out exactly which rules will
apply when.

In any case the Court of Appeal's reasons for distinguishing the *R&B* decision
in *Stevenson* are unconvincing. Both the UCTA provision considered in *R&B* and
the SoGA provision considered in *Stevenson* were originally found in the same legislation, the Supply of Goods (Implied Terms) Act 1973, and originated in the
same Law Commission Report (Law Commission 24: Exemption Clauses in
Contracts). It is almost unthinkable that it was intended that the expression 'in the
course of a business' should mean different things in the two contexts in which it
appears.

2.3.1.4 *Goods of a type ordinarily supplied for private use or consumption*

It should be noted that under the pre-implementation UCTA definition, it was not
only necessary to consider the capacity in which buyer and seller were acting, but
also to consider the nature of the goods which were the subject of the contract of
sale. According to the third element of the definition of 'dealing as consumer', the

goods had to be 'of a type ordinarily supplied for private use or consumption'. This requirement creates its own difficulties. For example, it is not clear what is a 'type' for this purpose. However, it serves an important function by limiting the scope of 'dealing as consumer', especially in light of the *R&B Customs Brokers* decision. As a consequence, if a buyer, who was not acting in the course of a business purchased goods from a seller who was acting in the course of a business, the buyer would nevertheless not be dealing as a consumer if the goods in question would not ordinarily be supplied for private use, notwithstanding the fact that in this particular situation they were. A seller selling goods not normally bought or used by consumers would therefore not have to worry about the rules applicable to consumer transactions.

2.3.1.5 *Goods*
As already noted, English law does not distinguish between consumer and non-consumer goods. Instead, goods are defined in section 61(1) SoGA:

Goods includes all personal chattels other than things in action and money, and in Scotland, all corporate moveables except money; and in particular, 'goods' includes emblements, industrial growing crops and things attached to or forming part of the land which are agreed to be severed before sale or under the contract of sale.

This definition is limited, like that in the Directive, to tangible moveable items. It does not cover 'things in action', which are items of intangible property such as debts, shares and intellectual property rights. Moreover, electricity is not goods.
    A difficult question which has as yet received no satisfactory answer is whether computer software can properly be classified as 'goods' for the purposes of this definition.

2.3.1.6 *The problem of software*
Many common consumer items, including but not only computer hardware, contain embedded software. It is not doubted that such items, such as VCRs, are 'goods' and it is submitted that the same should apply to computer hardware (see *Amstrad plc v Seagate Technology Inc.* (1998) 86 BLR 34). It seems, too, that a contract for the supply of hardware together with a software package is also 'goods' (*St Albans City and District Council v International Computers Ltd* [1996] 4 All ER 48 per Sir Iain Glidewell). The position of software sold alone is less clear. Strictly speaking 'software' is intangible, a set of encoded instructions, and all that the buyer of software purchases is a licence to use the software. Admittedly, software is often supplied, especially to consumers, on a physical medium such as a CD-ROM or floppy disk and it has tentatively been suggested that where software is supplied on a physical medium the contract can properly be classified as one for the sale of goods (per Sir Iain Glidewell in the *St Albans* case, above; strictly this view was *obiter*.) However, in a Scots case, *Beta Computers (Europe) Ltd v Adobe Systems Ltd* [1996] SLT 604, Lord Penrose, the Lord Ordinary, held that a

contract for the supply of software should not be regarded as a sale but as a contract *sui generis*, having some of the characteristics of a sale and some of a licence.

Clearly a contract for supply of software cannot be a sale for all purposes, since the 'seller' does not transfer property in the software to the buyer. In the same way, however, a bookseller does not transfer to the buyer property in the intellectual content of the book but no-one doubts that the book is goods. Clearly a CD-ROM is goods for some purposes. If the physical disk is so warped or scratched as to be unusable the goods are defective and the seller should be liable. The more difficult question is whether the seller of the physical medium, or licensor-supplier of the software program, should be strictly liable for the intellectual content of the program itself. Essentially this is a policy question, and since software is marketed commercially like any other product, and given its increasing importance to consumers in the modern world, there is a strong case for imposing strict liability on the supplier, at least in the case of a standard, mass-produced program. Imposing liability on the contractual supplier provides a conduit for liability (possibly) to be passed back to the software producer, and is no less justifiable than is the general imposition of liability on retailers. The distinction between software supplied on a physical medium and software supplied otherwise—for instance, downloaded on-line—is unattractive. There are therefore powerful arguments for bringing software, whether supplied on a physical medium within the scope of the Directive, and the SoGA implied terms, even if its supply does not involve a sale of goods for all purposes.

2.3.2 Scope of the Sale of Goods Act

As noted above, the Directive does not define 'sale', although it is clear from the Directive's legislative history that neither barter nor hire-purchase are covered. It is also likely that transactions which do not involve the transfer of property, such as hire, are excluded from the Directive. However, contracts which contain a service element, such as installing or manufacturing goods to order, are within the scope of the Directive.

In domestic law the SoGA 1979 applies only to contracts for the sale of goods, defined by section 2(1) as:

. . . a contract by which the seller transfers or agrees to transfer the property in goods to the buyer for a money consideration called the price.

The requirement that the contract be for the transfer of property excludes contracts of hire and hire-purchase where the contract is (initially in the case of hire-purchase) only for the transfer of possession, and the requirement that the consideration for that transfer be money excludes contracts of barter and exchange, where goods are supplied in return for a non-money consideration.

The distinctions between these various types of contract can be technical and sometimes difficult to draw. For instance, a contract of hire-purchase is functionally equivalent to a consumer conditional sale contract, both involving a supply of goods on credit, paid for by instalments, the creditor retaining property in the goods until payment as security. On the whole the tendency of English law in recent years has been to assimilate the treatment of different types of supply contract. Thus terms equivalent to those implied into contracts of sale by sections 13–15 of the SoGA, are implied into other supply contracts by other legislation (SoG(IT)A 1973: hire-purchase; SGSA 1982: barter; hire; other forms of supply) and broadly speaking consumers have the same rights in relation to the goods supplied under all forms of supply contract. However, the consumer's remedies for breach of the implied terms may vary according to the classification of the contract, the consumer having greater rights to terminate a non-sale supply contract than a sale. Generally, a consumer who acquires goods under a non-sale supply contract has rights at least as good as if he had bought them under a sale *strictu sensu*.

The most problematic distinction, and the most important for present purposes, however, is that between contracts of sale and contracts for work and materials. This impacts directly on the Directive's provisions relating to contracts to manufacture and supply and contracts to supply and install goods, discussed earlier. It has in the past been necessary to distinguish between contracts of sale and contracts of work and materials for various purposes and at different times different tests have been proposed. Broadly speaking the preferred test was to look to the 'substance of the contract'. If the principal objective of the contract was the supply of goods, with the skill or labour of the supplier being an ancillary element, the contract was one of sale. If on the other hand the principal element was the supplier's skill or labour, the contract was one for work and materials. On this basis contracts for a veterinary surgeon to inoculate an animal and for a hairdresser to apply hair dye to a customer have been held to be contracts for services, the supply of goods being ancillary (*Dodds & Dodds v Wilson & McWilliams* [1946] 2 All ER 691; *Watson v Buckley, Osborne, Garrett & Co Ltd* [1940] 1 All ER 174). On the same basis a contract for the service of a car would probably be classified as one for a service rather than for the supply of the parts.

The distinction between a contract of sale and one for the supply of a service is no longer as important as in the past. The SGSA 1982 applies to contracts for the transfer of goods and to contracts for the supply of a service. It implies into a contract for the supply of goods terms corresponding to those implied into contracts of sale by SoGA sections 13–15, and implies into a contract for the supply of a service an implied term that the service will be performed with reasonable skill and care (section 13). Significantly section 1(3) provides that the fact that services are also provided under the contract does not prevent its being a contract for the transfer of goods for the purposes of the Act, and section 12, which defines a contract for the supply of a service for the purposes of the Act similarly provides (section 12(3)) that the fact that goods are also transferred or bailed under a contract does not prevent its also being a contract for the supply of a service for the purposes of the Act.

The upshot is that where goods and services are supplied under a single contract the most natural classification of it will be as a contract for work and materials, governed by the 1982 Act, under which the seller is strictly liable for the materials supplied being in accordance with the contract description, of satisfactory quality and reasonably fit for the buyer's purpose and is also required to carry out the service element with reasonable skill and care.

2.3.2.1 *Contracts to manufacture and supply*

The 'substance of the contract' test for the categorisation of contracts breaks down when applied to contracts to manufacture and supply a finished product, and the categorisation of such contracts in English law has in the past been problematic, the courts applying different tests at different times, producing different results. Thus, for instance, a contract for a painter to paint a portrait has been held to be one for work and materials, on the basis that the substance of the contract was the painter's skill (*Robinson v Graves* [1935] 1 KB 579). However, in other cases the court has held that where a contract results in the transfer of property in a finished item the contract is properly construed as one of sale even though the supplier uses his skill to produce the finished item. So a contract for a dentist to make and supply a set of dentures was a contract of sale (*Lee v Griffin* (1861) 1 B & S 272; see also *Marcel Furriers Ltd v Tapper* [1953] 1 WLR 49: contract to manufacture and supply a coat) .

The modern tendency seems to be to treat a contract for the supply of a finished product as a sale, but it cannot be said with certainty that that will always be the case. The approach adopted remains important because although under a contract for work and materials the supplier is strictly liable for the quality, etc., of the *materials* supplied, he is not strictly liable for the quality of the finished item unless a term to that effect can be implied at common law. It may often in such cases be possible to imply such a term, for instance requiring the finished item to be reasonably fit for the buyer's purpose (see, e.g. *IBA v BICC Construction Ltd* (1980) 14 BLR 9, a commercial case), but such a term will only be implied if its implication would be necessary in the particular case. The remedies available to the customer for breach of contract by the supplier, and the supplier's freedom to exclude liability for breach of contract may also be affected by the categorisation of the contract.

The problem of classification is exacerbated where the supplier produces the finished item using materials supplied by the customer. As we have seen, the Directive treats such contracts as contracts of sale, but exempts the seller from liability for lack of conformity originating in the materials supplied by the consumer. It is not clear how English law would classify such contracts. However, the natural interpretation would probably be that the materials used remain at all times the consumer's property, the supplier providing his work, and possibly ancillary materials, to produce the finished product. To construe the contract as one of sale of the finished item would probably require it to be inferred that the consumer had first transferred the property in his materials to the supplier to enable the supplier to use them. Such an interpretation would be possible (see *Dixon v London Small Arms Co* (1876) 1 App Cas 632) but it would expose the consumer to the risk of misappropriation of the materials by the supplier or loss of them in the event of the supplier's insolvency.

2.3.2.2 *Contracts to supply and install*
We have seen that the Directive applies to contracts where goods are installed by or under the responsibility of the seller and installation forms part of the contract and have suggested above that this will apply wherever the seller has a contractual commitment to install the goods supplied.

It would be possible to apply a 'substance of the contract' test to such contracts so that in domestic law a contract would be classified purely as one of sale where the predominant element of the supplier's obligation is to supply the goods. However, the more natural approach, at least where the supplier is contractually obliged to install the goods, would be to treat the contract as one for work and materials covered by the 1982 Act, so that the supplier is strictly liable for the materials supplied and is required to perform the installation with reasonable skill and care, and that would seem to be the most likely interpretation of the various contracts considered in 2.2.2.2 above.

2.4 CHANGES MADE BY THE SSGCR 2002

Implementation of the Directive has required changes to be made to the definition of 'consumer' in the SoGA and related legislation, and a new definition of 'producer' to be introduced for certain purposes. The definition of 'auction sales' in UCTA has also been modified. On the whole, however, relatively few changes have been made to domestic law as a result of the matters considered above. As a result it is not clear that the Directive has been properly implemented.

2.4.1 Consumer

The DTI originally proposed to adopt a definition of consumer based on that in the Unfair Terms Directive, in the interests of producing a more coherent body of legislation. Since the Unfair Terms Directive defines 'consumer' more widely than does the Sales Directive, that would probably have been permissible in European law. Ultimately however it was decided not to adopt this approach, and for most purposes the SSGCR apply a modified definition of 'dealing as consumer', based on that in UCTA. However, they also introduce a separate, different definition of 'consumer' for other, limited purposes.

2.4.1.1 *'Dealing as a consumer'*

A number of changes have been made to the definition of 'dealing as a consumer' in section 12 UCTA in order to implement the Directive. A new sub-section 1A provides that where the buyer is an individual (as opposed to a legal person), the question of whether the goods are of a type ordinarily supplied for private use or consumption in section 12(1)(c) must be ignored. All that is necessary for the buyer to qualify as a consumer is therefore that

(a)   the buyer does not make the contract in the course of a business, and

(b)   the seller does do so.

This definition is more generous than that in the Directive. Under the Directive, a buyer will only then be a consumer if the goods are bought for a purpose which is not related to his trade, business or profession. The UCTA definition requires a stronger connection with a business before the buyer falls outside the definition of 'dealing as a consumer'. As the Directive expressly permits derogations from its provisions if they promote a higher level of consumer protection (Article 8(2); see chapter 1), the retention of the 'in the course of a business' formula is permitted.

As the law presently stands the test for determining whether the buyer is dealing in the course of a business is that set out in the *R&B Customs Brokers* case. Since that test permits a limited company to qualify as a 'consumer' in some circumstances it is important that the third limb of the definition of consumer, that the goods be of a type ordinarily supplied for private use or consumption, has been retained for transactions where the buyer is not an individual. This provision will therefore continue to restrict the situations in which a limited company can be considered to deal as consumer pursuant to the *R&B Customs Brokers* decision. As noted above, it is not clear which test is to be applied in determining whether the seller is acting in the course of a business under UCTA.

2.4.1.2 *'Consumer' in the SSGCR*

In addition to the changes made to section 12 of UCTA, there is a specific definition of 'consumer' in Regulation 2 of the SSGCR. This states that consumer 'means any natural person who, in the contracts governed by these Regulations, is acting for purposes which are outside his trade, business or profession'. However, as most of the provisions of the 2002 Regulations merely amend existing legislation, this definition only applies to Regulation 15 on consumer guarantees.

It is surprising to see that this definition uses the term 'natural person', derived from the Directive, rather than the word 'individual', used in the amendments to section 12 of UCTA . In the interests of consistency, it would have been preferable to use the same term in both provisions. In fact the definition of 'consumer' in Regulation 2 is taken not from the Directive but from the Unfair Contract Terms Directive, using the expression 'outside' in preference to 'not in the course of' his trade etc. As noted above, since this results in a slightly more generous definition of 'consumer', it is permissible.

2.4.2 Producer

A further change made by the SSGCR 2002 is that a definition of 'producer' has been inserted into the SoGA, SSGA and SoG(IT)A. This is copied from the Directive and defines 'producer' as 'the manufacturer of goods, the importer of goods into the European Economic Area or any person purporting to be a producer by placing his name, trade mark or other distinctive sign on the goods'. The definition in Article 1(2)(d) of the Directive refers to 'consumer goods' rather than simply 'goods'. However, no distinction is made in English law between consumer and non-consumer goods, and this restriction would therefore have been unnecessary.

2.4.3 Goods

The SoGA definition of goods was already broadly similar to that implicit in the Directive, and has not been changed. The status of computer software therefore remains unclear both in domestic law and under the Directive and will await clarification by the courts.

2.4.4 Auction sales

UCTA section 12(2) has been amended with the effect that where second-hand goods are sold at public auction which individuals have the opportunity of attending in person, a buyer who is an individual is nevertheless not to be regarded as dealing as a consumer. Consequently, those provisions in the SoGA and related legislation which only apply where the buyer is dealing as a consumer have no effect in such a case. Thus the new remedial scheme derived from the Directive and contained in SoGA Part 5A will not apply in such a case. In addition, although the terms in sections 13–15 SoGA are implied into a contract concluded at a public auction which individuals can attend in person, it may be possible to exclude these provided that the exclusion satisfies the tests of reasonableness under section 6 UCTA and fairness under the Unfair Terms in Consumer Contracts Regulations, 1999.

2.4.5 Contracts to manufacture and supply goods and to supply and install goods

Although the Directive applies only to contracts of sale, albeit in an extended sense as noted above, the DTI decided in implementing the Directive to extend some of its provisions to some types of non-sale supply contract, continuing the modern policy of seeking to assimilate the law governing different types of supply.

Changes corresponding to those described above have therefore been made to the legislation governing other types of supply contract. For example, the terms implied into contracts of sale by sections 13–15 SoGA are also implied into contracts for the transfer of property in goods other than sale by the corresponding sections in the Supply of Goods and Services Act 1982, and also into contracts for the supply of goods on hire-purchase by the Supply of Goods (Implied Terms) Act 1973. Changes made to the implied terms are made to all of these measures. However, the new remedies introduced by the Directive are only made available, in addition to contracts of sale, for contracts for the transfer of property in the goods. We have already noted the difficulties of amending legislation dealing with transactions other than sale through regulations adopted under the European Communities Act 1972 (see chapter 1 at 1.3.3.2).

No special provision has been made in the SSGCR to implement either Article 1(4) or 2(5) of the Directive, the only concession being to extend the definition of 'non-conformity' to cases where goods are installed by the seller and the installation is effected without reasonable skill and care in breach of the term implied by section 13 SGSA 1982.

It seems that this is not enough to implement the Directive. There is sufficient flexibility in the case-law and statutory provisions to allow them to be manipulated and applied in a way which more or less satisfies some of the requirements of the Directive. However, as we have noted, this is likely to be regarded as insufficient to satisfy the UK's EC law obligations. Moreover it seems clear that in some regards the existing legislation cannot be interpreted in a way which satisfies the Directive. This is one of the most significant gaps in the implementing legislation and we will return to this point as we examine the relevant substantive provisions in later chapters.

3

GOODS MUST BE IN CONFORMITY
WITH THE CONTRACT

3.1 INTRODUCTION

The core provision of the Directive is Article 2 which requires the seller to deliver goods 'which are in conformity with the contract of sale'. As the recitals to the Directive state, 'the principle of conformity with the contract may be considered as common to the different national legal traditions' of the EU Member States. Indeed, the concept is familiar not only to the laws of the EU Member States, but to almost all legal systems. In the UK the concept is given effect through statutory implied terms in sections 13–15 of the Sale of Goods Act 1979 and the corresponding legislation governing other contracts for the supply of goods. Those implied terms require the goods

    (a) if sold by description, to correspond with that description;

    (b) to be of satisfactory quality;

    (c) if the buyer makes known to the seller the purpose for which he requires the goods, to be reasonably fit for that purpose; and

    (d) if sold by sample, to correspond with the sample.

Similar provisions can be found in the laws of most countries, and there are broadly corresponding provisions in both the Vienna Convention and its predecessor, the Uniform Law on International Sales. The requirements of the Directive—unlike, say, the introduction of the concept of 'good faith' in the Unfair Terms Directive—should therefore come as no great shock to the common law. There are nevertheless small but significant differences between the provisions of the Directive and those of the prior English law.

This chapter will provide a brief overview of the Directive's conformity requirement before examining the pre-implementation domestic law. It will then consider the Directive's provisions in more detail and finally examine how they have been implemented in the UK.

3.2 THE DIRECTIVE

In its original *Green Paper on Consumer Guarantees and After Sales Service* the Commission proposed a requirement that goods should be required to conform to the consumer's 'legitimate expectations', described as 'a dynamic concept to be assessed taking all of the circumstances into account and, notably, the provisions of the contract, the presentation of the product, the price, the brand, the advertising or any information provided on the product, the nature of the product, its purpose, the laws and regulations concerning the product, and other features' (p 86). However, it seems that although this approach was generally welcomed by consumer representatives, 'professional circles' took 'a dim view' of it, and when a draft Directive was published in 1995, the requirement that goods conform to the consumer's legitimate expectations had been replaced by one that the seller deliver goods which conform to the contract, with a test of conformity based on the provisions of the Vienna Convention. This approach was said to be 'in conformity with most modern legal systems' and, confusingly, a 'new and shared concept of conformity of the goods with the contract' (p 11). The approach was to create a rebuttable presumption of conformity if goods satisfied certain requirements. This approach was carried through into the final text of the Directive, albeit with a number of significant changes of wording. Thus Article 2 of the Directive provides that:

1. The seller must deliver goods to the consumer which are in conformity with the contract of sale.
2. Consumer goods are presumed to be in conformity with the contract if they:
    (a) comply with the description given by the seller and possess the qualities of the goods which the seller has held out to the consumer as a sample or a model;
    (b) are fit for any particular purpose for which the consumer requires them and which he made known to the seller at the time of conclusion of the contract and which the seller has accepted;
    (c) are fit for the purposes for which goods of the same type are normally used;
    (d) show the quality and performance which are normal in goods of the same type and which the consumer can reasonably expect, given the nature of the goods and taking into account any public statements on the specific characteristics of the goods made about them by the seller, the producer or his representative, particularly in advertising or labelling.

3. There shall be deemed not to be a lack of conformity for the purposes of this Article if, at the time the contract was concluded, the consumer was aware, or could not reasonably be unaware of, the lack of conformity, or if the lack of conformity has its origin in materials supplied by the consumer.

Article 2(1) thus lays down the seller's basic duty: to deliver goods which conform to the contract. Under English sales law, and presumably under the corresponding laws of most other legal systems, the seller's basic duty is to deliver the goods. The Directive, however, does not address the duty to deliver which is presumably left to domestic law. Thus the buyer has no remedy under the Directive if the seller fails to deliver at all. However, the Directive clearly takes the duty to deliver for granted, because the general requirement that the goods should conform to the contract qualifies the seller's duty to deliver the goods: the seller must deliver goods which conform to the contract. Article 2 paragraph 2 then establishes a rebuttable presumption that the goods do conform to the contract if certain requirements are satisfied. Article 2(3) qualifies that general presumption by disapplying it in certain situations. Article 2(4) further qualifies the presumption by allowing the seller in certain circumstances to escape responsibility for public statements as referred to in Article 2(2)(d). Article 2(5) extends the conformity requirement by treating a lack of conformity resulting from incorrect installation of the goods as a lack of conformity in the goods in certain situations.

3.2.1 The Vienna Convention

As noted already (see 1.2), the conformity test in the Directive was heavily influenced by the provisions of the United Nations Convention on Contracts for the International Sale of Goods. Generally we might question whether an international convention concerned solely with *commercial* transactions was an appropriate model for a Directive concerned solely with the protection of consumers. However, as the Directive notes, and as we have observed above, the principles upon which the CISG is based are themselves widely recognised in domestic legal systems.

It may be useful to set out the corresponding provision, Article 35, of the CISG for comparison. Article 35 provides as follows—

(1) The seller must deliver goods which are of the quantity, quality and description required by the contract and which are contained or packaged in the manner required by the contract.

(2) Except where the parties have agreed otherwise, the goods do not conform with the contract unless they–

  (a) are fit for the purposes for which goods of the same description would ordinarily be used;

  (b) are fit for any particular purpose expressly or impliedly made known to the seller at the time of the conclusion of the contract, except where the circumstances show that the buyer did not rely, or that it was unreasonable for him to rely, on the seller's skill and judgement;

(c) possess the qualities of goods which the seller has held out to the buyer as a sample or model;

(d) are contained or packaged in the manner usual for such goods or, where there is no such manner, in a manner adequate to preserve and protect the goods.

(3) The seller is not liable under subparagraphs (a) to (d) of the preceding paragraph for any lack of conformity of the goods if at the time of the conclusion of the contract the buyer knew or could not have been unaware of such lack of conformity.

As can be seen, although the language of the Directive differs in some regards from that of Article 35 of the CISG, the two provisions are broadly similar. The main differences are the inclusion in the CISG of specific provision for the packaging of the goods, which may be of particular importance in international commercial transactions, and the inclusion in Article 2(3) of the Directive of a special exclusion of the conformity requirement where the lack of conformity originates in materials supplied by the buyer.

3.2.2 No general principle

As we have noted, the Commission's *Green Paper* proposed a more broadly based general requirement that goods should comply with the consumer's 'legitimate expectations'. That approach was rejected in favour of the more detailed requirement in Article 2. However, it is clear that the general principle underlying the Article 2 conformity requirement is that the goods should conform to the buyer's reasonable, or legitimate, expectations. That is clearly implicit in Article 2(1) which requires the seller to deliver goods which conform to the contract. The law of contract is concerned with the protection of reasonable expectations. Unpacking the language of Article 2(1) we may therefore say that the goods delivered must conform to the buyer's reasonable expectations derived from the contract.

That correspondence with reasonable, or legitimate, expectations is the underlying principle of Article 2 is confirmed by the language of Article 2(2)(d) which specifically requires that the goods 'show the quality and performance which are normal in goods of the same type and which the consumer can reasonably expect', and the principle is implicit in Article 2(3) which provides in mandatory terms that there shall be deemed not to be a lack of conformity in respect of any matter of which the consumer was aware, or could not reasonably be unaware, even if that matter would otherwise amount to a lack of conformity: if the consumer is aware of a defect in the goods he cannot claim that he *reasonably expected* the goods to be free of that defect.

As we have observed the reason for abandoning the general principle of compliance with legitimate expectations in favour of the more detailed requirement based on the CISG was a concern that the general requirement lacked substance and was perhaps too open textured. In particular it might create uncertainty until a sufficient body of explanatory case-law had developed. It is however unfortunate that the general principle was abandoned altogether. It is clear that the requirements of Article 2 are neither a necessary nor a sufficient test of conformity with the contract and explicit recognition of the principle on which the Directive is based might have facilitated the application of the conformity test.

3.2.3 A rebuttable presumption of conformity

Article 2 adopts a slightly peculiar approach. Having set out the general requirement of conformity in Article 2(1), Article 2(2) creates a presumption that goods conform to the contract if they satisfy the requirements set out in sub-paragraphs 2(a)–(d). It does not, as such, require goods to comply with the requirements of Article 2(2).

It is important to emphasise that the presumption of conformity created by Article 2(2) is rebuttable: in other words goods which satisfy Article 2(2) may nevertheless be held not to be in conformity with the contract. This is not explicitly stated in the substantive provisions of the Directive. It is, however, implicitly confirmed by recitals 6 and 7. Recital 6 states that the Directive is not intended to impinge on 'the provisions and principles of national law relating to contractual and non-contractual liability'. Recital 7 indicates specifically that the 'additional national provisions may be useful to ensure that the consumer is protected in cases where the parties have agreed no specific contractual terms'. Recital 8 however makes the point explicit, stating that:

... in order to facilitate the application of the principle of conformity with the contact, it is useful to introduce a rebuttable presumption of conformity with the contract covering the most common situations; whereas that presumption does not restrict the principle of freedom of contract;

and continues to state that the elements of the presumption may be used to determine the lack of conformity of the goods with the contract 'in the absence of specific contractual terms'.

3.2.3.1 *The Vienna Convention*
Although Article 2 is modelled on Article 35 of the Vienna Convention the two instruments take different approaches to the conformity requirement. As we have noted, the Directive creates a rebuttable presumption that the goods *do* conform to the contract provided they satisfy certain stipulated requirements. The Vienna Convention, on the other hand, adopts the opposite approach and states that 'unless the parties have agreed otherwise' the goods do *not* conform to the contract unless they satisfy certain, broadly analogous, requirements. In short the Vienna Convention creates a rebuttable presumption of non-conformity if goods do not comply with the requirements of Article 35.

3.2.3.2 *The presumption is rebuttable*

It is important to recognise that a lack of conformity may arise other than through the goods' failure to correspond with Article 2(2) because a lack of conformity triggers the Directive's remedial scheme. As recitals 7 and 8 indicate, goods which satisfy Article 2(2) will nevertheless lack conformity with the contract where they do not conform to one of the express terms of the contract. What is not clear, however, is whether all breaches of express terms give rise to a lack of conformity so as to trigger the Directive's remedial scheme. In English law contract terms are categorised as conditions, warranties and innominate terms. Under a contract for the sale of goods breach of a condition always entitles the buyer to reject the goods and terminate the contract. Breach of a term classified as a warranty, on the other hand, only gives rise to a right to damages and not to a right to reject the goods and terminate the contract. The consequences of a breach of a term classified as innominate depend on the seriousness of the breach, the buyer being entitled to reject the goods and terminate the contract only if the consequences of the breach are so serious as to deprive him of substantially the whole benefit of the contract. The terms implied into the contract of sale by the Sale of Goods Act are all categorised by the Act either as conditions or warranties—all but two being conditions—but the classification of express terms will depend on the intention of the parties as identified by the court, and it is clear that a court may be inclined to classify an express term as 'innominate' in order to maintain remedial flexibility.

It is clear that there is no room for this type of categorisation under the Directive: breach of any term—warranty, condition or innominate—may be said to give rise to a lack of conformity and thus to trigger the remedial scheme of the Directive. The significance of this should not be underestimated. The consumer's 'long-stop' remedy for lack of conformity under the Directive is to 'rescind' the contract and seek a refund of the price (Article 3(5); see 4.2.5). In other words, the effect of the Directive will be that in some cases a consumer may now be entitled to reject goods and obtain a refund of the price for a breach of express warranty or innominate term. Admittedly, rescission under Article 3 is a remedy of last resort and is only available where neither repair nor replacement is available or where both have been unsuccessful. Moreover the right of rescission is restricted, the Directive providing that the consumer is not entitled to have the contract rescinded if the lack of conformity is minor (Article 3(6)), but it would seem that this imports a *de minimis* restriction: a breach may be more than 'minor' without being so serious as to deprive the consumer of substantially the whole benefit of the contract, and it may therefore be that in the future consumers will in effect be entitled to reject, in appropriate circumstances, for breaches which would not have justified rejection in the past.

But can breach of all express terms give rise to a lack of conformity? Typically a contract will include express terms governing such matters as the fundamental nature of the goods, the date of delivery and the quantity to be delivered. Can the buyer invoke the Directive's remedial scheme in the event of late, or early, delivery or delivery of the wrong quantity? This could be significant. If non-timely delivery or delivery of the wrong quantity constitutes delivery of goods not conforming to the contract the buyer might be entitled to require the seller to 'replace' the goods under the Directive—e.g. by requiring the seller to recover and then redeliver the goods at the right time, or in the right quantity. As we have seen above, the CISG expressly refers to quantity in Article 35. The Directive makes no mention of the issue. It is clear, however, that issues of delivery were intended to be excluded from the scope of the Commission's original Green Paper which observed that 'questions pertaining to . . . the obligation to deliver . . . are conceptually distinct from the notion of guarantee'. Although this approach may be criticised from a purely English law perspective, and indeed, although the conceptual connection between delivery and the conformity of the goods with the contract is recognised in the Directive's final text, there is nothing to indicate that it was ever intended to bring issues relating to quantity or the time of delivery within the scope of the Directive. It is submitted therefore that delivery of the wrong quantity and/or delivery at the wrong time does not involve a lack of conformity with the contract.

3.2.3.3 *Goods conform to the contract despite not complying with Article 2(2)*
It has been suggested that goods which satisfy the requirements of Article 2(2) may nevertheless be held not to be in conformity with the contract. Conversely it is submitted that goods which do not satisfy the requirements of Article 2(2) may in an appropriate case still be in conformity with the contract. As noted above, Article 2(3) recognises limitations to the conformity requirement in certain circumstances. In addition, recital 8 recognises that the issues listed as aspects of conformity in Article 2(2) may not all be relevant in every case. Thus it states that 'the elements mentioned in the presumption are cumulative; . . . if the circumstances render any particular element manifestly inappropriate, the remaining elements of the presumption will nevertheless apply'. It is submitted, however, that it will be for the seller to prove that a particular element is inappropriate if he wishes so to argue. Article 2(2) does not as such impose a requirement that goods should comply with its provisions (unlike the implied terms of the Sale of Goods Act). Thus although it may well be difficult for the seller to persuade a court that goods which do not comply with the requirements of paragraphs (a)–(d) of Article 2(2) are in conformity with the contract, it is at least possible that that may be the case.

3.2.3.4 *The burden of proof*
Although there is no reference to the burden of proof in Article 2 it is submitted that the effect of defining the conformity requirement in terms of a rebuttable presumption of conformity is to throw the burden of proof in the first instance onto the seller to show that the goods do satisfy the requirements of Article 2(2). The consumer will initially raise the issue by alleging that the goods are not in conformity with the contract, indentifying the particular defect, and claiming one of

the remedies available under the Directive. Where the alleged lack of conformity is non-compliance with description or unfitness for purpose the consumer may also have to assert the manner in which the goods do not conform. If this analysis is correct, satisfaction of the requirements of Article 2(2) is, in effect, a defence for the seller to a claim by the consumer that the goods are not in conformity with the contract. If the seller can discharge that burden the burden of proof then passes to the consumer to rebut the presumption of conformity by showing that the goods fail to comply with some other express requirement of the particular contract. This is in sharp contrast with the position in English law where the onus is on the consumer to show that the goods do not conform to the requirements of the contract.

3.3 ENGLISH LAW PRIOR TO IMPLEMENTATION OF THE DIRECTIVE

As we have noted, the concept that under a contract of sale the seller must deliver goods which conform to the contract is familiar to most legal systems. In English law it is given effect primarily through the terms implied into contracts for the sale of goods by sections 13–15 of the SoGA 1979. Those terms require that:

 (a) where the goods are sold by description, they should correspond with that description (s 13);

 (b) the goods should be of satisfactory quality (s 14(2));

 (c) the goods should be fit for the buyer's purpose where he makes that known to the seller (s 14(3)); and

 (d) where goods are sold by sample, the goods should correspond with the sample (s 15).

Similar terms are implied into other contracts for the supply of goods by analogous provisions of other legislation (see Supply of Goods (Implied Terms) Act 1973, sections 9–11 (hire purchase); Supply of Goods and Services Act 1982, sections 3–5 (other supply contracts) and sections 8–10 (hire)).

 Taken together the effect of the statutory implied terms may be said to be to require the goods to conform to the buyer's reasonable, or legitimate expectations, and it is clear that when the implied terms were developed in English law in the 19th century that was their underlying rationale. This is implicitly recognised in sections 34 and 35 of the Act which deal with the buyer's loss of the right to reject the goods on the grounds of acceptance. Section 34 provides that when the seller tenders delivery he is bound to afford the buyer 'a reasonable opportunity of examining the goods for the purpose of ascertaining whether they are *in conformity with the contract*' and section 35(2) similarly provides that the buyer is not to be taken as having accepted the goods so as to lose the right to reject them until he has had such opportunity of examining them. Put another way, a convincing case can be made for seeing the implied terms as being concerned with the protection and promotion of good faith. If the buyer's expectations are reasonable, the seller must reasonably be aware of them, and a reasonable seller, being aware of the buyer's expectations, cannot in good faith expect or require the buyer to accept goods which do not meet those expectations.

3.3.1 Historical development

The implied terms emerged in English law gradually over a period of some 60 or so years commencing around the turn of the 19th century. Prior to that the guiding principle of the common law was '*caveat emptor*'—let the buyer beware. The buyer had no right of redress against the seller if goods proved defective unless he could show either that the seller had given an express warranty of quality, or that the seller had been fraudulent. *Caveat emptor* was however not known either to the mediaeval common law or Roman law. Nor was it a principle of the law merchant. It appears to have emerged as a principle of English law in the 16th or 17th century. (The case generally cited as its origin in sale law is *Chandelor v Lopus* (1603) Cro. Jac. 4.) In 1633 Coke contrasted the common law rule with that of the civil law:

Note that by the civil law every man is bound to warrant the thing he selleth or conveyeth, albeit there be no express warranty . . .; but the common law bindeth him not for *caveat emptor*. (Coke Litt (1633) 102a; L.2 C.7 S.145)

Caveat emptor flourished with the development of ideas of free trade. Yet, by the start of the 19th century the doctrine was already in decline and in a series of cases the English courts gradually developed the principle that where the buyer bought goods without prior examination they should conform to certain minimum implied requirements, given effect through the contract as implied terms. (For discussion of the emergence of the implied terms see Mitchell (2001).)

Although it is difficult to extract one coherent principle from the 19th century case-law, by the time the law of sale was codified in the Sale of Goods Act in 1893, the statutory draftsman, Sir Mackenzie Chalmers, was able to identify in it a series of implied terms, which required that:

(a) where goods were sold by description they should correspond with the description (section 13);

(b) where the buyer made known to the seller the purpose for which he required the goods, the goods should be reasonably fit for that purpose (section 14(1));

(c) where goods were sold by description, the goods should be of merchantable quality; and

(d) where goods were sold by sample the bulk should correspond to the sample and be free of defects not apparent on a reasonable inspection of the sample.

As a result although the Act stated *caveat emptor* to be the governing principle, it was eroded almost out of existence and the common law and civil law were, broadly speaking, more or less aligned.

The 1893 Act was essentially a codification (albeit with some modifications) of the prior case-law. Most of that case-law had been concerned with disputes between merchants. However, the late Victorian era saw the early development of the modern consumer society and during the 20th century the courts had to apply the law to consumer transactions. The result was to extend the scope of the implied terms, particularly of the merchantable quality requirement. However, despite statutory reform including, in 1973, the introduction of a definition of 'merchantable quality', there was by the 1980s a widespread view that the law was insufficiently attuned to the needs and expectations of consumers. As a result, in 1994, the Supply of Goods and Services Act was passed to implement recommendations made by the Law Commission in its 1987 report 160, 'Sale and Supply of Goods'. Amongst the reforms effected by the 1994 Act was the replacement of the requirement that goods be of merchantable quality by a requirement that goods be of 'satisfactory quality'. A list of factors which could, where appropriate, be taken into account in applying the new requirement was also added to the legislation.

3.3.1.1 *Implied terms in contracts other than sale*
The SoGA 1979 applies only to contracts of sale. However, similar terms are now implied into all contracts for the supply of goods, by the Supply of Goods (Implied Terms) Act 1973 (sections 9–11: hire-purchase) and the Supply of Goods and Services Act 1982 (sections 3–5: contracts for the transfer of goods). Unless otherwise stated in the following discussion of English law statements about the implied terms in contracts of sale apply equally to the corresponding implied terms in other forms of supply contract.

3.3.2 Significance of the implied terms

The implied terms are the cornerstone of private law consumer protection in English law. Their significance derives from several features.

1) They arise automatically, by implication. The requirement that goods correspond with description applies to all cases where goods are sold by description, including private sales. The implied requirements that goods be of satisfactory quality and reasonably fit for the buyer's purpose only apply where goods are sold in the course of a business (see 2.3.1.3), but subject to that the implied terms arise automatically and apply to all goods supplied under the contract.

2) The terms are all classified as conditions, with the consequence that in the event of a breach by the seller the buyer is entitled to reject the goods and obtain a full refund of the price paid.

3) Attempts to exclude the implied terms or liability or remedies for their breach are controlled by the Unfair Contract Terms Act 1977. Where the buyer deals as a consumer any attempt to exclude or restrict the terms etc. is wholly ineffective (UCTA 1977 section 6—contracts of sale and hire purchase; UCTA sec-

tion 7—other contracts for supply of goods: see 5.3.1). Moreover any attempt to exclude or restrict the implied terms is a criminal offence (Consumer Transactions (Restrictions on Statements) Order 1976. The 1976 Order was made under the now-repealed Part II of the Fair Trading Act 1973, but the Enterprise Act 2002, which replaces the 1973 Act, preserves the Order).

3.3.3 Goods must correspond with description

Section 13 of the SoGA provides that 'where there is a contract for the sale of goods by description, there is an implied term that the goods will correspond with the description.' The implied term applies to all sales, regardless of the status of seller or buyer. Thus where goods are sold by a private seller there is an implied term that they correspond with any description by which they are sold.

3.3.3.1 *Sale by description*

It may be that originally 'sale by description' was limited to cases where the buyer bought goods which he had no prior opportunity to examine. However, partly in order to extend the scope of the original merchantable quality term (which in the 1893 Act applied only where goods were sold by description), the courts gave 'sale by description' an extended meaning. Thus it was held that there could be a sale of specific goods by description (*Varley v Whipp* [1900] 1 QB 513) and even where the buyer saw and selected the goods in a self-service context (*Grant v Australian Knitting Mills Ltd* [1936] AC 85, PC: see now SoGA section 13(3)).

On the other hand, a sale is not a sale by description merely because descriptive words are used in negotiations or in the contract. The goods must be sold *by* description, and the courts have held that in order to bring the implied term into play the description must identify an essential commercial characteristic of the goods (*Ashington Piggeries Ltd v Christopher Hill Ltd* [1972] AC 441, [1971] 1 All ER 847, HL) and be such that the buyer would reasonably be expected to rely on it. Thus in *Harlingdon & Leinster Ltd v Christopher Hull Fine Art Ltd* [1991] 1 QB 564, [1990] 1 All ER 737, CA the Court of Appeal held that where a painting was sold as being by German expressionist painter Gabriele Münter, the attribution to Münter did not form part of the contractual description for the purposes of section 13. The seller made the attribution in reliance on the description in a 1980 auction catalogue and made clear to the buyer that he had no particular expertise in the area. In contrast the buyer did claim specialist expertise in expressionist painting. The Court of Appeal held that there could not be a sale by description unless the description was influential in the sale, so as to become an essential term of the contract, and so there could not be a sale by description where the parties could not reasonably expect the buyer to rely on the description

Even within the bounds of these restrictions it is clear that the court has considerable latitude to determine what is the description by which the goods are sold. Goods may be described broadly or in great detail. The description may be oral or

written, and may be given by the seller or derived from sales or promotional material which the seller expressly, or impliedly, adopts. The essence of a sale by
description it is suggested, is reasonable reliance: was the description such that a
reasonable buyer would rely on it as defining the goods to be supplied? Once however it is determined that goods are sold by description, they must exactly comply
with the description by which they are sold. Liability is strict and exact compliance is required.

3.3.4 Goods must be of satisfactory quality

Section 14(2) of the SoGA requires that where the seller sells goods in the course
of a business there is an implied condition that the goods supplied under the contract are of satisfactory quality. Unlike the correspondence with description term
in section 13 the satisfactory quality term only applies where the seller sells in the
course of a business. It therefore does not apply on a private sale, when *caveat
emptor* is still the governing principle. On the other hand it has been held that in
this context any sale *by* a business is a sale in the course of a business. There is no
requirement of regularity. So when a fisherman sold off a trawler the sale was in
the course of a business so as to attract the implied term (*Stevenson v Rogers* [1999]
1 All ER 613; see 2.3.1.3).

The term applies not merely to the goods sold but to the goods 'supplied under
the contract'. Thus it has been held that it applies to goods mistakenly supplied in
purported performance of the contract (*Wilson v Rickett, Cockerill & Co* [1954] 1
QB 598, [1954] 1 All ER 168), and to returnable packaging which was supplied but
not sold to the buyer (*Geddling v Marsh* [1920] 1 KB 668).

3.3.4.1 *Satisfactory quality*
Prior to 1994 the Act required goods to be of merchantable quality. Section 14(6)
of the SoGA 1979 provided that:

> Goods of any kind are of merchantable quality . . . if they are as fit for the purpose or pur-
> poses for which goods of that kind are commonly bought as it is reasonable to expect hav-
> ing regard to any description applied to them, the price (if relevant) and all the other
> relevant circumstances.

As noted above, however, concern was expressed that the concept of 'merchantable quality', with its apparent reference to saleability, was inappropriate for
consumer transactions, and that it failed to take full account of qualities which a
consumer might require in goods. In 1994 therefore the requirement was replaced
by the current requirement that the goods supplied be of satisfactory quality.
Section 14(2A) of the 1979 Act now provides that:

> goods are of satisfactory quality if they meet the standard that a reasonable person would
> regard as satisfactory, taking account of the description of the goods, the price (if relevant)
> and all the other relevant circumstances.

3.3.4.2 *Factors relevant to the assessment of quality*
This definition is expanded by section 14(2B) which states that:

The quality of goods includes their state and condition and the following (among others) are in appropriate cases aspects of the quality of goods—

  (a) fitness for all the purposes for which goods of that kind are commonly supplied;
  (b) appearance and finish;
  (c) freedom from minor defects;
  (d) safety; and
  (e) durability.

These factors are intended to reflect some of the more important aspects of consumer expectations of goods. It is clear, however, that these factors are neither necessary nor sufficient conditions for goods to be regarded as being of satisfactory quality. Section 14(2B) expressly states that these factors are aspects of quality 'in an appropriate case'. Thus goods are not necessarily unsatisfactory merely because they lack (say) durability. The key factor again appears to be the buyer's reasonable expectation. Thus in *Thain v Anniesland Trade Centre* (1997) SLT (Sh Ct) 102, it was held that a second-hand Renault, which was some five years old and had done some 80,000 miles, bought for £2995, was of satisfactory quality even though the gear box failed shortly after purchase. It was found as fact that the gear box failed due to wear and age so that at the time of sale it was likely to fail at any time; that such wear was not unusual in a car of this age, but that it had not actually begun to fail at the time of sale. The car therefore lacked durability but the court found that it was nevertheless of satisfactory quality because, on the facts, durability was not a quality which a reasonable person would expect of a car of this age and price.

Equally, and conversely, other factors may be relevant in an appropriate case and may make goods unsatisfactory. Thus prior to 1994 it was established that warnings and instructions could be relevant in the assessment of goods' quality and, in particular, that inaccurate, misleading or incomplete instructions could make goods unmerchantable (see *Wormell v RHM Agriculture (East) Ltd* [1987] 3 All ER 75; [1987] 1 WLR 1091—goods held not unmerchantable on the facts. See generally McLeod (1981) LQR 550). There seems no reason why the same principle should not apply in the assessment whether goods are of satisfactory quality.

Similarly compliance with appropriate technical standards adopted by the BSI may be a relevant factor when assessing whether goods are of satisfactory quality (see most recently, *Britvic Soft Drinks v Messer UK Ltd* [2002] EWCA Civ 548; [2002] 2 All ER Comm 321 (CA)). Goods which do not correspond with such a standard will generally not be of satisfactory quality (*Medivance Instruments Limited v (1) Gaslane Pipework Services Limited (2) Vulcana Gas Appliances Limited* (unreported; judgment of 18 April 2002)). However, the mere fact that goods do comply with a relevant standard does not mean that they are of satis-factory quality (*Central Regional Council v Uponor Ltd* (1996) SLT 645).

3.3.4.3 *Exclusion of the satisfactory quality requirement*

Although exclusion of the satisfactory quality term is prohibited by UCTA 1977 section 6, the seller may avoid liability in two situations. SoGA section 14(2C) pro-vides that the implied term

does not extend to any matter making the quality of goods unsatisfactory—

(a) which is specifically drawn to the buyer's attention before the contract is made,

(b) where the buyer examines the goods before the contract is made, which that exami-nation ought to reveal.

In effect therefore the buyer cannot complain of matters of which he has actual or constructive notice. The limitations in section 14(2C) are however of limited scope. The first only applies if the particular defect (etc.) is specifically drawn to the buyer's attention, although there is no requirement that the seller or his agent bring it to the buyer's attention. However, a general notification that goods are of a lower than normal quality may serve to lower the quality standard under section 14(2A). Thus, for instance, if crockery is sold as 'seconds' from a factory shop at a price lower than the normal full retail price, the consumer will be unable to com-plain of quality defects which one might reasonably expect to find in crockery sold as 'seconds', the description operating to lower the quality standard reasonably expected.

The second exception is equally limited. It applies only if the buyer does in fact examine the goods, in which case he cannot complain of defects which *that* examination ought to have revealed. Thus if the buyer chooses to examine the goods prior to purchase he must do so with reasonable care or take the conse-quences. There is, however, no obligation to examine the goods at all, although it may be that if the buyer leads the seller reasonably to believe that he has examined the goods he will be estopped from denying that he has done so. The buyer's exam-ination precludes him from complaining of defects which *that* examination ought to reveal. This is a curious formula. On the one hand it is clear that a cursory examination does not preclude the buyer from complaining about defects which a more thorough examination would have revealed. So, for instance, if a car buyer drives it a short distance he will not be precluded from complaining of an overheating problem which would have manifested itself had he driven a longer distance, or a defect which would have been revealed by a full mechanical exami-nation. On the other hand the test cannot be wholly subjective. It surely cannot lie in the buyer's mouth to say 'I carried out a full mechanical examination but did so negligently and therefore failed to discover the defect. Because of the negli-gent way I carried it out the defect could never have been revealed by the exami-nation.'

3.3.5 Reasonable fitness for purpose

The third implied term, in SoGA section 14(3), requires that, where the seller sells goods in the course of a business and the buyer makes known the particular purpose for which the goods are being bought, the goods must be reasonably fit for that purpose 'except where the circumstances show that the buyer does not rely, or that it is unreasonable for him to rely, on the skill or judgement of the seller'.

3.3.5.1 *Notification of purpose*
In order to rely on the fitness for purpose term the buyer must notify the seller of his purpose. He may do so expressly or impliedly. Where goods have a common use and the buyer makes no counter-indication it will be implied that they are purchased for their common purpose. So, for instance, the term applied where a buyer bought a hot-water bottle without indicating that it was purchased for any special purpose. It was implied that the buyer intended it for its normal purpose for which it was unfit (*Priest v Last* [1903] 2 KB 148; see also *Grant v Australian Knitting Mills Ltd* [1936] AC 85, PC). In most consumer transactions, this will mean that goods must not only be of satisfactory quality in accordance with the term implied by section 14(2), but also be fit for their ordinary purposes, as well as any particular purposes made known to the seller, in accordance with section 14(3). Both implied terms will be relevant and a consumer will generally be advised to plead a breach of both.

It is sufficient that the buyer indicates his purpose to the seller's agent authorised to receive such notification. Although this is not expressly stated in section 14(3) it must follow on general agency principles. Section 14(3) does mention one particular case of agency. Section 14(3)(b) provides that 'where the purchase price or part of it is payable by instalments and the goods were previously sold by a credit broker to the seller' it is sufficient if the buyer indicates his purpose to the credit broker. This covers the familiar situation where goods are supplied to the consumer on credit terms by a finance company which first acquires the goods from a dealer who also arranges the credit transaction (thus acting as a credit broker). Motor vehicles are often supplied on this basis. In such a case the consumer typically deals exclusively with the dealer rather than with his contractual supplier, the finance company. It is sufficient in such a case that the consumer indicates his purpose to the dealer.

3.3.5.2 *Particular purpose*
In order to rely on the implied term in section 14(3) the buyer must make known to the seller or his agent the particular purpose for which the goods are being bought. It is settled that the reference to 'particular purpose' does not require that the buyer indicate a special purpose, and the section applies equally where goods are purchased for their normal purpose as where they are purchased for an abnormal or special purpose.

On the other hand the section only requires that the goods be reasonably fit for the purpose indicated. Thus if the buyer does have a special purpose he must indicate it to the seller in order to rely on the section 14(3) term. This requirement has proved problematic over the years and has given rise to a number of difficult cases. In *Griffiths v Peter Conway Ltd* [1939] 1 All ER 685, CA a consumer purchased a Harris Tweed coat and contracted dermatitis from wearing it because she had especially sensitive skin. It was found as fact that the coat would have been perfectly suitable for a person of normal sensitivity. It was held that there was therefore no breach of the section 14(3) term because the coat was reasonably fit for the buyer's indicated purpose. In order to rely on the fitness for purpose term the buyer would have had to indicate her special sensitivity (of which she was in fact unaware). The result was the same where the buyer bought a camshaft for fitting to the engine of a named fishing vessel. The camshaft proved unsuitable because of the particular characteristics of the vessel, although it could be, and was, used satisfactorily in other similar engines. (See *Slater v Finning* [1997] AC 473, [1996] 3 All ER 398.) Thus if a consumer buys a new tyre for his car, specifying the make and model, and the seller supplies a tyre which is generally suitable for that make and model of car, the tyre is reasonably fit for the buyer's stated purpose even if, because of an unknown defect in the steering of the buyer's car, it proves unsuitable for that particular car and wears out prematurely. These decisions can be contrasted with that in the (non-consumer) case of *Ashington Piggeries Ltd v Christopher Hill Ltd* [1972] AC 441, [1971] 1 All ER 847, HL where an animal food manufacturer bought herring meal to be used in the manufacture of feed for mink. Due to chemical contamination the herring meal was toxic. It would be poisonous to all animals but was especially, and fatally, toxic to mink. The supplier knew that the meal was to be used in the manufacture of animal feed but not that the feed was to be used for mink. The House of Lords held that on these facts, because the meal was toxic to all animals, it was unfit for the purpose indicated by the buyer, manufacturing animal feed. The seller was therefore liable for the buyer's loss.

3.3.5.3 *Buyer must rely on seller*
In order to rely on the section 14(3) term the buyer must rely on the seller. However, reliance will rarely be an issue in consumer transactions. Where a consumer purchases from a retailer 'reliance will in general be inferred from the fact that a buyer goes to the shop in the confidence that the tradesman has selected his stock with skill and judgement' (per Lord Wright in *Grant v Australian Knitting Mills Ltd* [1936] AC 85 at 99).

All that is required is that the buyer rely on the seller's skill or judgement. Reliance is not limited to cases where the buyer relies on the seller to advise on the goods' suitability for his purpose. There was therefore a breach of the implied term where a consumer agreed to buy a car and, before the sale agreement was finalised, discovered a defect and returned the car to the seller's agent for repair. It was held that at the time the agreement was completed the buyer was relying on the skill of the agent to repair the car (*R and B Customs Brokers Ltd v United Dominions Trust Ltd* [1988] 1 All ER 847, [1988] 1 WLR 321, CA). In *Jewson v Kelly* (QB, 2 August 2002), the seller based his advice largely on product information supplied by the manufacturer of a heating boiler, but was nevertheless held liable because the decision to supply the boilers was still made by the seller. The Court of Appeal allowed Jewson's appeal and held that on the facts there was no breach of either the section 14(2) or 14(3) terms. The court did not however consider in any detail the question of the seller's reliance on promotional material provided by the manufacturer in advising on the goods' suitability for the buyer's purpose. *Jewson* was not a consumer case. It is submitted that in a consumer case a seller who identifies goods as fit for the consumer buyer's purpose on the basis of the manufacturer's promotional material should be liable for the breach of the section 14(3) term. We can note that this would be consistent with the increased emphasis on the relevance of manufacturer's public statements in assessing the goods' conformity with the contract.

The buyer's reliance on the seller need not be total. In an appropriate case the buyer may rely partly on the seller's skill or judgement and partly on his own. In such a case the implied term is engaged and is breached if the goods prove unfit for the buyer's purpose because of some matter within the area of reliance on the seller. Thus for instance in the *Ashington Piggeries* case the mink breeder sued the feed manufacturer for supplying toxic meal. The breeder had supplied the formula for the mink food but relied on the seller to obtain and use suitable ingredients in its manufacture. The meal was toxic due to a defect in one of the ingredients used by the manufacturer. The manufacturer was therefore liable because the lack of fitness originated within the area of his responsibility. The result would have been different had the meal been toxic because of an error in the buyer's formula.

The requirement of reliance on the seller seems to have reduced in significance in recent case-law. In *Britvic Soft Drinks v Messer UK Ltd* [2002] 1 Lloyd's Rep 20 (HC), Messer, a supplier of carbon-dioxide contaminated with benzene was held liable for a breach of the terms implied by section 14(2) and (3). Messer argued that they did not manufacture the gas nor test it themselves before supplying it to Britvic, the buyer, as Britvic were aware, and Britvic had therefore not relied on Messer's skill or judgement. At first instance, Tomlinson J rejected this, holding that it was 'sufficient that a buyer relies upon the skill or judgement of his immediate seller or any person from whom that seller has acquired the goods' (p 41). This seems to be a very generous interpretation of this provision. Although the outcome (finding a breach of the term implied by section 14(3)) is undoubtedly correct, the reasoning does not convince. Although Britvic knew that Messer did not test for benzene, it was accepted that no-one would have thought to carry out such testing because the presence of benzene was not anticipated. On that basis, Messer's argument that there was lack of reliance would fail (see also paragraphs 86–88 of the judgment of the trial judge in *Jewson v Kelly* (QB, 2 August 2002) for similar criticism of

Tomlinson J's observations. The Court of Appeal in *Britvic Soft Drinks* did not have to deal with this point. See also Sealy (2003) 62 CLJ 260.).

3.3.5.4 *Reliance must be reasonable*

The second proviso to section 14(3) is that the buyer's reliance on the seller must be reasonable. Clearly the reasonableness of reliance is connected to the requirement that the buyer notify the seller of his purpose with sufficient precision to allow the seller to exercise his skill or judgement. If the buyer has insufficiently indicated his purpose he cannot reasonably rely on the seller to supply goods fit for it. However, even where the buyer has sufficiently indicated his purpose it may be unreasonable for him to rely on the seller for other reasons. It is nevertheless submitted that it will rarely be unreasonable for a consumer to rely on a retailer, although it may be possible for the seller to avoid liability by disclaiming relevant expertise, thus making it unreasonable for the buyer to rely on him.

3.3.5.5 *Standard: reasonable fitness for purpose*

If it applies the term implied by section 14(3) requires that the goods supplied under the contract must be reasonably fit for the purpose indicated by the buyer. Absolute fitness is not required. The standard is therefore flexible and factors such as the degree of precision with which the purpose is specified and the price paid are likely to be relevant in determining the degree of fitness required to satisfy the implied term.

3.3.6 Sale by sample

Where goods are 'sold by sample' two further terms are implied (SoGA section 15). They require

(a)   that the bulk will correspond with the sample and

(b)   that the goods will be free from any defect making them unsatisfactory which would not be apparent on a reasonable examination of the goods.

The Act provides, unhelpfully, that a sale is 'by sample' 'where there is an express or implied term to that effect'. Case-law has interpreted the section as applying where a sample is used to define the subject matter of the contract. In such a case therefore the sample performs much the same function as the description where goods are sold be description, although it is clear (SoGA section 13(2)) that a sale may be by description *and* sample.

3.4 THE DIRECTIVE'S CONFORMITY REQUIREMENT

There are four elements to Article 2(2). As noted above, they are cumulative. Thus the goods delivered must satisfy all four elements, or as many of them as are appropriate in a particular case, in order to be presumed to be in conformity with the contract. However, as already noted there is no reason why goods which do not comply with all four paragraphs of Article 2(2) should not be held to be in conformity with the contract in an appropriate case.

3.4.1 Compliance with description and sample

Article 2(2)(a) provides that the goods are presumed to be in conformity with the contract if they comply with the description given by the seller and possess the qualities of the goods which the seller has held out to the consumer as a sample or a model. Article 2(2)(a) therefore creates two requirements which must be satisfied in an appropriate case if the goods are to be presumed to be in conformity with the contract. The goods must comply with the description given by the seller AND (where appropriate) possess the qualities which the seller has held out to the consumer as a sample or a model. Article 2(2)(a) is thus analogous to the terms implied by SoGA sections 13 and 15.

3.4.1.1 *Compliance with description*
Article 2(2) seems to require absolute correspondence with description to raise the presumption of conformity. Reasonable correspondence will not do. On the other hand, if as suggested above, the principle underlying the Directive is compliance with the buyer's reasonable expectations it must be the case that in certain circumstances the buyer is only entitled to expect reasonable compliance. An example might be provided by facts analogous to those of the old English commercial case of *Arcos Ltd v E. A. Ronaasen & Son* [1933] AC 470, HL, in which the buyer contracted to buy half-inch-thick timber staves. The seller delivered staves which varied in thickness, most being between one-half and nine-sixteenths of an inch thick. It was held that the goods delivered did not correspond to the contract description. The case is generally criticised, primarily on the grounds that the consequence of classifying the breach as one of the implied condition that goods should correspond with description was to trigger the buyer's right to reject the goods and, on the facts of the case, enable the buyer to escape from a bad bargain. One solution might be to interpret the contract description in such a case as being implicitly qualified by 'about' or some similar qualifier. It is suggested that in a case such as *Arcos* it might be relatively easy to infer such a qualification. Certainly it would seem reasonable that a court should be able to uphold the traditional approach of not taking account of *de minimis* variations from contract specification. However, the point may be moot under the Directive. The consumer's remedies under the Directive are the rights to have the goods repaired or replaced, or to rescind the contract or demand a reduction in price. Yet, the rights to repair and replacement are not available if they would be disproportionate, taking account of the costs imposed on the seller and the significance of the lack of conformity, and the right to rescind the contract is not available if the lack

of conformity is minor. On facts such of those or *Arcos* it might therefore be that the consumer's only remedy under the Directive would be a reduction of the contract price which, on those facts, might be minimal. In addition, because of the way Article 2 is constructed, it would be open to a court to find that goods do conform to the contract even though they do not precisely and absolutely correspond with the description.

Rather more difficult is the question when is a description 'given' by the seller? As noted above, the corresponding provision of English law, SoGA section 13, which applies where goods are 'sold by description' has been held to require that the description plays an influential part in the sale by defining the essential commercial characteristics of the goods. (See *Ashington Piggeries Ltd v Christopher Hill Ltd* [1972] AC 441, [1971] 1 All ER 847, HL; *Harlingdon & Leinster Ltd v Christopher Hull Fine Article Ltd* [1991] 1 QB 564, [1990] 1 All ER 737, CA.) Essentially the requirement is that the description must be such that a reasonable person would consider it contractual. As a result not all descriptive words applied to goods form part of the sale description, it being recognised that some descriptive words have no contractual effect and others may be contractual but not part of the description. Article 35 of the CISG refers to goods being of the 'description required by the contract'. On its face Article 2(2)(a) of the Directive would seem capable of requiring absolute correspondence with all descriptive words. Again, however, if the underlying principle is recognised as a requirement of correspondence with the buyer's reasonable expectations there may be scope for restricting the scope of Article 2(2)(a) to those descriptions which a reasonable person would regard as contractual.

There is however a further question. In the consumer context, where goods are generally sold pre-packaged, and especially where goods are sold in a self-service environment, much of the consumer's expectation is shaped not by the seller of the goods but by the manufacturer. To take a simple example, if C purchases a television set in a self-service electrical store, the description on which he relies may be primarily the one on the set's packaging and therefore the manufacturer's. Is that description 'given' by the seller? It is submitted that it ought to be so regarded, with the result that if the set proves not to correspond to the description on the packaging the consumer should be entitled to complain of a lack of conformity with the contract. To take another example, if the consumer buys a tin of wood stain described on the tin as 'quick drying', the description 'quick drying' should be regarded as 'given' by the seller so that there is a lack of conformity if the stain does not do 'exactly what it says on the tin'. However, the point is not clear, since statements made by manufacturers in advertising and sales promotion are taken into account under Article 2(2) paragraph (d) under which there is provision for the seller to disassociate himself from the manufacturer's statements.

3.4.1.2 *Compliance with sample*
At first impression there would seem to be only a limited role for the second aspect of paragraph (a), that the goods must possess the qualities of the goods which the

seller has held out as a sample or model. The corresponding provision of SoGA, section 15, refers to a 'sale by sample' and has been restricted to cases where a sample is used as a substitute for description to define essential commercial characteristics of the goods. It is generally assumed that sales by sample are rare in the consumer context. However, the language of the Directive is potentially wider. It does not require the sale to be 'by sample', but merely that the seller 'hold out goods' as a sample or model. It is submitted that it would include cases where, for instance, shop or window displays are used to sell goods, which might not be covered by SoGA section 15.

3.4.2 Fitness for buyer's purpose

The goods must be 'fit for any particular purpose for which the consumer requires them and which he made known to the seller at the time of conclusion of the contract and which the seller has accepted'.

Again, as in the corresponding provision of the CISG, and unlike SoGA section 14(3), the requirement is absolute: for the presumption to arise, the requirement is that the goods be fit for the consumer's purpose, not that they be reasonably fit. However, the language of paragraph (b) departs in several significant respects from that of Article 35(b) which requires that the goods

(b) are fit for any particular purpose expressly or impliedly made known to the seller at the time of the conclusion of the contract, except where the circumstances show that the buyer did not rely, or that it was unreasonable for him to rely, on the seller's skill and judgement.

Again, however, the degree of any unfitness may go to the determination of the remedy available to the consumer under the Directive, and it would be open to a court to find that goods which are reasonably fit for the consumer's purpose are in conformity with the contract.

The Directive's requirement of fitness is in any case subject to two preconditions. First, the buyer must make his purpose known to the seller 'at the time of the conclusion of the contract'. Second, the seller must have 'accepted' the buyer's purpose.

3.4.2.1 *Buyer's purpose made known*

The first requirement is fairly straightforward. It seems clear enough that it is sufficient that the consumer has made his purpose known to the seller at some time before conclusion of the contract. Similarly, although the Directive does not expressly say so, it is submitted that the first requirement is satisfied if the consumer has made his purpose known to the seller's agent with actual or apparent authority to receive notification. Given that most consumer sales take place in a retail environment and are effected by employees of the seller any other reading would emasculate the provision in modern commercial circumstances.

Presumably, as has been held under SoGA section 14(3), it will be sufficient if the buyer impliedly makes his purpose known. However, there is under the Directive a separate requirement of fitness for normal purpose, so that it will be unnecessary to invoke the fitness for purpose requirement where the buyer buys goods for their normal purpose.

3.4.2.2 *Seller accepts buyer's purpose*

The second pre-requisite is rather more problematic. It is not enough that the consumer make his purpose known to the seller. The seller must 'accept' it. It is not clear what this means, but it seems to require that the seller assent to the purpose indicated by the buyer. It is not clear, however, if this requires express assent or if the seller can be held to have impliedly accepted the buyer's purpose. What if the seller remains silent in the face of the buyer's statement of purpose? For instance suppose that the buyer purchases a coloured wood stain and informs the seller conversationally 'I'm going to paint the dog's kennel'. The seller makes no response. The stain is wholly unsuitable because it is toxic to animals. Can the seller be said to have accepted the buyer's purpose? It is submitted that the requirements of the CISG are here superior and, curiously, more favourable to the buyer. They, like the corresponding requirements of SoGA section 14(3), require that the consumer rely on the seller's skill and judgement, and that such reliance be reasonable. In the example just given it is submitted that if the seller possesses, or can reasonably be expected to possess, expertise relevant to the goods sold, the consumer can reasonably expect to be able to rely on the seller's skill and judgement and such reliance will relatively easily be assumed. It is difficult to conceive of a situation in which the seller accepts the buyer's purpose and yet it could be held that the buyer's reliance on the seller is unreasonable. If the buyer communicates his purpose and the seller expressly assents to it, it will relatively easily be inferred that the buyer relied on the seller's skill or judgement and that it was reasonable for him to do so. The Directive's requirement that the seller accept the consumer's purpose seems unduly protective of the seller, and inconsistent with a principle of protecting the buyer's reasonable expectations which it has been submitted underpins Article 2.

3.4.2.3 *Reliance on the seller*

Article 2(2)(b) may also be narrower than CISG Article 35(2)(b). The corresponding provision of the English Sale of Goods Act, section 14(3), like CISG Article 35, requires the buyer to rely on the seller's skill or judgement. It has been held that this need not involve reliance on advice on the goods' suitability for the buyer's stated purpose, so that the section was triggered where, prior to conclusion of the contract of sale, the buyer returned the goods to the seller's agent for repair and could therefore be said to be relying on the agent's skill or judgement to effect the repair. There would seem to be no scope for such a decision under Article 2(2).

3.4.3 Goods are fit for the purposes for which goods of the same type are normally used

The third aspect of conformity is fitness for normal purpose. A similar requirement appears in Article 35 of the CISG and as the basal requirement of the English Sale of Goods Act requirement in section 14(2) that goods should be of satisfactory quality. The language of Article 2 differs, however, from both in several regards.

3.4.3.1 *An absolute requirement*

The first thing to be noted about Article 2(2)(c) is that (unlike SoGA section 14(2)) it requires absolute fitness for normal purposes to raise the presumption of conformity. Under SoGA section 14(2B) goods are of satisfactory quality if they meet the standard that a *reasonable person* would regard as satisfactory. Fitness for all normal purposes is an aspect of quality 'in an appropriate case'. It is therefore clear that under the English legislation goods may be satisfactory even if not fit for all normal purposes (although there may still be a breach of the term implied by section 14(3)), if the circumstances make fitness for all purposes inappropriate—e.g. because the seller makes it clear that the goods are unfit for some normal purposes—so that a reasonable person would not expect them to be fit for all common purposes. On the face of it the language of the Directive would seem to leave no room for such a qualification to the fitness requirement. This may however be more apparent than real. If, as suggested earlier, the underlying principle of Article 2 is conformity with the buyer's reasonable expectation, Article 2(2)(c) may in reality impose a qualified requirement. As we have noted, recital 8 of the Directive anticipates that there may be cases in which some elements of the conformity requirement are inappropriate and therefore inapplicable. (In passing we should note, however, that the corresponding provision of the CISG seems to impose an absolute requirement.)

It must also be borne in mind that although Article 2(2)(c) imposes an absolute requirement of fitness, the effect of fitness for normal purpose under the Directive is to raise a presumption that the goods are in conformity with the contract. The absence of absolute fitness does not necessarily mean that the goods are *not* in conformity with the contract. It would be possible for a court to find that goods which are reasonably, although not absolutely, fit for the normal purpose of similar goods are nevertheless in conformity with the contract. The difference in effect between Article 2(2)(c) and section 14(2) may therefore be relatively slight.

3.4.3.2 *Fitness for normal use*

The second point we may note is that the requirement is one of fitness for the purposes for which goods of the same type are normally used. This mirrors the language of the CISG, but differs from the wording of the English SoGA which requires fitness for the purposes for which goods of the same description are commonly *supplied*. The emphasis in the Directive is thus, in effect, on the buyer's, rather than the seller's expectation. There may however be another point. Goods are frequently *mis*used for purposes for which they are not intended by the manufacturer or retailer. To take a familiar example, a screwdriver's intended purpose is to drive screws into wood and other materials. However, it is well known that screwdrivers are widely used for other purposes and, especially, as levers, for instance, to remove the lids from paint tins. If S sells B a screwdriver which is fit for driving screws but not for prising off the lids of paint tins, is it in conformity with the contract? The language of the Directive would suggest not: the screwdriver is not fit for one of the purposes for which goods of that type are normally used. Is the position changed if the goods are supplied with appropriate instructions and/or warnings? Such instructions and warnings can be taken into account in deciding if goods are defective for the purposes of the Product Liability Directive (85/374/EC) and implementing legislation (Consumer Protection Act 1987 section 3(2)(a); see chapter 8)). Again, however, on the face of the Directive there would appear to be nothing which allows the warning to be taken into account. The position would be different if the underlying principle of reasonable expectations were overtly recognised in the text: if the supplier gives a clear warning that the screwdriver is not suitable for use as a lever, the consumer cannot reasonably expect it to be fit for that purpose. This seems an eminently reasonable result. One way to reach it might be to read the reference to 'purposes for which goods of that type are normally used' as excluding cases of *misuse,* reading the word 'normally' as importing a normative requirement, effectively as 'properly', rather than 'commonly'. However, it seems that this is not what the Directive intends. Other language texts of the Directive use language which does not carry any normative implication. (The German text uses 'gewöhnlich', roughly translated as 'commonly'; the Italian version uses 'abitualmente'; the Spanish 'ordinariamente', and the French 'habituellement'.)

3.4.3.3 *Goods of the same type*
The language of Article 2(2)(c) raises another problem. The goods must be fit for the purposes for which goods of the same *type* are normally used. What are goods of the same 'type'? The CISG uses the expression 'goods of the same description', which suggests a closer similarity between the goods and those with which they are being compared. In contrast the English SoGA requires fitness for the purposes for which goods of the same 'kind' are commonly supplied. Is a plastic handled screwdriver the same type of goods as a wooden handled one? Is a motor car a motor car or is there a difference between (say) a 4 × 4 off road vehicle and a family saloon? If there is a difference (and it is submitted there is) are all 4 × 4s of the same type or are (say) a Land Rover Discovery and a Toyota Rav 4 of the same type?

An excessively wide definition of 'type' may produce unreasonable results. Thus in one sense we may term all motor cars goods of a common 'type'. It would, however, clearly be unreasonable to expect a super-mini to be fit for the same purposes as a 4 × 4 off road vehicle, or to be capable of towing a caravan, which might be a common purpose of a larger car. On the other hand, an overly narrow interpretation of 'type' may have similarly unreasonable results. If we postulate an extreme case, suppose that a particular make of car is incapable of being driven in the rain. It would surely not lie in the seller's mouth to say that since all cars of that make are incapable of being driven in the rain, they conform to the contract. The 'type' must be wider than the particular make. How, then, are we to decide between a narrow 'type' and a wide 'type'? The definition of the 'type' of goods to which a particular item belongs must, it is suggested, be to some extent context sensitive. The key, it is suggested, is again the consumer's reasonable expectation.

3.4.4 Quality and performance

Article 2(2)(d) requires that the goods show the quality and performance which are normal in goods of the same type and which the consumer can reasonably expect, given the nature of the goods and taking into account any public statements on the specific characteristics of the goods made about them by the seller, the producer or his representative, particularly in advertising or labelling.

This fourth aspect of the conformity requirement has no analogue in the CISG. On the other hand it bears some similarity to the test of satisfactory quality introduced into English law by the Sale and Supply of Goods Act 1994 and now contained in SoGA section 14(2A). Like that legislation, it recognises that consumers have wider expectations than mere fitness for purpose. There is however no equivalent of the list of factors to be considered in assessing the quality of the goods which appears in SoGA in section 14(2B) (the European Parliament's proposal to introduce a list identical to that in section 14(2B) was rejected), and it is submitted that in this regard the Directive is inferior to the domestic legislation.

That this is a test based on the consumer's reasonable expectation is expressly recognised. Again the test is partly based on a comparison with the norm for goods of the same 'type' raising again the problems discussed above. A number of observations can be made about this provision.

3.4.4.1 *Factors to be considered*
The Directive identifies two factors in particular as shaping the consumer's reasonable expectations: the nature of the goods and public statements made by the seller or producer, including in advertising. It is not clear what is meant by 'the nature of the goods'. Presumably the 'nature of the goods' is different from their 'type'. One factor which will clearly be relevant here is whether the goods are sold as new or second-hand. Recital 8 expressly recognises that 'the quality and performance which consumers can reasonably expect will depend *inter alia* on whether the goods are new or second-hand'. Presumably in the same way the fact that the goods are sold as 'seconds', 'shop-soiled', 'ex-display' and so on

would also be relevant when assessing the quality the consumer can reasonably expect.

3.4.4.2 *Public statements, advertising and promotional material*
The reference to advertising and similar statements is also significant, recognising that in the context of modern mass marketing of consumer goods consumer expectations are very largely shaped by advertising, and, in the case of manufactured goods, advertising by the manufacturer rather than the retailer. There was no corresponding provision in the domestic SoGA, although it is submitted that a court could, and in an appropriate case, would have taken such statements into account when making the assessment of quality (*cf. Jewson v Kelly* (2002), above).

It would however be unreasonable to fix the retailer with liability for all promotional statements by the manufacturer, especially in the context of the single market where consumers are being encouraged to shop outside their home state. Article 2(4) therefore exempts the seller of goods for liability for public statements about the goods if he can show that

(a) he was not, and could not reasonably have been aware of the statement; or

(b) at the time of conclusion of the contract the statement had been corrected (it is not necessary that the correction be by the seller); or

(c) the consumer's decision to buy the goods could not have been influenced by the statement.

This last exemption might apply where, for example, a particular promotional statement had been made in one or more Member States but not in the consumer's home state. It is for the seller to prove that the consumer's decision could not have been influenced by the statement and that is likely to be a difficult burden to discharge.

3.4.4.3 *Minor and cosmetic defects*
No mention is made in Article 2(2)(d) of freedom from cosmetic or minor defects. It is submitted that this is unfortunate. Consumers generally want, and reasonably expect, goods to be free of minor or cosmetic defects. For instance, it is submitted that a purchaser of a new car might justifiably complain if the car were delivered with scratched paintwork or a minor oil leak. Arguably these factors are impliedly included in the reference to quality and performance, but it would have been better if they had been expressly referred to.

3.4.4.4 *Price*
Another factor of which no mention is made is the price of the goods. Again it is submitted that common sense suggests that the price is relevant to the quality and performance reasonably expected by the consumer. It would be unreasonable, for instance, to expect the same standards of a £10 pair of shoes as of a £100 pair. It

must also be correct that paying a higher price can result in increased quality expectations (see, e.g., *Rogers v Parish (Scarborough) Ltd* [1987] QB 933, [1987] 2 All ER 232). However, the absence of any express reference to price in the Directive leaves it open to question whether it can be taken into account in assessing conformity. Significantly, the first draft of the Directive did expressly refer to price as a factor to be considered in assessing the quality and performance reasonably to be expected, suggesting that the absence of any reference to price in the final text of the Directive is deliberate. Of course a lower price may not always result in a lower expectation. For instance a consumer may reasonably believe that goods being sold cheap are a bargain, or are reduced or at sale price. It is submitted nevertheless that in an appropriate case price may be a relevant factor in shaping the consumer's reasonable expectations and can properly be taken into account. It may, for instance, be possible to argue that cheaper goods are of a different type from similar but more expensive items so that, for instance, a £100 pair of hand-made Italian leather shoes would be considered to be goods of a different type from a £10 plastic-soled pair.

3.4.5 Extension of the conformity requirement

As we have already noted, a contract for the supply of goods to be manufactured or produced by the seller is a contract of sale for the purposes of the Directive. Therefore under a contract for the manufacture and supply of goods the conformity requirement applies to the finished goods supplied under the contract, and not merely to the materials used. Thus if, say, a boat builder contracts to make and supply a boat to the consumer, the builder is strictly liable for any lack of conformity of the finished boat to the contract, whether that lack of conformity originates in the materials used or in the boat builder's work in its construction. However, the supplier may avoid liability where the lack of conformity originates in materials supplied by the consumer (see below).

It is not clear how, prior to the Directive, English law would have dealt with this situation. The contract for the seller to produce an item from materials supplied by the buyer would have been capable of being analysed in at least three ways—

(a) as a contract for the supply of labour only;

(b) as a contract for work and materials, the consumer supplying the materials to the supplier who would then supply them back under his contract; or

(c) as a contract for the supply of the finished product, the consumer first supplying the materials to the supplier.

In the first case the supplier would be required to perform the work with reasonable skill and care but would have no liability for the materials or for the quality of the finished product. In the second the supplier would be required to perform the work with reasonable skill and care and would be strictly liable for the quality of the materials supplied. In the third case the supplier would be strictly liable for the quality of the finished product. Thus in the second and third cases the supplier would, directly or indirectly, be strictly liable for the quality of the materials originally supplied to him by the consumer. Moreover, since the supply of the materials by the consumer to the supplier would not be in the course of a business it would not attract the implied satisfactory quality or fitness for purpose terms and there might thus be no way for the seller to pass back liability to the consumer. The Directive's solution avoids this difficulty and produces an outcome fairer to the supplier.

3.4.5.1 *Defective installation*

Article 2(5) of the Directive creates two further extensions of the supplier's liability. First, where the contract is for goods supplied to be installed by the seller or 'under his responsibility', any lack of conformity resulting from incorrect installation 'shall be deemed to be equivalent to lack of conformity of the goods'.

Example 1 S contracts to supply and install a fitted cooker. The cooker is delivered and installed by a sub-contractor. Once fitted the cooker fails to work properly because it is incorrectly wired in. The supplier is strictly liable. Installation of the cooker forms part of the contract of sale. The goods were installed under S's 'responsibility'. The lack of conformity resulting from incorrect installation is therefore deemed to be a lack of conformity of the goods.

Example 2 S, a joiner, contracts to manufacture, supply and fit a door. When fitted the door fails to close properly because it is badly hung. S is strictly liable. Installation of the goods forms part of the contract of sale and the goods were installed by S.

In addition, S would also be strictly liable if the lack of conformity were found to result from

(a) the materials used in the manufacture of the door;

(b) defective workmanship in its manufacture.

In cases where goods are manufactured and supplied or supplied and installed it will therefore no longer be possible for the supplier to avoid liability by arguing that the goods, or materials used in their manufacture, were of the required quality and requiring the consumer to prove negligence in manufacture or installation. The consumer will be able to say 'The finished item, as installed, does not conform to the contract, and you, the supplier, are therefore liable'.

From a UK perspective these are important provisions because in English (and Scots) law prior to the Directive, whilst the seller of the cooker would have been strictly liable for the quality etc. of the cooker, he would have been subject only to negligence liability in respect of its fitting, and the joiner would have been strictly liable only for the quality etc. of the materials used in the door's manufacture, and subject to negligence liability in respect of the workmanship in its manufacture and/or hanging.

3.4.5.2 *Installation by the consumer*

Article 2(5) applies to a second situation and imposes strict liability on the seller where goods are installed by the consumer if a lack of conformity results from incorrect installation which is due to 'a shortcoming in the installation instructions'.

This provision raises a number of tricky questions. Its scope may be wider than at first appears. Much will depend on the interpretation of the word 'installation'. Clearly Article 2(5) would apply to a cooker supplied for home installation or a door supplied for the consumer to hang. It is submitted that notwithstanding the use of the word 'installation' it should also apply to goods supplied for home assembly (the word used in the German text is 'montage' which translates as 'assembly'). Alternatively where goods for home assembly, such as self-assembly furniture, are supplied with inadequate instructions it may be possible to argue that the instructions are part of the goods so that the instructions themselves must satisfy the conformity requirement. Further examples of goods supplied for consumer installation could, it is submitted, include motor car parts supplied for consumer installation, paint supplied for consumer application and computer software supplied for installation on the consumer's computer. Overall, it is submitted that 'installation' should be given a wide meaning so that consumers will generally be entitled to expect adequate, comprehensible instructions for the use of goods supplied.

It is clear that if goods intended for consumer installation are supplied with misleading, incomplete or inaccurate instructions and as a result of the consumer following them the goods as installed do not conform to the contract in the terms of the Directive, the seller is liable. It is less clear that the seller is liable where the goods are supplied without installation instructions. In that case it may be possible to argue that the goods were not intended for consumer installation. It is not clear what criteria are to be used to determine when goods are intended for consumer installation. It is submitted that here again a reasonable expectation test may be appropriate: if a consumer would reasonably expect that the goods are intended for consumer installation, then the supplier will be liable for any lack of conformity resulting from a shortcoming in installation instructions, including the total absence of such instructions. In determining what the consumer can reasonably expect the context in which the goods are supplied should be relevant. Thus if goods are supplied by a DIY store, it would be a natural assumption that they are intended for consumer installation.

On the other hand the test of adequacy of instructions must be objective. If instructions would be adequate for a reasonably competent consumer to effect correct installation, then it ought to be possible to argue that there is no shortcoming in the instructions even if the particular individual consumer has found them impossible to follow or understand. However, nowadays it is common for consumers to buy a range of, often quite complex, items for self installation, including (for instance) gas and electrical appliances, central heating and so on. If such items are intended for consumer installation the supplier will be liable under this provision if any shortcoming in the instructions results in the goods, as installed, not complying with the conformity requirement. It is suggested that if there is any doubt about the manner in which or by whom the goods will be installed the safe course for the supplier is to ensure that he supplies either adequate instructions to enable the consumer to effect installation or a suitably clear and prominent instruction/warning that the goods are not suitable or intended for consumer installation.

3.4.6 Limitations on the conformity requirement

In general the Directive prohibits suppliers from contracting out of the conformity requirement. The status of contractual exclusions of liability is considered in chapter 5. However, although the liability imposed by the Directive is strict it is not absolute. Several limitations to the seller's liability are recognised.

3.4.6.1 *Acceptance of the consumer's purpose*
The requirement that goods be fit for the consumer's purpose (Article 2(2)(b)) applies only if the consumer makes that purpose known to the seller and the seller 'has accepted' it. The seller can therefore avoid liability under this head by refusing to 'accept' the consumer's stated purpose. Thus where the consumer states his intention of using goods for a purpose other than their common one the seller may be advised to disclaim knowledge of their suitability.

3.4.6.2 *Lack of conformity originates in consumer's materials*
As noted earlier, a contract for goods to be manufactured and supplied, such as a contract to build and supply a boat, is a contract for the sale of the finished product for the purposes of the Directive, so that the seller is liable for any lack of conformity in the finished product whether it originates in the materials used or in the seller's workmanship. However, Article 2(3) provides that the seller is not liable for any lack of conformity which 'has its origin' in materials supplied by the consumer. It achieves this result by providing that in such a case there is deemed not to be a lack of conformity. Thus if, say, the consumer asks a joiner to build a set of book shelves out of some old oak planking supplied by the consumer, there is deemed to be a contract for the sale of the finished shelves and the joiner is liable for any lack of conformity in the finished shelves. If, however, the finished shelves are rotten or warped because of defects in the wood supplied by the consumer, the joiner is not liable. It is submitted that this is entirely consistent with what we have here identified as the principle underlying the conformity requirement, that goods

should conform to the consumer's reasonable expectations. The seller may however not entirely escape liability. In some cases—including perhaps the example just given—it might be possible that the supplier will owe the consumer a duty of care to warn of any lack of suitability in the materials so that the supplier will be liable in negligence for failure to warn even if not strictly liable for lack of conformity under the Directive.

3.4.6.3 *Consumer aware of lack of conformity*

Article 2(3) creates a second, broader limitation on the seller's liability. In effect it provides that the consumer cannot complain of any lack of conformity if, at the time the contract was concluded, he was aware of it or could not reasonably have been unaware of it. This is broadly analogous to the restrictions on the satisfactory quality term in SoGA section 14(2C), but, it should be noted, applies to all of the aspects of conformity under the Directive. Thus the seller can avoid liability for any lack of conformity or defect by drawing it to the consumer's attention. Similarly the supplier should not be liable for patent defects. It is submitted however that defects etc. should be drawn to the consumer's attention in specific terms. Thus if, say, the consumer buys ex-display goods which are openly on display and are marked as 'ex-display' he may not be able to complain of a lack of conformity by reason of the goods having surface marks or scratches. The description 'ex-display' may also lower the standard of performance and quality expected under Article 2(2)(d). However, the consumer would still be entitled to complain in respect of functional defects not specifically drawn to his attention.

3.4.6.4 *Public statements about the goods*

As we have noted earlier, the quality and performance expected of the goods is judged by reference, *inter alia*, to the 'public statements on the specific characteristics of the goods', such as advertising and promotional statements, made by the seller, the producer or his representative. However, Article 2(4) provides that the seller is not bound by such statements if he shows that

(a) he was not and could not reasonably have been aware of the statement in question;

(b) at the time of conclusion of the contract the statement had been corrected; or

(c) that the consumer's decision to buy the goods could not have been influenced by the statement.

Clearly the third limb of Article 2(4) is entirely consistent with the general principle of protecting the consumer's reasonable expectations. However, the first two limbs seem to look rather to the seller's expectations. The first may be particularly important in the context of cross-border transactions. If, say, a manufacturer makes a particular claim for his goods in advertising in Germany, and a consumer, having seen that advertisement, buys the goods from a retailer in the UK, the UK retailer will not be held liable on the basis of the goods' failure to comply with the advertising claims if he can show that he neither knew nor could reasonably be expected to know of the advertisement in question. In such a case a consumer cannot reasonably expect the retailer to be adopting and endorsing the manufacturer's statements.

It is not at all clear what the second limb of Article 2(4) requires. Clearly if the retailer can show that he corrected the statement to the particular consumer, he will escape liability. What, however, if it is shown that the statement has been corrected by a statement directed to the general public of which the particular consumer is unaware? It is submitted that the seller should also escape liability in that situation. If it were necessary that the correction should always come to the attention of the particular consumer buyer the situation would always be covered by the third limb of Article 2(4), the consumer's decision to buy not being influenced by the original statement.

3.4.7 When is conformity judged?

Under the CISG the goods delivered by the seller must conform to the contract at the time when risk passes from seller to buyer. Although the position is not clear, the better view is that the position is the same in English law. Risk passes with property (section 20 SoGA). The time of the passing of property depends primarily on whether the goods are 'specific' (identified and agreed upon when the contract is made) or 'unascertained' (as where the particular goods to be delivered are *not* identified when the contract is made). Under a contract for specific goods, in the absence of any contrary provision, property in and risk of loss of the goods passes when the contract is made (SoGA section 18, rule 1). Under a contract for unascertained goods, property and risk pass when goods of the contract description are unconditionally appropriated to the contract by one party with the consent of the other (section 18, rule 5). Broadly speaking, therefore, the effect is that risk of loss of or damage to goods passes to the buyer under English law at the latest when goods are unconditionally appropriated to the contract, which will normally happen when goods are irrevocably earmarked for the buyer, for instance by being despatched to him by post.

Under the Directive, however, it seems that the goods' conformity with the contract is judged at the time the goods are delivered by the seller to the buyer. The draft Directive (Article 3(2)) explicitly provided that the time when conformity was to be judged was the moment of delivery. There is no corresponding provision in the final text but it is implicit that conformity is judged at the time of delivery. Thus Article 2(1) provides that the seller must deliver to the consumer goods which are in conformity with the contract of sale; Article 5 provides that the seller is liable for any lack of conformity which becomes apparent within two years as from the delivery of the goods, and Article 5(3) provides that there is a rebuttable presumption that any lack of conformity which becomes apparent within six months of delivery existed at the time of delivery.

It is therefore reasonable to assume that the intention, albeit not expressly stated, is that conformity with the contract is to be judged at the time of delivery. The seller is therefore liable for latent defects present at the time of delivery which manifest themselves within two years as from the date of delivery. Normally where a lack of conformity only becomes apparent after the date of delivery the buyer must prove that it was present at the time of delivery, but where a lack of conformity becomes manifest within the first six months after delivery the buyer can rely on the rebuttable presumption in Article 5(3) with the result that the burden of proof is thrown onto the seller to prove that the defect was not present at the time of delivery. If the seller succeeds in so doing, of course, he will avoid liability.

3.4.7.1 *Delivery*

What, though, does delivery mean? There is no definition in the Directive, so that presumably the concept is left to domestic law, at least until the ECJ gives a Community definition in Article 234 proceedings. English law recognises that delivery may be actual or constructive. Goods are actually delivered when physical possession of them is transferred. They are constructively delivered when the means of control is transferred or the seller acknowledges that he holds them to the buyer's order as bailee for him by attorning for them. In domestic law, therefore, goods can be delivered without coming into the buyer's actual possession. Thus where goods are despatched to the buyer by post they may be said to have been delivered when despatched.

Although the position is far from clear it is suggested that the reference to delivery in the Directive refers to actual, rather than constructive delivery. The explanatory memorandum to the draft Directive indicated implicitly that conformity was to be judged at the time of actual, physical receipt of the goods. The issue will, of course, be relatively unimportant in the majority of domestic transactions where the consumer takes receipt of the goods immediately the contract is made. It will, however, assume crucial significance if either physical delivery is delayed or the transaction is at a distance—for instance, over the Internet or by mail order—and performed by the seller delivering goods by post or courier. This, of course, is exactly the type of transaction which, in the context of the single market, the Directive was intended to encourage. Essentially the question can be re-phrased as 'Who bears the risk of loss in the course of delivery?'. The point may be illustrated by two examples.

Example 1   C buys a refrigerator from S. S agrees to deliver the goods to C's home. The goods are marked with a sticker showing C's name and address. Whilst the refrigerator is in transit S's delivery van is involved in a collision and the refrigerator is damaged. S is liable for any lack of conformity which exists at the time of delivery. Arguably, however, the refrigerator was constructively delivered to C when the contract of sale was concluded and it was marked with C's name and address. If therefore 'delivery' includes 'constructive delivery' any damage done to the goods after this time cannot affect the goods' conformity with the contract (although C may, of course, have a claim against the carrier if he is responsible for the accident, or possibly against the person who caused the accident). Conversely if 'delivery' connotes 'actual delivery' then the goods' conformity with the contract is not judged until the refrigerator reaches C so that if the damage done in the collision results in the refrigerator no longer conforming to the contract C can invoke the Directive's remedies on that ground.

Example 2 C orders a CD player over the Internet. S despatches a player by courier. The player is constructively delivered to C when despatched. On arrival the player is found to have been damaged in transit. If conformity is judged at the date of constructive delivery the relevant date will be the date when the player was despatched so that C will be unable to complain in respect of the damage in the post. If on the other hand 'delivery' is actual delivery, conformity is not judged until the goods reach C, in which case account can be taken of the damage suffered in transit.

Once again the notion of the consumer's reasonable expectation may be helpful. It is submitted that in cases such as these the consumer will reasonably expect to receive goods which are in conformity with the contract, suggesting that the time at which conformity is to be judged is the date of actual delivery of the goods.

3.4.7.2 *Delivery and risk*

There is however a further complication. As already noted, prior to the Directive English law tested the goods' conformity with the contract at the time when risk passed from seller to buyer. The notion of risk, after all, is used to allocate between seller and buyer responsibility for loss of or damage to goods. Now, in English law, risk passes, *prima facie*, with property and property can pass separately from physical delivery. For instance, if we take the example of the refrigerator above, the contract would in English law be one for specific goods. Property would therefore, in the absence of any agreement to the contrary, pass when the contract was made, and risk would, *prima facie* pass at the same time. In fact the SoGA quite explicitly recognises that risk may pass separately from delivery. Section 20(1) of the SoGA provides that:

Unless otherwise agreed, the goods remain at the seller's risk until the property in them is transferred to the buyer, but when the property in them is transferred to the buyer the goods are at the buyer's risk whether delivery has been made or not.

In the second example above, of the CD player, the contract would be one for unascertained goods. Under such a contract, property passes when goods of the contract description are unconditionally appropriated to the contract by one party with the other's consent. Case-law indicates that in the example the CD player would be appropriated to the contract when despatched to the buyer, so that the buyer would again bear the risk of loss in transit.

In short, under domestic law prior to the Directive the buyer would generally bear the risk of loss of or damage to goods in transit. It has been suggested above that the Directive requires the goods to be in conformity with the contract when they are physically delivered into the buyer's possession. The difficulty with this view, however, is that recital 14 to the Directive states that 'references to the time of delivery do not imply that Member States have to change their rules on the passing of risk', whereas if the view proposed above is accepted, the Directive does require a change to the existing domestic rules on the passing of risk. It is submitted that notwithstanding this difficulty the above view, that the time at which conformity is to be judged under the Directive is the time of actual delivery of goods to the consumer, is to be preferred. It is consistent with the Directive's underlying objectives of consumer protection and promotion of the Single Market. Recital 14 is at best an ambiguous and weak pointer in the opposite direction.

3.5 UK IMPLEMENTATION OF THE DIRECTIVE

As has been indicated above, the provisions of Article 2 of the Directive are broadly analogous to those of the pre-existing domestic law contained in the Sale of Goods Act 1979 and, specifically, in the implied terms derived from SoGA sections 13–15, and the corresponding provisions of the SoG(IT)A and SGSA. Moreover the Directive and the UK implied terms can be seen as based on the same underlying general principle, that the goods should conform to the buyer's reasonable expectations. The view of the UK government seems to have been that the existing domestic law was already, broadly speaking, functionally equivalent to Article 2 of the Directive, and that only minimal changes to the existing regime were necessary to implement the Directive. The main amendments made by way of implementation have been

(a) to add new sections 14(2D), 14(2E) and 14(2F) to deal with the Article 2(2)(d) provisions on the effect on quality of public statements relating to the goods and

(b) to add new provisions to sections 20 and 32 of the Act, dealing respectively with the passing of risk and delivery of goods to a carrier, intended to implement the Directive's rule that conformity is judged at the time goods are delivered to the consumer.

Corresponding changes have been made to the implied terms provisions of the SoG(IT)A and SGSA, even though they were not strictly required by the Directive. The potentially *ultra vires* nature of these changes was noted in chapter 1.

The provisions of English law described earlier in this chapter therefore remain largely unchanged. In some instances the result of this is that English law provides consumers with a higher level of protection than is required by the Directive. In one or two instances it may be that as a result of this approach the UK regulations have not fully implemented the Directive's requirements.

3.5.1 No conformity requirement

No attempt has been made to implement the general requirement in Article 2(1) of the Directive that the seller must deliver to the buyer goods which are in conformity with the contract. The assumption seems to have been that the conformity requirement is given sufficient effect by the implied terms, as modified to implement the specific provisions of Article 2 of the Directive.

As noted earlier, conformity with the contract requires more than that the goods conform to the terms of Article 2(2) of the Directive. In fact the Directive does not, as such, require that the goods conform to the requirements of Article 2(2). Satisfaction of those requirements raises a rebuttable presumption that the goods *do* conform to the contract, but it would be possible under the Directive for a consumer to show that notwithstanding the satisfaction of the requirements of Article 2(2) the goods do not conform to the contract because (for example) they do not satisfy an express term of the contract. In contrast, SoGA positively requires that the goods do conform to the implied terms, which, broadly speaking, correspond to the requirements of Article 2(2). In theory, at least, it is therefore possible to envisage situations in which there is a breach of the implied terms corresponding to the requirements of Article 2(2), giving rise to liability under SoGA, and yet the presumption of non-conformity would be rebutted under the Directive.

Insofar as the possibility outlined above would give consumers stronger rights under English law than under the Directive, the UK approach to implementation is permitted by EC law. However, there may be cases in which the absence of a general requirement of a conformity requirement in English law produces a result less favourable to the consumer than under the Directive. The significance of goods being not in conformity with the contract is that it triggers the Directive's remedial regime. Goods which do conform to the requirements of Article 2(2) may nevertheless not be in conformity with the contract if, for instance, they fail to conform to an express term of the contract. The remedial provisions of the Directive are given effect by means of a new Part 5A inserted into the SoGA and corresponding provisions inserted into the legislation applicable to other types of supply contract. New section 48F provides that 'For the purposes of this Part, goods do not conform to a contract of sale if there is, in relation to the goods, a breach of an express term of the contract or a term implied by section 13, 14 or 15 above.' Breach either of an express term or of a statutory implied term therefore amounts to a lack of conformity for this purpose. What, though, if the goods do not correspond to a term implied into the contract by the common law? In that case there would be a breach of contract but not a lack of conformity for the purposes of Part 5A. Although it must be conceded that it will be relatively rare in a consumer contract that a matter not covered by either the statutory implied terms or an express term will be covered by a common law implied term, it is submitted that there is a gap in the UK implementation of the Directive. For instance, it has been noted that a contract to make and supply goods may be construed as a contract of work and materials under which the statutory implied terms will apply to the materials used but there may be a common law term requiring the finished item to be reasonably fit for the buyer's purpose. Breach of that term would not amount to a lack of conformity under the UK legislation.

3.5.2 The aspects of conformity

As we have observed, the requirements of Article 2(2) are, broadly speaking, functionally equivalent to the implied terms in sections 13–15 SoGA and on the whole the approach of the UK government has been that no amendment to the implied terms was necessary to implement Article 2(2). As we have observed above, however, there are subtle differences between the Directive's and the domestic provisions, which may raise doubts as to whether the Directive has been properly implemented. Insofar as there are such differences a domestic court interpreting the provisions of the SoGA in future will of course have to interpret them, so far as possible, in accordance with the Directive. There may nevertheless be a question in EC law whether the UK has done sufficient to implement the Directive.

3.5.2.1 *Article 2(2)(a)—Description and sample*
No amendment has been made to section 13 or 15 of the SoGA to implement Article 2(2)(a). On the face of it, however, the SoGA requirement in section 13 that goods must be 'sold by description', as it has been interpreted by the domestic courts, appears to be narrower than the Directive's reference to 'the description *given by* the seller', which would appear to be capable of taking in descriptions not concerned with essential commercial characteristics of the goods.

Similarly there appear to be differences between the Directive's requirement that the goods 'possess the qualities of the goods which the seller has held out to the consumer as a sample or model' and the SoGA requirement that where goods are 'sold by sample' the bulk must 'correspond with the sample in quality' and the goods will be free from any defect making them unsatisfactory not discoverable on reasonable examination of the sample. First, the seller may hold out goods as a 'sample or model' without the sale being one 'by sample' in the relatively narrow sense of SoGA section 15. Second, the requirement that the goods 'possess the qualities' of the sample or model appears to be rather broader than the combined requirements of section 15 that the bulk correspond with the sample 'in quality' and be free of hidden defects. The Directive seems to require that the goods and the sample have the same attributes. Section 15 seems better suited to commercial than consumer transactions. It may therefore be necessary in future to interpret section 15 in accordance with the Directive in consumer cases.

3.5.2.2 *Article 2(2)(b)—Fitness for buyer's purpose*
Similarly no change has been made to section 14(3) to implement Article 2(2)(b). There are however several differences between the two provisions.

It has been suggested earlier that the Directive should be read as permitting the consumer to make his purpose known

(a) by implication as well as expressly and

(b) to an agent of the seller.

Insofar as by expressly permitting both of these possibilities section 14(3) differs from the Directive, it is more favourable to the consumer and no problem of non-implementation arises.

There are however rather more significant differences between the pre-conditions for the application of the two requirements. Article 2(2)(b) applies if the buyer

(i) makes his purpose known to the seller and

(ii) the seller accepts it.

Section 14(3) applies if the buyer (i) makes his purpose known to the seller and (ii) he relies on the seller's skill or judgement and (iii) it is reasonable for him to do so. It is not clear what is required for the seller to 'accept' the buyer's purpose, but it would seem that it would be possible for the buyer, acting reasonably, to rely on the seller's skill or judgement even where the seller has not accepted the buyer's purpose, whereas it is unlikely that if the seller 'accepts' the buyer's purpose the buyer would be held not to have relied on the seller. Again it would seem therefore that section 14(3) is more favourable to the consumer than the Directive.

3.5.2.3 *Article 2(2)(c)—Fitness for normal purpose*
No change has been made to section 14(2) to implement Article 2(2)(c). There are however differences between the two provisions. First, as noted above, Article 2(2)(c) requires the goods to be fit for the purposes for which goods of the same type are normally used. The corresponding requirement in section 14(2) appears in section 14(2B) which provides that '*in an appropriate case* ... fitness for all the purposes for which goods of the kind in question are commonly supplied' is an aspect of quality. The first thing we may note, therefore, is that section 14(2B) does not absolutely require fitness for all common purposes in all cases. Fitness for all common purposes is only required in 'an appropriate case'. Given however that, as noted earlier, the Directive recognises that in an appropriate case goods may conform to the contract without satisfying all aspects of Article 2(2), there is probably little functional difference between the two provisions in this regard.

Next, it is not clear that the Directive's reference to 'goods of the same *type*' is the same as section 14(2B)'s reference to 'goods of the *kind* in question'. Given however that neither expression has any clear meaning the two can probably be given the same effect.

More problematic is the difference between the Directive's requirement that goods be fit for the purpose for which similar goods are 'normally used' and section 14(2B)'s requirement that goods be fit for the purposes for which similar goods are 'commonly supplied'. (Significantly in earlier drafts of the Regulations it was proposed to add a reference in section 14(2B) to the purposes for which goods are normally used.) Since, as noted earlier, goods may be commonly misused for purposes for which they are not commonly supplied, the Directive would seem on this point to be more generous to the consumer than is section 14(2B) and it may be that it is arguable that this aspect of Article 2 has not been properly implemented, in particular in light of recent ECJ case-law requiring a clear transposition of provisions which grant rights to consumers (see C-144/99 *Commission v Netherlands*, chapter 1). However, insofar as 'fitness for normal use' requires something different from 'fitness for purpose for which commonly supplied' it may be that a court could consider it as one of the other relevant circumstances under section 14(2A).

3.5.2.4 *Article 2(2)(d)—Quality and performance*

There is no direct analogue to Article 2(2)(d) in the SoGA. The view seems to have been taken that it is largely given effect by the requirement that goods be of satisfactory quality, as explained and expanded in section 14(2A) and section 14(2B). Conversely there is no equivalent in the Directive to the list of 'aspects of quality' contained in section 14(2B). It is suggested that nothing turns on this. The factors there listed, or similar ones, would be likely to be taken into account by a court assessing whether goods are in conformity with the contract under the Directive. Certainly similar factors were considered by the English courts prior to the introduction of section 14(2B) in 1994 when making an assessment whether goods were of merchantable quality. Insofar as they do refer to matters not mentioned in the Directive they would seem to be more favourable to the consumer and their retention is therefore permitted.

Article 2(2)(d) requires the goods to show the 'performance' which is normal in goods of the same type. Neither section 14(2A) nor section 14(2B) refers expressly to the goods' performance. However, the list in section 14(2B) is not an exhaustive list of the factors relevant to the assessment of quality and the references to quality, durability and fitness for normal purpose, coupled with the reference in section 14(2A) to 'all other relevant circumstances' should be sufficient (if there were any doubt) to allow a court to take account of the goods' performance. Indeed, the doctrine of indirect effect (see chapter 1) would require domestic courts to adopt such an interpretation of section 14(2).

The retention in section 14(2A) of the reference to price as a factor which may be relevant to the assessment of quality should not be controversial. As noted earlier, there is no express reference to price in the Directive. However, it was suggested earlier that price must be relevant to quality and, arguably, is implicitly brought into the Directive's assessment by the reference in Article 2(2)(d) to the consumer's reasonable expectation. At least insofar as a higher price may lead to an expectation of superior quality, reference to price may in some cases favour the consumer.

3.5.2.5   *Article 2(2)(d)—Public statements about the goods*

Rather surprisingly in view of the general approach to implementation of Article 2(2) it was felt that express provision should be made for the Directive's reference to public statements about the goods. Three new sub-sections 14(2D), 14(2E) and 14(2F) have therefore been added. Their wording is at times rather convoluted and it must be questioned whether it was necessary to include them at all.

Section 14(2D), closely following the language of the Directive, provides that 'if the buyer deals as consumer . . . the relevant circumstances' to be considered in making the assessment of quality under section 14(2A) 'include any public statements on the specific characteristics of the goods made about them by the seller, the producer or his representative, particularly in advertising or on labelling'. Section 14(2E) then gives effect to Article 2(4) of the Directive which provides that in certain circumstances the seller is not bound by public statements about the goods. The language of section 14(2E) differs from that of Article 2(4) in one significant respect. Section 14(2E) provides that a public statement about the goods is not to be considered a relevant circumstance when assessing the quality of the goods if, before the contract was made, the relevant statement had been withdrawn or corrected *in public*. It thus seems that it is not necessary for the withdrawal or correction to come to the attention of the particular buyer provided that there has been some public correction before the contract. It is not clear what the qualification 'in public', which has no equivalent in the Directive, requires. The degree of publicity which must be given to the correction is not indicated in the Regulations, but it is submitted that in order for the seller to rely on a correction or withdrawal reasonable steps must have been taken to publicise it at least to the same degree as the original statement about the goods. A separate question is whether it is sufficient for the correction or withdrawal of a false statement to be made privately to the particular consumer but not to the public generally. It would be surprising if a consumer could base a claim that goods are unsatisfactory on a public statement which he knew to have been expressly corrected before the contract was made and it would seem that in such a case the existing provision in section 14(2C)(a) ('any matter . . . which is specifically drawn to the buyer's attention before the contract is made') would apply to prevent the consumer relying on the public statement as making the goods unsatisfactory.

It is not clear that these new provisions were necessary in order to implement the Directive, since it would in any case have been open to a court to consider them as part of the relevant circumstances. This appears to be tacitly recognised by section 14(2F) which provides that:

Subsections (2D) and (2E) above do not prevent any public statement from being a relevant circumstance for the purposes of subsection 2A above (whether or not the buyer deals as consumer . . .) if the statement would have been such a circumstance apart from those sub-sections.

Since the factors listed in section 14(2B) are aspects of quality 'in an appropriate case', it might have been rather easier simply to have added reference to public statements to that list.

3.5.3 Article 1(4): Goods to be manufactured

The UK implementing regulations contain no provision to implement Article 1(4) of the Directive which, as noted above, provides that contracts for the supply of consumer goods to be manufactured or produced are to be treated as contracts for the sale of goods for the purposes of the Directive, the UK government having apparently taken the view that Article 1(4) merely reflects the existing common law position. However, as explained earlier (see 2.3.2.1), the treatment of such contracts in English law is unclear, different approaches to contracts to manufacture and supply having been taken at different times, and the better view is that at least some contracts which would not be classified as sales under existing domestic law are required to be treated as sales for the purposes of the Directive. At the very least the opportunity should have been taken to clarify English law. This deficiency in the Regulations can to some extent be made good by courts adopting the approach to classification favoured in *Lee v Griffin* (1861) 1 B & S 272, according to which any contract which results in the transfer of property in the finished item is to be classified as a contract for sale of that item, and it can therefore be expected that courts will adopt this approach. However, given the uncertainty of domestic law on the point and the absence of any clear implementing provision it may be said that in this respect the UK has failed properly to implement the Directive.

3.5.4 Article 2(3): Limitations to the conformity requirement

Article 2(3) of the Directive contains two limitations on the seller's liability, pro-viding that there is deemed not to be a lack of conformity if

(a) at the time the contract was concluded the consumer was not, or could not reasonably have been, unaware of the lack of conformity or

(b) if the lack of conformity originates in materials supplied by the consumer.

The implementing regulations contain no provision to implement either of these limitations.

The first limitation is partly covered by the existing section 14(2C) which provides that the satisfactory quality term does not extend to matters specifically drawn to the buyer's attention before the contract is made or, where the buyer examines the goods, to matters which that examination ought to have revealed. In both instances the consumer either will be, or ought reasonably to be, aware of the relevant matter. However, section 14(2C) only limits the operation of the satisfactory quality term. Article 2(3) of the Directive is much wider and limits the application of all aspects of the conformity requirement. Arguably, therefore, English law is again more favourable to the consumer than is the Directive. Again, however, the differences may be more apparent than real. If a consumer purchases goods in circumstances where they know, or ought to know, that the goods do not correspond with their description or are not fit for the buyer's purpose, as the case may be, it would be open to a court to hold that the sale was not one by description, reliance on the description in the circumstances being unreasonable, or that the buyer did not, or it was unreasonable for him to, rely on the seller's skill or judgement in relation to the goods' fitness for purpose.

The failure to implement the second part of Article 2(3) is more significant. As noted earlier, it is not clear how a contract where the consumer supplied some or all of the materials to be used in the manufacture of a finished item would be analysed. If regarded as a contract purely for work, the seller would have no liability for defects originating in the materials. However, in at least some cases such a contract could be construed as one for sale of the finished item, or for work and materials with the supplier supplying back to the consumer the materials initially supplied by the consumer. In such a case the supplier would be strictly liable for the conformity with the contract of the materials and/or the finished product, and would have no means of redress against the consumer. The problem is the more acute because, as we have suggested above, the Directive treats all contracts for the supply of goods to be manufactured as contracts for the sale of goods. It seems clear that the second part of Article 2(3) was intended to protect the supplier by qualifying his liability under a contract to manufacture and supply a finished product where the finished item is manufactured partly or wholly from the consumer's materials. The UK has failed to implement either provision and as a result would seem to have exposed the seller in such cases to wider liability than would be the case under the Directive.

3.5.5 Article 2(5): Non-conformity due to incorrect installation

The UK Regulations similarly do not seem adequately to implement Article 2(5) which in certain circumstances treats a lack of conformity resulting from incorrect installation of the goods either by the seller or by the consumer, as a lack of conformity in the goods themselves.

3.5.5.1 *Installation by or under the responsibility of the seller*
As noted earlier, a contract to supply and install goods would in most cases be categorised in English law as a contract for work and materials or, possibly, as involv-

ing two separate obligations for supply of goods and their installation. In either case the supplier's duty in respect of the installation would be to carry it out with reasonable skill and care. It is not clear that this is sufficient to satisfy the Directive. The Directive seems to require that

(a) a lack of conformity arising from incorrect installation be treated as a lack of conformity in the goods, and

(b) a lack of conformity be judged in the same way as a lack of conformity in the goods themselves, which seems to mean that the seller should be strictly liable for the lack of conformity.

The UK Regulations seek to implement the first part of Article 2(5) by inserting a new section 11S(b) into the Sale and Supply of Goods Act 1982, which provides that:

Goods do not conform to a contract for the supply or transfer of goods if . . .
(b) installation of the goods forms part of the contract for the transfer of the goods, and the goods were installed by the transferor, or under his responsibility, in breach of the term implied by section 13 below . . .

Section 1(3) of the 1982 Act provides that a contract may be a contract for the transfer of goods whether or not services are also supplied, and section 12(3) provides similarly that a contract may be one for the supply of services whether or not goods are also transferred. A contract under which goods are transferred and services supplied is thus a contract both for the transfer of goods and for the supply of a service. The term implied by section 13 provides that in a contract for the supply of a service the service will be performed with reasonable skill and care. The effect of section 11S, which appears alongside the new provisions in the 1982 Act which implement the Directive's remedial scheme, is therefore that if the seller installs the goods negligently, in breach of the term implied by section 13, the goods do not conform to the contract, with the result that the consumer is entitled to the range of remedies derived from the Directive. This however is not what the Directive requires. It states that a lack of conformity in the goods which results from 'incorrect installation' is to be treated as a lack of conformity in the goods themselves, so as to trigger the remedial scheme. An example may illustrate this.

Example S contracts to supply and install a built-in oven. S follows the manufacturer's instructions but due to a reasonable, non-negligent misreading of them installs the oven incorrectly so that it fails to perform as efficiently as it would if properly installed.

The intention of the Directive seems to be that in such a situation S would be liable to the consumer. Although S was not negligent, installation was 'incorrect' and, as a result the oven fails to conform to the contract. The position would be the same if as a result of incorrect installation the oven did not match the display model in the supplier's show-room or the manufacturer's advertising. The trigger for liability is not incorrect installation as such, whether negligent or non-negligent, but non-conformity of the goods with the contract resulting from 'incorrect installation'. The Directive does not define 'incorrect installation' but there is no indication that it intends to import a negligence standard into the Directive. This is borne out by the second part of Article 2(5) which deals with 'incorrect installation' by the consumer due to inadequacies in the installation instructions. This part would clearly apply where the consumer has followed the installation instructions provided and has nevertheless installed the goods 'incorrectly'. It is difficult to see how a consumer could in such a case be said to have acted negligently. Again this emerges more clearly from some of the other language texts of the Directive: the German text uses 'unsachgemäss', which means 'improper'; the French 'defectueux' (incomplete or imperfect), and the Italian 'defectuosa'. This is entirely consistent with the approach of the Directive that the supplier of goods should be strictly liable for their conformity with the contract. In contrast the UK legislation equates 'incorrect installation' with a lack of reasonable skill and care and makes that the sole trigger for the remedial scheme. Although in many cases incorrect installation will be the result of negligence, that will not necessarily be the case.

The UK approach gives rise to several further difficulties. Under SGSA section 13 the consumer must prove negligence by the supplier (although in many cases, especially if the goods as installed fail to work properly, he may be able to rely on the principle of *res ipsa loquitur*). Under the Directive the consumer merely has to prove non-conformity and, as suggested earlier, it may be that the burden of proof will initially be on the supplier to show that the requirements of Article 2(2) are satisfied so as to give rise to the presumption of conformity. In addition under the Directive any attempt by the seller to exclude or restrict the consumer's rights arising from the Directive are ineffective. However, exclusion or limitation of liability for breach of the term implied by SGSA section 13 is permitted subject to a test of reasonableness. This is not permitted by the Directive.

3.5.5.2 *Installation by the consumer*
The UK Regulations contain no provision to implement the second aspect of Article 2(5), that a lack of conformity resulting from incorrect installation by the consumer due to 'a shortcoming' in the installation instructions shall be deemed to be equivalent to a lack of conformity in the goods. As we have noted earlier, it would seem that in English law goods supplied with inadequate or misleading instructions may be deemed not to be of satisfactory quality. This, however, is not what the Directive requires. Under domestic law the lack of installation instructions may lead to the goods being held not to conform to the contract. The Directive requires that the consumer have the remedies it provides available to him where the goods as installed do not conform to the contract *as a result of* inadequacies in the installation instructions. The difference may be subtle and in many cases the English law approach will produce similar results to the Directive.

Indeed, in some respects the English approach may be said to be more favourable to the consumer since if instructions are inadequate there is a lack of conformity even if they do not result in incorrect installation by the consumer. On the other hand the Directive makes it clear that the consumer is entitled to invoke its remedial scheme, including by demanding repair or replacement of the goods, after installation. A consumer who receives goods with inadequate installation instructions but nevertheless proceeds to try to install them may be held as a result to have accepted the goods thereby losing the right to reject them derived from the Sale of Goods Act. Some confirmation that installation in such a case does not prevent the buyer invoking the Directive's remedial scheme is probably needed to satisfy the Directive. Moreover the domestic position is at best unclear, the proposition that instructions are relevant to quality being derived from case-law. It is not at all clear that this is sufficient to satisfy EC law.

3.5.6 The time of conformity

As we have noted, the Directive expressly judges conformity of the goods with the contract at the time of their delivery to the consumer, and, although the position is not clear, it would seem that 'delivery' means *actual* physical delivery of the goods into the buyer's possession. In contrast the better view seems to have been that, prior to implementation of the Directive, English law required goods to conform to the contract at the time when risk passed from seller to buyer, which would normally occur at the same time as the transfer of property and could occur without physical delivery. Three new provisions have been incorporated into the SoGA in order to align domestic law with the Directive. It is however not clear that they do so.

First, a new section 48A provides that the remedial scheme derived from the Directive is available to the consumer if 'the goods do not conform to the contract at the time of delivery'. Second, a new subsection (4) has been added to section 20, dealing with the passing of risk from seller to buyer, providing that where the buyer deals as consumer the normal rule that risk passes with property is disapplied and the goods remain at the seller's risk 'until they are delivered to the consumer'. Third, a new subsection 32(4) has been inserted to deal with the situation where the seller is authorised or required to send the goods to the buyer and delivers them to a carrier for that purpose. The normal rule in that situation is that delivery to the carrier is deemed to be delivery to the buyer. Section 32(4) however disapplies this rule where the buyer deals as consumer and expressly provides that in that case delivery to the carrier is not delivery to the buyer. The result clearly is that where the seller is authorised or required to send the goods to the buyer, for instance where they are supplied by mail order, the goods are not 'delivered' to the buyer until they reach his possession, when conformity with the contract will be assessed, and the seller bears the risk of loss or damage to the goods whilst in transit.

These provisions go some way to satisfying the apparent requirements of the Directive. One difficult problem remains, however. The SoGA defines 'delivery' as 'voluntary transfer of possession from one person to another' and it is clear that 'delivery' may be actual or constructive. It is possible to envisage situations in which the seller remains in physical possession of goods after property in them has passed to the buyer and is deemed therefore to have made constructive delivery of them. If, as suggested earlier, the Directive requires conformity to be judged at the time of actual, physical delivery of the goods, section 48A is insufficient to satisfy the Directive.

3.6 CONCLUSION

The requirement in the Directive that goods should be in conformity with the contract is broadly similar in its effect to the requirements of the SoGA implied terms. As we have demonstrated, however, at the level of detail there are significant differences between them and many differences remain after implementation of the Directive by the SSGCR 2002.

Many of the difficulties and unresolved issues in the law arise from deficiencies in the Directive itself. In a number of areas insofar as there are differences between domestic law and the Directive, domestic law is more favourable to the consumer, and the difference is therefore permitted due to the minimal nature of the Directive's harmonisation objective. In other cases it may be possible to construe domestic law consistently with the Directive by means of the doctrine of indirect effect. In some areas, however, this may not be possible and there appear to be genuine gaps in the implementing legislation. In particular the treatment of contracts to make and supply goods and contracts to supply and install goods appears to be inadequate to satisfy the Directive and may raise a risk of liability for non-implementation.

4

REMEDIES

4.1 INTRODUCTION

The previous chapter examined the requirement that goods must be in conformity with the contract. The second main substantive provision of the Directive relates to the remedies available to the consumer if he has been supplied with goods that are not in conformity with the contract. Article 3 of the Directive contains a relatively complex system of remedies, under which if the seller delivers goods not in conformity with the contract the consumer may be entitled to have the goods repaired or replaced, or to have the contract rescinded and the price refunded, or to keep the goods and have a partial refund of the price.

Primacy is given in the remedial hierarchy to the remedies of repair or replacement. This is in sharp contrast to the position in English law where the buyer's principal remedies are rejection of the goods and termination of the contract and/or a claim for damages. The Directive here betrays its civil law roots. In effect the consumer's primary remedies under the Directive are to have the contract properly performed by having goods repaired or replaced, with the right to escape the contract by rescinding it available only as a 'long-stop' option. Rights of repair and replacement—rights of 'cure'—are effectively forms of specific performance and specific performance is the principal remedy for breach of contract in civilian systems, reflecting the maxim *pacta sunt servanda*. In contrast in English law, whilst lip service is paid to the notion of *pacta sunt servanda*, the principal remedy for a breach of contract is an award of damages. In the law of sale it is relatively easy for a consumer buyer to escape the contract in the event of non-conformity of the goods delivered. English law prior to the Directive recognised no right for the buyer to demand and at best only a limited right for the seller to insist on cure of a defective performance. Specific performance of a sale contract is rarely if ever awarded. Introduction of the Directive's rights to require cure by way of repair or replacement of non-conforming goods is therefore a radical departure for English contract law.

There are some broad similarities between the remedial regime of the Directive and that of the CISG. Certainly the CISG recognises rights for the buyer to insist on cure of a defective performance by repair or replacement of non-conforming goods, in addition to the rights of price reduction and rescission of the contract. However, the CISG regime is considerably more sophisticated and complex than that of the Directive and it seems more likely that the two regimes share common roots than that that in the Directive is derived directly from that in the CISG.

It should be noted that the Directive refers to repair, replacement, rescission and price reduction as 'rights' of the consumer, rather than as remedies. This may, in fact, be a more appropriate description of the various things a consumer can ask for under Article 3. Indeed the same may be true of English law, where it may be more accurate to say that in the event of a breach of condition by the seller the buyer has the *right* to reject the goods and terminate the contract and/or a *right* to damages. These are secondary rights which arise as a result of the seller's failure to perform his primary obligations. (See the analysis by Lord Diplock in *Photo Productions Ltd v Securicor Transport Ltd* [1980] AC 827, [1980] 1 All ER 556, HL.) However, this chapter will continue to use the term 'remedy' on the basis that the rules set out in Article 3 are used to make good a lack of conformity.

After examining the provisions of the Directive we will consider the remedial scheme of English law prior to its implementation and then consider how the Directive has been implemented. It will be necessary to consider separately the impact of the Directive on contracts of sale and on contracts for the supply of work and materials.

4.2 THE REMEDIAL REGIME IN THE DIRECTIVE

This part will analyse the Directive's remedial regime as contained in Article 3. It will be seen that this in itself is unusually complex for a consumer protection measure and that there are a number of ambiguities regarding its scope. A later section will consider how this has been implemented into English law. It can, however, be noted at the outset that the implementation has managed to complicate further an already complex system of rules.

4.2.1 Seller's liability

A preliminary point is that only the final seller is liable to the consumer for a lack of conformity (Article 3(1)). The original *Green Paper* proposals that manufacturers should be directly liable to the consumer for any lack of conformity in the goods were not pursued. A consumer can therefore not pursue any claims against the manufacturer or importer of goods which are not in conformity (in contrast with the position under the Product Liability Directive and the Consumer Protection Act 1987). Conversely, it is not possible for a seller to avoid his obligations under this Article by suggesting that a consumer should bring a claim against somebody else. Chapter 8 will consider in detail the arguments for and against a system of manufacturer liability.

4.2.2 Prerequisites to a claim

In order for the consumer to claim one of the rights provided for in Article 3 of the Directive a number of pre-requisites must be satisfied. First, the goods must be not in conformity with the contract. If it can be shown that the goods satisfy the requirements of Article 2 it will rebuttably be presumed that they are in conformity with the contract. In effect it is presumed that all that the contract requires is conformity with the Article 2 requirements. Second, the lack of conformity must manifest itself within two years of delivery of the goods. Third, it must be established that the lack of conformity was present at the time the goods were delivered to the consumer. Fourth, it may be necessary for the consumer to give notice of the lack of conformity to the seller.

4.2.2.1 *Manifestation of non-conformity*
Generally, the seller is liable for all instances of non-conformity which appear within two years from the date the goods were delivered to the consumer. By way of derogation, Member States may provide that, in the case of second-hand goods, a consumer and seller may agree on a reduced period of seller's liability, but this may not be less than one year (Article 7(1)). This one/two year time period is not a limitation period for bringing a claim against the seller, but rather a manifestation period. It is clear that the seller is only liable for a lack of conformity which existed at the time the goods were delivered. However, a defect or other lack of conformity may not be immediately apparent and only be revealed after a period of using the goods. Provided this occurs during this two-year period, the seller will be liable. Of course, this entails that if, under national legislation there is a limitation period, this needs to be a minimum of two years from the time of delivery so as not to undermine the manifestation period, and Article 5(1) so provides.

In principle, the seller can offer the consumer any of the four remedies of repair, replacement, price reduction or rejection (Recital 12). Seller and consumer may agree on any remedy, regardless of specific legal entitlements, by way of settlement of the consumer's claim. However, the consumer is not required to accept this proposal. If he chooses not to do so, then Article 3 comes into play.

4.2.2.2 *Non-conformity at the date of delivery*

Although the seller is liable for any lack of conformity which manifests itself within two years from delivery of the goods, the consumer is only entitled to rely on the rights provided by Article 3 if the lack of conformity was present at the date of delivery. The burden of proving that any lack of conformity was present at the time of delivery is normally on the consumer. By way of derogation, however, where a lack of conformity becomes apparent within six months of delivery of the goods, it is rebuttably presumed that the goods were not in conformity with the contract at the time of delivery (Article 5(3)). Where the presumption applies it has the effect of reversing the burden of proof and it is then for the seller to prove that the lack of conformity was not present at the time of delivery. The presumption does not, however, apply where it would be incompatible with either the nature of the goods or the nature of the lack of conformity (Article 5(3)). A seller seeking to rebut the presumption will often seek to do so by arguing that because of either the lack of conformity or the nature of the goods the lack of conformity must have, or is likely to have, arisen after the date of delivery. However, it seems that Article 5(3) requires the court to take notice of its own motion of the fact that the presumption is incompatible with either the lack of conformity or the nature of the goods and therefore to disapply the presumption without the need for the seller to raise the point.

When, then, will the presumption be incompatible with the nature of the goods? Clearly it will be where the goods in question have a life expectancy of less than six months, as, for instance, in the case of groceries such as fruit and vegetables which will inevitably deteriorate in quality almost from the date of purchase, and will often not survive for more than a week or so. The presumption in this case would clearly not be compatible with the (perishable) nature of the goods. (Note though that such goods would still not conform with the contract if they deteriorate more quickly than reasonably expected as, for example, if fruit has gone mouldy within a few hours of delivery.) Similar suggestions may be made in the case of fashion items such as shoes, which may be designed to last no more than a few months. If such shoes were to wear out after four or five months of regular use, it may be difficult to argue that they were not in conformity at the time of delivery.

Equally, the presumption will not apply where it would be incompatible with the nature of the lack of conformity. For example, if a dent is discovered in the bodywork of a car five months after delivery it may have been present at the time of delivery but it is more likely to have been caused by one of a number of factors thereafter, and it would be preposterous to presume that it existed at the time of delivery. The presumption would be incompatible with the nature of the particular 'lack of conformity' which is much more likely to have been caused by the consumer or a third party after delivery.

There may be some overlap between the tests for establishing whether goods are in conformity with the contract, and whether the burden of proof should be reversed, particularly in considering whether a lack of conformity is compatible with the nature of the goods. In particular, both may require an assessment of the durability reasonably expected of the goods. 'Durability' is, of course, not expressly an aspect of conformity, but will fall within Article 2(d) as an aspect of quality and performance which a consumer can reasonably expect (see 3.4.4).

4.2.2.3 *Notification of the lack of conformity*

Article 5(2) gives Member States the option to provide that a consumer must inform the seller of the lack of conformity within a period of two months from the date on which he discovered it. This is immediately problematic. Article 5(1), providing for the two year 'manifestation period', provides that the seller is liable for any lack of conformity which 'becomes apparent within two years as from delivery'. Under Article 5(2) on the other hand the two-month notification period runs from the date on which the consumer detected the lack of conformity. The combined effect seems to be to favour the less diligent consumer. Provided that the lack of conformity becomes apparent within the two-year period the requirement of Article 5(1) is satisfied even if the consumer does not notice the lack of conformity at that time (although a consumer who fails to notice an apparent lack of conformity may fall foul of any domestic limitation period). On the other hand the two-month notification period will not begin to run until the particular consumer has become aware of the lack of conformity.

A further problem arises under Article 5(2). How is the seller to prove the date when the individual consumer became aware of the lack of conformity rather than the date when he could, or should, have become aware of it?

4.2.3 The remedial hierarchy

Article 3 provides for four remedies. The relationship between them is one of the most difficult and controversial aspects of the Directive. It will be useful to set out the text of the key provisions.

3(2) In the case of a lack of conformity, the consumer shall be entitled to have the goods brought into conformity free of charge by repair or replacement, in accordance with paragraph 3, or to have an appropriate reduction made in the price or the contract rescinded with regard to those goods, in accordance with paragraphs 5 and 6.

3(3) In the first place, the consumer may require the seller to repair the goods or he may require the seller to replace them, in either case free of charge, unless this is impossible or disproportionate.

A remedy shall be deemed to be disproportionate if it imposes costs on the seller which, in comparison with the alternative remedy, are unreasonable taking into account the value the goods would have if there were no lack of conformity, the significance of the lack of conformity, and whether the alternative remedy could be completed without significant inconvenience to the consumer.

Any repair or replacement shall be completed within a reasonable time and without any significant inconvenience to the consumer, taking account of the nature of the goods and the purpose for which the consumer required the goods.

3(5) The consumer may require an appropriate reduction of the price or have the contract rescinded:
if the consumer is entitled to neither repair nor replacement, or
if the seller has not completed the remedy within a reasonable time, or
if the seller has not completed the remedy without significant inconvenience to the consumer.

It thus seems that Article 3 provides for a two-stage hierarchy of remedies. In the first instance, the consumer is entitled to require the seller to repair or replace the goods. Only if neither of those is available, or if the seller fails satisfactorily to complete the required remedy, can the buyer resort to the 'second stage' remedies of rescission or price reduction. The objective is to hold both parties to their bargain, so primacy is given to requiring the seller to cure his defective performance. The Green Paper originally proposed a scheme under which the choice of remedy would be, primarily, for the seller. The final scheme is more structured but, as will be seen, may still, in practice, prioritise the seller's interests.

Before considering further the relationship between the remedies it will be useful to consider what each entails.

4.2.4 Stage 1: Repair or replacement

Repair is defined as 'in the event of lack of conformity, bringing consumer goods into conformity with the contract of sale' (Article 1(2)(f)). Replacement is not defined. It is submitted that what is intended is direct replacement of the conforming goods with goods which *do* conform to the contract. Recital 16, which proposes that replacement will generally be impossible in the case of second-hand goods, suggests that replacement must be with an identical item (albeit one conforming to the contract).

It remains open to the parties to agree for the seller to replace the contract goods with different goods—for instance, if goods of the contract description are no longer available it would be possible for the parties to agree that the seller should replace them with the closest available substitute, which might be a more up-to-date model. However, it is submitted that replacement by a non-identical substitute is not 'replacement' within the meaning of Article 3(3) and can only be provided with the agreement of both parties.

Repair and replacement must both be provided free of charge. Article 3(4) provides that 'free of charge' refers to 'the necessary costs incurred to bring the goods into conformity, particularly the cost of postage, labour and materials'.

The basic position is that a consumer has the right to choose between repair and replacement. However, there are two significant qualifications to this which effectively undermine the consumer's rights. The buyer cannot require the seller to repair or replace the non-conforming goods if, in either case, the remedy is impossible or disproportionate (Article 3(3), final part). It will therefore be necessary first to consider whether it is possible to provide the remedy chosen by the consumer and secondly, whether it is disproportionate in comparison to another remedy.

4.2.4.1 *Impossible to repair*

Repair may be impossible for several reasons. An obvious example is where the lack of conformity is so severe that repair would simply not be an option (e.g. a vase which has been shattered). Some products may by the nature of their design be impossible to repair (such as a faulty disposable camera). Repair may also be impossible if (say) spare parts necessary for the repair are no longer available. It is submitted, however, that 'impossibility' should be narrowly construed so as to avoid unduly limiting the availability of repair which is intended to be one of the buyer's primary remedies. In cases of impracticability, such as, for instance, where the seller does not have the necessary staff or tools to effect repair, the question should be whether the remedy would be disproportionate. Repair will also generally be impossible where the non-conformity consists of the goods failing to correspond with their description: a 12″ television screen cannot be repaired so as to become a 36″ screen.

The Directive speaks of the consumer requiring the seller to repair the goods. It is submitted, however, that this should not be read as requiring the seller personally to effect repair. It should be sufficient if the goods are repaired by the seller or by someone on his behalf. What should be required is that the seller take responsibility for getting the goods repaired—restored to conformity with the contract (Recital 10).

It is not clear how effective repair has to be. The definition requires that the goods are brought into conformity with the contract. It has been suggested that:

[o]bviously, this does not mean that they have to be in a brand-new state. The definition requires repair, which is so effective that the goods compared to the requirements of the contract would have been acceptable originally. (Staudenmeyer (2000), p 555)

This statement cannot be taken at face value. If the initial sale was of 'brand new goods', goods which are not in 'brand new' condition would not conform to the contract. The point, it is submitted, is that the repair must cure the lack of conformity which is established—or presumed—to have existed in the goods at the date of delivery. The consumer is not, however, entitled to have the seller 'repair' other defects in the goods which do not amount to a lack of conformity or which did not exist, or cannot be shown to have existed at the date of delivery. Thus, for instance, if the handle falls off a china teapot, it may be possible to 'repair' the teapot by gluing back the handle, but this would not bring the teapot into conformity with the contract, because it would not give the consumer what he bargained for. On the other hand, if a car breaks down three months after delivery, by which time its paint work has become scratched in everyday use, the consumer is entitled to have the breakdown repaired and its cause remedied, but not to have the scratches made good, even though the scratches may be such that the car would have lacked conformity with the contract had they been present at the date of delivery. The same would be true if the car *had* been scratched at the date of delivery but, because of the particular circumstances of the case—perhaps because the car was sold as second-hand—the scratches would not have amounted to a lack of conformity.

There is a second issue, not addressed by the Directive. Suppose that the consumer demands repair in respect of a particular lack of conformity but the goods are, unknown to either party, also affected by another defect which would amount to a lack of conformity? Suppose, for instance, that the consumer buys a new car and discovers that the radio is defective. He returns the car to have the radio repaired under Article 3. Unknown to the consumer the car also has an engine defect which has not yet manifested itself. On a strict reading of Articles 1(2)(f) and 3(2) if the seller repairs the radio he has not 'repaired' the goods because, due to the unknown engine defect, the car is not in conformity with the contract. This is important because, as we shall see, failure by the seller satisfactorily to complete repair of the goods triggers the consumer's right to claim one of the two 'second stage' remedies of rescission or price reduction. It is submitted, however, that it would be a nonsense in such a case to say that the seller has failed to repair. The problem lies in the Directive's defintion of repair. It would have been more sensible to define it in terms of making good the particular lack of conformity identified by the buyer.

One final point about repair may be noted. We have seen that in certain circumstances the Directive treats as a lack of conformity in the goods any lack of conformity resulting from incorrect installation, including where the incorrect installation was by the consumer and resulted from a deficiency in the installation instructions. It would seem that in such cases 'repair' may require the seller actually to re-install the goods, including where initial installation was by the consumer. This may prove problematic for, e.g., DIY stores who supply goods for consumer installation, although we would repeat our earlier comment that it does not seem necessary for the seller to effect repair personally. It may be, however, that in such cases repair would be considered disproportionate and therefore be unavailable.

4.2.4.2 *Impossible to replace*

The instances where replacement will be impossible are likely to be few in number. Again it is submitted that 'impossibility' should be strictly and narrowly construed to exclude cases of difficulty or impracticability. The fact that the seller's stock of a particular item is exhausted does not make replacement impossible if substitute goods can be obtained from another supplier. The fact that that might be difficult or expensive may make replacement 'disproportionate' but does not make it impossible.

Similarly 'legal impossibility' should not preclude replacement. Replacement will be impossible if the contract goods are unique, as for instance where the contract is for sale of a particular piece of antique furniture. It cannot, however, be intended that replacement should be considered impossible merely because the contract is for 'specific' goods. In many cases the consumer, strictly speaking, contracts to buy a particular specific item. For instance in a self-service store where the consumer takes one of a number of identical items from a shelf and takes it to a check-out to pay for it, the contract is strictly speaking for the particular item presented at the check-out. That fact should not rule out replacement. Many consumer goods are mass-produced and therefore generic. It will not matter to the consumer whether he obtains a particular unit of a generic product, and it will be possible to provide a replacement. If this view is accepted it seems that replacement will only then not be possible where the product in question has gone out of production.

However, replacement may often be impossible in the case of second-hand goods. Recital 16 to the Directive states that 'the specific nature of second-hand goods makes it generally impossible to replace them'. Significantly this does not absolutely exclude the possibility of replacement in the case of second-hand goods. Here the question of the precise definition of 'replacement' becomes crucial. As we have noted the Directive does not define 'replacement' and it is not clear whether a replacement item has to have the exact same characteristics (other than the non-conformity!) as the non-conforming one. Take the example of a second-hand car: although no two used cars are the same, it is perfectly possible that the seller may have a similar car which would meet the consumer's needs and could therefore be offered as a replacement. Slight variations need not rule out the possibility of replacement, although this will, of course, depend on the nature of the variations. In the example of the second-hand car, there is no reason why a car of the same model and colour, but with a marginally different mileage, should not be considered as an adequate replacement.

If, however, the right of replacement is to have the goods replaced with an identical item, replacement under the Directive will only be possible where such an identical substitute is available, and therefore not in the case of second-hand goods. On the other hand it must be borne in mind that the Directive preserves the right of the parties to agree on any remedy they choose. There is therefore nothing to prevent the parties agreeing on the seller's replacing non-conforming goods by a near-identical substitute—say a newer model of higher specification, or a similar second-hand car. It should be noted though that in such a case the replacement is supplied under a contract. The arrangement could be analysed either as a variation of the original agreement or as a settlement of the consumer's claim, in which case the contract would be one of barter, the seller supplying the replacement item in consideration for the consumer's agreement to release his non-conformity claim. This in turn has important consequences for the consumer's rights. There is a new contract of supply and whilst contracts of barter are not covered by the Directive they are covered by the SSGCR 2002.

Overall, it is submitted that circumstances where either remedy will be 'impossible' will be rare. However, either remedy may be unavailable even if possible if it is 'disproportionate'.

4.2.4.3 *Disproportionality*

If 'impossibility' is narrowly construed the key factor limiting the availability of the remedies of repair and replacement is likely to be that neither is available as of right if it is 'disproportionate'. Determining when a remedy is 'disproportionate' is one of the most difficult aspects of the Directive. Article 3(3) provides that a remedy is deemed to be disproportionate 'if it imposes costs on the seller which, in comparison with the alternative remedy, are unreasonable'. In making the assessment whether the costs of a particular remedy are unreasonable, three factors are to be taken into account:

1. the value the goods would have had if they had been in conformity with the contract,

2. the significance of the lack of conformity, and

3. whether the alternative remedy could be completed without significant inconvenience to the consumer.

It is clear, then, that the test is an objective one and this is confirmed by Recital 11 to the Directive. Making the assessment involves making two comparisons. It is meaningless to speak of a remedy as being 'disproportionate' in the abstract. It must be disproportionate in comparison to something and it is submitted that the comparison here is between the cost to the seller of providing the given remedy and the benefit of it to the buyer. However, the structure of and the factors listed in Article 3(3) suggest that in making that assessment the seller's interests are prioritised over those of the buyer. Insofar as the test involves a comparison between the remedies of repair and replacement it has some similarities with the test used in domestic law to determine whether to award damages for breach of contract assessed on the 'cost of cure' (i.e. repair) or 'difference in value' (i.e. replacement) basis (see *Ruxley Electronics and Construction Ltd v Forsyth* [1996] AC 344, [1995] 3 All ER 268, HL). The test might perhaps more familiarly (although no more precisely) be expressed in English by asking if the buyer has a 'legitimate interest' in insisting on the particular remedy.

Once the cost/benefit assessment of the chosen remedy has been made, the second comparison becomes relevant. It is to be noted that the test is not whether the costs of the remedy in question are unreasonable *per se* but whether they are unreasonable in comparison with those of the alternative remedy. The Directive therefore requires an assessment to be made of the cost/benefit balance of the comparator remedy and then the costs and benefits of the two to be compared.

It is clear that applying the test of disproportionality requires a comparison between the costs and benefits of two remedies—that demanded by the consumer and 'the alternative'. But which remedies may be compared? It is clear from the location of the disproportionality test in Article 3(3) that one of the comparators will always be either repair or replacement. There is no room for application of the test as between rescission and price reduction. Nevertheless, two interpretations are possible, one narrow and one wider. The narrow view is that the test applies only as between repair and replacement. The wider view would allow a comparison of repair or replacement with the other remedies provided for by Article 3, to consider whether repair or replacement is disproportionate as compared to price reduction or rescission. It is not at all clear which interpretation is correct, and there are arguments for both interpretations. The location of the 'disproportionality' test in the middle of Article 3(3), which is concerned solely with repair and replacement, seems to support the narrow view. Price reduction/rescission are introduced in Article 3(5). If it had been intended to apply the disproportionality test to all the remedies, it would have made more sense to include it in a separate sub-paragraph following Article 3(5). The language of Article 3(3) also lends some support to this view. Article 3(3) requires a comparison to be made between the costs of the buyer's chosen remedy and 'the alternative remedy' which, in its context in Article 3(3), seems to suggest a comparison of repair with replacement and *vice versa*. If a general comparison with the other remedies available under Article 3 were intended it would be more natural to refer to a comparison between the costs of the chosen remedy and those of 'another' or 'any other' remedy. Recital 22 uses similar language to Article 3(3). The words 'the alternative' could however be read as referring to 'the particular alternative remedy with which the chosen remedy is compared'. Further support for the narrow view is provided by Article 3(5) which uses the expression 'the remedy' to refer to repair and replacement. Similarly, Recital 10 states that in the case of non-conformity consumers should be entitled to have the goods brought into conformity with the contract by repair or replacement 'or, failing this, to have the price reduced or the contract rescinded', again suggesting that the primary remedies are repair and replacement and implying, perhaps, that any comparison should be made between them. It must be conceded, however, that this provides at best only weak support for the narrow view. Some support for the wide view is provided by Article 3(5) which provides that one of the circumstances in which price reduction or rescission is available is 'if the consumer is entitled to neither repair nor replacement'. The consumer is not entitled to repair or replacement where the remedy in question is impossible or disproportionate. If the disproportionality test involves a comparison between only repair and replacement it is difficult to see how both could be disproportionate. Similarly if one is impossible, it is difficult to see how the other could be considered 'disproportionate' on this basis. If therefore the comparison is only between repair and replacement the only circumstances in which both remedies would be unavailable would be where both are impossible. But Article 3(5) does not refer to both being impossible but to the consumer being entitled to neither remedy. Article 3(5) would make more sense if the assessment of disproportionality did permit a comparison between repair/replacement on the one hand and price reduction/rescission on the other.

Perhaps the strongest reason for favouring the narrow view is policy. If the wider view were adopted the consumer would generally be restricted to the remedies of price reduction and rescission. The costs of these, and especially price reduction, will generally be much lower for the seller than those of repair or replacement, so that repair or replacement will generally be 'disproportionate' in comparison with price reduction/rescission. But this would undermine the overall thrust of the remedial regime, which is very much focused on ensuring performance of the seller's obligations. It should also be borne in mind that although the Directive no doubt seeks to avoid imposing excessive burdens on business, it is intended to be a consumer protection measure. An interpretation whose practical effect will often be to restrict the consumer's choice of remedies should be rejected. Nevertheless, the only safe conclusion is that overall the position is rather unsatisfactory and a clearer structure to the proportionality test would have been desirable.

Assuming, then, that the relevant comparison is between repair and replacement, the first question is therefore to consider which of repair or replacement is going to be less costly for the seller to provide. In some instances, such as where the goods are of low value, replacement will often be less costly than repair. However, in most cases it is likely that the cost of repairing a product will be lower than that of providing a replacement. A seller who has to replace a defective item will be left with that item on his hands. Even if the defective item can be repaired it cannot be resold as 'new' at its full price.

Example   Suppose, for instance, that S sells a new item for £100. It proves defective and will cost £50 to repair. The consumer demands a replacement. If S provides a replacement and repairs the defective item his costs will be £150. Suppose he resells the repaired item as 'nearly new' for £80. His net loss is £70. If, on the same facts, the consumer had accepted repair of the original goods S's loss would be only the cost of repair—£50.

There will of course generally be some difference between costs of repair and replacement. However, mere difference in cost is not enough to make one remedy disproportionate in comparison with the other. In order to be regarded as disproportionate the costs of one remedy must be unreasonable compared to those of the other. Recital 11 emphasises that this requires that such costs are *significantly* higher:

In order to determine whether the costs are unreasonable, the costs of one remedy should be significantly higher than the costs of the other.

Of course, the question whether the costs imposed by a particular remedy are unreasonable is not the sole determinant that that remedy is disproportionate.

The costs to the seller must be balanced against the benefits to the consumer. The second factor to consider is therefore the value the goods would have had if there were no lack of conformity. The fact that the goods in conformity with the contract would be of low value will tend to limit the availability of repair. Where the cost of providing repair would, because of the cost of labour and parts required, exceed the market value of the goods themselves, the remedy would be disproportionate. In that case, providing a replacement (or price reduction/ rescission, subject to the discussion in the previous paragraph) may offer a better solution. Conversely if the goods would be of high value if they conformed to the contract, even an expensive repair may not be disproportionate.

Alternatively, where there is only a small difference in value between the goods as delivered and their market price, it may be that replacement would be regarded as disproportionate if repair could be effected easily and at low cost. In this respect, the second factor overlaps with the third.

The cost of the chosen remedy must also be weighed against the significance of the lack of conformity. This is likely to overlap to some extent with the previous factor, and the two will often have to be read together. For instance, if the effect of the particular lack of conformity is to make the goods useless, even relatively expensive repair may be justified, if the goods, in conformity with the contract, would be of high value. Conversely replacement may be more appropriate if the goods are of low value. On the other hand a relatively minor lack of conformity might not justify expensive repair, especially if, contrary to the views above, comparison with the remedies of price reduction and rescission is permitted. In some cases the lack of conformity may be so severe that there is little point in attempting repair. In contrast, if a particular lack of conformity is very slight, repair may be more appropriate than replacement.

Finally, the degree of inconvenience that may be caused to the consumer by the provision of the particular remedy must be considered. This is the only factor which takes into account the consumer's interests when assessing whether a remedy is disproportionate. It may result in the consumer being able to insist on a remedy which would otherwise be considered disproportionate. Suppose, for instance that S supplies a washing machine which breaks down. The cost of repair is far cheaper than that of replacement and on cost alone replacement would be considered disproportionate. However, repair will involve waiting several weeks for spare parts and then a day during which repairers will take apart the washing machine on the consumer's kitchen floor. The inconvenience to the consumer might be such as to favour replacement. The position might be different if the supplier were in a position to take away the defective machine for repair and provide the consumer with a substitute in the interim.

Assuming that, as suggested above, the comparison required by the disproportionality test is between repair and replacement, it seems that repair is likely to be the more commonly available remedy, replacement often being disproportionate in comparison. Repair may therefore be regarded as the primary remedy under the

Directive. However, there will also be particular cases where replacement would be the more appropriate remedy. If however a wider comparison between repair or replacement on the one hand and rescission and price reduction on the other is permitted it is likely that repair and replacement will often be unavailable and the primary remedy will be price reduction.

4.2.4.4 *Provision of remedy within reasonable time and without inconvenience*

Article 3(3) requires that any repair or replacement be provided within a reasonable time and without any significant inconvenience to the consumer. The seller's failure to comply with this requirement is one of the grounds on which the consumer may demand either rescission of the contract or reduction of the price (Article 3(5)). It is however not clear if the consumer can ask for a replacement if repair has not been satisfactorily effected, or *vice versa* (Bianca, 2002, paragraphs 73–4). There is nothing in the Directive which expressly prevents a consumer who has requested repair from going back and requesting replacement instead, or *vice versa*, provided that both remedies were possible and neither disproportionate when the consumer made his initial choice of remedy. The better view is therefore that the consumer's choice of repair or replacement is not a once-and-for-all election, so that if replacement is still possible and would not be disproportionate compared to repair, it may be possible for the consumer to ask for a replacement if repair has not been, or cannot be, provided satisfactorily.

The Directive does not specify whether the consumer must have given the seller the opportunity to repair or replace and waited for a reasonable period of time to have passed (or a significant inconvenience caused) before an alternative remedy may be considered, or whether this can be done in anticipation of the seller's failure to do so. Article 3(5) suggests that the former is the case, because it is phrased in terms of the seller not having completed the remedy. However, if a seller by his actions makes it obvious that he will not comply, there seems no good reason why the consumer should be made to wait until a reasonable time has expired and, perhaps by analogy with the familiar English doctrine of anticipatory breach (also found in the CISG) the consumer should be able to move immediately to the appropriate 'second stage' remedy.

In determining whether repair or replacement has been effected within a reasonable period and without significant inconvenience, account is to be taken of the nature of the goods and the purposes for which the consumer required the goods. For example, it would undoubtedly be a significant inconvenience if a consumer were made to wait for two months for a repair of his refrigerator. Similarly if the goods were acquired for a particular purpose, say a video camera bought to record a family wedding, repair might be inappropriate if it could not be completed until after the wedding. Once again, there appears to be some duplication of aspects of the proportionality test—whether the provision of a remedy would cause a 'significant inconvenience' is relevant in both contexts. Other factors may be relevant. For instance, as suggested above, one factor which might be relevant is whether the seller is able to provide a temporary replacement whilst the consumer waits for repair or replacement of his goods (e.g. a courtesy car). If this were so, it might make an otherwise unreasonable period/significant inconvenience acceptable. However, the Directive rightly does not lay down a specific rule in this respect, because having a temporary replacement may nevertheless be a significant inconvenience in particular circumstances.

4.2.4.5 *Conformity of repaired or replacement goods*
The Directive is silent on the important question of the consumer's rights in relation to repaired or replacement goods. A proposal by the Parliament to include a provision expressly stating that 'the same provisions' should apply to goods supplied by way of replacement as to newly supplied goods (there was no mention of repaired goods) was rejected.

Presumably since the purpose of repair or replacement is to bring the goods into conformity with the contract (Article 3(2)) the goods as repaired or replaced should conform to the terms of the original contract. But when does time begin to run for the purposes of determining the manifestation period or the reversed burden of proof in relation to repaired or replacement goods? Suppose, for instance, that three months after delivery goods break down due to a latent defect, and the seller provides a replacement, which in turn breaks down four months later. Can the consumer rely on the presumption, in Article 5(3) of the Directive, that the lack of conformity in the replacement was present at the date of delivery and thus on the reversed burden of proof? Common sense would suggest 'Yes': the goods have broken down only four months after delivery, and the basis for the presumption is that the fact of early breakdown leads to the inference that the defect was present all along. On the other hand it is now seven months after delivery of the original goods, and a strict reading of the Directive could lead to the conclusion that the six-month time limit always runs from the date of original delivery. The same problem arises in relation to repaired goods. If goods are repaired within the six-month period and then manifest a different defect, the six-month and two-year periods should run from the date of first delivery. But if the goods break down a second time because of a failure of the repair—for instance because a replacement component fails—a case can be made for saying that the periods should run from the date of repair.

4.2.4.6 *Risk of loss*
The Directive is silent on another matter of practical importance. Although it is made clear that the seller must provide the remedy 'free of charge' (see above) the practicalities of returning the goods to the seller for repair/replacement are not addressed. In particular, if goods are returned for repair or replacement, who should bear the risk of loss of or damage to them in transit? This may be a particularly significant issue in the context of the Directive which, as we have seen, is intended to encourage consumers to engage in cross-border transactions. In the

era of e-commerce it is quite likely that the seller will often be a distant one, possibly based in another country with no local retail outlet or even no retail outlet at all. We have seen that the Directive effectively requires the seller to bear the risk of loss during initial delivery, and it is submitted that the combined logic of that provision and the requirement that the seller should provide repair or replacement free of charge suggest that the risk of loss in transit should be borne by the seller. However, the failure of the Directive to deal with this problem—which was highlighted in several discussions of the proposals which led to it—is to be regretted.

4.2.5 Stage 2: Price reduction or rescission

If neither repair nor replacement produce the desired result, or neither is available, it may be possible for the consumer to obtain a partial or full refund of the purchase price through the second stage remedies of price reduction and rescission.

4.2.5.1 *When do price reduction and rescission become available?*
Rescission and price reduction are available in three situations:

(a) where the consumer is entitled to neither repair nor replacement;

(b) where repair or replacement is available but the seller has not completed the repair or replacement within a reasonable time;

(c) where repair or replacement is available but the seller has not completed the repair or replacement without significant inconvenience to the consumer (Article 3(5)).

Broadly speaking, therefore, the 'second stage' remedies are available where:

(a) neither repair nor replacement is available or

(b) where despite one or both being available the seller has failed to complete the remedy satisfactorily.

A consumer will be entitled to neither repair nor replacement if both are impossible and/or disproportionate. We have considered above the question whether the test of disproportionality permits a comparison between the costs of repair/replacement and rescission/price reduction and tentatively concluded that it does not. If this view is correct, condition (a) of Article 3(5) will normally only be satisfied if both repair and replacement are impossible; they cannot both be 'disproportionate' if the only comparison permitted is with each other. It may, however, be possible to envisage situations in which one is impossible and the other disproportionate, as for instance where repair would be very expensive in comparison with the original value of the goods and replacement is impossible, because manufacture of the contract goods has been discontinued. If, however, contrary to our earlier analysis, an assessment of disproportionality does permit a comparison between the first and second stage remedies there will be cases where both repair and replacement will be disproportionate and the second stage remedies will therefore be available much more frequently.

As will be noted, 'significant inconvenience to the consumer' is relevant in both Article 3(3) to the assessment whether repair or replacement is 'disproportionate' and in Article 3(5) to the availability of rescission and price reduction. Article 3(3) requires a judgment to be made prospectively, before repair or replacement has been attempted, whether the proposed remedy can be effected without 'significant inconvenience'. If it cannot (or perhaps more likely, if at that time it seems that it cannot) that fact goes to the assessment of proportionality and may result in the proposed remedy being wholly unavailable. (Note that prospective significant inconvenience does not allow the consumer to refuse the remedy.) Article 3(5), on the other hand, applies where there has been an attempt at repair or replacement and requires an *ex post facto* assessment whether it has been effected without significant inconvenience. In effect it allows the consumer who has opted for repair or replacement to withdraw his election and opt for one of the second stage remedies instead. (In passing we may note that it seems odd that the *a priori* assessment under Article 3(3) does not seem to permit account to be taken of the time likely to be taken to effect the proposed remedy. The separate reference to the time taken to effect the remedy in Article 3(5) indicates that delay *per se* does not amount to 'significant inconvenience'.)

In many cases the factor which causes inconvenience to the consumer will be the time taken to effect a remedy. A typical situation might be where the seller takes more than a few days to repair non-conforming goods, and a replacement product is not available. Then it may be argued either that the repair has not been effected within a reasonable time or that the attempt has caused significant inconvenience to the consumer, or both.

Rescission will not be available where the lack of conformity is minor (Article 3(6)). In that case, the only remedy available to the consumer is price reduction because, *ex hypothesi*, repair or replacement will not be available in a case where rescission and price reduction are. There is no guidance on when a lack of conformity will be minor. We have suggested earlier (3.2.3.2) that perhaps something akin to a *de minimis* resctriction is intended. After all, the ratio of the significance of the lack of conformity to the cost of remedying it will have already been considered in deciding if repair or replacement will be disproportionate so as to make rescission available. A comparison may perhaps be drawn with section 15A of the English Sale of Goods Act which, in relation to *commercial* transactions provides that the buyer may not reject goods, even for breach of condition, if the breach is so minor that it would be unreasonable to reject.

It is not clear whether in assessing whether a lack of conformity is 'minor' account can be taken of the consequences of the lack of conformity. In the *Bernstein* case in England (*Bernstein v Pamsons Motors (Golders Green) Ltd* ([1987] 2 All ER 220)) a car engine seized up after only about 140 miles, due to a blockage in the lubrication system. The seller sought to argue that the defect was only minor and therefore did not make the car unmerchantable. The argument was (rightly) rejected partly on the grounds that the consequences—and potential consequences—of the defect were far from minor and the consumer could justifiably claim that his confidence in the car had been shaken. It is, however, not clear that the same approach could be taken under the Directive. (Note that the identical issue would be unlikely to arise since the particular defect in issue in *Bernstein* would be readily repairable, as indeed it had been repaired in the case.)

It must be borne in mind that the minor lack of conformity provision only comes into play when the consumer is claiming rescission, which means that it has already been determined that repair and replacement are not available or they have been attempted and failed. There may be instances where repair/replacement are not available and yet the lack of conformity is minor. One instance might be where goods are supplied with a minor, irreparable cosmetic defect—say a mark on the casing of a TV set or hi-fi product—and the particular item is discontinued and therefore irreplaceable. Or a similarly irreplaceable vase is supplied with a small chip in the glaze on its base. Generally however a minor lack of conformity is likely to be capable of cure by repair or replacement, so that rescission will probably only be considered because the seller has failed to repair or replace the non-conforming item within a reasonable time or without a significant inconvenience. In such cases the 'minor defects' restriction on the right of rescission may be detrimental to the consumer. In the case of a 'minor' lack of conformity there may be less urgency for the seller to provide a remedy, especially if the consumer can still use the goods for the time being, and the seller may therefore delay the provision of a remedy because he does not regard it as a priority. In the meantime the consumer will still have non-conforming goods. In such a situation the threat of rescinding the contract if the seller does not perform his obligations may be an important lever in the bargaining process to pressurise the seller into performing his obligations.

4.2.5.2 *Price reduction*

Price reduction is the one remedy on whose availability there are no restrictions in the Directive. It is therefore the consumer's only absolute entitlement. It might be thought that price reduction will be inappropriate where there is a major lack of conformity because the amount by which the price is reduced in such a case may fall not far short of a full refund. In such a case full rescission may seem the more appropriate remedy. However, a consumer may prefer to keep goods even with major lacks of conformity, especially if (say) he has had the goods for some time before the lack of conformity manifests itself, if the price is reduced appropriately.

The Directive offers no guidance on how the amount of any price reduction should be calculated. There are two possibilities:

(a) a flat-rate deduction of the difference between
(i) the value the goods would have had had they conformed to the contract, and
(ii) the value of the goods as delivered, or

(b) a proportionate reduction of the purchase price, in the same ratio as the value of the goods as delivered bears to the value they would have had, had they conformed to the contract.

It was noted in chapter 1 that the Directive borrows from the Convention on Contracts for the International Sale of Goods 1980 (CISG), and it would be reasonable to assume that the right to price reduction in the Directive would follow similar principles to those in the CISG (Twigg-Flesner & Bradgate, 2000; Bianca, 2002). The price reduction remedy under the CISG may be regarded as quasi-restitutionary, intended to prevent the seller receiving full payment where he has not performed in full. Accordingly, it adopts the proportionate reduction approach. A number of examples may illustrate this:

Example 1   A consumer buys goods from a seller for £100. Had the goods been in conformity with the contract, they would have been worth £100, but the goods as delivered are defective and are worth only £80. A flat-rate deduction would give the consumer £20. A proportionate reduction based on the ratio that the actual value of the goods bears to their value had they conformed to the contract would mean that the consumer would have to pay 80/100 of the contract price, which would also result in a £20 deduction.

Example 2   Again, the consumer buys goods for £100, but had the goods conformed to the contract of sale, they would, in fact, have been worth £120—for example because they were bought in a sale. A flat-rate reduction based on the difference between the actual value of the goods and the value had they been in conformity would mean that £40 is subtracted from the contract price and the consumer would pay £60. The proportionate reduction approach would require the consumer to pay 80/120, which is £66.66. This example might be relevant where goods are bought during a sale period.

Example 3   Finally, assume that even if the goods had been in conformity with the contract, they would have been worth less than the contract price, e.g., £90. The flat-rate reduction would mean that the contract price is reduced by £10 (£90–£80), and the consumer would have to pay £90. The proportionate reduction approach would require the consumer to pay 80/90, i.e., £88.89.

Although the differences between the amounts of the reduction produced by the two different approaches are small in these examples, the point is that the proportionate reduction rules work in the consumer's favour where he has made a bad bargain, but where he has made a good bargain the flat-rate deduction approach may produce a more favourable result. In the consumer context the difference between the two approaches should not be overstated as the sums involved will usually be small, but it is nevertheless important to understand that neither approach necessarily favours the consumer in every case. It might therefore be possible, consistent with the objective of the Directive, to argue that the court should adopt whichever approach produces a result most favourable to the consumer in the particular case. In practice, however, where disputes are dealt with by the parties, the flat-rate deduction approach may be easier to apply. In fact any price reduction is likely to be calculated by the parties on a fairly *ad hoc* basis because of the difficulty of assessing the value of non-conforming goods.

4.2.5.3 *Rescission*

As already noted, a consumer cannot rescind the contract if the lack of conformity is minor, although it is not clear when this will be the case. Other than this there is little guidance in the Directive on the meaning or operation of 'rescission', and it seems that the detailed operation of the right of rescission is left to domestic law (see the Council Common Position of 24.9.98). We may note in passing that from an English law perspective the use of the word 'rescission' may be unfortunate. 'Rescission' is already used in several senses which tends to result in confusion, and it has been authoritatively suggested that its use should be restricted to *rescissio ab initio* where parties are restored to their pre-contract positions, normally because of some defect in the formation of the contract, in order to distinguish it from termination for breach, which operates prospectively (see *Johnson v Agnew* [1980] AC 367 at 393). What the Directive provides is a remedy for non-conformity—effectively a remedy for breach. It may be, however, that the right provided is closer to true *rescissio ab initio* than to termination for breach.

If a consumer does rescind, he should be given a refund of the purchase price. Although not specified in Article 3 itself, Recital 15 states that Member States may provide that account may be taken of the use the consumer has had of the product. Consequently, a consumer may not get back the full purchase price. This provision is justifiable on the basis that a consumer may have had the goods for a period during which they performed as intended, as for instance where a latent defect only manifests itself after some time. However, it may be difficult to determine in a particular case (a) whether the seller should make a deduction at all and (b) if so, the amount. After all, where goods are affected by a latent defect the consumer's use or enjoyment of the goods may have been affected. Much will depend on the nature of the lack of conformity. If a latent defect merely means that the goods are less durable, and wear out earlier than they should have done, it may be appropriate to reduce the buyer's refund to take account of the use he has had of the goods before they break down. If, however, a latent defect affects performance before it is discovered, the amount of any reduction of the consumer's refund should reflect the value of the (sub-standard) use he has had of the goods. This is a further element of the remedial regime where more guidance would have been welcome.

Although nothing specific is stated in the Directive, it seems that a precondition to rescission is that the consumer must be able to return the non-conforming product, unless this is not possible because of the lack of conformity (e.g. defective brakes leading to a car crash in which the car is destroyed: Bianca, 2002, paragraphs 46–48).

4.2.5.4 *Scope of the rights of price reduction and rescission*

The precise scope of the rights of price reduction and rescission allowed by Article 3 is not clear. Article 3(5) refers generally to the consumer's right to require 'an appropriate reduction of the price or have the contract rescinded'. However, Article 3(2) provides that 'In the case of a lack of conformity, the consumer shall be entitled . . . to have an appropriate reduction made in the price or the contract rescinded *with regard to those goods* . . .'. The italicised words seem to qualify the preceding reference to the right to have the contract rescinded so as to restrict the right of rescission to the goods affected by the lack of conformity, although no such restriction appears in Article 3(5). The effect seems to be that where several items are sold together and only some are affected by a lack of conformity the buyer is only entitled to rescind the contract with regard to those goods. This immediately creates one potential difficulty. Suppose, for instance, that the consumer buys a pair of shoes and one of them has a loose heel. Can the seller argue that only the one defective shoe is affected by the lack of conformity so that, if the right to rescind is available, the consumer is only entitled to rescind the contract in relation to that shoe? Such a result would be nonsensical. It could be avoided by interpreting the 'goods' affected by the lack of conformity as the pair of shoes, perhaps by adopting something akin to the concept of a 'commercial unit' used in the Sale of Goods Act according to which a 'commercial unit' means 'a unit division of which would materially impair the value of the goods or the character of the unit' (SoGA section 35(7)). What though of the case where several separate items are purchased together as a single package, as for instance where the consumer purchases a computer, printer and scanner intending to use them together? If the printer lacks conformity and cannot be repaired or replaced, should the consumer be entitled to rescind the whole contract, or only to rescind the contract in relation to the printer? It is submitted that where the remaining items not affected by the lack of conformity cannot be used properly without the non-conforming item the consumer should be entitled to rescind the whole contract. An alternative approach, which would give effect to the consumer's expectations, would be to look to the manner in which the goods are sold and, where goods are sold as a package, treat the relevant goods as the package. Thus in the example of the computer equipment referred to above if the goods are sold as a single package at a composite price the consumer should be able to rescind the whole contract if any part of the package lacks conformity.

It is not clear whether a similar restriction applies to the right of price reduction, and the language of Article 3(2) is ambiguous in this respect. Grammatically the words 'with regard to those goods' could be read as governing only the immediately preceding reference to 'the contract rescinded' or the whole of the preceding sub-clause, referring to both 'an appropriate reduction in the price or the contract rescinded'. Where goods are sold as a package it may be difficult to attribute a price to each element of the package, and it is submitted that the more natural reading of Article 3(2) is that the consumer is entitled to an 'appropriate' reduction of the overall package price (which might be more than the price of the particular non-conforming item).

4.2.6 Consequential losses

A significant gap in Article 3 is the absence of any provision dealing with consequential losses. The Directive requires that a remedy is made available to a consumer without any cost, but there may be losses in addition to the cost of returning the product for repair or replacement. For example, a defective freezer may cause the loss of all the food it contains. A faulty washing machine may ruin a load of clothes. If a car is supplied with defective brakes as a result of which it is involved in a collision the car may be damaged and the driver and passengers injured. There are differences between the laws of the Member States as to the extent to which and basis on which damages may be recovered for such losses in a claim for breach of contract. The question of whether to award damages for consequential losses, and the conditions on which these may be claimed, has therefore been left to the Member States, although it is notable that the CISG adopts a rule similar to the English law rule, and permits recovery of damages to put the buyer in the same position as if the contract had been performed, subject only to a remoteness of damage limitation. (CISG Article 74. Note however that an award of damages under Article 74 would not include compensation for death or personal injury resulting from a breach of contract. See CISG Article 5.)

4.2.7 No combination of remedies

One of the striking features of the Directive is that although there is a very complex system for determining which remedy is available to the consumer in different circumstances there is no provision for a combination of remedies and it appears that such combination is not permitted. This seems unfortunate as a combination of the Directive's remedies may sometimes be necessary to provide the consumer with satisfactory redress. Suppose, for instance, that a consumer buys a new car. It performs unsatisfactorily and after several months breaks down. The defect is repaired. However, the performance of the car prior to repair has been impaired by the defect—perhaps its fuel efficiency has been lower than it should have been. In order to provide the consumer with full redress they should receive a partial refund of the price in recognition of the reduced value of the use of the car. Or it may be that the defect can be repaired but that the repair will not restore the goods to perfect condition. On a strict interpretation of Article 3, this might mean that repair, as defined (bringing the goods into conformity with the contract) is impossible. However, the consumer might be willing to accept repair, provided that he is given some allowance in price to reflect the less than perfect condition of the repaired goods. In these and other similar cases a combination of repair and price reduction would best provide the consumer with an acceptable remedy but this possibility is not provided for in the Directive, other than through Recital 12 according to which the seller may offer the consumer any of the four remedies— but even this provision does not seem to anticipate a combination of remedies. A solution might, of course, be available in domestic law by means of an award of damages in addition to the award of repair or replacement.

4.2.8 A 'right' of cure?

As we have observed, consistent with the emphasis of civilian law on which it is based, the Directive emphasises the preservation of the contractual relationship between the parties, prioritising the rights of repair and replacement. It has there-fore effectively created a 'right' for the seller to insist on cure in consumer transac-tions. In contrast with the position in English law the consumer has no absolute right to a refund. In the first instance he is only entitled to repair or replacement.

The primacy given to repair and replacement suggests that a seller can have at least two, and possibly more, attempts at performing his obligations under the contract of sale to deliver goods which are in conformity with the contract. Admittedly, the seller does not in terms have the right to repair or replace a non-conforming product, because the Directive is phrased in terms of consumer enti-tlement. In practice, however, it will often be the seller who has the choice of remedy. Provided that either repair or replacement is possible and not dispropor-tionate the consumer is not entitled to demand price reduction or rescission unless and until the seller has attempted and failed satisfactorily to effect repair or replacement. The test of disproportionality emphasises the seller's interests and the cost of the proposed remedy. Moreover it must be borne in mind that most disputes will be resolved, not in court, but by a consumer complaint and negotia-tion with the seller. In practice therefore the consumer will often have to settle for what the seller is prepared to provide. The consumer's right to demand 'cure' can very quickly elide into the seller's right to insist on cure. Although it may be desir-able in principle that consumers should be held to their original bargain, the seller will have had the opportunity of fulfilling that bargain when making the original delivery. Why should he get a second (and even a third?) chance? The emphasis on cure may tie a consumer to a contract with a seller who may ultimately be unable to provide conforming goods.

4.3 REMEDIES IN ENGLISH LAW

Before implementation of the Directive, English law provided the buyer of goods with, broadly speaking, three remedies in the event of his receiving goods not

conforming to the contract. However, one of those remedies, specific performance, is rarely available and even more rarely awarded. Although the position is
not clear the better view is that a right of cure was not available in domestic law;
certainly any right which was recognised was relatively limited. In addition there
were important differences between the remedies available under different types of
supply contract.

4.3.1 The remedies in the Sale of Goods Act 1979

As we have noted, the delivery of goods not conforming to the contract amounts
in the terms of domestic law to a breach of contract. Prior to implementation of
the Directive the buyer's rights under a contract of sale governed by the Sale of
Goods Act 1979 in the event of a breach by the seller were

(a) to reject the goods and treat the contract as repudiated;

(b) to claim damages; and

(c) to have the contract specifically performed.

All three rights remain available after implementation of the Directive.

4.3.1.1 *Rejection and termination*
The buyer's remedies for breach of contract by the seller depend on the
classification of the term broken and the consequences of the breach. The buyer
is in all cases entitled to claim damages for breach of contract. However, SoGA
section 11(3) indicates that if the term broken is classified as a condition the buyer
is entitled to reject the goods and treat the contract as repudiated. In contrast,
where the term broken is classified as only a warranty (defined as 'an agreement
with reference to goods . . . the subject of a contract of sale, but collateral to the
main purpose of such contract'—SoGA section 61) the buyer is entitled to damages for losses caused by the breach, but not to reject the goods and terminate the
contract.

Most cases of goods lacking conformity with the contract will be covered by the
implied terms in SoGA sections 13–15, considered in chapter 3, above. The
implied terms are all classified, in England and Wales, as conditions. It follows
therefore that in the event of a breach by the seller of any of the implied terms in
sections 13–15 the buyer is *prima facie* entitled to reject the goods and terminate
the contract.

However, a lack of conformity may also result from a breach of an express or
implied term of the contract. The classification of such terms depends on the
intention of the parties and in many cases an express term may be classified as a
mere warranty. Alternatively express terms may be classified as innominate, so
that the remedies available to the buyer in the event of their breach depend on the
seriousness of the breach and its consequences. In practice most express terms in
sale contracts are likely to be classified as innominate. The buyer is entitled to

reject goods for breach of an innominate term if the consequences of the breach are so serious as to deprive the buyer of substantially the whole of the benefit he was intended to obtain from the contract.

4.3.1.2 *Loss of the right to reject*
Breach of condition or serious breach of an innominate term therefore gives the buyer the *right* to reject the goods and terminate the contract. He is not obliged to do so. Rejection is at the buyer's option and it is open to the buyer to opt instead to accept the goods as delivered and simply claim damages for the breach. The measure of such damages is considered below.

If the buyer elects to accept the goods he loses the right to reject them. However, the buyer may in certain circumstances also be deemed to have accepted the goods and thus lose his right of rejection and termination (section 11(4) and sections 34–35). The buyer is deemed to have accepted the goods in three situations:

(a) if he expressly intimates his acceptance;

(b) if he does some act inconsistent with the seller's ownership of the goods; this would include any act which involves the buyer treating the goods as his own, such as using them, consuming them, repairing or attempting to repair them, or dealing with them as owner;

(c) if, after the lapse of a reasonable time he retains the goods without indicating that he is rejecting them (section 35).

It will thus be apparent that the buyer may, quite inadvertently, be deemed to have accepted goods complete with defects of which he is unaware. Indeed, prior to 1994 it was possible for the buyer to be deemed to have accepted goods without having had the opportunity to discover any defects. However, important changes were made to the law on acceptance by the Sale and Supply of Goods Act 1994, to make the law more appropriate to consumer needs. Thus the SoGA now provides that the buyer is not to be deemed to have accepted the goods by express intimation or by doing an act inconsistent with the seller's ownership unless he has first had a reasonable opportunity of examining them to ascertain whether they are in conformity with the contract (section 35(2)) and cannot be deprived of this right to examine the goods by any contract term, waiver or otherwise. Thus a buyer who signs a delivery note 'accepting' the goods without first being given the opportunity of examining them may nevertheless reject them if on examination they prove not to be in conformity with one of the implied conditions. Moreover the Act also provides that the buyer is not to be deemed to have accepted goods *merely* because he asks for or agrees to their repair by the seller or under an arrangement with the seller, or delivers them to a third party by way of resale or other disposition (section 35(6)). So if the consumer receives defective goods and, without discovering the defect, makes a gift of them to a relative, it can no longer be argued that by that act alone he has accepted the goods and lost the right to reject. Nor, if the goods

prove defective does the buyer lose the right to reject the goods if he asks the seller
to repair them or arrange for their repair. (The position may be different if the
buyer attempts repair himself or makes his own arrangements for repair.)

In most cases, however, the buyer loses the right to reject goods simply by lapse
of time. This is especially problematic where goods are affected by a latent defect.
For a long time a leading case in this area was the decision of Rougier J. in
Bernstein v Pamsons Motors (Golders Green) Ltd ([1987] 2 All ER 220). Here the
consumer had bought a new car but during the three weeks following the purchase
he was ill and drove the car only about 140 miles. The car then seized up due to a
blockage in the lubrication system. The judge held that the car was unmerchantable (now unsatisfactory) but that the right to reject had been lost by the
consumer's retaining it beyond a reasonable time without rejecting it. He observed
that whether a reasonable period of time has passed would depend on the nature
and complexity of the goods. However, the nature and speed with which a defect
could have been discovered was irrelevant because it was desirable for the seller to
be 'able to close his ledger reasonably soon after the transaction is complete' (p
230).

The *Bernstein* decision has been widely and frequently criticised as being hard
on the consumer—it may be questioned whether three weeks was a reasonable
period within which a seller should consider a deal closed in the case of a sale of a
new car—and inconsistent with the recognition of durability as an aspect of quality. In 1994, however, a new section 35(5) was inserted into the SoGA, providing
that the factors relevant to an assessment of whether a reasonable time to reject
the goods has elapsed include whether the buyer has had a reasonable opportunity
of examining the goods to ascertain if they are in conformity with the contract. In
effect, therefore, the buyer must have had a reasonable opportunity to examine the
goods before he can be taken to have accepted them. This, however, does not mean
that the buyer must have had a reasonable time to discover the particular defect in
the goods of which he complains and it is not clear to what extent it would change
the outcome of *Bernstein*. The principle in *Bernstein* that the complexity and
nature of the goods is relevant in determining what is a reaonable time was applied
in *Peakman v Express Circuits Ltd* (1998, unreported) and in *Truk UK Ltd v
Tokmakidis GmbH* [2000] 1 Lloyd's Rep 543, both non-consumer cases. In *Truk*,
the court noted that *Bernstein* was a harsh decision on the facts and held that the
passage of six months did not preclude rejection in that case. In *Clegg v Anderson*
[2003] EWCA Civ 320, [2003] 1 All ER (Comm) 721 the Court of Appeal went further and held that *Bernstein* no longer represented the law in relation to acceptance. It is not entirely clear to what extent *Bernstein* has been overruled, but it is
submitted that the nature and complexity of the goods will continue to be a relevant factor in considering whether the consumer has had a reasonable opportunity to examine the goods. The practical effect of these changes may therefore be
limited, and it is by no means certain that *Bernstein* would be decided differently
today.

The Court in *Clegg* also considered the effect on the right to reject of the buyer's agreement to the seller's attempt to repair the goods. In *Clegg*, a yacht worth around £250,000 had been delivered with a keel that was significantly heavier than specified. The consumer tried out the vessel, but made it clear that he expected the seller to consult with the manufacturer and to propose how the problem could be rectified. It was suggested that the keel should be repaired by shaving off the excess lead to reduce its weight, and engineers were sent by the manufacturer to do this, but the consumer did not want to rush into making a decision and requested further information about safety certification and related matters. Eventually, he decided to reject the yacht. At first instance, it was held that the right to reject had been lost because the consumer had taken the yacht out to sea and had told the seller that he liked it. This, together with various other acts, meant that the buyer had accepted the yacht. The Court of Appeal, however, concluded that it was clear that the consumer had constantly demanded information about how the problem could be solved, and consequently had not yet accepted the yacht. All that the buyer was doing was 'seeking information which the seller has agreed to supply which will enable the buyer to make a properly informed choice between acceptance, rejection or cure, and if cure, in what way' (paragraph 75, Hale LJ). Nor did the time taken to request, agree to and carry out repairs count as part of the reasonable time for rejection under section 35(4) (paragraph 63). It was therefore still possible to reject and terminate the contract.

Thus the fact that a consumer uses goods (even though they do not comply with the implied terms) and requires the seller to repair any defects will not necessarily mean that he has accepted them. Asking the seller to repair a fault may therefore stop the time for rejection from running, effectively giving the consumer a longer period than would otherwise be regarded as reasonable to exercise his right of rejection. This is logical—asking the seller to repair a fault cannot be deemed acceptance. If the seller refuses to carry out repairs, the consumer may then reject the goods and terminate the contract. If the seller attempts repair but is unsuccessful the position is the same. The consumer's position should be all the stronger where, as in *Clegg*, he has not reached the point of requesting repair but is still at the stage of exploring his options.

4.3.1.3 *Partial rejection*

Prior to 1994 the rule was that if several items were supplied under a single contract the buyer had to accept or reject all of them, unless the contract was severable so that in effect the obligations to deliver and pay for the separate items could be treated as separate from one another. Thus if only some of the goods supplied under a single, non-severable contract were defective, the buyer had to choose either to accept or reject all of them. If he accepted any of the goods he accepted them all. (In practice of course sellers would generally not take the point and would be willing to allow the buyer to reject only the defective goods and keep the rest.) However, section 35A SoGA, introduced in 1994, now provides a more flexible regime and provides that in any case where some or all of the goods are affected by a breach of contract the buyer may

(a) reject all of the goods,

(b) accept all of the goods, or

(c) reject some and accept the rest,

provided that he at least accepts all of the goods not affected by the breach. The only restriction on this right of 'partial rejection' is that the buyer may not reject goods which form part of a 'commercial unit', defined as 'a unit division of which would materially impair the value of the goods or the character of the unit'. So, for instance, a consumer may not reject one shoe from a pair, one encyclopaedia from a set or a defective component from a motor car (Law Commission, *Sale and Supply of Goods*, 1987, paragraph 6.12).

4.3.1.4 *The effects of rejection*

If the consumer elects to reject the goods for breach of condition the effect is to put the seller in the same position as if he had not delivered the goods to the consumer at all. The consumer is therefore entitled to a full refund of the price paid, with no reduction on the grounds of any use the consumer may have had of the goods. Use of the goods either constitutes acceptance and bars rejection altogether or has no effect at all. The claim for a refund is a restitutionary one on the basis that the consumer paid the price for a consideration which has wholly failed, and, therefore, does not require the consumer to prove loss or to mitigate his losses. However, the consumer is not limited to a claim for a refund. Since rejection puts the seller in the position of not having delivered the consumer can also claim damages for non-delivery, so that if he must pay a higher price to buy equivalent goods from another supplier he may recover damages in respect of that 'market loss'. Damages are also available for any other losses caused by the goods, so that, for instance, if a consumer buys a car which proves to have defective brakes which cause the car to roll down the drive into the wall of the consumer's house, injuring the consumer, the consumer is entitled to reject the car and recover its price and claim damages to cover

(a) the damage to the house,

(b) his own injuries, and

(c) the extra cost (if any) or buying a replacement car elsewhere.

The right to reject is therefore a potent weapon, even if it is available for only a relatively short time after delivery. Where the buyer has not already paid for the goods rejection is a self-help remedy, and the buyer can exert considerable leverage on the seller by the simple expedient of withholding payment.

4.3.1.5 *A right to cure?*

As noted earlier the SoGA speaks of a breach of condition, such as one of the implied terms in sections 13–15, giving the buyer the right to 'reject the goods and treat the contract as repudiated'. If the buyer is entitled to treat the contract as repudiated he is entitled, in turn, to repudiate his own obligations under it and thus to terminate it.

There is a tendency amongst some commentators to roll rejection and termination together and treat them as one right. The better view, however, seems to be that the two are separate rights which can be exercised separately. Thus in the event of a breach of condition the consumer can reject the goods *and* terminate the contract, *or* simply reject the goods without treating the contract as repudiated. If the buyer chooses to treat the contract as repudiated and terminate it he is entitled to a refund of the price if paid. If, however, he chooses to reject without terminating, he keeps the contract 'alive' and therefore binding on both parties. In that case the seller may have an opportunity to 'cure' his initial breach by providing replacement goods or repairing the original goods. To this extent it may therefore be accurate to speak of the SoGA as giving the buyer a right to request 'cure' of a defective performance by the seller. It should be noted, however, that this 'right' is only *enforceable* to the extent that the buyer may be able to obtain specific performance of the seller's delivery obligation. In practice specific performance of sale contracts is very rarely ordered.

Can the seller, though, insist on curing a defective performance? The consumer may, of course, accept an offer of cure by repair or replacement rather than insisting on a refund, in which case the repair or refund is provided pursuant to a contract between the parties. But can the seller require him to accept cure? Some commentators favour a different analysis of the rights of rejection and termination, according to which the buyer is always entitled to reject goods for breach of condition but cannot terminate the contract unless the seller's breach is repudiatory or the time for delivery has expired. It may be that this analysis has little application to consumer transactions where the contract will rarely provide for the seller to have an extended delivery period, where a breach of condition by the seller may well be regarded as repudiatory, or where it may be possible to imply a term that the seller should make only one tender in performance of the contract. However, if this analysis were to be accepted it would mean that the seller, at least in some instances, has a right to cure a defective performance. There is, however, relatively little support for this analysis in the case-law, certainly outside the field of international documentary sales, and in *Clegg v Anderson* [2003] EWCA Civ 320, [2003] 1 All ER (Comm) 721 the Court of Appeal recently emphasised that it is for the consumer to decide whether to exercise his right of termination or whether to let the seller attempt to rectify defects in the goods delivered. The consumer is not required to act reasonably in rejecting the goods and terminating the contract, rather than choosing damages or cure (per Hale LJ at paragraph 74), an analysis which tends to support the view that, at least in an ordinary domestic sale, there was no right, prior to implementation of the Directive, for the seller to insist on being allowed to cure a defective performance.

4.3.2 Damages

Although a lack of conformity may initially involve a breach of condition, if the consumer accepts or is deemed to have accepted the goods, a breach, even of a condition, will be treated as a breach of warranty only, with the result that the consumer will not be entitled to reject the goods or treat the contract as repudiated. However, the consumer is always entitled to claim damages for any breach of contract, whether the term broken is a condition, an innominate term or a warranty. In each case damages are assessed by reference to the difference, as at the date of delivery, between the value of the goods as delivered and the value the goods would have had had they corresponded with the contract (section 53(3)). This 'difference in value' measure may be easier to apply to commercial contracts where there may well be a market for different grades of goods. Where the goods are repairable the difference in value may be represented by the cost of curing the defect by repair, and this may often be the appropriate measure in consumer cases, provided that it is not unreasonable to have the goods repaired (*Ruxley Electronics and Construction Ltd v Forsyth* [1996] AC 344; [1995] 3 All ER 268, HL). As noted earlier, the consumer will additionally be entitled to damages for any other losses caused by the seller's breach of contract, including damage to property and personal injury.

4.3.2.1 *Price reduction*
Prior to implementation of the Directive the SoGA did not provide for a remedy of price reduction as such. However, where the buyer has a claim against the seller for damages for breach of warranty, including where there is a breach of condition but the buyer has accepted the goods, section 53(1)(a) permits the buyer to 'set up against the seller the breach of [contract] in diminution or extinction of the price'. So if the seller delivers defective goods, and the consumer has not already paid the price, the consumer may withhold some or all of the price, and plead the breach of warranty as a defence to any action by the seller for the unpaid amount.

Section 53(1)(a) in effect provides the buyer with a simple self-help means to enforce a claim for damages and thus obtain redress. It does not as such constitute a separate price reduction remedy, although in practice it may have much the same effect, especially if price reduction is calculated on the flat-rate deduction basis (see 4.2.5.2, above). The right asserted is however the right to damages, assessed as above. This becomes apparent where the buyer has already paid the price when the right to withhold payment is useless and the buyer must assert his right by pursuing a separate action for damages.

4.3.3 Specific performance

The SoGA recognises that a court may order specific performance of a contract of sale. However, specific performance is regarded as an exceptional remedy in common law jurisdictions, partly on the grounds that it is economically inefficient to force a reluctant contractor to perform his obligations and generally more efficient to compensate the buyer by an award of damages enabling him to go out into the market place and buy replacement goods. Thus specific performance of sale contracts is only very rarely awarded.

Its availability is limited by two factors. SoGA section 52 provides that the court may make an order for specific performance 'in any action for breach of contract to deliver specific or ascertained goods'. Outside these circumstances the court has no jurisdiction to award specific performance. Goods are 'specific' when identified and agreed upon at the time of sale. They are ascertained if the goods to be delivered, although not initially identified, are identified after the contract is made. Section 52 precludes specific performance of a contract for wholly unascertained goods where the goods to be delivered have not yet been identified.

We are concerned with the situation where the seller has delivered goods which do not conform to the contract. In that situation the goods will always be either specific or, at the least, ascertained so that the court will have jurisdiction to award specific performance. However, although there is no case-law on the point, it seems that all that the court could order would be delivery of the particular specific or ascertained goods the subject of the contract. It might be possible on that basis to order the seller to repair and re-deliver the defective goods but it would not appear to be possible to order him to deliver replacement goods.

The point may, however, be academic because it is clear that even where the court has a jurisdiction to award specific performance of a sale contract it will rarely do so. Specific performance is an equitable remedy and will normally only be granted if there is no other adequate remedy available. In particular it will not be awarded if damages would provide a sufficient remedy (*Co-operative Insurance Society v Argyll Stores (Holdings) Ltd* [1998] AC 1, p 11). In the case of most consumer goods, which are mass-produced and generic, an award of damages will enable the consumer to obtain a replacement in the market, or to have the goods repaired. Thus the courts have refused specific performance even of contracts for relatively rare items (see e.g. *Cohen v Roche* [1927] 1 KB 1—a set of chairs in that case) on the grounds that they are ordinary articles of commerce. Specific performance of the obligation to deliver will only be awarded if the item in question is unique, or almost unique (e.g., where there is only one, or a very small number of, other such products in existence—*Behnke v Bede Shipping Co.* [1927] 1 KB 640).

In the present context, however, a further restriction comes into play. The court will not normally order specific performance of an obligation if that would require the court to supervise performance. Where we are concerned with delivery of non-conforming goods, specific performance would involve an order to the seller to cure his defective performance. But if replacement goods are available the goods will not be unique and specific performance will not be available (unless, possibly, the seller is the only supplier of that type of item), and repair will normally have to be supervised by the court.

In short, specific performance would appear to have no significant role to play in the present context prior to implementation of the Directive. Its limited role also underlines the point that prior to implementation domestic law did not recognise an enforceable right for the buyer to insist on cure of a defective performance. As we shall see, the position is changed as a result of the SSGCR 2002.

4.3.4 Remedies for breach of other forms of supply contract

As we have noted elsewhere, goods may be supplied under a range of different transactions which fall outside the SoGA, including contracts of hire-purchase, exchange, barter, work and materials and so on. The position now is that terms corresponding to those implied into contracts of sale by SoGA sections 13–15 are implied into all contracts for the supply of goods, so that broadly speaking the supplier of goods is generally subject to the same liability in respect of the goods supplied regardless of the legal characterisation of the supply contract. (As we have noted, however, it may still be necessary to categorise the contract in order to determine what are the goods supplied to which the terms relate: see 2.3.2.) A breach of those terms will, in addition, generally give the consumer similar rights to damages to those which arise for breach of a sale contract.

However, although the supplier may be subject to the same implied obligations in respect of the goods, there are important differences between the remedies available to the consumer under a contract of sale and other types of supply contract. In particular the concepts of 'rejection' and 'acceptance' have no place in contracts of supply other than sale. Under contracts of barter, exchange, work and materials and hire-purchase breach of a condition relating to the goods allows the consumer to treat the contract as repudiated. The language of 'rejection' does not appear in the legislation governing these types of supply but in effect if the consumer terminates the contract he will reject the goods. However, the concept of loss of the right to reject through 'acceptance' applies only to contracts of sale. Under all other contracts the general contract rule applies, that the victim of a breach of condition, or a serious breach of an innominate term, is entitled to terminate the contract unless he opts to affirm it and, importantly, he will not be taken to have affirmed the contract unless *with knowledge of the breach* he does some act which indicates his intention to continue with its performance. The consumer who acquires goods pursuant to a contract of barter, work and materials or hire-purchase will therefore not lose his rights of rejection and termination simply due to the passage of time, or by inadvertently doing an act inconsistent with the supplier's ownership (and, recognising the functional equivalence of conditional sale and hire-purchase, the same rule applies to conditional sales where the price is payable by instalments and the buyer deals as consumer within the terms of the Unfair Contract Terms Act 1977: SoG(IT)A 1973 section 14(1)). He thus cannot lose his rights before he is aware of their existence.

The point is illustrated by the case of *Farnworth Finance Facilities v Attryde* ([1970] 1 WLR 1053, CA) in which a consumer had taken on hire-purchase of a motorcycle which proved to have several defects. Nevertheless, the consumer used it for about four months and covered some 4,000 miles. During this time, attempts were made to repair the defects, but eventually, the consumer terminated the contract. The Court of Appeal held that the consumer had not affirmed the contract and was therefore entitled to terminate it. The position may now be similar in the case of a contract of sale by virtue of section 35(6) SoGA, especially in view of the decision of the Court of Appeal in *Clegg v Anderson* [2003] EWCA Civ 320, [2003] 1 All ER (Comm) 721, but the decision nicely illustrates the difference between the two types of transaction. A consumer who acquires goods under a contract of sale may have a less extensive right to reject the goods for breach of contract than if the goods were supplied under a contract of a different type.

There are also differences between the consequences of termination under sale and other forms of supply contract. As we have seen, a consumer who rejects goods under a contract of sale is entitled to a full refund of the price paid on a restitutionary basis. In contrast a consumer who rejects under a contract of hire-purchase is not entitled to a full refund of instalments paid to the supplier, because those instalments are treated as payments for the hire of the goods. The consumer having had some use of the goods, albeit of an inferior quality than bargained for, is not entitled to a refund but only to damages to compensate for the difference between the value of the use enjoyed and the value of the use which should have been provided.

It is not clear which rule applies to other forms of supply contract. In a case of barter or exchange the consumer should be entitled to the return of the consideration he provided. In the case of a contract for the supply of work and materials it will be necessary to decide if the breach in relation to the goods supplied is such as to give rise to a total failure of the consideration provided by the consumer.

4.4 THE IMPLEMENTATION OF THE DIRECTIVE'S REMEDIAL REGIME INTO ENGLISH LAW

As noted previously, one of the broad policies underlying the introduction of the Directive into UK law was that there should be no reduction in existing levels of consumer protection. It was also decided that the existing policy of seeking to assimilate the consumer's rights under different types of supply contract should be continued and, as we have seen, changes to reflect the requirements of the

Directive's conformity requirement were therefore made to the wording of the statutory implied terms not only in the SoGA but also in the SGSA 1982 and the SoG(IT)A 1973, even though not strictly required by the Directive.

As outlined above, however, the process of assimilation has not been carried through to the remedial schemes applicable to contracts for the supply of goods, where there are differences between the regimes applicable to sales and other forms of supply. Implementation of the Directive might have provided an opportunity to review those differences and align the rules applicable to the different types of contract. However, since that would have involved going considerably further than required to implement the Directive it probably could not have been done by regulations under the European Communities Act and would have required primary legislation (see chapter 1). The DTI rejected that option on the grounds that to align the remedies regimes on the model of the SoGA acceptance/rejection scheme would reduce the rights of consumers under other forms of supply contract, contrary to the declared policy of maintaining existing levels of protection, whilst to extend the rights of buyers to reject goods under a sale contract would impose additional burdens on sellers.

Nevertheless some changes were necessary to the remedial scheme under the SGSA 1982 because of the Directive's application to contracts to produce and supply goods and to supply and install goods, which might be covered by the 1982 Act. As a result it is now necessary to consider separately the remedies available to the consumer

(a) under contracts for the sale of goods covered by SoGA 1979,

(b) under contracts for the supply of goods covered by the SGSA 1982 and

(c) under contracts of hire-purchase covered by the SoG(IT)A 1973.

4.4.1 Sale of Goods Act 1979

Consistent with the policy described above the approach of the implementing Regulations has been to make the new remedies based on the Directive available in consumer cases alongside the pre-existing remedies, rather than to replace the existing remedies. Consumers therefore continue to be entitled to rights to reject and terminate the contract, claim damages and seek specific performance of the contract as described above. Since this gives consumers additional rights not available under the Directive, it is permitted by EC law. However, although the existing short term right to reject the goods may be considered to be more favourable to consumers than the Directive's remedies in certain circumstances, especially because of its familiarity, simplicity and potency, it would not have been enough simply to have retained the existing remedies without implementing the Directive's remedial scheme which is more favourable to the consumer in certain circumstances, including by giving the consumer enforceable rights to repair and replacement. The result is to create a further distinction between the rules applicable to consumer and non-consumer sales and to produce a regime which is unlikely to be readily accessible to consumers.

4.4.1.1 *Scope*

Article 3 has been implemented by inserting into the SoGA a new Part 5A, containing six new sections, 48A–48F. The provisions of Part 5A apply only

(a) to consumer contracts which, in England and Wales means that the buyer 'deals as consumer' within the terms of the definition in UCTA section 12 (see chapter 2) where

(b) the goods do not conform to the contract at the time of delivery.

Section 48F provides that goods do not conform to the contract for the purposes of Part 5A if there is 'a breach of an express term of the contract or of a term implied by section 13, 14 or 15'. As we have noted elsewhere (see chapter 3) this is both too wide and too narrow. First, on its face it would mean that delivery of the wrong quantity or at the wrong time, both of which involve a breach of an express term, would amount to a lack of conformity triggering the Part 5A remedial scheme. Second, it omits any reference to common law implied terms so that a breach of a common law implied term relating to the goods will not amount to a lack of conformity for this purpose (see chapter 3 for a full discussion). Section 48B then provides for the remedies of repair and replacement; section 48C for the remedies of rescission and price reduction; section 48D deals with the relationship between the new remedies and the pre-existing SoGA remedial scheme and section 48E with the powers of the Court.

4.4.1.2 *Presumption of non-conformity*

As we have noted the Directive provides that any lack of conformity which manifests itself within six months of the date of delivery of the goods is rebuttably presumed to have existed at the time of sale, effectively reversing the burden of proof. This is a valuable provision for consumers who would otherwise bear the burden of proving that a lack of conformity was present at the date of delivery, as is the case under the pre-existing domestic law. Although a court may be prepared to draw inferences from the nature of the goods and of the lack of conformity—e.g., a dishwasher that breaks down after being used only a few times will very probably not have been of satisfactory quality at the time of sale—it may be difficult in some cases for the consumer to discharge this burden and it may be necessary to obtain expert evidence etc. During the consultation process prior to implementation of the Directive, the DTI considered whether to extend the reversed burden of proof to claims for the existing remedies of damages and rejection/termination. Ultimately however it was persuaded not to do so, presumably to avoid increasing burdens on business. It is not at all clear that in fact extending the reversed burden would have resulted in a significantly increased burden for business. In many cases the court will draw an appropriate inference that a defect which manifests itself within six months was present at the time of delivery as a matter of common sense. However, as implemented, the reversed burden will only apply to the new remedies (section 48A(3)) so that a consumer who wishes to reject the goods and terminate the contract, or claim damages, will, strictly speaking, have to prove that the goods did not conform with the contract at the time of delivery whereas if he seeks repair or replacement of the goods on the grounds of the same lack of conformity he can rely on the statutory presumption.

4.4.1.3 *Limitation on availability*

We have noted that the Directive makes its remedial scheme available only where a lack of conformity manifests itself within two years of the date of delivery. Under English law the normal limitation period applicable to claims in contract is six years, and that is the limitation period applicable to a claim for damages for breach of a contract of sale. The DTI recognised that to introduce a further two-year manifestation period alongside the existing six-year limitation period would be confusing and therefore decided not to implement the Directive's two-year manifestation period restriction. Since the result is, theoretically at least, advantageous to consumers, this is permitted by EC law. It should impose few additional burdens on business since damages, which would be available for the full six-year period in any case, will normally represent the cost of repair or replacement of the goods. Moreover, it should be borne in mind that where a defect manifests itself more than six months after delivery the consumer will bear the burden of proving that the lack of conformity was present at the date of delivery, and that is likely to become increasingly difficult with the passage of time. Even if the consumer can overcome that hurdle, the longer the period between delivery and the consumer making a claim the more likely it is that repair or replacement will be impossible or disproportionate, and any claim for a refund following rescission is likely to be reduced to take account of the consumer's use of the goods.

4.4.1.4 *Repair and replacement*

Section 48B provides for the remedies of repair and replacement. The language of the section for the most part follows that of the corresponding parts of the Directive but with some significant changes.

As in the Directive, 'repair', but not 'replacement' is defined. A new provision inserted in SoGA section 61 defines repair as 'to bring goods into conformity with the contract'. All the difficulties arising from this definition and discussed above are thus imported into English law. Similarly the earlier discussion of 'replacement' applies here. An additional point must however be made. As noted above in the discussion of specific performance, in English law contracts may be either for specific or unascertained goods. Many consumer contracts made in the face-to-face retail environment, especially in self-service stores, will actually be for specific goods. The significance of this is that under a contract for specific goods the buyer is only entitled to receive and the seller only entitled to supply the particular item contracted for. It is therefore difficult to see how, conceptually, there could be a right to replacement under a contract for specific goods. And, although under a contract for unascertained goods the particular goods to be supplied under the contract are not identified at the time the contract is made, they must be identified subsequently, before property can pass to the buyer, when the goods to be supplied become 'ascertained'. Thereafter the position is much the same as under a contract for specific goods—both parties are committed to buying and selling that particular item. No doubt this is a theoretical rather than a real practical problem. The statute says that the consumer is entitled to demand a replacement and common sense can overcome the conceptual objections just described. However, the existence of the problem underlines the difficulties of patching the new legislation into the existing legislative framework. Significantly a similar problem was identified in German law where it was overcome by creating a new category of 'generic' goods (see Micklitz, 2002).

Section 48B(2) provides that if the buyer requests repair or replacement the seller must provide the remedy within a reasonable time and without causing significant inconvenience to the buyer, taking into account the nature of the goods and the purpose for which they were required (section 48B(5)), and must bear any necessary costs incurred in effecting the repair or replacement. These provisions closely follow the language of the Directive. However, section 48B(3) departs from the language of the Directive in a significant respect. The section provides for the non-availability of the remedies of repair and replacement in cases of impossibility or disproportionality. Rather curiously the section provides that the consumer '*must* not' require ('may not' would seem more appropriate) the seller to repair or, as the case may be, replace the goods if that remedy is impossible or disproportionate. In discussing the Directive earlier in this chapter we observed that it is not clear whether the disproportionality test requiring a comparison of the costs of a particular remedy with an alternative required a comparison only between repair and replacement *inter se* or also permitted a comparison with the costs of rescission and/or price reduction. Section 48B(3) deals with this point quite explicitly and provides that the consumer may not require repair or replacement where that remedy is impossible, or disproportionate in comparison with the other remedy, or disproportionate in comparison with price reduction or rescission. The implementing legislation thus avoids the ambiguity which exists in the text of the Directive. However, it is by no means clear that this is the correct interpretation of the Directive and if the analysis proposed earlier is accepted section 48B(3) goes further in restricting the consumer's rights than the Directive permits. It is likely significantly to weaken the position of the consumer seeking repair or replacement, because those remedies will generally be more burdensome and thus disproportionate in comparison with price reduction. It is submitted that this could be regarded as an incorrect implementation of the proportionality test.

Finally, section 48D deals with the relationship between remedies. Some such provision was required, particularly because of the decision to retain the pre-existing remedies. However, section 48D has no equivalent in the Directive and insofar as it restricts the remedies available to the consumer it too may lead to the UK being held to have improperly implemented the Directive. Section 48D provides that where the consumer has asked for repair or replacement he must give the supplier a reasonable time in which to effect the repair or replacement before

(a) seeking the alternative remedy or

(b) exercising the right to reject the goods and terminate the contract.

The implementing legislation therefore implicitly answers in the affirmative the question not answered by the Directive, whether a consumer who has requested repair can subsequently request replacement, or *vice versa*. He can, but not until he has given the seller a reasonable time to effect the first remedy. We may however note in passing two curiosities about the language of section 48D. Section 48D(2)(a) provides that the buyer who has sought repair or replacement may not reject the goods and terminate the contract for breach of condition. The expression 'reject the goods and terminate the contract' is not used elsewhere in the SoGA. Section 11(4) refers to the right to reject the goods and treat the contract as repudiated. We may note, too, that on its face section 48D(2)(a) would preclude the buyer terminating for a breach not related to the conformity of the goods, such as late delivery amounting to a breach of condition. On the other hand it will not prevent the consumer rejecting the goods and terminating the contract on the grounds of a serious breach of an innominate term. Presumably what is intended is that the consumer may not reject the goods and terminate the contract on the grounds of the lack of conformity in respect of which he has sought repair or replacement.

4.4.1.5 *Rescission and price reduction*
The remedies of rescission and price reduction are provided for by section 48C. Again the language of the implementing provision departs in a number of ways from that of the Directive.

Section 48C also seems to depart from the text of the Directive in another respect which may be prejudicial to consumers. Section. 48C(1) is as follows:

(1) If section 48A above applies, the buyer may—
(a) require the seller to reduce the purchase price of the goods in question to the buyer by an appropriate amount, or
(b) rescind the contract with regard to those goods.

'The goods in question' for this purpose are the goods which under section 48A are not in conformity with the contract. The result therefore is that where only some of the goods supplied under a contract are affected by a lack of conformity the buyer is entitled to rescind the contract, or obtain a price reduction, only in relation to the affected goods. It seems clear that the Directive imposes a similar restriction on the right of rescission. It is however not clear that under the

Directive the right of price reduction is so limited. (See the discussion at 4.2.5.4 above.) Article 3(2) of the Directive provides that

In the case of a lack of conformity, the consumer shall be entitled . . . to have an appropriate reduction made in the price or the contract rescinded with regard to those goods. . .

The difference between the Regulations' reference to an 'appropriate reduction' and the Directive's reference to a reduction 'by an appropriate amount' may be purely semantic. The key question for present purposes is whether the words 'with regard to those goods' in Article 3(2) of the Directive govern both the rights of price reduction and rescission, or only the right to rescission. The Directive could be read in either way and it seems to have been assumed in the drafting of the SSGCR that the restriction applies to both rights. However, the alternative reading is at least as likely and it was suggested earlier (see 4.2.5.4) that it would be the preferable reading. It may therefore be that by limiting the right of price reduction to the particular goods affected by a lack of conformity, the SSGCR do not properly implement the Directive. (It should be noted however that since the text of the Directive itself is ambiguous here, the UK should not incur liability for incorrect implementation in this regard.)

An example may illustrate the problem. Where several items are purchased together but are intended to be used separately (as, for instance, where the consumer buys a washing-machine, microwave and a toaster under a single contract), reducing the purchase price of the defective item alone may produce a fair result. However, if several items are bought as a package to be used together—as for instance where the consumer buys a laptop computer, printer and scanner as a package—and a lack of conformity in one prevents them being used together, then reducing the price only of the defective item may not adequately compensate the consumer. It is suggested that in such a case the price reduced should be that of the overall package supplied under the contract and not merely of the individual item. Perhaps a distinction should be drawn similar to that drawn in domestic law between entire and severable contracts. Relevant factors would be the manner in which the goods are sold and priced so that, for instance, if the computer package referred to above were offered as a package at a combined price the package would be treated as 'the goods in question'. In contrast if the consumer put the 'package' together himself, even if he intended to use them together, the contract would be treated as one for three separate items.

As noted, the right to rescind the contract is similarly limited to a right to rescind with regard to the goods affected by the non-conformity, and we have suggested that this may be inconsistent with the Directive. We may also note that as a result, rescission under section 48C differs from the right to reject the goods for breach of condition which, as we have seen, permits the buyer to reject all the goods delivered under a non-severable contract, even if only some of them are affected by the breach. In addition where only some of the goods supplied under the contract are affected by a lack of conformity there is nothing on the face of the legislation to prevent the consumer rescinding in such a way as to split a 'commercial unit'. It cannot however be intended that where, say, one of a pair of shoes lacks conformity, the consumer can only rescind in relation to that shoe, and it would be necessary in such a case to read the reference to 'the goods in question' as referring to the whole commercial unit, and it might be possible to take a similar approach where several items are bought together as a package, as in the case of the computer package considered above.

Section 48C(3) takes up the option provided for in Recital 15 of the Directive and provides that if the consumer does rescind the contract any reimbursement may be reduced to take into account the period of use the consumer may have had of the goods before the lack of conformity manifested itself. This is a novel provision for English law which would normally restrict restitution to cases of *total* as opposed to partial failure of consideration. As noted previously, it may be difficult to determine the appropriate amount by which the refund should be reduced.

There is no provision in the SSGCR directly corresponding to Article 3(6) of the Directive, restricting the right of rescission in cases of minor conformity, but the court has a general discretion to impose conditions on any remedy it awards (section 48E(6)) which would include power to reduce the amount of any refund in any amount it thinks just.

Section 48C contains no guidance on how the amount of any price reduction is to be calculated (see above, 4.2.5.2), and this may prove as problematic as has calculation of the amount of compensation or indemnity payable to a commercial agent under the Commercial Agents (Council Directive) Regulations 1993. It may be that the courts will have to seek guidance from the practice of courts in other Member States.

4.4.1.6 *Powers of the court*

Section 48E sets out the powers of the court in proceedings for a remedy under Part 5A. As noted earlier, the rights of repair and replacement are effectively forms of specific performance, but English law has traditionally been reluctant to award specific performance of sale contracts and the court's power to do so under the SoGA is limited. Section 48E(2) SoGA therefore gives the court extensive powers to order specific performance of the rights to repair and replacement. There is no power for the court to enforce a claim for rescission or price reduction but they will presumably be available under the court's inherent power. The Directive and the Act both treat rescission, in particular, as a unilateral act, as it is where, for instance, a contract is rescinded by the victim of a misrepresentation.

Curiously, however, sections 48E(3) and (4) then give the court a wide discretion on the consumer's application for any remedy under Part 5A to award any other remedy under Part 5A in substitution 'if it considers that another remedy under sections 48B or 48C is appropriate'. This is a wide discretion for which there appears to be no basis in the Directive. It would mean, for instance, that if the consumer requests replacement of defective goods and, although replacement is neither impossible nor disproportionate, the seller refuses to provide a replacement, the court could order price reduction in lieu on the grounds that it would be 'more appropriate'. This would appear to be a clear breach of the Directive. In order to avoid this result the court would have to interpret section 48D in a more restricted manner and exercise its discretion strictly in accordance with the remedial hierarchy in the Directive itself.

As noted above, the UK took the option permitted by the Directive to provide for any refund of the price payable to the consumer on rescission of the contract to be reduced to take account of the consumer's use of the goods, and section 48E(5) gives the court power to make such a reduction. Also as noted above the court has power to make such a reduction under section 48C(3) and this provision therefore seems to be otiose. Finally, section 48E(6) allows the court to make any order 'unconditionally or on such terms and conditions as to damages, payment of the price and otherwise as it thinks just'. Again this is a wide discretion. It would permit the court to award damages in addition to any of the Part 5A remedies, and would also, apparently, enable the court to refuse to permit the buyer to rescind the contract in the case of a minor lack of conformity, as permitted by Article 3(6) of the Directive. It would also, on its face, be sufficiently wide to allow the court to adjust the amount of any refund to the buyer in a case of rescission. The court already has power under sections 48C(3) and 48E(5) to reduce the amount of any refund to take account of the consumer's use of the goods, but section 48E(6) would seem to permit the court to take account of a wider range of factors, including perhaps the conduct of the consumer and to make a further adjustment of the refund accordingly.

4.4.1.7 *Relationship with existing remedies*
As we have noted, in order not to reduce existing levels of consumer protection it was decided to retain the existing SoGA remedial regime alongside the new regime derived from the Directive. This approach creates a number of difficulties, for instance resulting in two sets of apparently similar remedies existing in parallel. The right to rescind the contract derived from the Directive is apparently very similar in effect to the right to reject the goods and terminate the contract derived from the SoGA. Similarly the Directive's right of price reduction is similar in effect to the buyer's right to withhold payment and set up a claim for damages against the seller's claim for the price. The Directive's primary remedies of repair and replacement are, however, based on an entirely different philosophy from that underlying the SoGA right of rejection. Under SoGA the buyer's primary remedy is to be released from the contract; under the Directive it is (in effect) to have it specifically enforced by demanding cure. On the other hand a demand for repair or replacement necessarily involves as a pre-requisite that the buyer has first rejected the goods as delivered. But if the analysis of the operation of the right of rejection under the SoGA advanced earlier (4.3.1.5) is accepted, rejection without termination, thus permitting an attempt at cure, is possible under the prior domestic law.

There are also important differences, especially between the SoGA rights to reject and terminate and the Directive right to rescind the contract. First, if there is a breach of condition, the buyer's right to reject under the Act is absolute and results in a refund of the price in full, the court having no discretion to impose conditions. Second, as we have noted, the right to reject may be far more favourable to the consumer where several items are supplied under a single contract, allowing the buyer to reject all of the goods and not merely those affected by the lack of conformity. Third, the buyer is entitled after rejection to bring a claim for loss of bargain damages to compensate for the extra cost (if any) of purchasing a replacement elsewhere. It is not clear that such damages are available following rescission where it would seem that they are, at best, available at the court's discretion.

Broadly speaking, therefore, the buyer who receives non-conforming goods has a range of options, many of which are mutually inconsistent. For instance he may reject the goods and keep the contract alive by demanding repair or replacement, or reject the goods and terminate the contract. The implementing legislation therefore needs some mechanism to reconcile these inconsistent rights.

As noted above, the provision intended to address this problem is section 48D(2)(a) which provides that if the buyer has requested repair or replacement he cannot seek to reject the goods and terminate the contract for breach of condition without first allowing a reasonable time for the repair/replacement to be effected. Some of the difficulties of this provision have been highlighted above. We may note here that the restriction on the right to reject is conceptually meaningless. The buyer who requests repair or replacement has necessarily already rejected the goods as delivered. What is needed is merely a restriction of the right to terminate the contract on the grounds of the lack of conformity giving rise to the claim for repair.

Section 48D(2)(a) effectively suspends the consumer's SoGA right to terminate the contract where he asks for repair/replacement. If the repair/replacement is not effected within a reasonable time the right to terminate revives. This, it is submitted, is the effect of section 35 of the Act, although again it requires some manipulation of the language of the section to produce this effect. Section 35(6)(a) provides that a buyer will not be 'deemed to have accepted the goods merely because he asks for, or agrees to, their repair by . . . the seller'. During the consultation on the proposed implementation of the Directive it was proposed to amend section 35(6)(a) by adding the words 'or replacement' after repair. This proposal was however deemed unnecessary on the grounds that a consumer seeking replacement must already have rejected the original goods. There is however nothing in the section to preserve the buyer's right to terminate the contract and at common law it would certainly be possible to argue that a buyer who having received non-conforming goods asked for their replacement was thereby electing not to terminate the contract. Moreover there is nothing in section 35 to prevent the buyer being held to have accepted the goods by lapse of time whilst waiting for the seller to effect repair or replacement. It will therefore be necessary to fall back on reasoning similar to that in *Clegg v Anderson* to preserve the consumer's right to reject and ultimately terminate the contract where he has initially requested repair or replacement.

Section 48D does not address the relationship between the new remedies and the consumer's right to claim damages. The availability of damages in addition or as an alternative to any of the new remedies in Part 5A is covered by the court's general discretion in section 48E(6) to make any order under that section 'on such terms and conditions as to damages . . . as it thinks just'. The consumer may have claims on two different bases. It is clear that damages for consequential losses, such as for damage to other property or personal injury caused by the non-conforming goods, should be fully available as they are not covered by the new scheme in Part 5A. What, though, of damages for loss of bargain? Prior to implementation of the Directive the primary measure of damages would be the difference in value between the goods as delivered and the goods as they should have been had they conformed to the contract. In effect in many cases such damages amount to the economic equivalent of repair or replacement. To award such damages in full where the consumer obtains repair or replacement from the seller would therefore effectively give the consumer double compensation. However, there may be cases where repair or replacement does not adequately cover all of the consumer's losses. For instance, the consumer may need to be compensated for loss of use of the goods during repair, or for loss of enjoyment of them prior to repair or replacement. Damages should be available in addition to repair, replacement or, indeed, rescission to cover such losses. (Presumably if the court awards price reduction it will take such factors into account when fixing the amount of the reduction.)

What is less clear is whether the consumer who has requested repair or replacement can withdraw that request and claim damages instead, perhaps to enable him to obtain repair elsewhere. The consumer may prefer this course of action if, for instance, he has no confidence in the seller's ability to effect a satisfactory repair. This possibility is not provided for by section 48D. There are two possible ways of resolving this: either a claim for damages is ruled out altogether once a consumer has opted for repair/replacement, or the right to damages is restricted in a similar manner to the right to terminate and can only be exercised once the seller has had a reasonable time in which to comply. It is suggested that the latter is the only sensible interpretation. The consumer's interests must be balanced against those of the seller. It would be unreasonable to permit the buyer to claim damages when the seller has already begun to effect a repair or has taken steps to obtain a replacement.

In addition to such conceptual difficulties, the position regarding the burden of proof is now rather unsatisfactory. A consumer who seeks a remedy under the new Part 5A can rely on the presumption that a lack of conformity which manifests itself within six months of delivery was present at the time of delivery, unless this is incompatible with the lack of conformity or the nature of the goods. This puts the burden on the seller to prove that the goods were in conformity at the time of delivery. However, a consumer who wishes to terminate the contract for breach of condition, or claim damages, cannot rely on this presumption. As a result, such a consumer will still have to prove that there was a breach of condition at the time that risk passed. This is likely to cause some considerable confusion, and it would have been preferable to apply the same rules irrespective of the remedy the consumer is seeking.

4.4.2 Supply of Goods and Services Act 1982

As we have already explained the Directive is largely concerned with contracts of sale in the narrow, legal sense and not with the other forms of contract by which goods may be supplied. It does, however, extend to two other types of contract—contracts for the supply and installation of, and contracts to manufacture and supply, goods—which, in domestic law, might be classified not as sales but as contracts for work and materials. As we have noted, the DTI opted not to extend the new remedial regime under the Directive to all forms of supply (although application of the regime to contracts of hire-purchase, in particular, where the law on affirmation effectively gives the consumer a long term right of rejection, would in fact have imposed little significant extra burden on suppliers). It was however necessary to ensure that the Directive's regime would apply to contracts for supply and installation and contracts to manufacture and supply. A simple solution would have been to adopt the approach of the Directive and simply state that such contracts are to be classified for remedial purposes as contracts for the sale of goods, and that a lack of conformity in the finished product or, in the case of a supply and install contract, in the goods as installed resulting from incorrect installation, should be treated as a lack of conformity in the goods so as to trigger the remedial scheme. This was not the approach adopted, however. Instead the SSGCR insert a new Part 1B into the SGSA 1982 which, as explained earlier, applies to most forms of non-sale supply other than hire-purchase. As will be seen, it is not at all clear that this adequately implements the Directive.

The new SGSA Part 1B consists of six sections, sections 11M–11S, very largely corresponding to the new provisions inserted in Part 5A of SoGA examined above. For the most part, therefore, the comments made above apply with appropriate modifications to the provisions of Part 1B. The new scheme applies to contracts for the transfer of goods where the transferee deals as consumer (or, in Scotland, the contract is a consumer contract) and the goods do not conform to the contract. As under the corresponding provisions of SoGA the expression 'deals as consumer' is to be interpreted in accordance with the definition in section 12 UCTA 1977. The key issues in relation to Part 1B are therefore the meaning of 'contracts for the transfer of goods' and 'lack of conformity'.

4.4.2.1 *Contract for the transfer of goods*
The 1982 Act applies to two main categories of supply contract:

(a) contracts for the transfer of goods involving the transfer of property in goods from supplier to customer, and

(b) contracts of hire.

Both are covered by Part 1 of the 1982 Act. Although it is not explicitly stated it seems clear that the new provisions in Part 1B apply only to contracts for the transfer of property in goods. Certainly the line taken in the pre-implementation consultation was that the new remedial regime would not be applied to contracts of hire (if it were the exclusion of hire-purchase would be even more anomalous), and new section 11S, which defines 'lack of conformity' for the purposes of the new provisions, refers only to a beach of the terms implied by sections 3, 4 and 5 of the Act which apply to contracts for the transfer of goods (the corresponding terms in relation to hire contracts being found in sections 8–10). Curiously, however, although for the most part the language of Part 1B refers to 'transferor', 'transferee' and 'contract for the transfer of goods', section 11S refers to goods not conforming to 'a contract for the *supply* or transfer of goods' (emphasis added).

According to section 1 of the 1982 Act a contract for the transfer of goods is 'a contract under which one person transfers or agrees to transfer to another the property in goods' other than

(a) a contract for sale of goods;

(b) a hire-purchase contract;

(c) a contract for transfer of property in exchange for trading stamps on their redemption;

(d) a transfer made by deed for no consideration; and

(e) a contract intended to operate by way of mortgage, pledge, charge or other security.

Section 1(3) adds that the fact that services are also provided under the contract does not prevent its also being a contract for the transfer of goods for the purposes of the Act. Part II of the 1982 Act applies to contracts for the supply of services. Section 12, which defines a contract for the supply of a service for the purposes of the Act contains a corresponding provision that the fact that goods are also transferred or bailed under a contract does not prevent its also being a contract for the supply of a service for the purposes of the Act. A contract which involves the transfer of property in goods AND the supply of services is therefore covered by both parts of the Act. The upshot appears to be that the new remedial scheme will apply to all contracts for the transfer of property in goods, whether alone or together with services, covered by Part 1 of the 1982 Act.

The new remedial scheme will therefore apply to contracts for supply by way of barter or exchange and to contracts for the supply of goods and services together under a contract for work and materials, but not to contracts excluded from the scope of Part 1. In some respects this goes further than required by the Directive which does not apply to contracts of barter or exchange. (The potential constitutional problems which this may create were noted in chapter 1.) Moreover it seems that, intentionally or otherwise, the new remedial scheme will also now apply to all contracts for the supply of work and materials. Thus, for instance, if a consumer takes his car to have new tyres fitted and the tyres are not of satisfactory quality the consumer will now be entitled to have the tyres replaced, relying on the new remedial scheme. Similarly if he takes the car to be serviced and defective components are installed, he may be entitled to have the components repaired or replaced. Arguably such contracts might be categorised under the Directive as contracts for the supply and installation of goods, and therefore be covered by its provisions. The implementing provisions may however go further than the Directive by covering all contracts for supply of work and materials.

Example   C contracts with S, a decorator, for S to decorate the outside of C's house, supplying all paint and materials. The decorator uses paint which, unbeknown to either party, is of inferior quality and very quickly begins to peel off. It might be possible to construe the contract as one to supply and install paint, in which case it would be covered by the Directive, but this seems to require a somewhat extended interpretation of 'install'. On the other hand the contract clearly is one for the supply of work and materials under which the supplier is strictly liable in domestic law for the quality of materials supplied. It would appear to be a contract for transfer of property in the paint with the result that the remedies of repair and replacement would be available to the consumer. In theory at least, therefore, it may be open to C to require S to replace the defective paint.

The new Part 1A was deemed necessary to satisfy the Directive's extension of its provisions to contracts

(a) to manufacture and supply, and

(b) to supply and install goods.

Both could be classified by English law as contracts for work and materials. Thus although they may go further than required by the Directive, the new provisions are capable of applying its remedial scheme to such contracts. Whether or not they do so properly depends on whether there is a lack of conformity so as to trigger the availability of the remedial scheme.

4.4.2.2 *Goods not in conformity with the contract*
New section 11S defines lack of conformity for the purposes of Part 1B. It provides that goods do not conform to a contract for 'the supply or transfer of goods' if

(a) there is, in relation to the goods, a breach of an express term or of a term implied into the contract by SGSA sections 3, 4 or 5; or

(b) 'installation of the goods forms part of the contract for the transfer of goods and the goods were installed by the transferor, or under his responsibility, *in breach of the term implied by section 13 below*' [emphasis added].

This is clearly intended to implement Article 2(5) of the Directive by making the Directive's remedies available where goods installed by the supplier lack conformity with the contract as a result of incorrect installation. It seems, however, that this is not sufficient to implement the Directive. Section 13 of the 1982 Act requires that, where the contract is one for services (including one where goods are also supplied) the supplier must perform the service with reasonable skill or care. The effect of section 11S is therefore that the consumer can rely on the new remedial regime where the supplier has performed the installation *negligently*. However, what the Directive requires is that the consumer be entitled to invoke its scheme where the goods, as installed, lack conformity with the contract due to incorrect installation and, as explained earlier, this does not seem to require the consumer to prove negligence in installation (see 3.5.5). The UK provisions therefore seem to adopt a *lower* standard of protection than the Directive, which is not permissible under EC law.

Nor is it clear that the new provisions implement the Directive in relation to contracts to manufacture and supply. The Directive requires its remedies to be available to the consumer under such a contract if the goods as supplied do not conform to the contract. The difficulty is that a contract to manufacture and supply a finished item—say a contract with a joiner to manufacture and supply book-cases—could be categorised in English law either as a sale of the finished item or as a contract for work and materials. If the contract is categorised as a sale there is no difficulty: the finished product must be in conformity with the contract, and if not the supplier may be required to repair or replace it, and so on. If however the contract is classified as one of work and materials it is the materials, not the finished product, which, are the goods for the purposes of section 11M and which therefore must be in conformity with the contract. Suppose, then, that the finished product is not fit for its intended purpose due to defective manufacture. The SGSA requires the materials used to be in conformity with the contract but on these facts there is no lack of conformity in the materials. Even if the consumer can prove lack of reasonable care in manufacture, that does not amount to a lack of conformity because breach of the term implied by section 13 SGSA only amounts to a lack of conformity if the contract is one for supply and installation of goods and the negligence relates to the installation. It would take an extended (although not impossible—see the discussion earlier: 3.5.5) reading of 'installation' to apply it to this situation. If the contract is properly categorised as one for work and materials the court might well be prepared to imply into it a further term that the finished item should be of satisfactory quality, reasonably fit for the consumer's purpose and so on. But breach of that term will not amount to a lack of conformity so as to make the Part 1B remedies available because a lack of conformity does not arise from breach of a term implied at common law.

To avoid these difficulties and make the Directive's remedial scheme available to the consumer the court would have to classify the contract as one of sale of the finished item, which is what Article 1(4) of the Directive requires. We have suggested earlier that the case-law on classification of contracts is sufficiently flexible to permit that. However, the case-law is not settled and there are conflicting decisions. It is clear therefore that reliance on the case-law is insufficient to satisfy EC law requirements in relation to implementation (see Chapter 1). It therefore seems to us that the implementation of the Directive in this regard is seriously defective.

4.4.2.3 *Application of the remedial scheme*
Part 1B provides for the same remedies—repair, replacement, rescission of the contract and price reduction—as are provided for by SoGA Part 5A and the earlier discussion of the remedies applies here. However, their application to contracts of work and materials under the 1982 Act gives rise to a number of additional issues.

In the first instance the consumer's remedial rights are again to require the supplier ('transferor') to repair or replace the goods (SGSA section 11N). Once again this seems to be both more and less than the Directive requires. As we have noted under a contract for work and materials governed by the 1982 Act the goods supplied are the materials. The primary effect of section 11N is therefore that under a contract for work and materials such as a contract to service a car, if the parts supplied are not in conformity with the contract the consumer is entitled to have them repaired or replaced. Presumably in order to effect replacement in such a case it will not be enough for the supplier to supply a replacement part leaving it to the consumer to refit it. In order to effect repair or replacement in such a case it will therefore be necessary for the supplier to refit the part in question. If it becomes necessary to enforce compliance the court will therefore have to order specific performance of a service, which traditionally the courts have been reluctant to do. The court in fact has no express power to order specific performance of the service element of the contract but presumably the court could order refitting of the replacement part pursuant to its general power (section 11R) to make an order conditional on such terms and conditions as it thinks just.

Again, however, the real difficulties arise in relation to the types of contract the new provision is mainly intended to cover, contracts for the manufacture and supply and for the supply and installation of goods. The court's power under section 11N is to order repair, or replacement of the goods, which must be the goods transferred under the contract. Once again difficulty arises from the fact that a contract to make and supply goods may be classified as one for work and materials. We have noted above that there are difficulties in bringing such a contract within the remedial regime in a way which satisfies the Directive. If those difficulties can be overcome a further one arises. The court's power is to order repair or replacement of the goods transferred. If the contract is classified as one for work and materials the court therefore only has power to order repair or replacement of the defective materials used. If therefore there is a defect in the finished product due to poor workmanship the court has no power under section 11N to order repair. Again the difficulty can be overcome by the court classifying the contract as one for sale of the finished item but again it is submitted that this possibility is insufficient to satisfy EC law, at least in the absence of an established and unambiguous line of cases (see chapter 1).

Similar problems arise in relation to contracts for supply and installation. The court's only power is to order repair or replacement of the goods. This follows the wording of Article 3(3) which provides that the consumer may require the seller to repair the goods. However, the Directive requires its remedial scheme to apply to cases where there is a lack of conformity in the goods as installed as a result of incorrect installation. Suppose that under a contract to supply and fit a cooker the supplier installs it incorrectly so that it does not work properly. There is however nothing wrong with the cooker itself which will work satisfactorily if re-installed. What is needed to remedy the lack of conformity therefore is repair of the installation. The court has no specific power to order that. One solution might be to give an extended meaning to 'replace' so that the court could order the supplier to 'replace' in the sense of re-install the cooker, but this is unsatisfactory. The alternative, and probably the better solution, requires the power to order repair of the goods to be read as extending to 'repair of the goods and their installation as appropriate'. A purposive approach to the legislation, consistent with the Directive, may permit this. It could be argued that, because the inadequate installation means that the goods themselves are not in conformity with the contract, 'repair' of the goods requires that the installation is corrected. In other words, since installation is treated as an aspect of the conformity of the goods, 'repair' of the goods encompasses repair of the installation. This does, however, involve stretching the statutory language.

Further difficulties arise from transposition into the SGSA of the language used in the SoGA and the relationship between the new remedies and those (still) available under the prior law. A minor point to note is that section 11Q, dealing with the relationship between the new remedies and the old (equivalent to SoGA section 11D) provides that if the transferee requires the transferor to repair or replace the goods he may not 'reject the goods and terminate the contract'. Strictly speaking, however, the transferee under a contract of work and materials does not have a right to 'reject' the goods. This may however be a semantic point. The word 'reject' does not appear in the 1982 Act but a transferee who treats the contract as repudiated must, in effect, reject the goods. More problematic is the impact of requesting repair or replacement on the consumer's rights under the prior law. In the SoGA the buyer may point to section 35 which provides that he is not to be taken to have accepted the goods merely because he agrees to their repair by the seller. We have noted earlier that this provision is inapt to deal with the mischief at which it is aimed. There is however no corresponding provision in the SGSA to prevent the buyer's request for repair or replacement under section 11N being construed as affirmation of the contract so as to prevent the buyer subsequently seeking to treat the contract as repudiated. The point may be less significant here because the right under section 11P to seek rescission of the contract if the repair or replacement is not satisfactorily effected is more closely analogous to the general contractual right to treat the contract as repudiated than it is to the right to reject under a sale contract, and there is no doubt that the right to rescind is not prejudiced by a request for repair or replacement. However, it is not clear that loss of bargain damages are available to a buyer who rescinds under section 11P, so it may be that the common law right to terminate for breach is more favourable to the buyer than the statutory right to rescind. It is therefore to be hoped that a court would infer that request for repair or replacement under the statute does not amount to affirmation, and if repair or replacement were not provided in accordance with section 11N, a consumer would be allowed to terminate the contract.

4.5 COMMENTARY AND CONCLUSION

The length of this chapter reflects the complexity of the remedial schemes under contracts for sale and supply of goods resulting from implementation of the Directive. The Directive's scheme is in itself complex and, in places, unclear. The complexity is only increased by the hybrid scheme produced by grafting the Directive scheme onto the pre-existing domestic regime. Appended to this chapter is a chart which attempts to summarise the composite remedial scheme, from which the complexity of that scheme will be apparent. The problem is yet further exacerbated when one takes into account that there are different schemes applicable to

(a) contracts of sale,

(b) contracts of hire and hire-purchase and

(c) other contracts for the transfer of goods.

This complexity is in itself unsatisfactory in a measure directed at consumers. It must be borne in mind that disputes arising out of consumer supply transactions are rarely litigated, but are generally dealt with by face-to-face negotiation. What consumers—and indeed sellers—need is clear and comprehensible rules under which rights can be asserted and claims settled without the need for legal advice. However, even consumers and suppliers with the benefit of legal advice will find that some provisions of the legislation are unclear. The great advantage of the pre-implementation SoGA scheme, with its short term but absolute right to reject, coupled with long-term rights to damages, was that it provided a relatively clear and comprehensible framework of rights within which the parties could negotiate a settlement. The consumer's right to reject and demand a refund gave him a powerful bargaining lever which might enable him to negotiate repair or replacement, and the availability of damages would allow him, if he preferred to keep the goods, to buy repair or replacement elsewhere.

Much of the uncertainty originates in the Directive itself. For instance the references to remedies being 'disproportionate', 'significant inconvenience' and 'minor defects' are all necessarily imprecise and one anticipates that they may well be used by suppliers to steer consumers towards the weaker long-stop remedy of price reduction. However, the deficiencies in the Directive have been magnified and augmented by the way in which it has been implemented into English law. Moreover, it seems that in a number of respects the UK implementation does not satisfy European law. For example, the provisions intended to extend the remedial scheme to contracts to supply and install and to manufacture and supply seem inadequate to satisfy the Directive and it would seem that it will not be enough to satisfy the Directive to point to the possibility of compliant interpretation by manipulation of the common law. In addition, the complexity and ambiguity within the system would be unlikely to find favour with the European Court of Justice, should it be asked to rule on the correctness of the UK's implementation in Article 226 enforcement proceedings. Recent case-law involving the implementation of the Unfair Contract Terms Directive (see chapter 1) has made it clear that legal certainty is important and that consumers should be able to ascertain their rights from the legislation itself. This will be very difficult indeed, as this chapter has demonstrated.

Insofar as there are ambiguities in the Directive itself—and the lengthy analysis of Article 3 above has demonstrated that there are many ambiguities within that Article—the UK would not necessarily be at fault for having adopted a particular interpretation of Article 3 if that interpretation would be reasonable. For example, although the present writers take the view that the proportionality test in Article 3(3) is limited in its application to determining which of repair and replacement might not be available, it is possible to give this a wider reading, and the UK would not necessarily be found in breach for having done so in section 48B(3) SoGA. However, in some respects, the UK has exacerbated these problems, either by changing the scope of the remedies emanating from the Directive or in trying to fit old and new remedies together. These are serious problems.

4.5.1 A better solution?

A possibly tidier integration of old and new remedies might have been achieved by including the right to reject and terminate and to claim damages in Part 5A and restricting the existing sections in the SoGA to non-consumer transactions. Consumers would thus be subject to a new scheme under which they would have an initial choice of two remedies: reject the goods or claim damages/price reduction. If a consumer chose to reject the goods, he would have a further choice either

(a) to terminate the contract or

(b) to choose between repair and replacement,

provided that if more than a reasonable time had elapsed after delivery the right to terminate the contract would not be available if the lack of conformity was minor, and the court would have the power to reduce any refund of the price to reflect the consumer's use of the goods. It would be open to the seller to offer to repair/replace but the consumer would have the absolute right to reject that offer and choose instead to terminate. If the consumer did opt for repair or replacement the seller would be obliged to provide it within a reasonable time and without significant inconvenience. If this was not done, the consumer would be entitled to terminate the contract, unless the lack of conformity was minor, in which case a reduction of the purchase price would be given instead. On this view, the right to terminate (or to rescind) would maintain its position as an initial remedy. The rules on 'acceptance' would be abandoned, but the restriction on termination for minor lack of conformity and the power to reduce the amount of refund in the case of long term rejection would be utilised so as to limit the right to terminate. This would avoid the difficulties now posed by having both an initial right to terminate and a subsequent right to rescission, as well as some of the clashes between rejection and repair/replacement.

Table 4.1—The remedial regime after the implementation of the Guarantees Directive

RIGHT	WHEN AVAILABLE	CONDITIONS	RESTRICTIONS ON AVAILABILITY	NOTES
Rejection	Only for a short time after delivery	Goods not in conformity with contract at date of delivery in breach of condition	Right lost where goods accepted	Rejection results in a full refund of the price paid. Consumer must always prove lack of conformity present at date of delivery
Repair/ replacement	Up to six years after delivery	Goods not in conformity with contract at date of delivery	Not available if either (a) impossible or (b) disproportionate	Lack of conformity manifesting in first six months presumed to have been present at delivery
Rescission	Up to six years after delivery	Whenever (a) goods delivered not in conformity with contract AND (b) repair/ replacement impossible or ineffective	Not available for 'minor defects'	Rescission leads to refund of price; amount of refund can be reduced to take account of use of goods. Lack of conformity manifesting in first six months presumed to have been present at delivery

Table 4.1 (*Cont.*)

RIGHT	WHEN AVAILABLE	CONDITIONS	RESTRICTIONS ON AVAILABILITY	NOTES
Refund	Up to six years after delivery	Whenever (a) goods delivered not in conformity with contract AND (b) repair/ replacement impossible or ineffective		Refund may be total or partial
Damages	Up to six years after delivery	Whenever goods not in conformity with contract, in breach of contract		May include compensation for additional, or consequential losses, including property damage, injury, disappointment, loss of amenity etc.

Table 4.2—Remedial Regime for contracts to supply and install goods

RIGHT	WHEN AVAILABLE	CONDITIONS	RESTRICTIONS ON AVAILABILITY	NOTES
Repudiation (equivalent to rejection)	Only for a short time after defect discovered	Only where there is either (a) breach of condition in relation to the goods supplied or (b) failure to take reasonable care in installation which has serious consequences	Right lost if consumer affirms contract after discovering breach	Consumer entitled to full refund of price
Repair/ replacement	Up to six years after installation	Where (a) breach of express term or statutory implied condition in relation to the goods installed or (b) installation not effected with reasonable skill and care	Not available if (a) impossible or (b) disproportionate	Not clear what 'repair' means in this context

Table 4.2 (*Cont.*)

RIGHT	WHEN AVAILABLE	CONDITIONS	RESTRICTIONS ON AVAILABILITY	NOTES
Rescission	Up to six years after installation	Where (a) either (i) breach of express term or statutory implied condition in relation to the goods installed or (ii) installation not effected with reasonable skill and care AND (b) repair/replacement impossible or ineffective	–	Rescission leads to refund of price; amount of refund can be reduced to take account of use of goods.
Price reduction/ refund	Up to six years after installation	Where (a) either (i) breach of express term or statutory implied condition in relation to the goods installed or (ii) installation not effected with reasonable skill and care AND (b) repair/replacement impossible or ineffective	–	Refund may be total or partial
Damages	Up to six years after installation	Whenever breach of contract in relation to goods supplied or manner of installation	–	Will cover costs of repair or replacement. May include compensation for additional, or consequential losses, including property damage, injury, disappointment, loss of amenity etc.

5

EXCLUSION OF LIABILITY

5.1 INTRODUCTION

The Directive confers on consumers the right to receive goods which are in conformity with the contract of sale. However, the grant of such rights is impotent if they can be excluded by agreement. On the other hand, respect for party autonomy decrees that a contracting party should be the best judge of his own interests and should therefore be free to waive his rights, wholly or in part. The principle of freedom of contract, by which respect for party autonomy is recognised in the law of contract, is common to the legal systems of all the Member States. Adherence to freedom of contract would permit the consumer's rights to be excluded by suitably worded contract terms. Such exclusion might be unobjectionable in cases where the exclusion is freely negotiated, perhaps on the basis of the consumer accepting a lower standard of performance in return for a reduction of the price. It has however long been recognised that in the consumer context 'freedom of contract' is often illusory. Contracts are made on standard terms prepared by or for the seller and geared to the protection and promotion of the seller's interests over those of the consumer. Such terms are presented to the consumer on a 'take it or leave it' basis so that the consumer generally has no choice about the terms of the contract. Indeed, even where a contract document is proffered most consumers generally pay it little heed. Even if a consumer were otherwise inclined to examine the terms, the retail environment often implicitly discourages such examination, and any attempt to negotiate terms would almost certainly be rebuffed. The result, widely recognised, is that the terms on which consumer (and, indeed, many business) contracts are made are 'negotiated' in no real sense at all.

All this is well known. There is therefore a need in the field of consumer protection to balance the competing needs of providing appropriate levels of protection and maintaining respect for freedom of contract. In general it has been recognised that the need for consumer protection trumps that for respect for freedom of contract and the law has therefore developed a range of techniques for controlling exclusion clauses and similar terms in contracts, especially with consumers, both at common law and under statute and at both the domestic and European levels. The Directive follows this familiar approach and invalidates terms which attempt to exclude or restrict the rights it gives to consumers. There were already stringent controls on such terms in UK domestic law and implementation of the Directive therefore required relatively little new provision. It may be however that the implementation has in some respects not gone far enough to satisfy the requirements of the Direcetive.

5.2 THE DIRECTIVE'S PROVISIONS

The tension described above between the values of freedom of contract and the needs of consumer protection is apparent in the Directive. Thus Recital 8 introducing the 'rebuttable presumption of conformity with the contract' (see 3.2.3.2) continues 'that presumption does not restrict the principle of freedom of contract'. However, Recital 22 recognises the limitations of freedom of contract and provides that:

the parties may not, by common consent, restrict or waive the rights granted to consumers, since otherwise the legal protection afforded would be thwarted. . .

The policy reflected in Recital 22 is given effect in Article 7 of the Directive which provides that:

Any contractual terms or agreements concluded with the seller before the lack of conformity is brought to the seller's attention which directly or indirectly waive or restrict the rights resulting from the Directive shall, as provided for by national law, not be binding on the consumer.

The parties therefore cannot contract out of the protection provided by the Directive.

5.2.1 Scope of the control

The only qualification of Article 7 is a provision permitting the parties on a sale of second-hand goods to derogate from the Directive's provisions by agreeing that the period during which the seller is liable for any lack of conformity is less than the two-year period provided for by Article 5(1), provided that the agreed period is not less than one year. Subject to this Article 7 imposes a blanket prohibition on exclusion or restriction of the rights given to consumers by the Directive. It clearly invalidates contract terms which seek to exclude or restrict the consumer's right to receive goods which are in conformity with the contract under Article 2, or the remedial rights granted by Article 3 where the goods supplied are not in conformity with the contract. There are however many other, more subtle ways of restricitng rights than by crudely excluding them, and it is submitted that Article 7 should therefore be given a broad, purposive interpretation to avoid its prohibition on exclusion of the consumer's rights being side-stepped and consumers thus being denied their rights. Domestic courts have adopted just such an approach when applying the Unfair Contract Terms Act 1977 (see below 5.3.1) and it is submitted that the wording of Article 7 supports such an approach. It covers

(a) contract terms or agreements;

(b) concluded before the lack of conformity is brought to the seller's attention; which

(c) directly or indirectly;

(d) waive or restrict the rights resulting from the Directive.

5.2.1.1 *Contract terms or agreements*
The prohibition on contract terms waiving or restricting the rights resulting from the Directive is straightforward. It may be noted that the Directive does not use the language of 'exclusion' or 'exemption' which would be familiar to an English lawyer but speaks instead of a term 'directly or indirectly waiving' the consumer's rights. The intention is however clear enough. A term in the contract of sale excluding the conformity requirement, or qualifying it by excluding any of its elements is ineffective. The same applies to a term excluding or restricting any of the remedial rights. Thus a term excluding the right to repair or replacement, or providing that in the event of the goods proving to be non-conforming the seller will repair or replace them but will not refund the price, is of no effect. So too is a term providing for a shorter liability period than the two years provided for in the Directive (subject to the special provision for sales of second-hand goods referred to above) or a term excluding the presumption that a defect manifesting itself within the first six months after delivery was present at the time of delivery, or a term requiring the consumer to bear carriage costs incurred in returning goods for repair or replacement.

It makes no difference whether the contract, or the particular term, is on standard terms or is freely negotiated. The term is in all cases ineffective. Effectively it is presumed that the consumer's expectations reflected in the conformity requirement are so fundamental that the consumer cannot intend to renounce them.

5.2.1.2 *Directly or indirectly waive or restrict*
The prohibition applies to terms which 'directly or indirectly' waive or restrict the consumer's rights. Thus a term which does not exclude or restrict rights but which

imposes on them any additional condition, or makes it more difficult for the consumer to enforce them, should also be ineffective. The Directive is (regrettably) silent on the way in which a request for repair or replacement is to be made but adopting the approach suggested here a contract term providing, for instance, that the consumer must give notice of a defect in a particular form, or in order to obtain a refund or replacement must return the goods in person to the supplier's head office would be invalid. It is not clear whether a term requiring the consumer seeking a remedy to return the goods to the place where purchased would be valid. Where the supplier is a retail chain with more than one outlet there seems to be no good reason for such a requirement which might be inconvenient for the consumer—especially given the Directive's objective of encouraging consumers to make use of the Single Market and therefore, for instance, to shop whilst travelling—and it is submitted that such a provision should therefore also be invalidated.

The reference to 'terms . . . which directly or indirectly waive . . . the rights resulting from this Directive' does create one difficulty. Article 2(3) provides that there is not deemed to be a lack of conformity if at the time the contract was concluded the consumer 'was aware, or could not reasonably be unaware of, the lack of conformity'. Article 2(3) therefore anticipates that if a matter which would otherwise constitute a lack of conformity is drawn to the consumer's attention the consumer cannot complain that the goods lack conformity on account of that matter. Can the seller draw the consumer's attention to such matters by contract term or is such a term invalidated by Article 7? One possible way to reconcile the two provisions is to read Article 2(3) as part of the definition of the rights given to the consumer by the Directive, so that a disclaimer drawing a lack of conformity to the consumer's attention for the purposes of Article 2(3) is therefore outside the scope of Article 7 as it does not waive rights resulting from the Directive. However, such an approach would tend to frustrate the Directive's objective by enabling the seller to draw attention to matters which would otherwise constitute a lack of conformity by means of small-print terms in the contract and then argue that the consumer was aware or could not have been unaware of them. It cannot be intended, for instance, that Article 7 can be evaded by including in the contract a term such as:

It is acknowledged that all defects in the goods have been drawn to my attention and that I buy them as seen

or

the buyer acknowledges that in selecting the goods he has not indicated to the seller that they are required for any particular purpose.

It is submitted therefore that the overriding provision is Article 7. A contract term which has the effect of waiving, restricting or otherwise excluding the consumer's rights under the Directive, including a provision acknowledging that what would otherwise be a lack of conformity has been drawn to his attention, is ineffective in accordance with Article 7. In order to shelter behind Article 2(3) the seller cannot rely on a contract term reciting that matters have been drawn to the consumer's attention but must show that they have in fact been so. The reference in the contract will at best provide rebuttable evidence that that is the case.

5.2.1.3 *Terms or agreements*

Article 7 is not limited to contract terms which waive or restrict the consumer's rights. It also applies to 'agreements concluded with the seller before the lack of conformity is brought to the seller's attention'. In other words the consumer's rights under the Directive cannot be excluded by a term in the sale contract, nor by a term in any other contract, nor by a totally separate contract. An agreement concluded *after* the relevant lack of conformity is drawn to the seller's attention is valid. Thus if the consumer complains of a lack of conformity and then agrees with the seller to have the goods repaired, the agreement is binding on the consumer and, provided that the repair is completed free of charge, within a reasonable time and without significant inconvenience to the consumer, the agreement is effective to exclude the consumer's alternative remedial rights under Article 3. The same would apply to an agreement to accept any other remedy in settlement of the consumer's claim.

Such agreements are however only effective if made after 'the lack of conformity is brought to the seller's attention'. Thus if the buyer compromises a claim, he is bound by the compromise in relation to that claim but it cannot preclude the consumer making a further claim if a second lack of conformity later manifests itself. Suppose, therefore, that the consumer buys a new car and after a month identifies a number of minor defects. He returns the car to the seller and agrees to have it repaired. The agreement includes a term to the effect that the seller agrees to provide the repair in 'full and final settlement of all claims which the buyer has, or may have against the seller on the grounds of lack of conformity in the goods'. The agreement will be effective to prevent the consumer making any additional claim in relation to the particular lack of conformity complained of. Suppose, however, that two months later the gear box breaks down due to a latent defect present at the time of sale. The seller cannot rely on the agreement to exclude the consumer's right to make a further claim in respect of the defective gear box.

It is submitted that the word 'agreement' should be given a broad interpretation. One's natural inclination might be to think of bilateral agreements, but it is submitted that the prohibition in Article 7 should be read as applying to unilateral acts of waiver so that, for instance, if the consumer were to sign a delivery note acknowledging the goods to be in conformity with the contract and purporting to waive any rights under the Directive, it should be ineffective to deprive the consumer of any rights under the Directive.

5.2.1.4 *Rights resulting from this Directive*

As noted above the prohibition on exclusions applies to any term or agreement concluded between the consumer and the seller which directly or indirectly waives or restricts 'rights resulting from this Directive'. It is therefore not limited to agreements excluding the consumer's rights against the seller. An agreement between the seller and consumer to the effect that the manufacturer's guarantee is not to be binding would also be invalidated on this basis.

5.2.2 Evasion by choice of law

Article 7(2) seeks to prevent sellers evading the Directive's provisions by including a choice of law clause in the contract. It requires Member States to

take the necessary measures to ensure that consumers are not deprived of the protection afforded by this Directive as a result of opting for the law of a non-member State as the law applicable to the contract where the contract has a close connection with the territory of the Member States.

Similar provisions appear in Article 6(2) of the Unfair Terms Directive (93/13/EEC) and Article 12(2) of the Distance Selling Directive (97/7/EC).

Article 7(2) seems to be restricted to circumstances where the contract expressly provides for the choice of law of a non-Member State. Where the rules of private international law determine that the law of a non-Member State applies, Article 7(2) has no application and the consumer will therefore not be able to rely on the Directive.

The expression 'close connection with the territory of the Member States' is not defined in this Directive or in the others in which it appears, and it is in some ways problematic. A similar concept, of a contract having a close connection with a country, is used in some circumstances to determine the law applicable to a contract under the Rome Convention on the law applicable to contractual obligations. It would, however, be inappropriate simply to transpose into the Directive the interpretation of that concept from the Convention, because the Convention, although entered into by all the Member States, is not part of the *acquis communitaire*, and the ECJ has not, at present, been given jurisdiction to interpret its provisions. The concept of 'a close connection with the law of the Member States' should therefore be given an autonomous EC interpretation in accordance with the general principles of EC law.

5.2.3 Relation with other controls on unfair terms

To the extent that Article 7 invalidates exclusion and similar clauses it overlaps the provisions of the Unfair Terms Directive. The Annex to the Unfair Terms Directive includes an indicative list of terms which may be considered unfair— (the so-called 'grey list'), although in C-478/99 *Commission v Sweden* [2002] ECR I-4147, the ECJ emphasised that a term include in that list would not inevitably be unfair. Amongst them are a number of terms which would have the effect of excluding or restricting the requirement that goods be in conformity with the contract. They include terms:

(b) inappropriately excluding or limiting the legal rights of the consumer *vis-à-vis* the seller or supplier . . . in the event of total or partial non-performance or inadequate performance by the seller or supplier of any of the contractual obligations;

(k) enabling the seller or supplier to alter unilaterally, without a valid reason, any characteristics of the product to be provided;

(m) giving the seller or supplier the right to determine whether the goods or services supplied are in conformity with the contract . . .

Under the Unfair Terms Directive a term is unfair and therefore not binding on the consumer if, contrary to the requirement of good faith, it creates a significant imbalance in the rights and obligations of the parties to the detriment of the consumer (Article 3(1)). Terms of the type listed above are therefore not automatically invalidated by the Unfair Terms Directive but are subjected to the test of fairness. In contrast terms which waive or restrict the consumer's rights under the Sales Directive are automatically invalid. In effect therefore Article 7 creates a 'black list' of wholly ineffective or 'automatically unfair' terms. Moreover in one important respect it is wider than the Unfair Terms Directive for whereas the latter applies only to terms which have not been individually negotiated, Article 7 applies to all terms or agreements which purport to waive or restrict the consumer's rights, whether individually negotiated or not.

5.3 EXISTING PROVISIONS OF DOMESTIC LAW

As we have noted throughout, domestic law in the area covered by the Directive was already well developed, and there were already in place strict controls on the exclusion or restriction of the SoGA implied terms and liability for their breach. Indeed, English law could be said to be somewhat over-endowed in this area, with the result that there were already several layers of control on exclusion and similar clauses. First, an exclusion clause will only be effective at common law if it is effectively incorporated into the contract and on its proper construction it covers the breach. In the past the courts have adopted a strict, *contra proferentem*, approach to the construction of exclusion clauses, according to which any ambiguity in the clause is interpreted contrary to the interests of the party seeking to rely on it. In the past these rules have been manipulated to seek, so far as possible, to minimise the abuse of exclusion and similar clauses so that, for instance, adoption of a *contra proferentem* approach has sometimes resulted in contract terms being given an artificially strained construction. In the field of consumer contracts, however, the significance of the common law controls is nowadays much reduced because the courts have statutory powers to control exclusion and similar clauses under the Unfair Contract Terms Act 1977 and the Unfair Terms in Consumer Contracts Regulations 1999 (UTCCR). The main significance of the common law controls today is therefore in the context of business to business contracts. They are therefore considered in chapter 9, below, where we consider the position of retailers.

The 1999 Regulations, which implement the EC's Unfair Contract Terms Directive (93/13/EEC) and replace earlier Regulations made in 1994, apply to contracts between sellers/suppliers and consumers and require that

(a) any written contract presented to a consumer be expressed in 'plain and intelligible language' (regulation 7(1)) and that if there is any doubt about the meaning of a written term, 'the interpretation which is most favourable to the consumer shall prevail' (regulation 7(2)); and

(b) that an unfair term in a contract between a seller or supplier and a consumer shall not be binding on the consumer (regulation 8).

A term is unfair for this purposes if it has not been individually negotiated and contrary to the requirement of good faith, it causes a significant imbalance in the parties' rights and obligations arising under the contract, to the detriment of the consumer.

The controls imposed by the 1999 Regulations on contract terms are generally important. In the present context however their significance is much reduced because the UCTA 1977 imposes much more stringent controls on the effectiveness of exclusion and similar clauses in consumer sale contracts.

5.3.1 Unfair Contract Terms Act 1977

UCTA section 6 provides that:

as against a person dealing as consumer, liability for breach of the obligations arising from

(a) section 12, 14, or 15 of the [SoGA 1979] (seller's implied undertakings as to conformity of goods with description or sample, or as to their quality or fitness for a particular purpose) . . .

cannot be excluded or restricted by any contract term (s 6(2)(a))

Terms covered by section 6(2)(a) are therefore automatically invalid. There is no question of their being justified as 'fair' or 'reasonable'.

5.3.1.1 *Types of clause covered*
Any attempt to exclude or restrict the statutory implied terms is therefore wholly ineffective, and there are similar prohibitions on attempts to exclude the corresponding terms relating to the goods under contracts of hire-purchase (section 6(2)(b)) and other contracts for the supply of goods under which possession or ownership of goods passes (section 7). Moreover, section 13 of UCTA expands its reach to a wide range of clauses which have the effect of restricting or excluding liability. Section 13 provides that:

To the extent that this Part of this Act prevents the exclusion or restriction of any liability it also prevents–

(a) making the liability or its enforcement subject to restrictive or onerous conditions;
(b) excluding or restricting any right or remedy in respect of the liability, or subjecting a person to any prejudice in consequence of pursuing any such right or remedy;
(c) excluding or restricting rules of evidence or procedure

The prohibition on exclusion clauses in section 6 therefore applies to clauses which

• exclude the implied terms, either in their entirety or partially;

• exclude or limit liability for their breach, so that a clause which states 'no refunds in any event' is invalid as excluding the buyer's right to reject the goods and treat the contract as repudiated; so too is a clause which limits the seller's liability in damages in the event of a breach;

• require claims to be notified within a specified time;

• restrict rules of evidence, such as a term providing that no refunds will be given without production of a receipt: where there is a breach of condition the buyer is entitled to reject the goods and treat the contract as repudiated, thus obtaining a refund of any monies paid. It is necessary for the consumer to prove that he purchased the goods from the seller but he may use any evidence, including oral testimony, to do so. The requirement of a receipt therefore excludes the normal rules of evidence;

• providing that the consumer's signature on a delivery note shall be conclusive evidence that goods were delivered in satisfactory condition.

Decisions of the courts have further widened the ambit of the 1977 Act by adopting a purposive approach to its interpretation, holding, for instance, that a reflexive indemnity clause which requires A to indemnify B against B's liability to A should be treated as an exclusion of B's liability (*Phillips Products Ltd v Hyland* [1987] 2 All ER 620, [1987] 1 WLR 659, CA; *cf. Thompson v T Lohan (Plant Hire) Ltd* [1987] 2 All ER 631). Similarly it has been held that a clause restricting rights of set-off and similar rights is subject to the Act (*Stewart Gill v Horatio Myer Ltd* [1992] QB 600, [1992] 2 All ER 257), so that a clause in a sale contract requiring the buyer to pay the price in full and not to withhold payment on grounds of any allegation that the goods are defective, unsatisfactory etc. would be subject to the Act and ineffective where the buyer deals as consumer.

5.3.1.2 *Deals as consumer*

UCTA section 6 only invalidates an exclusion where the buyer deals as consumer. In other cases terms are subjected to a test of reasonableness. As we have noted, prior to implementation of the Directive UCTA section 12 provided that a person dealt as consumer for the purposes of section 6 if three conditions were satisfied:

(a) the buyer did not make the contract in the course of a business, or hold himself out as so doing,

(b) the seller did make the contract in the course of a business, and

(c) the goods were of a type ordinarily supplied for private use or consumption.

As noted in chapter 2, in *R & B Customs Brokers Co Ltd v United Dominions Trust Ltd* ([1988] 1 All ER 847; [1988] 1 WLR 321), the Court of Appeal held that a person *bought* goods 'in the course of a business' for the purposes of UCTA where either

(i) the purchase was an integral part of the business, or

(ii) there was a sufficient degree of regularity of similar purchases.

Thus on the facts of that case a limited company whose business was shipping brokerage and freight forwarding was dealing as consumer when it bought a car for the use of its directors under a conditional sale agreement, since the car was not integral to the company's business and the company had previously bought only one or two cars on credit terms.

As noted in chapter 2, in *Stevenson v Rogers* ([1999] 1 All ER 613) the Court of Appeal adopted a different approach to the interpretation of the phrase 'in the course of business' for the purposes of section 14 SoGA and held that for the purposes of that section any sale by a business is a sale in the course of a business. In so doing the Court distinguished the decision in *R&B*. Thus although there are difficulties reconciling the two decisions, it is clear that for the present *R&B Customs Brokers* remains good law at least so far as the definition of *buying* 'in the course of a business' for the purposes of UCTA section 6 is concerned.

The third element of the definition of 'deals as consumer' in section 12, requiring that where the contract was for the sale or supply of goods the goods had to be of a type ordinarily supplied for private use or consumption, therefore had a significant role to play in restricting the scope of the definition. A person buying goods not of a type ordinarily supplied for private use or consumption could not be dealing as a consumer. As we have noted, however, the concept of goods 'of a type ordinarily supplied for private use or consumption' was not an easy one to apply.

5.3.1.3 *Contracts for work and materials*
The controls in UCTA sections 6 and 7 apply to the statutory implied terms in contracts for the sale and supply of goods which require the goods supplied to conform to the contract description and sample and be of satisfactory quality and fit for the buyer's purpose. We have seen earlier (see 2.3.2 and 3.5.5) that where a contract involves a supply of goods and labour, whether under a contract to perform a service or to use work and materials in the production of a finished item, the contract will normally be subject to an implied term that the work element will

be performed with reasonable skill and care (SGSA 1982, section 13). UCTA also controls terms which seek to exclude or restrict that term or liability for its breach and by section 2 provides that:

(a) liability for death or personal injury caused by negligence can never be excluded or restricted by any contract term or notice; and

(b) liability for other forms of loss or damage caused by negligence can be exclued or restricted only in so far as the exclusion (etc.) satisfies the test of reasonableness.

'Negligence' is defined as including 'any obligation, arising from the express or implied terms of a contract, to take reasonable care or exercise reasonable skill in the performance of the contract' and 'any common law duty to take reasonable care or exercise reasonable skill' (UCTA section 1(1)). The result is that under a contract for the supply of work and materials a contract term excluding or limit-ing the supplier's liability for loss other than death or personal injury resulting from breach of the implied contractual duty to perform the service with reason-able skill and care will be effective if it satisfies the test of reasonableness. The test of reasonableness in this context is that the term be a fair and reasonable one to have been included in the contract, the assessment being made as at the time of contracting. The effects are best illustrated by an example.

Example   S contracts with B to supply and install double glazing at B's house. The con-tract is one for supply of work and materials, and therefore includes implied terms that (a) the windows and other materials supplied will conform to the contract description, be of satisfactory quality and reasonably fit for the buyer's purpose and (b) S will perform the installation with reasonable skill and care. Any term in the contract purporting to exclude S's liability in respect of the quality, etc., of the materials will be ineffective. On the other hand a term excluding or restricting S's liability in respect of the installation work may be valid if reasonable and therefore effective to exclude liability for loss other than death or personal injury. Thus if on completion of the work it is found that the windows do not close properly, S will be liable if it is shown that that is due to his failing to exercise reasonable skill or care in installation but he may be able to rely on a term in the contract excluding or limiting his liability if the term satisfies the test of reasonableness.

5.3.2 Regulatory control

The provisions in UCTA sections 6 and 7 provide consumers with strong protec-tion against terms which seek to exclude or restrict the statutory implied terms in contracts for the sale of goods. However, a supplier might be tempted nevertheless to include such terms in its contracts with consumers on the basis that, even though ineffective as a matter of law, such terms might effectively deter consumers ignorant of the law from bringing a claim or could be used to rebut claims at the negotiation stage. This is recognised and in order to provide further protection against such use of invalid exclusions there are additional controls on the use of exclusion clauses invalidated by sections 6 and 7.

5.3.2.1 *Consumer Transactions (Restrictions on Statements) Order 1976*

The Consumer Transactions (Restrictions on Statements) Order 1976 (SI 1976/1813) makes it a criminal offence for a person acting in the course of a business to purport to apply to a consumer transaction a term invalidated by UCTA section 6 (regulation 3). (The Order was made under Part II of the Fair Trading Act 1973 in relation to previous statutory controls on exclusion clauses (in the Supply of Goods (Implied Terms) Act, 1973) and has been continued in force with amendments. The FTA 1973 was itself repealed by the Enterprise Act 2002, but the Order has been preserved for the time being and remains in force.)

The prohibition applies to the inclusion of an invalidated term in a notice or advertisement or on goods or their packaging or in a document supplied to the consumer. It should be noted, however, that the prohibition applies to contracts for the sale and hire-purchase of goods but not to other forms of supply contract.

The Order further requires that where a supplier supplies to a consumer goods bearing, or a document containing, a statement about the consumer's rights against the supplier, there must be included, in 'close proximity' to the statement in question, a further clear and conspicuous statement that the consumer's statutory rights are not affected (regulation 4).

The CT(RS)O thus imposes criminal penalties for the purported use of contract terms invalidated by UCTA section 6. As a result such terms are now used less often than in the past although the OFT's *Unfair Terms Bulletins* regularly feature terms which seek to exclude the implied terms.

5.3.2.2 *Unfair Terms in Consumer Contracts Regulations 1999*

As noted earlier there are further controls on the use of unfair terms in the Unfair Terms in Consumer Contracts Regulations 1999. As also noted earlier, as between supplier and consumer the UTCCR have relatively little impact, because the UCTA sections 6 and 7 impose much more stringent controls on the use of exclusion and similar clauses. First, UCTA, unlike the UTCCR, is not limited to standard terms and UCTA section 6 will therefore invalidate a term in a contract between a business and a consumer purporting to exclude the SoGA implied terms even if the term was freely negotiated. Second, the effect of sections 6 and 7 of UCTA is wholly to invalidate exclusion clauses of the type to which they apply where the clause appears in a contract between a business and a consumer. In contrast the UTCCR never wholly invalidate a term but subject it to a test of fairness. Although a term excluding the statutory implied terms in a consumer sale contract is unlikely ever to be regarded as fair, such a clause is at least potentially valid under the UTCCR.

The UTCCR do nevertheless play an important role in controlling the use of unfair terms in consumer sales contracts because, as noted earlier, the Regulations do not only apply as between an individual consumer and a supplier but also permit the Director General of Fair Trading and any other 'qualifying body' as defined by the Regulations to take action under the Regulations to prevent the use of unfair terms. The list of 'qualifying bodies' in the Regulations includes a number of regulatory bodies, such as the various industry regulators for utility industries, and the Consumers' Association, but the lead role in enforcement is taken by the Unfair Terms Unit of the Office of Fair Trading. The OFT has power under the Regulations to seek undertakings from businesses and, if necessary, to obtain injunctions to prevent anyone using or recommending the use of an unfair term, including a term invalidated by the UCTA. Whilst therefore the UCTA may invalidate a term in a particular contract, the OFT can use its powers under the UTCCR to prevent the continued use of the offending term.

5.3.3 Other controls

As explained elsewhere (see 4.3.1) the consumer's primary remedy for breach of the statutory implied terms under the SoGA is to reject the goods and treat the contract as repudiated. However, the right to reject is lost if the consumer has accepted the goods. Section 35 SoGA provides that the consumer is not to be taken as having accepted the goods by express intimation of acceptance, or by doing in relation to the goods an act inconsistent with the seller's ownership, unless he has first had a reasonable opportunity of examining them for the purpose of determining whether they are in accordance with the contract (section 35(2)). Section 35(3) provides that a buyer who deals as consumer cannot be deprived of this right to examine the goods by any agreement, waiver or otherwise. A provision in a delivery note providing that the consumer accepts the goods as delivered as being in conformity with the contract is thus of no effect and will not preclude the consumer subsequently rejecting them.

5.4 THE SSGCR

As will be apparent from the preceding discussion, domestic law already imposed strict controls on suppliers' freedom to exclude or restrict the statutory implied terms in sale and supply contracts prior to implementation of the Directive. Consequently the view was taken that relatively little was needed by way of implementation of Article 7. However, as will appear below, it may be that in a number of respects the implementation does not go far enough.

5.4.1 The definition of 'consumer'

The only change made to implement Article 7 was to amend the definition of 'dealing as consumer' in UCTA section 12 by removing the requirement that the goods be of a type ordinarily supplied for private use or consumption in cases where the buyer is an individual, as explained in chapter 2. There is a corresponding amendment to the provisions of the Act applicable in Scotland.

The result is that for the purposes of UCTA an individual deals as consumer in any particular contract if he neither makes nor holds himself out as making the contract in the course of a business and the seller or supplier does make the contract in the course of a business. A limited company buying goods can still deal as a consumer, in accordance with the decision in the *R&B Customs Brokers* case if it satisfies both these requirements and, in addition, the goods are of a type ordinarily supplied for private use or consumption.

It remains the case that a person does not deal as consumer if, even though he does not contract in the course of a business, he holds himself out as so doing. Thus if, say, a person buys goods for private use but does so using a business cheque or credit card—perhaps to take advantage of a business discount—he is not dealing as consumer for the purposes of UCTA. This seems reasonable enough; after all the supplier in such a case will reasonably believe that he is dealing with a business. However, there is no corresponding provision in the Directive and unless a person who holds himself out as acting in the course of a business can be said to be acting 'for purposes which are related to his trade, business or profession' it may be that there is here a failure properly to implement the Directive.

5.4.2 Delivery notes

It was suggested above that Article 7 should probably be given a wide, purposive interpretation and that the reference to 'contractual terms or agreements concluded with the seller' should be given a wide construction, which would include delivery notes so as to invalidate a provision in a delivery note by which the consumer purports to waive the right to complain of a lack of conformity in the goods or to pursue any remedy for such lack of conformity. We noted above that a term in a delivery note by which the buyer purports to waive the right to examine goods for the purposes of determining whether they are in conformity with the contract is invalidated by SoGA section 35(3) and that a consumer therefore cannot be deprived of the right to reject goods for breach of condition under the SoGA by signing a delivery note unless he has first had a reasonable opportunity of examining the goods.

There is however nothing to prevent a consumer being held to have waived the rights arising from Article 3 of the Directive. UCTA section 6 applies only to contract terms. A waiver in a delivery note or similar document would not be a contract term but a unilateral statement. We suggested above (5.2.1.3) that Article 7 of the Directive should be read as prohibiting such a waiver. This is probably not a significant gap. Should the matter arise we would expect a court to hold that, in light of the wording and purpose of the Directive, the rights arising from it are incapable of being waived. Any other reading would drive a significant hole in the consumer's protection under the Directive. However, if this reading of the Directive is correct there is here another gap in the implementing provisions.

5.4.3 Settlement and compromise agreements

We suggested above that Article 7 extends to compromise and settlement agreements insofar as they purport to exclude the consumer's rights in relation to a lack of conformity not brought to the seller's attention at the time the agreement is made. Insofar as they purport to exclude the consumer's rights under the terms implied by SoGA sections 13–15 or remedies for the breach of those terms such agreements would appear to be within the scope of UCTA sections 6 and 7.

5.4.4 Build and supply contracts

Under the Directive a contract to manufacture and supply an item is treated as a sale of that item (Article 2(4); see 2.2.2.1). As we have noted elsewhere, this provision has not been specifically implemented and this seems to us to be a major gap in the implementing regulations. It seems to have been assumed that the Directive's requirements are satisfied by existing legislation. However, as we have noted elsewhere (see 2.4.5) if such an arrangement is regarded as a contract for work and materials the supplier has no statutory liability for the quality etc. of the finished item. Instead his liability is limited to

(a) statutory undertakings that
  (i) the materials used will conform with the contract description and sample, be of satisfactory quality and reasonably fit for purpose; and
  (ii) that he will perform the work of manufacture with reasonable skill and care; and

(b) (possibly) a common law undertaking that the finished item will be of satisfactory quality, reasonably fit for purpose and so on.

We have noted already that this is insufficient to satisfy the Directive. As we noted above (5.3.1.3) liability for breach of the implied undertaking that work will be performed with reasonable skill and care can be excluded, subject to the test of reasonableness, under UCTA section 2. Moreover, even if the contract were held to contain implied terms relating to the quality etc. of the finished item, those terms would arise at common law. Their exclusion would therefore not be covered by UCTA section 6. Arguably a term excluding any such implied term—for instance by providing that the supplier's liability shall be limited to supplying materials etc. corresponding with the statutory implied terms and carrying out the work with reasonable skill and care and that the supplier gives no undertaking in respect of the quality or fitness for purpose of the finished product—would prevent any such term arising. A term cannot normally be implied at common law where its implication would contradict an express term of the contract. If so, such an exclusion would escape all statutory control. Even if this is not the case, the term would at most be subject to control under UCTA section 3 under which a term by which the supplier purports to exclude or restrict liability for breach of contract or in respect of all or part of his contractual obligation to be entitled to render no performance or a performance substantially different from that reasonably expected of him is subjected to a test of reasonableness. In short, even if the supplier were to be subject to any liability in respect of the finished product it would be possible for him to exclude or restrict that liability. This appears to be inconsistent with the Directive and there is therefore here a failure of implementation.

5.4.5 Contracts for the supply and installation of goods

A similar difficulty emerges in relation to contracts for the supply and installation of goods. As we have noted (3.4.5) the Directive provides that where goods are to be installed by or under the responsibility of the seller any lack of conformity resulting from incorrect installation is to be treated as a lack of conformity in the goods (Article 2(5)). This provision has not been specifically implemented, with the result that the supplier's liability for installation in domestic law is limited to the statutory undertaking in SGSA section 13 to perform the installation with reasonable skill and care. We suggested earlier that this is insufficient to satisfy the Directive. A consequence of this approach is that the prohibition on exclusion of liability in UCTA sections 6 and 7 does not apply. Instead any attempt by the supplier to exclude or limit his liability for negligence in the work of installation will be subject to UCTA section 2 which permits exclusion etc. of liability for negligence which results in loss other than death or personal injury, provided that the exclusion satisfies the test of reasonableness. This seems to be inconsistent with the Directive which requires that lack of conformity resulting from incorrect installation be treated as a lack of conformity in the goods and that no exclusion or limitation of the supplier's liability be permitted.

5.4.6 Avoidance by choice of law

As noted earlier, Article 7 requires Member States to 'take the necessary measures' to ensure that consumers are not deprived of the Directive's protection as a result of choosing the law of a non-Member State as the law of the contract where the contract has a close connection with the territory of the Member States. There is no corresponding provision in the domestic implementing regulations. Section

27 of the UCTA contains a similar anti-avoidance provision which provides that:

This Act has effect notwithstanding any contract term which applies or purports to apply the law of some country outside the United Kingdom where

(a) the term appears to the court . . . to have been imposed wholly or mainly for the purpose of enabling the party imposing it to evade the operation of this Act; or

(b) in the making of the contract one of the parties dealt as consumer, and he was then habitually resident in the United Kingdom, and the essential steps necessary for the making of the contract were taken there, whether by him or by others on his behalf.

This is clearly insufficient to satisfy Article 7(2). First it is limited to cases where the consumer is resident in the UK, whereas Article 7(2) invalidates choice of law clauses where the contract has a close connection with the territory of the Member States. Moreover, section 27 only prevents the use of a choice of law clause to evade its controls on exclusion and similar clauses. Nothing in section 27 prevents the parties choosing the law of another state and thus evading the application of the Sale of Goods Act or other legislation. If the statutory implied terms do not apply to the transaction there is no need for them to be excluded.

It is clear that what Article 7 requires is some provision which prevents the consumer being deprived of the rights derived from the Directive. UCTA section 27 is clearly insufficient to satisfy that requirement. What is required is an equivalent to regulation 9 of the Unfair Terms in Consumer Contracts Regulations 1999 which provides that:

These Regulations shall apply notwithstanding any contract term which applies or purports to apply the law of a non-Member State, if the contract has a close connection with the territory of the Member States.

A similar provision appears in regulation 25(5) of the Consumer Protection (Distance Selling) Regulations 2000 (SI 2000/2334). Given the use of almost identical provisions in these two measures the omission of an appropriate implementing provision from the SSGCR is all the more surprising. The position is not redeemed by the Rome Convention on the law applicable to contractual obligations, given effect in the UK by the Contracts (Applicable Law) Act 1990. Article 5 of the Convention provides that a choice of law shall not have the effect of depriving the consumer of the protection of the mandatory rules of law of the place where he has his habitual residence. However, Article 5 only applies in restricted circumstances, essentially where the consumer's entry into the contract has been solicited in some way by the supplier or the consumer's order was received by the supplier in the consumer's country of habitual residence. It would therefore not apply if, for instance, the consumer were to seek out the supplier to contract with him, and its application to contracts made over the Internet may be problematic.

In fact the provisions of the Rome Convention in combination with those of the UCTA give rise to a further difficulty. Under UCTA section 26 the Act's controls on exclusion and similar clauses do not apply to 'international supply contracts', defined as contracts for the sale of goods or under or in pursuance of which the possession or ownership of goods passes and 'made by parties whose places of business (or, if they have none, habitual residences) are in the territories of different states' (section 26(3)), and

(a) the goods are to be carried from the territory of one state to another; or

(b) the acts constituting offer and acceptance were done in different states; or

(c) the contract requires the goods to be delivered to a state other than that where offer and acceptance took place.

UCTA section 26 applies to consumer and non-consumer contracts. The result is that if a consumer in the UK orders goods from an overseas supplier and one of the conditions in (a)–(c) is satsifed the contract is an international supply contract and, regardless of any choice of law clause in the contract, the consumer is unprotected by the provisions of the UCTA. The Law Commission has recommended the removal of section 26 (see Law Commission Consultation 164, 2002, paras 5.67–5.69). Its retention means that there is another, serious gap in the UK implementation of the Directive.

5.5 CONCLUSION

Article 7 of the Directive is, on its face, relatively straightforward. Given the existence of several layers of control over exclusion and similar clauses in domestic law, especially in sale of goods contracts, it might have been thought that its implementation would be unproblematic. In fact, as demonstrated in this chapter, partly as a result of reliance on existing legislative provisions, and partly as a result of the problematic approach taken in the implementing regulations to 'build and supply' and 'supply and install' contracts, there are in fact a number of serious gaps in the UK implementation of Article 7. The Law Commission is undertaking a review of the law governing exclusion clauses and unfair terms, with a view to simplifying and rationalising the law and, no doubt, the gaps we have here identified can be filled as part of wider reform of the law. However, in the meantime we must conclude that in this area the Directive has, in a number of significant respects, not been properly implemented.

6

THIRD PARTIES

6.1 INTRODUCTION

Amongst the most radical proposals in the Commission's original *Green Paper* was one to make the 'legal guarantee'—the seller's legal undertaking relating to the quality etc. of the goods supplied to the consumer—run with the goods so that it would be enforceable not only by the original purchaser but also by third parties into whose hands the goods should come. The result would have been to enable donees and second-hand purchasers to claim against the original seller (and, under the proposals in the *Green Paper*, the manufacturer) if the goods failed to meet their legitimate expectations. Such a development would have recognised that many consumer goods are not bought solely for the personal use of the buyer. Some are bought as gifts and are never intended for the use of the buyer. Other, particularly high value, items are bought with an eye to their eventual resale on the second-hand market at some stage, and, indeed, in the case of some goods, such as motor cars, their second-hand saleability may be treated by the original seller and manufacturer as a marketing feature of the goods. Moreover giving third parties the legal right to enforce the seller's quality and related undertakings would have aligned law with everyday practice, for sellers generally do permit third parties, at least donees, to invoke at least some of the rights of the buyer under the contract of sale.

Introduction of such a scheme would have raised a number of difficult issues. In the context of the *Green Paper*, which proposed a broad requirement that goods should conform to the buyer's legitimate expectations, it might be relatively easy to accommodate a scheme of third party enforceability. The third party would be entitled to complain if the goods failed to meet his legitimate expectations. Similarly it is relatively easy to apply the core requirements, whether in domestic law or under the Directive, that goods should meet the quality standard a reasonable person would expect and should be reasonably fit for their common purposes, to a scheme extending protection to third parties: third parties would have the same broad quality expectations as the original purchaser. However, other aspects of the conformity requirement depend on circumstances surrounding the original sale. The goods are required to comply with the description given to the buyer, and to be reasonably fit for the buyer's intended purpose. How would those requirements apply in favour of a third party? Clearly a third party could not reasonably complain if the goods were not fit for *his* intended purpose if that were not known to the seller at the time of the original sale. Should the third party be entitled to a remedy if the goods were not fit for the original buyer's stated purpose if that purpose was not shared by the third party? How would the exceptions to the conformity requirement, which prevent the buyer complaining of defects etc. in the goods drawn to his attention at the time of sale—to which there are corresponding provisions in domestic law—apply in relation to a claim by a third party? Would the scheme apply where the original purchaser was not a consumer but he resold the goods to a private individual—as where, for instance, an accountant bought a computer for his practice but sold it second-hand to a private individual for domestic use?

Such difficulties are not insuperable. Third-party schemes have been introduced in a number of countries including some common law jurisdictions. For example, section 24 of New Zealand's Consumer Guarantees Act 1993 (NZCGA) provides that:

Where a consumer acquires goods from a supplier and gives them to another person as a gift, that person may, subject to any defence which would be available to the supplier against the consumer, exercise any rights or remedies under this Part of this Act which would be available to that person if he or she had acquired the goods from the supplier, and any reference in this part of this Act to a consumer shall include a reference to that person accordingly.

As a result, a person who receives goods as a gift, is able to rely on the provisions of the NZCGA with regard to quality and remedies as if they had bought the goods.

A scheme for third-party rights was even mooted for the UK in the DTI's 1992 consultation *Consumer Guarantees*. However, ultimately this proposal was not pursued and similarly it was decided not to pursue the Green Paper proposal and the final text of the Directive contains no provision for enforcement of the conformity requirement by anyone other than the original purchaser of the goods. This is clearly implicit in the definition of 'consumer' in Article 1 and the 'conformity' requirement in Article 2. A consumer is a person who 'in *contracts* covered by this Directive is acting for purposes . . .'. A 'consumer' must therefore be a party to a contract and it is therefore clear, that a third party donee of goods cannot be a consumer for the purposes of the Directive. Moreover, since the core of the conformity requirement in Article 2(1) is that 'the seller must deliver goods to the consumer . . .' it is clear that the Directive only applies to the contract between the seller and the first consumer purchaser. A second-hand buyer from an original consumer purchaser is therefore not protected by the Directive. (It should be noted that sales of second-hand goods are not as such excluded from the Directive. If second-hand goods are sold by a business seller to a consumer buyer the Directive applies as between that seller and buyer, although the fact that the goods are second-hand will be relevant to the determination whether they are in conformity with the contract by lowering the level of the consumer's reasonable expectation: see 3.4.4.1.) The Directive does not however preclude Member States giving rights to third parties. In fact it may be possible for some third parties to enforce a contract against the original seller under UK domestic law.

6.2 THE POSITION IN DOMESTIC LAW

Until recently the fundamental obstacle to a third party enforcing a contract of sale against the original seller in English law was the doctrine of privity of contract according to which a contract may only be enforced by and against a party to the contract. Thus if C bought goods from R as a gift for T, and the goods proved not to correspond with the contract description or not to be of satisfactory quality, T had no legal right to enforce the contract against R and, as a matter of law, could neither claim damages nor reject the goods and claim a refund of the price. The position was exacerbated by two further rules which operated to restrict the rights of C, the original purchaser. The general rule of English contract law is that a party to a contract can recover damages only in respect of his own losses, and not in respect of losses suffered by a third party. Thus as a matter of strict law C could not enforce the contract by claiming damages on behalf of T. Moreover, until 1994 the mere fact of C's having given the goods to T could have been treated as acceptance of the goods by C so as to prevent C rejecting the goods and obtaining a refund.

The privity restriction can, of course, be evaded where in buying the goods C acts as T's agent, or if C effects an assignment to T of his rights under the contract of sale. However, agency is unlikely to be applicable where C buys goods as a gift for T, and, similarly, a resale by C to T would be inconsistent with C being T's agent. It would at least in theory be possible for C to assign his rights to T, whether T is a donee or second-hand purchaser of the goods. However, a legal assignment must be in writing, signed by the assignor, and notice of the assignment must be given to the person against whom the right assigned is enforceable (Law of Property Act 1925, section 136). An assignment which fails to satisfy these requirements may take effect as an equitable assignment but the position of an equitable assignee is generally unsatisfactory and the formal requirements for a full, legal assignment mean that it is of little practical use in the consumer context.

In practice, of course, retailers would often not seek to rely on the strict legal rules. In particular a retailer would often be willing to exchange faulty goods at the request of a third party donee of the goods provided that they could produce evidence that the goods were originally purchased from the retailer. But any refund provided in such circumstances was provided on a voluntary basis rather than as of right. The position is however now modified in two important respects. First, it may now be possible for the third party, T in the example above, to enforce the contract between R and C by virtue of the Contracts (Rights of Third Parties) Act 1999. Second, the common law rule prohibiting recovery of damages in respect of a third party's loss has in recent years been subject to some modification.

6.2.1 Contracts (Rights of Third Parties) Act 1999

The Contracts (Rights of Third Parties) Act 1999 (C(RTP)A 1999) was passed to implement recommendations made by the Law Commission in its 1996 report 242, *Privity of contract: contracts for the benefit of third parties*. It modifies the common law doctrine of privity of contract by enabling a third party for whose benefit a contract is made to enforce the contract if certain conditions are satisfied.

6.2.1.1 *The legislative scheme*
Section 1 of the 1999 Act provides that:

(1) Subject to the provisions of this Act, a person who is not a party to a contract (a 'third party') may in his own right enforce a term of the contract if
  (a) the contract expressly provides that he may, or
  (b) subject to subsection (2), the term purports to confer a benefit on him.

(2) Subsection (1)(b) does not apply if on a proper construction of the contract it appears that the parties did not intend the term to be enforceable by the third party.

The third party can only enforce the contract on this basis if he is identified in it, by name, as a member of a class or by description (section 1(3)).

Where the Act applies its effect is very much to put the third party in the same position as if he had been a party to the contract. Thus if he is entitled to enforce the contract the third party is entitled to any remedy that would have been available to him in an action for breach of contract had he been a party to the contract (section 1(5)); the third party can only enforce the contract subject to and in accordance with any other relevant terms of the contract; and, in an action by the third party to enforce the contract, the promissor is entitled to raise any defence or set-off arising from the contract and relevant to the term enforced by the third party which he could have raised in an action by the other contracting party (section 3). It must be emphasised, however, that the third party is not a party to the contract. In particular whilst the Act allows the third party to take the benefit of the contract, it does not allow burdens to be imposed on any third party. Thus whilst A and B can contract for A to pay money to C and confer on C an enforceable right to payment, they cannot contract for C to make payment to A so as to impose an obligation on C.

The key to the legislative scheme is therefore the intention of the contracting parties. The third party is only entitled to enforce the benefit of a term in the contract if it appears that the contracting parties intended both to confer a benefit on him and that he should be able to enforce the term. In the absence of an express indication in the contract the ascertainment of the intention of the contracting parties is a matter of construction of the contract. The contracting parties can therefore include in the contract an express provision to the effect that the third party is not to be entitled to enforce the contract. Moreover the contracting parties generally remain free to vary or rescind the contract, including by extinguishing the third party's rights, unless and until

(a) he communicates to the promissor his assent to the relevant term, or

(b) the promissor is aware that he has acted in reliance on the term, or

(c) he has relied on the term and the promissor can reasonably be expected to have foreseen that he would do so (C(RTP)A section 2).

6.2.1.2 *Application to consumer sales*

It is clear that the scheme of the C(RTP)A could apply to consumer sales. The Act is closely based on the Law Commission's recommendations and in its report the Law Commission analysed a number of hypothetical situations and considered how the new Act would apply to them. They made it clear that in certain situations the Act would apply where a consumer C, contracts to buy goods from a retailer, R, as a gift for a third party, T. The Commission proposed the following scenario.

C, a consumer, contracts to purchase a three piece suite from retailer R, as a wedding present for a relative, T. C tells R that the suite is intended as a gift for T and contracts for the suite to be delivered direct to T's home. In these circumstances T would be entitled to enforce the contract, including by claiming damages for breach of the implied term that the goods should be of satisfactory quality, unless R could establish that on the proper construction of the contract it was not intended to confer an enforceable benefit on T. (paragraph 7.41, example 14)

It is therefore clear that there are circumstances in which the C(RTP)A could enable a third party donee of goods to claim against the seller where the goods supplied are not of satisfactory quality. There seems no reason to believe that the Act could not also be used where the third party's complaint is that the goods do not conform to the description by which they were sold or are not fit for the donee's purpose provided that that purpose was made known to the seller by the original buyer. However, it is equally clear that the scope for application of the C(RTP)A in the context of consumer sales is limited by a number of factors. It seems most unlikely that the Act could be invoked by a second-hand purchaser.

The core requirement of the Act is that the original parties should intend to confer an enforceable benefit on the third party. That requirement is unlikely to be satisfied in relation to a second-hand purchaser at the time of first sale. In any case, the scope for application of the C(RTP)A in favour of second-hand buyers is further limited by the requirement that in order to take the benefit of the contract the third party must be identified in the contract. Admittedly, such identification need not be specific; it would probably be enough if the contract is expressed to benefit 'second-hand' purchasers as a group, in particular because section 1(3) does not require the third party to be in existence at the time the contract is entered into. However, protection of second-hand purchasers as a group in this way would probably require an express reference in the contract, and the inclusion of such provisions is unlikely in practice.

It seems that the potential for application of the C(RTP)A even to donees is likely to be limited. First of all, the Act will not apply unless the original seller knows that the goods are intended as a gift for the intended beneficiary. The Law Commission indicated in its report that the Act would not apply if, in the above example, the suite were to be delivered to C's address and R was unaware that it was intended as a gift (see paragraph 7.42, example 15). It is not clear whether it is sufficient that the seller ought to know that the goods are intended as a gift for the third party. For instance, would it suffice that the consumer, C, asked for the suite to be delivered to T's address, and that the seller knows that it is not C's address? If not, would it make a difference if C said 'That's my daughter's address. She's getting married' without explicitly explaining that the suite is intended as a wedding gift? In some cases, depending on the nature of the goods and the circumstances of the case, R might reasonably argue that he thought that the goods were to be delivered to T's address for C's convenience and did not realise that they were intended as a gift. The Law Commission was clearly of the view that unless the goods are to be delivered to the intended donee it will be difficult to argue that it was intended that the contract should confer a benefit on the donee (see paragraph 7.41, note 31). The Act will therefore not assist the donee in the common situation where goods are delivered to the original purchaser and then, in turn, delivered by them to the intended donee. However, where the contract does require delivery direct to the donee there may be a further difficulty. As the Commission noted, in order to qualify as a contract of sale under the SoGA 1979 a contract must be for the transfer of property from seller to buyer (section 2(1) SoGA 1979). A contract between C and R for R to transfer property in goods to T would on this analysis not be a sale at all. It would therefore be necessary to construe the contract for the suite, above, as involving a transfer of property in the suite by R (seller) to C (buyer) and then by C to T, even though the suite is delivered direct to T. However, the problem here may be more apparent than real. The passing of property under a sale contract is not necessarily linked to delivery so that there would be no obstacle to the parties contracting for R to deliver to T and by so doing transfer property to C. In any case, the more natural analysis of the contract would be that in delivering to T's address R is fulfilling his obligation to deliver to C, by delivering in accordance with C's instructions. But even if property in the suite passes direct to T so that the contract between R and C is interpreted as not being a sale, it would still be a contract for the transfer of goods subject to the SGSA 1982.

6.2.1.3 *Remedies*

It thus appears that the scope for application of the C(RTP)A in favour of donees is probably very limited. If the donee can clear the hurdles of establishing that the contract was intended to confer on him a benefit and to be enforceable by him, what remedies would be available to him? The Act provides that 'there shall be available to the third party any remedy which would have been available to him in an action for breach of contract if he had been a party to the contract' (section 1(5)). Again the Commission's report is helpful. It makes clear that its intention was that the beneficiary should have available all *judicial* remedies for breach of contract, and that such remedies would not include termination or discharge of the contract for serious breach of contract by the promissor, on the grounds that 'termination is a self-help, not a judicial, remedy' (paragraph 3.32). On this basis it is submitted that the donee of goods would not be entitled to reject the goods and terminate the contract. It is submitted however that the donee would be entitled to the new remedies in SoGA Part 5A derived from the Directive. It was suggested earlier that the rights to repair and replacement are effectively forms of the right to specific performance, which is a remedy available to the beneficiary under the C(RTP)A. Moreover, the court has power to order repair, replacement, price reduction or rescission (SoGA section 48E). They can therefore be regarded as judicial remedies. One objection might be that the provisions in Part 5A are expressed as 'rights of [the] buyer', and the donee is of course not the buyer. However, the C(RTP)A makes available to the third party beneficiary all the remedies which would have been available to him had he been a party to the contract. Under a contract of sale the rights of the seller and buyer differ. The remedies available of a donee of the goods must be those which would have been available had he been a party to the contract *as buyer*, including therefore those provided for in Part 5A.

Even if the beneficiary can establish a right to enforce the contract against the original seller it must be borne in mind that the seller can raise against the donee any defence arising from the contract and relevant to the term being enforced which could have been raised in a claim by the buyer (C(RTP)A section 3(2)). This would include a right of set-off if, for instance, the buyer had failed to pay for the goods. Most importantly of all, however, it must be borne in mind that it is always open to the seller to exclude the beneficiary's right to enforce the contract and although UCTA section 6 renders ineffective any term by which the seller purports to exclude or restrict his liability to the original buyer for breach of the statutory implied terms relating to the goods, section 6 has no application to a clause excluding the seller's liability to a third party beneficiary.

It appears therefore that the C(RTP)A will rarely apply in the context of consumer sales so as to protect a second-hand buyer or donee of goods. It will be open to the seller to exclude any third party right of enforcement by an appropriate provision in the contract of sale. In the absence of some express provision in the contract the best that can be said is that the position of the third party will generally be unclear. The Law Commission did consider whether it should recommend a special regime to protect consumers which would have made it easier for third-party donees, amongst others, to enforce contracts for their benefit. The Commission declined to do so, partly because there were then proposals for such reform in the European Commission's *Green Paper*. It is therefore ironic that those proposals ultimately came to nothing.

6.2.2 Negligence

One way in which the restrictions of the privity doctrine can be evaded is by a claim in negligence. It is again clear, however, that such a claim will be of little assistance in the present context.

A consumer injured by a defective product can of course sue the person responsible for the defect in negligence in accordance with the principle of *Donoghue v Stevenson* [1932] AC 562. In order to succeed in such a claim it will be necessary to prove that the defendant was negligent and that that negligence caused the claimant's loss or injury. Such claims may lie against anyone in the distribution chain who can be shown to have been negligent, although in practice claims are most commonly brought against manufacturers. We consider claims against the manufacturer in chapter 8 (see 8.3.1.2). For present purposes the point to note is that although a claimant may recover damages in negligence for personal injury or damage to property, damages are not normally recoverable for pure economic loss and in the light of the House of Lords' decision in *Murphy v Brentwood DC* [1990] 2 All ER 908 (a buildings liability case) it is clear that a claim for the diminished value of a defective item, including a claim for the cost of repairing it, will normally be regarded as a claim in respect of 'pure economic loss' so as to be irrecoverable. In *Murphy* Lord Keith observed that to impose liability on the manufacturer of goods for such repair costs would 'open an exceedingly wide field of claims, involving the introduction of something in the nature of a transmissible warranty of quality' ([1990] 2 All ER 908 at 921).

Similarly although the producer of a defective product is strictly liable under the Consumer Protection Act 1987 for damage or injury caused by the product, no claim lies under the Act for the diminished value of the defective product itself (see 8.3.1.1).

6.2.3 Claims by the buyer

If the third party donee or second-hand purchaser of goods cannot claim against the original seller, what is the position of the original consumer purchaser? How are their rights under the contract affected by the disposition in favour of the third party?

6.2.3.1 *The buyer's right to reject*

The most fundamental right of the buyer where the seller delivers goods not in conformity with the contract is to reject them for breach of condition. As explained earlier (see 4.3.1.2), dealing with the goods by gift or resale is capable of being an 'act inconsistent with the seller's ownership' of the goods by which the buyer accepts the goods and therefore loses the right to reject them. However, the buyer is not taken to have accepted the goods on this basis until he has had a reasonable opportunity of examining them for the purpose of ascertaining whether they are in conformity with the contract (SoGA section 35(2)) and the buyer is not to be taken as having accepted the goods merely because he delivers them to another person under a sub-sale or other disposition. Where goods are purchased as a gift the original purchaser will often have no opportunity to examine them before giving them to the intended donee and any lack of quality, fitness etc. will only come to light after the gift. The likelihood therefore is that where a lack of conformity amounting to a breach of one of the statutory implied conditions is discovered by the donee, provided that the goods are returned by the donee to the original buyer, the buyer will not be deemed to have accepted the goods by 'inconsistent act' and should be able to reject them.

It must be borne in mind, however, that the buyer is also deemed to have accepted the goods and lost the right to reject them if he retains the goods beyond a reasonable time without intimating to the seller that he has rejected them (SoGA section 35(4)) and that in determining what is a reasonable time for this purpose account is taken of whether the buyer has had a reasonable opportunity of examining the goods for the purpose of ascertaining whether they are in conformity with the contract. Where goods are bought as a gift and are not examined by the original purchaser there will often be a delay before any lack of conformity is discovered by the intended donee. In that case it may be argued by the seller that the buyer has accepted the goods by lapse of time. However, the decision of the High Court in *Truk UK Ltd v Tokmakidis GmbH* [2000] 1 Lloyd's Rep 543 suggests that in assessing what is a reasonable time for this purpose a court will take account of the expectations of the parties. In *Truk* where the seller knew that the buyer bought the goods for resale the lapse of six months did not bar rejection, because it was found that that was a reasonable time for the buyer to take to resell the goods. Applying this reasoning in the consumer context it is submitted that where the seller of the goods knows, or ought to know, that the goods are bought as a gift, the reasonable time for examining the goods and rejecting them should include sufficient time for the goods to be delivered to the intended donee and for the donee to examine the goods to ascertain their conformity with the contract. If this reasoning is accepted, it may produce some surprising results. For instance, many consumers shop early for Christmas presents, beginning Christmas shopping in the early autumn. Retailers are aware of this and, indeed, encourage it. If the consumer buys goods in October as a Christmas gift and the retailer is aware, or ought reasonably to be aware, of that fact (e.g. because the goods are sold as a gift item), the consumer should not be taken to have accepted the goods by lapse of time until a reasonable time after Christmas.

It is submitted therefore that where goods are bought as a gift and the retailer is aware or ought reasonably to be aware of that fact the consumer's right to reject the goods should generally survive the transfer of the goods to the donee, at least where that happens within the period after sale which the retailer could reasonably expect. Where goods are resold, however, the position is likely to be different. Resale will not per se be an 'act inconsistent with the seller's ownership' so as to amount to acceptance, provided that the goods are returned to the consumer so that they are available for physical return to the original seller. It must be borne in mind that a consumer who resells goods will not be selling in the course of business and will therefore only be liable to take back non-conforming goods where they do not conform to the description by which they are sold (although the consumer may voluntarily take back goods where there is no legal liability to do so). The consumer who has resold goods may therefore not have them available for return.

In any case, resale by the consumer will normally take place some time after the original purchase by the consumer and the right to reject will therefore be lost by lapse of time. Resale by a consumer will generally not be anticipated by the original seller, so that time taken for the goods to be resold will not be taken into account in reckoning what is a reasonable time under SoGA section 35(5); indeed, if the consumer buys goods *for* resale he may well forfeit his status as consumer.

6.2.3.2 *Claim for third party's loss*

As noted above, (6.2) the general rule is that in the event of a breach of contract by one contracting party the other party can recover damages only in respect of his own loss. Thus if A contracts with B and B's defective performance causes loss to C, A can recover damages in respect of his own loss but not in respect of that suffered by C. So if a consumer contracts to buy goods and gives or resells them to a third party, the consumer buyer cannot recover damages in an action for breach of contract for the losses suffered by the third party.

A number of limited exceptions to this principle are recognised, however, and the law is currently in a state of development. It has for some time been recognised that an exception to the general principle applies in the case of contracts to supply services to a group, such as a contract for a meal in a restaurant or to provide a family holiday. Thus if A contracts with B for B to provide a holiday for A and his family, in the event of a breach of contract A can recover damages not only for his own losses but also for losses, in the form of disappointment and/or distress, suffered by the family members intended to benefit from the holiday (*Jackson v Horizon Holidays Ltd* [1975] 3 All ER 92, [1975] 1 WLR 1468, CA). This exception has so far only been applied in the context of contracts for services and its ambit is unclear but it could be applied, for instance, where a family member buys goods intended to provide entertainment for family use. Thus suppose that C buys a new television set in order for the family to watch the World Cup and the television set proves defective or not of satisfactory quality, C could recover damages not only for the cost of repairing the set but also for his own and his family's disappointment (subject of course to the normal rules on remoteness of damage).

In the 'family holiday' cases the intention is to provide a benefit to the contractor and to members of his family. It is not clear that this line of cases could be applied where the contracting party is not an intended beneficiary, as where C contracts with R for R to supply goods intended as a gift for T. However, a second, recent line of cases may enable C to recover damages in such a case. In *Linden Gardens Trust Ltd v Lenesta Sludge Disposals Ltd* ([1994] AC 85, [1993] 3 All ER 417) the House of Lords recognised that where A entered into a building contract with B for the development of a site and then, before completion of the building work transferred his interest in the site to C, A could enforce the contract against B by recovering damages for B's defective performance, A's damages being assessed by reference to the difference in value between the work contracted for and that provided. It was always anticipated by A and B that the property would be occupied by third parties who would have no right of action against the builder if the work was not satisfactorily performed.

The precise scope of this exception is unclear. In *Darlington B.C. v Wiltshier Northern Ltd* [1995] 3 All ER 895 the Court of Appeal applied it in a case where A contracted with B for B to do work on property owned by C. To date it has been applied in cases involving contracts for building work, but there would seem to be no reason in principle why it should not be applied where A contracts with B for B to supply goods to C. Indeed, in the most recent decision of the House of Lords, *Panatown Ltd v Alfred McAlpine Construction Ltd* [2000] 4 All ER 97, Lord Millett offered as an example of the rule's possible application a man buying a car as a gift for his wife (see at p 161). Expressed broadly the principle would seem to be that where A contracts with B for B to confer a benefit on C in circumstances where the contracting parties anticipate that C will have no right of action in the event of defective performance by B, A may enforce the contract by claiming damages even though A has personally suffered no loss as a result of the breach of contract. Thus in *Panatown* the majority of the House of Lords held that the principle did not apply where C had an independent right of action against B. One unresolved question is whether A, the contracting party, recovers for his own losses or for those suffered by C, the intended beneficiary. The majority in *Linden Gardens* and *Panatown* expressed no concluded view on this issue, but Lord Griffiths in

Linden Gardens and Lords Goff and Millett in *Panatown* favoured the view that A recovers for his own loss, his damages being the difference in value between the performance contracted for and that actually rendered. This is of course the basic measure of damages for breach of warranty of quality in a contract for sale of goods (see 4.3.2) and would be relatively easy to apply in the present context. It seems in principle correct that the contractual buyer should be able to claim on this basis notwithstanding that the goods are not intended for his benefit. It should be noted however that if this analysis is correct, A would not be able to recover in respect of consequential losses—such as damage to other property— suffered by C. Nor is it clear whether A is accountable to C for the damages recovered.

The discussion so far has been in terms of the buyer's ability to recover damages where he has disposed of the goods by way of gift. It is not clear whether the same reasoning would apply where the buyer disposes of the goods by way of second-hand sale. The rationale of the exception recognised in *Linden Gardens* is that the contracting parties were aware at the time of the contract that the goods would come into the hands of a third party who would have no personal right of action on the contract. That will rarely be the case in relation to a second-hand sale. On the other hand if the rationale of the exception recognised in these cases is that the buyer recovers damages in respect of his own loss in terms of the difference in value between the goods contracted for and the goods as delivered there is no reason to exclude a claim by the buyer in the event of the goods' having been resold. Even if the defect in respect of which the buyer claims has not reduced the resale price, it is clear that the buyer is entitled to damages equal to the full difference in value measure (*Slater v Hoyle and Smith Ltd* [1920] 2 KB 11, CA).

6.2.3.3 *Part 5A remedies*

As we noted above (see 4.1), the new remedies in Part 5A of the SoGA derived from the Directive are expressed as 'rights of [the] buyer'. There is nothing to restrict their availability to cases where the buyer has or retains a proprietary interest in the goods. There is therefore nothing on the face of the legislation to prevent a consumer who buys goods and gives them to a third party as a gift enforcing the contract by demanding repair, replacement, price reduction or rescission of the contract even after making the gift. Indeed, the same reasoning would apply wherever the original consumer has parted with the goods, so that it would be possible for the original consumer buyer to enforce the contract by demanding any of the Part 5A remedies even after the goods have been resold to a second-hand buyer. Since the purpose of the Part 5A remedies is to give the consumer the full benefit of his contract there seems to be no reason to restrict their availability to cases where the consumer has or retains property in the goods. If the goods as supplied were not in conformity with the contract and the consumer is able to return them for repair or replacement it is no business of the seller's that the goods are no longer the consumer's property.

6.2.4 Commercial practice

The point was made earlier that in practice retailers often do not take technical points on privity. In particular where goods are bought as a gift a retailer will often allow the donee to exchange the goods if they prove defective, at least if the donee has proof of the goods having been supplied by the retailer. Sometimes the retailer may act in ignorance of the fact that the donee is not the original purchaser of the goods, but often the retailer will allow exchange even where the full facts are known. In such a case the retailer's action is purely concessionary; there is no legal obligation to provide any remedy, but the retailer may choose to do so to maintain its commercial reputation. Of course, prior to the coming into force of the SSGCR 2002 consumers had no right to demand repair or replacement of defective goods, although retailers would often offer and consumers accept repair or replacement in settlement of the consumer's claim for a refund or damages. It seems reasonable to suppose that retailers and consumers, including both purchasers and donees, will continue to act in this pragmatic and sensible way now that the regulations have been introduced. This may however have unexpected implications.

It was suggested above that in certain circumstances where a consumer buys goods as a gift for a third party, the third party may now be entitled to enforce the benefit of the contract pursuant to the C(RTP)A 1999. The availability of the right of enforcement will depend on the construction of the contract and the intentions of the contracting parties and in many cases it will not be clear whether the third party is entitled to enforce or not. Now suppose that the goods prove defective and the third party seeks repair or replacement under the SSGCR. If the third party is entitled to enforce the contract, he will be in the same position as if he had bought the goods and repair or replacement will be provided as it would be to the original purchaser. Suppose however that it is not clear whether or not the third party is entitled to enforce. It is settled law that an agreement not to pursue or to compromise a claim can provide consideration to support a contract. It is not necessary that the claim be a good one, but only that the claimant honestly believe in the claim, that the claim be a reasonable one and that the claimant not conceal any material fact from the other party. Suppose, therefore, that the third party donee claims to be entitled to enforce the contract pursuant to the C(RTP)A 1999 and the retailer offers to repair or replace the goods in settlement of the third party's claim. The third party's agreement to accept the remedy offered in settlement of the claim will be consideration for the seller's agreement to repair or replace the goods as the case may be, so that the third party will be entitled to enforce the offer to provide a remedy. More importantly, however, if the goods are repaired or replaced the repair or replacement will be effected pursuant to a contract, which will be either a contract for the transfer of goods (replacement) or a contract for the supply of services or the supply of work and materials (repair). Where the seller replaces the goods there will therefore be implied conditions that the replacement goods correspond with description and are of satisfactory quality and reasonably fit for the donee's purpose (SGSA 1982 sections 3–4). Where the goods are repaired the seller will be subject to an implied contractual obligation to perform the repair work with reasonable skill and care (SGSA 1982 section 13) and there will be further implied conditions that any spare parts supplied correspond with description and are of satisfactory quality and reasonably fit for purpose. Moreover, since any goods supplied, whether by way of replacement or as part of a repair, are supplied under a contract for the supply of goods the donee will be entitled to invoke the remedies derived from the Directive pursuant to Part 1B of the SGSA 1982, including in the case of repair where there is a lack of conformity in any replacement part as a result of its being incorrectly installed (see 4.3.4). The result will be that although the seller might not have had any legal obligation to the donee in respect of the initial complaint, by agreeing to supply a remedy the seller enters into a contract and is exposed to potential liability for a period of six years from the date of the repair or replacement.

6.3 CONCLUSION

We have seen in this chapter that donees and second-hand purchasers are currently not directly covered by the provisions of the SoGA/SGSA, unless it can be established that the provisions of the Contracts (Rights of Third Parties) 1999 apply. However, even then a third party will not be able to benefit from the full extent of the original consumer's rights. Recent common law developments indicate that the law of damages is slowly moving towards allowing claims in third party situations, although it is early days yet and the legal position is far from settled.

The legal position of third parties is not satisfactory at present, which has been recognised both by the UK government and at the European level. Yet, the EC stepped back from its proposals in the Green Paper to introduce 'horizontal privity', whilst at the same time, the Law Commission chose not to address the issue, expecting the EC to act. As a consequence, the question of third party rights remains unresolved, and it is hoped that the Commission will consider putting forward proposals for 'horizontal privity' when it is due to report on the Guarantees Directive in 2006, or, failing that, that the UK will grasp the nettle and introduce third party rights directly, perhaps following the lead of the New Zealand CGA.

7

GUARANTEES

7.1 INTRODUCTION

In addition to the rights available under statute, consumers often enjoy further protection against defects in goods they have bought by virtue of voluntary guarantees given by a retailer or manufacturer. Most consumer goods such as domestic appliances or cars will be sold with a guarantee. In addition, it is now often possible for a consumer to purchase a so-called 'extended warranty', which is offered as an optional extension of the guarantee given by a manufacturer.

Guarantees usually duplicate some of the protection given to consumers under sales law, although the rights they give are generally not as extensive as those given by statute. From the manufacturer's or retailer's point of view a guarantee may nevertheless be a valuable selling point. It is commonly assumed that the fact that a guarantee is given on particular goods indicates that the manufacturer has sufficient confidence in them to offer the guarantee and that they therefore meet a reasonable level of quality. In addition, even if the rights they give are more limited than those provided by statute, guarantees may offer the consumer an alternative means by which to obtain redress if purchased goods prove faulty. It may be easier for a consumer to claim under a guarantee than to establish a right under the Sale of Goods Act, because a manufacturer or retailer may be more willing to honour their responsibilities under a guarantee which they have drafted, rather than to accept that they are liable to provide a remedy under sales law. The principal remedy offered under a guarantee will normally be repair or, possibly, replacement of the goods, remedies which hitherto were not available under the general law. It will often be more attractive, especially for a supplier, to repair defective goods than to have to provide a full refund to a consumer who rejects them. Equally, the guarantee may be more attractive to the consumer who would rather have the goods repaired than reject them for a refund.

Guarantees may therefore be an attractive alternative to the rights available under the general law for both consumers and retailers and manufacturers. However, if there is too much emphasis on the guarantee there is a danger that consumers may be misled as to the full extent of their legal rights. It is all too easy for consumers to be led to believe that the guarantee represents the sum of their rights, and for retailers to use the guarantee as a means of shuffling off liability for defects in the goods onto the manufacturer. The Directive regards guarantees as a competitive tool, allowing manufacturers and sellers to compete on the basis of the guarantees they offer (Recital 21). This overall perception of guarantees is evident in the substantive provisions on guarantees in the Directive.

7.1.1 Types of guarantee

It is possible to identify three types of guarantee: 'traditional' quality guarantees, extended warranties and satisfaction guarantees. In this section the salient features of these types of guarantee will be set out in fairly general terms. It should be borne in mind there may be variations with regard to particular aspects.

7.1.1.1 *'Traditional' guarantees*
The 'traditional' guarantee is usually given by a manufacturer against defects in workmanship and materials. Guarantees are commonly of a much shorter duration than the life expectancy of the corresponding goods, the most frequent period of coverage being 12 months after purchase. One explanation for this relatively short guarantee period is that the types of defects which the guarantee covers are most likely to become apparent during this period. After one year, the likelihood that other causes may have contributed to, or caused, a fault is significantly higher. However, it may be noted that certain categories of low-maintenance goods are now often accompanied by a longer-term guarantee (e.g. bedframes—20 year guarantees).

It is possible to identify a considerable degree of variation in the terms and conditions on which such guarantees are provided, often according to product sector. Some require that a registration card is returned before the guarantee can be relied upon. In order to claim under a guarantee, it may be necessary to return the goods to the seller, or the manufacturer, or an independent service centre. Some guarantors will assume all the costs associated with guarantee claims, whereas others will put at least some of the financial burden on consumers. This variation means that there is no standard form of guarantee which applies to all consumer goods.

7.1.1.2 *Satisfaction guarantees*

Satisfaction guarantees are provided free-of-charge and are generally of very short duration. A common period is 28 days. These guarantees are given to encourage consumers to try out a particular product on the basis that if they do not like it, they can return it to the guarantor, typically for a full refund of the price. It is not normally necessary for the consumer to claim that the product was defective in some way in order to invoke the guarantee. In many ways, such guarantees effectively offer the consumer a cooling-off period, provision of which is now common under legislation governing various types of consumer transaction such as contracts concluded at a distance, such as mail-order or on-line purchases, and where consumers may be subject to high pressure sales techniques (Consumer Protection (Distance Selling) Regulations 2000, implementing Directive 97/7/EC on the protection of consumers in respect of distance contracts (1997) O.J. L 144/19).

7.1.1.3 *Extended warranties*

Extended warranties are, essentially, a form of breakdown insurance. Consumers usually have to purchase such warranties separately, although some credit card companies offer extended warranty cover on goods purchased with their cards. Extended warranties are intended as an extension to the duration of the manufacturer's guarantee, but this is somewhat misleading because the terms on which an extended warranty is provided will often differ from those of the manufacturer's guarantee. In particular, many warranties will also provide cover against accidental damage, and may also cover ordinary wear and tear, neither of which is usually covered by a manufacturer's guarantee, which is only given against defects in workmanship and materials.

Extended warranties may be of some use in that they provide consumers with an easy means of dealing with faulty goods. However, in recent years, there has been considerable concern about the cost of extended warranties compared to the actual cost of repairs. There is evidence that at least some such warranties are sold at significantly inflated prices, and both the Department of Trade and Industry and the Office of Fair Trading have sought to raise awareness of these issues. The Competition Commission has been asked to investigate the market for extended warranties and its report was due at the end of September 2003 (see http://www.competition-commission.org.uk/inquiries/current/warranty/index.htm for details).

7.2 THE DIRECTIVE AND GUARANTEES

This section will analyse the provisions in the Directive which affect guarantees. Originally, these were referred to in the *Green Paper* as 'commercial guarantees' (to distinguish them from 'legal guarantees', the term used in the *Green Paper* to refer to the consumer's rights under the general law of sale). There, a number of proposals for the regulation of guarantees at the European level were made. These were largely disclosure-based and would have required that consumers be provided with clear information about the scope of any guarantee offered. In the absence of such information, a 'default' guarantee would have applied. In addition, it was suggested that there should be a European Guarantee which would have provided identical cover in all the Member States of the European Union, and that where goods are sold through a defined distribution network, all the members of such networks should be required to honour guarantees. Finally, guarantees should have provided a benefit that went over and above the protection given to consumers by their legal rights. As will be seen in the discussion which follows, few of these proposals survived, and those which did went through a process of considerable dilution between the *Green Paper* and the final Directive.

7.2.1 Definition

Article 1(2)(e) defines a guarantee as

any undertaking by a seller or producer to the consumer, given without extra charge, to reimburse the price paid or to replace, repair or handle consumer goods in any way if they do not meet the specifications set out in the guarantee statement or in the relevant advertising.

Several points about this definition should be noted. First, it does not include 'extended warranties', because it is made clear that a guarantee within the definition must be given free of charge. Extended warranties are normally paid for separately by a consumer. Moreover, many extended warranties are provided by insurance companies on behalf of a seller or manufacturer, rather than directly by the seller or manufacturer, whereas the definition in Article 1(2)(e) only covers undertakings given 'by a seller or producer'.

In the first draft of the Directive (COM (1995) 520 final), the definition was not restricted to guarantees given free of charge, and the explanatory memorandum expressly confirmed that extended warranties would be covered. However, in later drafts of the Directive, the scope of the definition was narrowed so as to exclude any guarantees for which a consumer has to pay separately.

Similarly, although it is not entirely clear, it seems that short-term money back guarantees ('satisfaction guarantees') are also not covered. Such guarantees do not normally provide any specifications that a product should meet (other than, perhaps, that the consumer will like the product). Rather, satisfaction guarantees are given to encourage consumers to try out particular goods without having to worry too much about not liking them and being left with an unwanted purchase. It therefore relates to the subjective attitudes of consumers towards the goods, rather than to any shortcomings that fall within the seller's or manufacturer's responsibility. This would suggest that such guarantees are not covered by the definition. However, it must similarly be noted that the definition refers to an undertaking 'to reimburse the price paid'. Price refund is the typical remedy offered by a satisfaction guarantee. As most guarantees tend to offer only repair or replacement of defective goods, it is possible that this was intended to cover satisfaction guarantees, although the exact position remains unclear.

Third, it extends to undertakings given by the seller or 'producer' of the goods. It therefore extends to guarantees given by the manufacturer, importer into the Community or own brander of the goods who by placing his name, brand etc. on the goods purports to be their producer (see the definition of 'producer' in Article 1(2)(d); see chapter 2 at 2.4.2). On the other hand, it is at least arguable that the definition excludes a non-manufacturing producer such as (say) the grower of agricultural produce. The definition of 'producer' in Article 1(2)(d) is expressed in exclusive terms, and includes only

(a) a manufacturer;

(b) an importer; and

(c) an 'own brander' of consumer goods.

It can be compared with the definition of 'producer' in the product liability directive (1985/374/EEC) as 'the manufacturer of a finished product, the producer of any raw material, or the manufacturer of a component part, and any person who by putting his name, trade mark or other distinguishing feature on the product presents himself as its producer' (Article 3(1)). To this extent the provisions of Article 1(2)(d) and Article 6 seem to reflect the limited scope of the original *Green Paper* which, it will be recalled, dealt only with 'consumer durables' suggesting a limitation to manufactured products. Although guarantees of non-manufactured produce are probably rare, it is possible to envisage scenarios in which a non-manufacturer producer might offer a guarantee. Repair of non-manufactured produce may be impossible but replacement or reimbursement of the price could be offered. For instance, a grower of organic fruit or producer of organic meat might offer consumers a money back guarantee. Even if such an undertaking otherwise fell within the scope of Article 1(2)(e) (the undertaking would most likely be a 'satisfaction guarantee') it would seem not to satisfy the requirements for being a 'guarantee' since the producer would seem not to be a 'producer' for the purposes of the Directive. Curiously, should a retailer offer an undertaking in relation to such produce it would fall within the scope of the Directive provided that it satisfied the other requirements of Article 1(2)(e).

Finally, the definition is not restricted to guarantees contained in a document enclosed with the goods, but may also cover guarantees given in advertising. The intention here seems to be twofold: first to make clear that statements in advertising may be relevant to the determination of the scope of any guarantee offered and, second, to include within the definition any undertakings given in general advertising. This (like the provision in Article 2(2)(d); see 3.4.4.2) recognises the influence that product advertising may have on consumers' purchasing decisions. Moreover, if guarantors are to compete with respect to their guarantees, advertising becomes an important avenue by which such competition may be pursued by advertising the availability and scope of any guarantee offered. It is therefore to be welcomed that references to a guarantee in advertising can be taken into account in determining the extent of the guarantor's obligations under the guarantee. On the other hand, it seems unlikely that it is intended that all advertising statements should be encompassed within the definition of 'guarantee'. A guarantee must contain an 'undertaking' by the seller or manufacturer. Many advertising claims are jokey in tone and not intended to be taken seriously. It is submitted that some limitation must be imported to the effect that the statement must be promissory and must be such that a reasonable consumer would expect that it was intended to be taken seriously.

7.2.2 Guarantees to be legally binding

The main provision on guarantees is Article 6. Perhaps the most significant aspect of this Article is Article 6(1) which states that:

A guarantee shall be legally binding on the offerer under the conditions laid down in the guarantee statement and the associated advertising.

It is clear, then, that the undertakings contained in guarantees are to be legally binding. The Directive does not, however, specify the legal basis of their enforceability. The natural reading must be that they are contractual. 'Undertakings', or promises, are normally enforced as contracts and, in most Member States, guarantees are already treated as contracts. This position is, however, not uniform: Scottish law, for example, also recognises a legally binding obligation called a 'unilateral promise', which is different from a contractual obligation in that it becomes binding from the moment it is made. In English law, even a unilateral contract must be accepted by the promisee before it becomes legally binding. In Scottish law, therefore, provided that a guarantee is construed as a promise, it could be legally binding as soon as it is made (see D. Cusine, 'Manufacturers' Guarantees and the Unfair Contract Terms Act' (1980) 25 *Juridical Review* 185). Secondly, the classification of guarantees as contractual would have made it clear that the provisions of Directive 93/13/EEC on Unfair Terms in Consumer Contract ('the Unfair Terms Directive') apply to the terms and conditions on which guarantees are provided. (A guarantee is almost always going to contain pre-drafted standard terms which would therefore be subject to the Unfair Terms Directive.) As it is, however, the absence of any specific reference to the legal basis of the enforceability of guarantees leaves Member States free to determine the basis of enforceability and opens up the unfortunate, if unlikely, possibility that in some jurisdictions, unfair contract terms legislation may not be applied to guarantees. This would be the consequence in Scottish law if guarantees are construed as promises rather than contracts, which would take these outside the scope of Part II of the Unfair Contract Terms Act 1977 (see Cusine, 1980).

A number of other observations can be made about Article 6. First, only the person giving the guarantee (the offerer) is bound by it. The consumer can therefore only enforce the guarantee against the offerer. This may be significant where a manufacturer gives a guarantee, but claims under the guarantee are to be handled by a seller, or an independent repair service provider. This is a common arrangement for 'brown' goods such as televisions or audio equipment. A refusal by a retailer or service provider to honour the guarantee would not give rise to a cause of action against them, but only against the manufacturer as the 'offerer' of the guarantee.

In contrast, Article 6(1) is not clear about the persons entitled to enforce the guarantee. On the one hand it does not restrict the benefit of a guarantee to the initial purchaser but on the other it does not expressly provide for its transferability to subsequent owners. The *Green Paper* expressly provided that guarantees should be transferable. In the absence of any specific rule in the Directive, it is therefore for Member States to decide whether guarantees should be transferable to subsequent owners of the goods, such as donees or second-hand purchasers. It will, in any event, be possible for the guarantor to include a term in the guarantee by which it becomes transferable. It would have been preferable to provide expressly that guarantees are transferable, as was proposed in the *Green Paper*.

Secondly, the guarantor is bound by the guarantee 'under the conditions laid down in the guarantee statement and the associated advertising'. As already noted, there seems to be nothing to prevent a guarantee being given in general advertising if the advertising contains an appropriate 'undertaking'. It is also possible that the guarantee statement may fail to include aspects of the guarantee mentioned in advertising. Article 6 makes clear that any such additional material would also be binding on the guarantor. However, the Directive does not provide for any conflicts between the guarantee statement and the associated advertising. One way to resolve such conflicts would be to let the guarantee document prevail (Malinvaud, 2002, paragraph 15), but this could be detrimental to the consumer who may have relied on the references to the guarantee in an advertisement. Moreover, it could, potentially, encourage guarantors to make generous promises in advertising and then retract these in the guarantee statement (which a consumer will very probably not have read before committing himself to a purchase). The better solution would be to resolve such conflicts in favour of the consumer and to allow the more favourable provision to prevail.

Thirdly, guarantees will only bind the offerer under the conditions set out in the guarantee and the relevant advertising. There is no explanation as to which 'conditions' are referred to here. It seems that two types of conditions may be relevant. The first relates to any steps the consumer may have to take before the guarantee becomes available to him. Guarantors often require a consumer to return a registration card in order to benefit from a guarantee. Alternatively, or in addition, it may be necessary for the seller to complete a section on the guarantee document to provide evidence of the date of purchase. If such conditions are not fulfilled, it seems that the guarantee will not be binding under Article 6(1). The second type of condition to which Article 6(1) applies are the terms and conditions on which the guarantee is made available to the consumer. Such conditions may relate to the duration of the guarantee period, the procedure for making a claim under the guarantee, the allocation of charges for parts and labour, aspects of the goods not covered by the guarantee, and maintenance and servicing requirements. There is nothing in Article 6 about the substantive content of any of these conditions, and it is therefore up to the guarantor to decide what sort of guarantee to provide. However, whatever the scope of the guarantee, it will only bind the guarantor to the extent specified in the guarantee document (and in advertising). A guarantor therefore has an almost unrestricted freedom to determine what sort of guarantee to offer. The only restriction in the Directive itself is Article 7, which provides that the rights of consumers under sales law cannot be restricted or excluded in any way (see chapter 5). Consequently, it would not be possible to use a guarantee to curtail or eliminate the protection given to consumers by virtue of Articles 2 and 3 of the Directive.

The Directive makes no attempt to control either type of condition. The absence of any mandatory requirement that the guarantor offer any particular type of cover is consistent with the policy of encouraging manufacturers and retailers to compete on guarantees. However, it is surprising that there is no negative control, such as for instance prohibiting unfair or onerous conditions or requiring that important conditions be specifically drawn to the consumer's attention. It is submitted that this is a failing in the Directive. Assuming that the guarantee is contractual it will, as noted, be subject to legal controls on contract terms and, in particular, on those derived from the Unfair Terms Directive.

7.2.3 Relationship with statutory rights

The mutual independence of the consumer's guarantee and statutory rights is underlined by the first paragraph of Article 6(2), which requires that a guarantee state

that the consumer has legal rights under applicable national legislation governing the sale of consumer goods and make clear that those rights are not affected by the guarantee.

This provision marks a step back from the proposals in the *Green Paper*, and also the first draft of the Directive (COM (1995) 520 final) which suggested that a guarantee should provide something additional over and above the rights granted by sales law. No such provision is found in the final version of the Directive. Obviously where a guarantee is given by a manufacturer, the mere fact that the guarantee is given will provide something 'additional' as manufacturers are generally not currently liable to consumers for product quality (see chapter 8). Consequently, a requirement that the guarantee provide something extra would have little effect. (The position would have been different under the *Green Paper* which proposed that manufacturers should be directly liable, jointly with retailers, on the so-called 'legal guarantee'.) However, as noted earlier, one of the dangers of guarantees is that they can be used as a means of denying consumers their rights under the general law, by creating the impression that the guarantee contains the sum of the consumer's rights. A requirement that the guarantee contain a clear statement that the consumer has rights under sales law additional to those in the guarantee, and that those rights are not affected by the guarantee, could be enough to make it clear to consumers that guarantees are not the full extent of their rights when something goes wrong with their goods.

7.2.4 Disclosure requirements

Article 6(2) further requires that the guarantee document

set[s] out in plain intelligible language the contents of the guarantee and the essential particulars necessary for making claims under the guarantee, notably the duration and territorial scope of the guarantee as well as the name and address of the guarantor.

This goes some way to compensating for the fact that guarantees are not necessarily subject to legal controls on unfair contract terms. The requirement that the guarantee set out the consumer's rights in 'plain, intelligible language' clearly mirrors the similar requirement in the Unfair Terms Directive. It is not clear however what this means. The natural reading would be that it imposes an objective standard of intelligibility. There is similarly no requirement that the guarantee be provided in the consumer's own language and in the context of the single market it may be undesirable or even impossible to impose such a requirement. For instance, a product might be bought by a consumer while travelling abroad. Or a product initially marketed in one Member State might be imported, without the manufacturer's knowledge, into another. On the other hand, it is true that many consumers only know their native language and from a purely consumer perspective it might have been desirable to ensure that a guarantee is provided in the consumer's native language (Malinvaud, 2002, paragraph 22). However, Member States are given the option in Article 6(4) to require that guarantees are drafted in one or more of the official languages of the European Community. This provision may be of greater significance for those Member States whose language is less common, unlike French, German or English, for example.

Article 6(2) is otherwise phrased in rather vague terms. There is no elaboration on what might be the 'contents' of the guarantee in addition to the aspects mentioned in the Article (duration, geographical scope, and the name and address of the guarantor). It may be assumed that this would also include details of what is covered, and any restrictions or conditions that apply.

It is necessary to set out the 'essential particulars' for making a claim under the guarantee. Again, this term is rather imprecise, and could refer to details of who to contact, whether to return goods to the seller or directly to the guarantor, whether the consumer has to pay for postage and so on. It is unfortunate that no further guidance has been provided.

7.2.5 Written availability

Article 6(3) states that:

On request by the consumer, the guarantee shall be made available in writing or feature in another durable medium available and accessible to him.

This provision is a further indication of the disclosure-based approach to guarantees adopted in the Directive. Recital 21 emphasises that guarantees are one aspect on which manufacturers (and sellers) may compete, and in order to promote such competition, consumers are encouraged to compare guarantees given with similar goods before deciding on a purchase. However, it may be questioned whether this provision will be of great practical application, because it does not seem that many consumers are interested in the details of a guarantee prior to purchase. Most consumers will, at best, be interested in whether a guarantee is offered at all. It may be argued that this is because there has, so far, been no obligation on a seller or manufacturer to provide details of guarantees in advance. However, the experience in the United States under the Magnuson-Moss Warranty Act 1975, which contains detailed pre-sale availability rules, suggests that only a small minority of consumers would take advantage of this provision in the pre-purchase context (see Twigg-Flesner, 2003b, chapter 6).

This provision may, nevertheless, be relevant, for instance, where goods are advertised with a guarantee, but no further details are provided, or where the product packaging refers to a guarantee, but gives no further details. A consumer could then ask that further details be made available. Of course, Article 6(3) is not restricted to the pre-purchase context. It may also apply at a later stage—for example where a consumer has encountered a problem with the goods, but has misplaced the guarantee document.

7.2.5.1 The meaning of 'durable medium'
The main difficulty with this provision is that there is no clear definition of what might be considered a 'durable medium'. The fact that the medium on which the guarantee is to be made available should be 'durable' suggests that it must be capable of retention for some time. Clearly, a paper-based guarantee document would satisfy this requirement. However, the medium must be 'accessible' to the consumer and it seems here that the requirement is subjective to the individual consumer. A consumer who is visually impaired, therefore, may be entitled to ask for an audio-tape or a Braille or large-print version of the guarantee document, as the document usually enclosed with the goods will almost certainly not be 'accessible' to that consumer. Guarantors will therefore have to ensure that their guarantee documents are available in such alternative formats.

It is perhaps more difficult to identify whether a medium is 'durable' in the context of electronic media. This is particularly important in the context of the Single Market and given the importance of electronic commerce in encouraging consumers to participate in it. Some electronic media, such as a CD-ROM or a floppy disk, will probably satisfy the requirement of 'durability'. On the other hand it is less clear whether the requirement would be satisfied by making guarantee terms available on a web site. The absence of any explanation in the Directive is a significant shortcoming.

Some guidance on the meaning of 'durable medium' for the purposes of the Guarantees Directive may be obtained by looking to other Directives which use the same concept. This must be subject to the proviso that phrases which are defined for the purposes of one particular measure may have a different meaning in the context of another measure. However, it has been suggested that where a phrase not defined in one Directive is defined in another, both should be given the same meaning to ensure uniform application of EC Law (see Advocate-General Tizzano in C-168/00 *Leitner v TUI Deutschland* [2002] ECR I-2631). (This issue was identified as requiring action at the European level in the Commission's *Action Plan on a More Coherent European Contract Law* (COM (2003) 68 final, paragraphs 19–24).) As the concept of 'durable medium' permeates a number of recent consumer protection directives, it is therefore arguable that it should be interpreted in the same way in all of these measures, as long as there are no conflicting definitions. The Directive on Distance Selling (Directive 97/7/EC OJ No L 144/19, 4.6.97) requires consumers in the context of distance sales contracts to be provided with certain information 'in a durable medium' but offers no definition of this phrase. On the other hand, Article 2(f) of Directive 2002/65/EC concerning the distance marketing of consumer financial services ((2002) O.J. L 271/16) defines 'durable medium' as follows:

'Durable medium' means any instrument which enables the consumer to store information addressed personally to him in a way accessible for future reference for a period of time adequate for the purposes of the information and which allows the unchanged reproduction of the information stored.

It is clear that this definition cannot apply in all respects for the purposes of Article 6(3) of the Consumer Guarantees Directive. In particular, it requires that the information be 'personally addressed' to the consumer, so that a statement in general advertising would not suffice. Nor, arguably, would an impersonal document or guarantee card included with the goods. This may be appropriate in the context of a contract for financial services where the particular 'financial product' may be tailored to the consumer's own personal circumstances. It would be less necessary in the context of guarantees, and it is submitted that both general advertising statements and impersonal guarantee cards would be acceptable for the purposes of the Guarantees Directive.

Leaving aside this aspect, the remainder of the definition may be of some help. It seems that the key is that the information is supplied in some form which enables the consumer to store it for future reference and reproduce it unchanged, at least for a period during which the consumer needs to access the information in an unchanged form. This could include information published on a web site, provided that the web site remains unchanged for the period during which the consumer requires the information (i.e., the guarantee period). However, the definition of 'durable medium' in Article 2 (12) of Directive 2002/92/EC on Insurance Mediation ([2003] OJ L 9/3) suggests otherwise. In addition to the paragraph already set out above, the definition in the Insurance Mediation Directive contains the following second sentence:

In particular, durable medium covers floppy disks, CD-ROMs, DVDs and hard drives of personal computers on which electronic mail is stored, but it excludes Internet sites, unless such sites meet the criteria specific in the first paragraph.

This is rather less helpful than it might be, because the reference to web sites is somewhat circular—such sites are not durable media as defined in the first paragraph unless they meet the definition in the first paragraph. It may therefore be safer to assume that publishing guarantee information on a web site will not in itself satisfy the Directive, but may do so if the information is capable of being downloaded and saved to disk, or printed out, by the consumer. Clearly a printout of the relevant site provided by the manufacturer, retailer or his agent would be enough. It seems reasonably clear that information about the guarantee supplied to the consumer by e-mail would satisfy the requirement, although this assumes that the consumer uses e-mail software which stores messages on the hard drive or floppy disk.

We must therefore conclude that the precise meaning of 'durable medium' remains unclear. It may be, of course, that this is intentional to allow for inclusion of new media which are currently not widely available.

What, then, is the scope of application for Article 6(3)? Although it is not limited to the pre-sale context, it seems that it will have the greatest relevance there. A consumer may wish to consult the guarantees given on a number of competing products as part of his purchasing decision. However, it seems likely that the number of consumers who will take advantage of this provision will be small, because most consumers decide on a purchase based on product-specific factors gained from other sources (such as reviews in specialist magazines or testing reports in *Which?* magazine).

7.2.6 Validity and enforcement

Article 6(5) states that a failure to comply with the requirements in Article 6 does not affect the validity of a guarantee and consumers can still rely on it. So if a guarantee fails to include any of the details required by Article 6(2), the guarantee will nevertheless be legally binding, although there it may be difficult to determine what the guarantee actually provides. There are, however, no specific sanctions provided for a failure to comply with any of the requirements of Article 6 (see e.g. Micklitz, 1999, p 488). The only sanction envisaged in the Directive is Article 10, which amends the Injunctions Directive to include the Consumer Guarantees Directive within its scope. Consequently, if a particular guarantor does not comply with the requirements of Article 6 and thereby harms the collective interests of consumers, it may be possible for the relevant enforcement authority to apply for an injunction to prevent him from continuing to do so.

7.3 ENGLISH LAW BEFORE IMPLEMENTATION OF THE DIRECTIVE

The Directive thus requires that any consumer guarantee given by a retailer, manufacturer, importer or own-brander

(a) be legally binding;

(b) be expressed in plain, intelligible language;

(c) be made available to the consumer; and

(d) make clear that the consumer enjoys statutory rights in relation to the quality etc. of the goods.

It does not, however, require that any guarantee be given or prescribe, other than as mentioned above, any particular content for inclusion in the guarantee.

Prior to implementation of the Directive English law contained only minimal controls on the content of guarantees. Like the Directive it contained no requirement for a retailer or any other party to give a guarantee. Most significantly of all there were doubts about the legal enforceability of guarantees.

7.3.1 No requirement to give guarantee

The policy of the Directive, as we have seen, is that guarantees should be an instrument of competition. There is therefore no positive requirement for any person to provide a guarantee and only minimal control on the contents of guarantees. The policy of domestic law is similar. A 1990 Consumer Guarantees Bill, promoted by the National Consumer Council, would have created a new class of 'Consumer Guarantee' with a prescribed minimum content and required that the sale of certain classes of consumer goods be accompanied by a clear statement whether or not the goods had the benefit of a 'Consumer Guarantee'. It would not, however, have required that goods actually have a guarantee. In effect, therefore, its aim was the provision of information to enable consumers to make informed choices. A consumer buying goods covered by a 'Consumer Guarantee' as defined would (in theory) know the rights that the guarantee would contain. However, even this modest measure was opposed by government and did not become law. In 1992 the

DTI published a consultation document, *Consumer Guarantees*, in which it observed that imposing a mandatory requirement on manufacturers to offer a guarantee or prescribing the content of guarantees 'would, in the Government's view, be unnecessarily bureaucratic and run the risk of creating loopholes that could be exploited by manufacturers seeking to avoid taking responsibility for the quality of their products. Such matters are best left to market forces operating in a free competitive environment' (DTI, 1992).

7.3.2 Legal enforceability of guarantees

Hitherto most academic discussion of guarantees has concentrated on their legal enforceability. A guarantee offered by a manufacturer, retailer or other person in the distribution chain is enforceable at common law, if at all, as a contract. For the guarantee to be enforceable it must therefore satisfy all the requirements necessary for creation of a valid contract. Specifically, there must be an offer by one party, accepted by the other, there must be consideration for the undertaking in the guarantee and the guarantee must be intended to be legally binding.

Although it is possible to envisage situations where the offer to contract on the terms of the guarantee is made by the consumer, the normal analysis is that the guarantee setting out the undertaking offered by the guarantor is offered by the prospective guarantor. Where a 'guarantee' is contained in general advertising or promotional material it may be open to question whether or not it is intended to be legally binding. We return to this question in the following chapter. Where a formal guarantee is given there will generally be little difficulty in establishing that it was intended to be legally binding. The key issues are therefore likely to be whether the guarantor's offer was accepted by the consumer and whether the consumer provided consideration for it. Since the guarantee will normally involve undertakings only by the guarantor, if it constitutes a contract at all it will be construed as a unilateral (or 'if') contract. Under such an arrangement the offeror gives an undertaking and offers to be legally bound by it if the offeree to whom it is addressed does some act in return. The offeree gives no undertaking, although the offeror's undertaking may be defined and qualified by conditions. Under such an arrangement the same act normally constitutes acceptance of the offer and provides consideration for the offeror's undertaking.

'Consideration' is normally defined as 'the price of a promise' and it is generally open to the offeror to name his own price. The law does not concern itself with the adequacy of the consideration provided so long as there is something which is either of benefit to the promissor or detriment to the promisee. Some guarantees require the consumer to do some act such as returning a registration card containing details of the product, where purchased and so on. Such an act is capable of providing consideration for the guarantor's undertaking. The information provided by the consumer may be of some commercial benefit to the guarantor; even if that is not the case, the detriment suffered by the consumer in completing and returning the card would be sufficient consideration. There is therefore no difficulty in finding that the guarantee is binding in such a case.

The situation is rather less clear where the guarantor does not require the consumer to do anything after purchase of the goods to register the guarantee etc. Provided that the consumer is aware of the guarantee before or at the time of purchasing the goods the consumer can be said to accept the offer of the guarantee by purchasing the goods, the guarantor being taken as having waived the need for communication of acceptance. The consumer would provide consideration for the guarantee by purchasing the goods, thus providing a benefit to the guarantor (who benefits from the sale of the guaranteed product) and suffering a detriment by virtue of paying the price for the product. (See the similar analysis in the classic case of *Carlill v Carbolic Smoke Ball Co Ltd* [1893] 1 QB 256; see also *Chappell & Co Ltd v Nestlé Co Ltd* [1960] AC 87, [1959] 2 All ER 701.) The position is however rather less clear where the consumer is not aware of the guarantee prior to purchase. This is quite a common situation where, for instance, a manufacturer provides a guarantee in a document packaged with the goods and the consumer is not required to do anything more, for instance to register the guarantee. Although the position is not clear it is generally accepted that a person cannot accept an offer of which he is ignorant (see *R v Clarke* (1927) 40 CLR 227; *cf. Williams v Carwardine* (1833) 5 C & P 566; *Gibbons v Proctor* (1891) 64 LT 594). In the situation described above, therefore, the consumer's purchase of the goods could not be regarded as acceptance of the offer of the guarantee or provide consideration for the guarantor's undertaking. Unless therefore it were possible to find some additional consideration provided by the consumer after purchase of the goods, the guarantee in this situation would not be legally binding according to orthodox contractual analysis.

It must be conceded that this problem has tended to be of rather greater academic than practical concern. Manufacturers have usually honoured their guarantee, regardless of the strict legal position, either because it was assumed that the guarantee was binding (as is the case in some other jurisdictions), or out of concern for commercial reputation and the potentially adverse effect on their business reputation of a refusal to honour a guarantee (see Collins, 1999).

7.3.3 Controls on the content of guarantees

Although there was therefore no requirement in domestic law to offer a guarantee or that any guarantee offered should be legally enforceable, it was recognised that controls on the content of guarantees were needed, *inter alia* to prevent consumers being misled as to their legal rights and to regulate the use of exclusion and similar clauses in guarantees.

7.3.3.1 *The relationship between statutory rights and guarantees*
As we have noted, one of the issues addressed by the Directive is the relationship between the consumer's rights under the general law and the rights derived from a

guarantee. The intention is that guarantees should provide consumers with additional rights. We have also seen that contractual restrictions on the seller's statutory liability for goods supplied are subject to strict control under the UCTA 1977 which generally renders them wholly ineffective. However, if it were possible to use a guarantee to restrict or even exclude the consumer's statutory rights, those rights would be undermined, the controls on exclusions of liability would be sidestepped, and the guarantee would effectively lower, rather than raise, the level of protection provided to the consumer. It is therefore necessary to ensure that guarantees do not limit in any way the protection given to consumers by the general law.

Any attempt in a guarantee to exclude or limit the SoGA implied terms or liability for their breach is invalidated by the combined effect of sections 6, 7 and 10 of the UCTA 1977. The provisions of sections 6 and 7 have already been examined. As we have seen they invalidate any clause in a contract between a seller or supplier of goods and a consumer by which the seller/supplier purports to exclude, restrict or limit the implied terms in the contract of supply or his liability for their breach. Section 10 prevents the evasion of these controls by means of a secondary contract. It provides that:

A person is not bound by any contract term prejudicing or taking away rights of his which arise under, or in connection with the performance of, another contract, so far as those rights extend to the other enforcement of another's liability which this Part of this Act prevents that other from excluding or restricting.

Although the precise scope of this provision is unclear it has been held that it does apply where a term in a contract between A and B purports to exclude or restrict rights B would otherwise enjoy under a separate contract with C (see *Tudor Grange Holdings Ltd v Citibank NA* [1992] Ch 53, [1991] 4 All ER 1). It would therefore apply to a term in a manufacturer's guarantee of goods which purported to exclude the consumer's rights against a retailer under the Sale of Goods Act. Curiously it is not clear that section 10 would apply where the guarantee was given by the retailer and purported to exclude or limit the retailer's liabilities under the separate supply contract. Section 10 refers to 'the enforcement of *another's* liability' and it is argued that 'another' must be a third party not privy to the contract in which the exclusion appears. It would be possible however to construe 'another' more widely as contrasting with the opening words of the section referring to 'a person' and thus as meaning any person other than the person not bound by the exclusion. But the point may be moot. If an exclusion in a retailer's guarantee of the retailer's liability under the contract of sale is not prohibited by section 10 it would almost certainly be caught by the language of UCTA section 6 which states simply that liability arising under the SoGA implied terms 'cannot be excluded or restricted by reference to any contract term' (UCTA section 7 is in similar terms).

Even in the absence of an outright exclusion or restriction of the consumer's rights, a guarantee may undermine the effectiveness of the statutory rights by creating the impression that it is the principal or even only statement of the consumer's rights. In the UK this is regulated by the Consumer Transactions (Restrictions on Statements) Order 1976. Although the Order was made under Part II of the Fair Trading Act 1973, which has been repealed by the Enterprise Act 2002, the Order itself has been preserved for the time being and remains in force. In essence, regulations 4 and 5 of the Order require that where a manufacturer, supplier or retailer gives any guarantee (or other promise), to do anything in the event of the goods proving defective or not fit for a purpose or not conforming with a description, there must also, in close proximity to the guarantee statement, be a clear and conspicuous statement to the effect that the consumer's legal rights are not affected in any way by the guarantee. The regulations extend to any statement of the consumer's rights against the person giving the guarantee, whether made on the goods or the container in which they are supplied or in a separate document.

In practice this has resulted in the inclusion in most guarantees of the familiar phrase 'This does not affect your statutory rights'. Such a statement does not, however, tell the consumer what these statutory rights might be and it is therefore difficult for a consumer who does not know what his rights are to consider whether the guarantee offers the most appropriate way of dealing with defective goods. The OFT has therefore taken the view that such statements are not sufficiently clear and precise to satisfy the Unfair Terms in Consumer Contracts Regulations 1999, and it suggests the inclusion, as a minimum, of a second statement summarising these rights, or directing consumers to their local Trading Standards Department for advice on their legal rights (regulation 7 UTCCR 1999; see Office of Fair Trading, *OFT 311—Unfair Contract Terms Guidance*, 2001, p 52 and p 164).

In addition, case-law under section 14(2) SoGA 1979 has made it clear that the existence of a guarantee is irrelevant in establishing whether goods are of satisfactory quality. In *Rogers v Parish (Scarborough) Ltd* ([1987] QB 933, CA, [1987] 2 All ER 232), decided under the precursor to the current section 14(2) which required goods to be of merchantable quality, the plaintiffs had purchased a new Range Rover for some £16,000. The vehicle suffered from a number of defects and, after a replacement provided by the supplier had proved no better, the plaintiffs eventually sought to exercise their right to reject the car and terminate the contract of sale. One of the arguments put forward by the seller was that the car as supplied was of merchantable quality because any defects could be remedied free of charge under the manufacturer's guarantee. This was rejected by the Court of Appeal. Mustill LJ noted that:

Surely the [guarantee] is an addition to the buyer's rights, not a subtraction from them, and, it may be noted, only a circumscribed addition since it lasts for a limited period and does not compensate the buyer for consequential loss and inconvenience. If the defendants are right a buyer would be well advised to leave his guarantee behind in the showroom. ([1987] QB 933 at 945)

Therefore, the availability of a guarantee has no bearing on the assessment of whether goods are of satisfactory quality.

It can therefore be concluded that the relationship between guarantees and legal rights is one of mutual independence. Guarantees cannot restrict the scope of the legal rights. Importantly, consumers may choose whether to pursue a remedy under a guarantee, or by claiming that there has been a breach of their legal rights. Choosing a guarantee first should not prevent a consumer from exercising his statutory rights subsequently if claiming under the guarantee has not resolved the problem.

7.3.3.2 *Exclusion clauses in guarantees*

The preceding discussion addressed the relationship between guarantees and the consumer's statutory contractual rights under the contract of sale or supply. A manufacturer who is not otherwise in a direct contractual relationship with a consumer may nevertheless be liable to the consumer for defects in the goods either under the Consumer Protection Act 1987 or in the common law of negligence (see chapter 8). Any attempt by a manufacturer to limit or exclude liability arising under the 1987 Act by any contract term or notice is wholly ineffective (CPA 1987 section 7) and thus any term in a guarantee purporting to exclude such liability will be ineffective.

Any term in a guarantee which purports to exclude or restrict liability for common law negligence will be subject to UCTA section 5. Section 5(1) renders ineffective any clause in a guarantee by which a manufacturer seeks to exclude or limit his liability for loss or damage caused by negligence during the manufacturing or distribution process. The section provides as follows:

In the case of goods of a type ordinarily supplied for private use or consumption, where loss or damage

(a) arises from the goods proving defective while in consumer use; and
(b) results from the negligence of a person concerned in the manufacture or distribution of the goods,

liability for the loss or damage cannot be restricted by reference to any contract term or notice contained in or operating by reference to a guarantee of the goods.

Goods are in 'consumer use' 'when a person is using them, or has them in his possession for use, otherwise than exclusively for the purposes of a business' (section 5(1)(a)).

For the purposes of this section, 'guarantee' is defined in section 5(2)(b) which provides that:

Anything in writing is a guarantee if it contains or purports to contain some promise or assurance (however worded or presented) that defects will be made good by complete or partial replacement, or by repair, monetary compensation or otherwise.

The section would therefore apply to terms in the type of guarantee considered in this chapter. However, the section is stated not to apply 'as between the parties to a contract under or in pursuance of which possession or ownership of the goods passed'. It would therefore not apply to a term in a retailer's guarantee. However, in such a case the retailer would be strictly liable for the goods under the contract of supply and any attempt to exclude that liability would be ineffective in accordance with the provisions already discussed.

The upshot is that section 5 invalidates any term in a guarantee given by a manufacturer or other party not privy to the actual contract of supply in which the guarantor seeks to exclude or limit his (or any other person's) liability in negligence under the principle of *Donoghue v Stevenson* [1932] AC 562 (see chapter 8). It should be noted that the section is limited to guarantees of goods 'of a type ordinarily supplied for private use or consumption' (see discussion above at 2.3.1.4) but that the phrase 'consumer use' is widely defined so that, for instance, if a solicitor were to buy a personal computer for home use, using it for his business and for leisure purposes, the computer would be in consumer use even if at the time of the loss or damage it was being used for business purposes.

Section 5 to some extent overlaps with section 2 of UCTA which applies to terms and notices which exclude or limit liability for loss or damage caused by negligence. Under section 2 liability for death or personal injury caused by negligence cannot be excluded at all; liability for other types of loss including damage to property can be excluded only insofar as the exclusion satisfies the requirement of reasonableness. Within its area of application section 5 therefore provides greater protection than does section 2 since it wholly invalidates any attempt by a manufacturer to exclude or limit liability for any kind of loss or damage, including damage to property or economic loss, resulting from negligence in manufacture. In contrast section 2 only wholly invalidates exclusion or restriction of liability for death or personal injury. On the other hand the scope of section 2 is wider than that of section 5 since it applies generally to any exclusion (etc.) of liability for negligence and is not limited to loss caused by negligence in manufacture. It would therefore extend to (say) a term in a guarantee purporting to exclude liability for loss caused by goods proving defective due to negligence in storage or distribution.

Notwithstanding these differences in the scope of the two provisions, there is a considerable degree of overlap between sections 2 and 5 of the UCTA. The Law Commission is in the process of reviewing the legislation on unfair contract terms, and in its 2002 consultation document suggested that in light of that overlap section 5 could 'safely be abolished' (Law Commission Consultation Paper No 166, *Unfair Terms in Contracts*, paragraph 4.27).

7.3.3.3 *Controls on terms in guarantees*

In addition to terms seeking to exclude liability under sales law or negligence, guarantees sometimes contain other terms which make claiming under the guarantee difficult or onerous for the consumer. Assuming that the guarantee is contractual its terms will be subject to other statutory controls under the Unfair

Contract Terms Act 1977 and the Unfair Terms in Consumer Contracts Regulations 1999 which may invalidate such terms.

(i) UCTA section 2   As outlined in chapter 5, UCTA section 2 restricts the effectiveness of contract terms which seek to exclude or restrict liability for loss caused by negligence, including both breach of a common law duty of care and breach of a contractual requirement to exercise reasonable skill or care. Liability for personal injury or death caused by negligence can never be excluded. Liability for other forms of loss—damage to property and economic loss—can be excluded but only in so far as the exclusion satisfies the requirement of reasonableness. Where repair work is carried out under a guarantee the person effecting the repair will normally be subject to a duty of care in respect of its performance. Where the guarantee is contractual the contract will be one for supply of a service under the Supply of Goods and Services Act 1982, and the duty of care will arise as an implied term of the contract, under section 13 SGSA. If the guarantee is not contractual the guarantor will nevertheless be subject to a tortious duty of care at common law. Any clause in the guarantee which purports to exclude or restrict the guarantor's liability for loss caused by breach of the relevant duty of care will therefore be subject to section 2 UCTA.

(ii) UCTA section 3   UCTA section 3 applies wherever one party to a contract deals (a) as a consumer or (b) on the other party's written standard terms of business. It will therefore potentially apply to manufacturers' and retailers' guarantees offered to consumers (and, since guarantees are normally provided on written standard terms, to guarantees offered to non-consumers). Applying section 3 to guarantees it provides that the guarantor cannot by reference to any term in the contract exclude or restrict his liability for breach of contract or:

claim to be entitled

(i)   to render a contractual performance substantially different from that which was reasonably expected of him or

(ii) in respect of the whole or any part of his contractual obligation, to render no performance at all

except in so far as the contract term satisfies the requirement of reasonableness. (see section 3(2)(b))

Section 3 is a potentially far-reaching provision. In particular the provisions of section 3(2)(b) quoted above are capable of particularly wide application. The key to the section is determining what performance 'was reasonably expected' by the consumer, and in *Zockoll Group Ltd v Mercury Communications Ltd* [1998] FSR 354 the Court of Appeal held that the proper approach to the section is first to determine the contractual performance reasonably expected without reference to the particular terms under challenge, on the grounds that any other approach would emasculate the section and 'frustrate the purpose of the legislation' (per

Lord Bingham MR at p 395). The result is that if a term in small print qualifies, restricts or removes a right which the consumer reasonably thinks is provided by the contract, the term is subject to the reasonableness test under the Act. Thus, for instance, if a manufacturer offers goods with a 'two year, no charge, parts and labour guarantee' and then in the small print of the guarantee provides that in order to take advantage of the guarantee the consumer must return the goods in their original packaging and pay all associated carriage costs it would be open to a court to hold the term subject to section 3, on the grounds that it purports to allow the manufacturer to offer a lesser guarantee than the consumer reasonably expected as a result of the 'headline' terms, and therefore subject the term to a test of reasonableness. It should be emphasised however that (a) it would be open to a court to find that such a term did not fall within section 3, on the grounds, for instance, that the performance offered was not substantially different from that expected, or that the consumer's expectation of a higher level of service was unreasonable (if, for instance, the terms of the guarantee were all prominently displayed); and (b) that such a term might nevertheless be considered reasonable. (However, the term in this example may be caught by the UTCCR 1999, and therefore not be binding on consumers.) It must also be borne in mind that by virtue of section 13 the UCTA does not apply only to exclusion clauses but to a range of other types of clause which have the effect of excluding or restricting liability or its enforcement (see 5.3.1.1).

(iii) The Unfair Terms in Consumer Contracts Regulations 1999   The Unfair Terms in Consumer Contracts Regulations 1999 (UTCCR) implement the EC's Unfair Contract Terms Directive (93/13/EEC) and replace earlier Regulations made in 1994. The Regulations apply to contracts between sellers or suppliers and consumers. However, 'seller or supplier' is defined broadly to refer to 'any natural or legal person who, in contracts covered by these regulations, is acting for purposes related to his trade, business or profession' (regulation 3(1)). They apply to all terms in such a contract which have not been individually negotiated (regulation 5(1)). They provide that:

A term shall always be regarded as not having been individually negotiated where it has been drafted in advance and the consumer has therefore not been able to influence the substance of the term. (regulation 5(2))

A guarantor will be a 'seller or supplier' for these purposes and since a guarantee will normally be drafted in its entirety by the guarantor, the terms of a guarantee will generally be subject to the Regulations.

Where they apply, the Regulations impose two levels of control over contract terms. First, they require the seller or supplier to ensure that any written contract term is expressed in 'plain and intelligible language' (regulation 7(1)) and provide that if there is any doubt about the meaning of a written term, 'the interpretation which is most favourable to the consumer shall prevail' (regulation 7(2)). Second, they provide that an unfair term in a contract between a seller or supplier and a consumer shall not be binding on the consumer (regulation 8). The test of fairness is laid down in regulation 5. It provides that:

A contractual term which has not been individually negotiated shall be regarded as unfair if, contrary to the requirement of good faith, it causes a significant imbalance in the parties' rights and obligations arising under the contract, to the detriment of the consumer.

In order to be judged unfair a term must therefore create a significant imbalance in the rights and obligations of the parties; that imbalance must be to the disadvantage of the consumer, looking at the contract as a whole; and the creation of the imbalance must be contrary to the requirement of good faith. As the House of Lords recognised in applying this test in *Director-General of Fair Trading v First National Bank plc* ([2001] UKHL 52, [2002] 1 All ER 97) consideration of whether an imbalance is contrary to 'good faith' requires consideration of both substantive and procedural issues. Some terms, such as those which purport to exclude or limit liability for death or injury caused by negligence, are inherently so unfair that their inclusion in a contract is always necessarily contrary to good faith. Other terms are not thus necessarily unfair and their fairness will depend on procedural aspects of good faith, defined by Lords Bingham and Steyn as requiring 'openness and fair dealing', and such terms may therefore be fair, even though they create a significant imbalance in the rights and obligations of the parties, if introduced openly and fairly into the contract.

Importantly for present purposes, the Regulations provide that if an individual term is judged unfair, the remainder of the contract remains in force and binding on the parties provided that it is capable of continuing in existence without the invalidated term (regulation 8(2)). Thus if a term in a guarantee were to be judged unfair under the Regulations the remainder of the guarantee would remain in force. A challenge to an individual term in a guarantee will therefore not deprive the consumer of his rights under the remainder of the guarantee. The most important feature of the Regulations, however, is that not only may they be relied on by individual consumers to challenge terms in contracts to which they are party, but they may be enforced by the Director General of Fair Trading and by any other 'qualifying body' as defined by the Regulations who may therefore take action under the Regulations to prevent the use of unfair terms. In addition to a number of regulators the list of 'qualifying bodies' in the Regulations includes the Consumers' Association.

Applying these provisions to guarantees, there can be no doubt that terms in guarantees may potentially be subject to the Regulations and therefore to challenge as unfair either by individual consumers or by the OFT. However, the application of the Regulations may be restricted by regulation 6(2) which provides that:

(2) In so far as it is in plain and intelligible language, the assessment of the fairness of a term shall not relate
(a) to the definition of the main subject matter of the contract; or

(b) to the adequacy of the price or remuneration, as against the goods or services supplied in exchange.

Pretty clearly this precludes assessment of the fairness of the guarantor's core undertaking in itself: a consumer cannot challenge the guarantee on the basis that (say) it only covers parts and not labour, or lasts only for 6 months rather than a year. Initially, however, the OFT took the view that the effect of regulation 6(2) was to severely limit the application of the Regulations to guarantees, observing that:

Regulation 3(2) [of the 1994 Regulations, equivalent to regulation 6(2) in the 1999 Regulations] provides that terms which define the subject matter of the contract cannot be assessed for fairness, provided that they are in plain and intelligible language. The conditions of a [guarantee] are likely to come within this exemption. (OFT, 1996, p 30)

If this were correct, then most of the terms of a guarantee would be outside the scope of the Regulations. Indeed, it would have the effect of removing exclusion clauses in a guarantee from the scope of the Regulations, because such clauses are part of the conditions on which a guarantee is provided. The result would be that the only terms open to challenge under the Regulations would be procedural terms relating to such matters as the procedure for making a claim. However, in *Director-General of Fair Trading v First National Bank plc* the House of Lords indicated that the exclusion in regulation 6(2) should be given a narrow interpretation and it is reassuring that since 1996 the OFT has moved away from this particular interpretation and has applied the UTCCR to a wide range of terms found in guarantees. A glance at the *Unfair Contract Terms Bulletins*, which are published at regular intervals by the OFT and detail terms found to be unfair, reveals the kinds of terms in guarantees which have been found to be unfair. These include terms which have the effect of limiting or excluding the legal rights of consumers under sales law, restrictions on transferability (double glazing), imposing unnecessary costs on consumers who wish to claim under the guarantee, confusing and misleading terms in a guarantee and a requirement to use the original packaging in which the goods were delivered if it becomes necessary to return these (see further Twigg-Flesner, 2003b, chapter 8). As a result the UTCCR have proved to be a very useful tool in ensuring that guarantees do not contain unfair terms and as such provided an important counterweight to the broad freedom given to guarantors in determining the scope of their guarantees.

7.4 THE SALE AND SUPPLY OF GOODS TO CONSUMERS REGULATIONS 2002

It is clear from the previous section that there has hitherto been relatively little legal regulation of guarantees. The implementation of Article 6 of the Directive has therefore caused fewer difficulties than that of other parts of the Directive. The rules on guarantees described above continue to apply alongside the new rules contained in the SSGCR, and in order to obtain a full picture of the law, this section should be read together with section 7.3. Moreover, as the SSGCR provisions closely follow Article 6 of the Directive, the points made in section 7.2 are also relevant.

7.4.1 Definition

The relevant provisions of the SSGCR apply to 'consumer guarantees' defined for the purposes of the SSGCR in regulation 2 thus:

'Consumer guarantee' means any undertaking by a person acting in the course of his business to a consumer, given without extra charge, to reimburse the price paid or to replace, repair or handle consumer goods in any way if they do not meet the specifications set out in the guarantee statement or in the relevant advertising.

This definition closely follows the definition of 'guarantee' in Article 1(2)(e) of the Guarantees Directive. Consequently, there is the same uncertainty with regard to its scope as identified previously in relation to Article 1(2)(e), and in particular whether 'satisfaction guarantees' are covered. However, in one respect, the definition in the SSGCR is wider than that in the Directive. The definition in the Directive only covers undertakings by a seller or a producer as defined (see 7.2.1), whereas that in regulation 2 includes undertakings by any person acting in the course of their business. It may therefore also include guarantees given by an importer of goods from elsewhere in the EU into the United Kingdom, or by a distributor. Importantly, it may also extend to 'extended warranty'-style guarantees which are given free of charge, such as the extended warranties given by credit card companies.

Guarantor is defined separately as 'a person who offers a consumer guarantee to a consumer' (regulation 2 SSGCR).

Whereas the definition of 'guarantor' is unproblematic, it is regrettable that the phrase 'in the course of his business' was used in regulation 2, rather than the phrase 'in the course of *a* business' more commonly found in domestic legislation. As we have suggested elsewhere (see chapter 2), 'in the course of *his* business' seems to have a narrower scope than 'in the course of *a* business'. There will therefore be a mismatch between the new provisions and other provisions of domestic law. For instance UCTA section 5 will apply to an exclusion of liability arising in the course of *a* business. There is no doubt that the Regulations satisfy the requirements of the Directive under which a guarantee is an undertaking given by a seller, defined as a person acting 'in the course of *his* trade, business or profession' but in other areas the DTI was prepared to go further in implementing the Directive than strictly necessary and in the interests of consistency it might have been preferable if the more familiar formula had been used. Moreover, the use of the phrase 'in the course of his business' will import into this area the uncertainty that currently exists in English law with regard to the test to be applied in establishing whether a particular transaction was effected in the course of business (see above 2.3.1.3). Thus, it is not clear whether the *R &B Customs Brokers* test, requiring some degree of regularity, or the *Stevenson v Rogers* test should apply for the purposes of regulation 2. However, as the person giving the guarantee must be acting in the course of *his*, rather than simply *a* business, it seems that the stricter *R & B* test would be appropriate here.

Only consumer guarantees which are given free of charge come within the scope of the definition. Extended warranties (other than, potentially, those given free-of-charge) are therefore not covered, because a consumer has to pay separately for those. It is, however, possible that separate legislation on extended warranties may be adopted as a result of the Competition Commission inquiry, noted above.

It can also be seen that it was decided to use the term 'consumer guarantee', rather than simply 'guarantee'—perhaps the DTI felt that because section 5 UCTA already defines 'guarantee' for the purposes of that section, there was a risk of confusion if there were two different definitions of the same term. During the implementation process, the DTI proposed amending the definition in section 5 UCTA to bring it into line with that in the Directive, but this proposal was abandoned. In the remainder of this chapter, the term 'guarantee' will include 'consumer guarantees' within the meaning of regulation 2 SSGCR.

7.4.2 Regulation 15—Guarantees legally binding

The key requirement of the Directive is that guarantees should be enforceable. As we have seen the enforceability of at least some guarantees at common law was not certain. The matter is now put beyond doubt by regulation 15(1) of the SSGCR which provides that:

Where goods are sold or otherwise supplied to a consumer which are offered with a consumer guarantee, the consumer guarantee takes effect at the time the goods are delivered as a contractual obligation owed by the guarantor under the conditions set out in the guarantee statement and the associated advertising.

The legal status of guarantees as contracts is therefore confirmed. A guarantee takes effect as a contractual obligation owed by the guarantor to the consumer. The approach seems to be to replicate as closely as possible the common law approach. The reference to a 'contractual obligation owed by the guarantor' rather than simply to 'a contract between guarantor and consumer' is perhaps intended to confirm that the contract is (in common law terms) unilateral (see 7.3.2 above), emphasising that it imposes no obligations on the consumer. There may be conditions to be satisfied if the consumer is to invoke the guarantee, but they are not enforceable as contractual obligations by the guarantor against the consumer. However, since this is a statutory contract there is no need to satisfy the common law requirements for creation of a contract. There is therefore no need to find that the consumer has accepted the guarantor's offer or provided consideration for it.

On the other hand, it is submitted that it will still be necessary to show that the guarantor's undertaking was intended to be legally binding, in the objective sense described earlier. Although it is not clear, it seems that the language of regulations 2 and 15 is wide enough to apply not only to formal guarantees provided packaged with goods but also to more general guarantees given in advertising and promotional literature, such as for instance the famous undertaking in *Carlill v Carbolic Smoke Ball Co* (although the particular advertisement in that case would not qualify as a consumer guarantee as it did not involve an undertaking to reimburse the price, replace, repair or otherwise handle the goods). A consumer guarantee must be an 'undertaking', indicating that the language must be promissory and, it is submitted, that it must be such that a reasonable consumer would think it intended to be taken seriously.

The statutory contract created by the guarantee is thus different in some respects from normal contracts. However, classifying the guarantor's obligation as contractual is instantly recognisable to an English lawyer (and not too controversial for Scottish lawyers), and, more importantly, means that guarantees will be subject to other legal rules applicable to contracts, including those on privity of contract, remedies for breach and, most importantly, the legislation on unfair contract terms.

7.4.2.1 *Parties to the guarantee and transferability*

A contractual obligation is normally owed to one or more particular persons, and is limited by the doctrine of privity of contract so that it can only be enforced by and against the contracting parties. The obligation created by regulation 15 is peculiar in that it is not stated to be owed to any particular person. As a result, although neither the Directive nor the SSGCR expressly so provide, it is arguable that regulation 15(1) permits the guarantee to be enforced not only by the initial purchaser of the goods but also by a subsequent owner, such as a donee or second-hand purchaser. As we have noted, the Directive is unhelpful on this point. Indeed, it does not as such require that the guarantee be contractual but merely that it be legally binding (see 7.2.2).

Regulation 15(1) states that 'where goods are sold or otherwise supplied to a consumer which are offered with a consumer guarantee, the guarantee takes effect as a contractual obligation owed by the guarantor under the conditions set out in the guarantee statement and the associated advertising'. There is nothing to limit the guarantor's obligation to the first purchaser. It is therefore at least arguable that where the guarantee expressly states that the benefit of the guarantee runs with the goods, the guarantee can be enforced in accordance with its terms not only by the initial purchaser but by subsequent owners of the goods. Even in the absence of such a provision, however, it may be that the benefit of the guarantee will pass with the goods. Nothing in regulation 15 requires the goods to be sold or supplied by a person acting in the course of a business. The only requirement is that (a) the goods are sold or supplied to a consumer and (b) that the goods are offered with a consumer guarantee. 'Consumer' is defined in regulation 2 as 'any natural person who, in contracts covered by these Regulations, is acting for purposes which are outside his trade, business or profession'. The contracts covered by the SSGCR for this purpose must include the contractual guarantee under regulation 15(1) because, since all other provisions of the Regulations simply amend existing primary legislation, the definition of 'consumer' in regulation 2 only applies to regulation 15. The relevant definition of 'consumer' therefore does not require that the party with whom the consumer deals is acting in the course of a business (cf. section 12 UCTA, which requires the seller to be acting in the course of a business—see chapter 2). As a result, provided that goods are supplied to a natural person acting for purposes which are outside his trade, business or profession regulation 15 on its face applies regardless of whether the person selling or supplying the goods is acting in the course of a business. Thus, if A (a consumer) sells or supplies goods to B (another consumer, such as a second-hand purchaser), B would be a consumer for the purposes of regulation 15(1) and on the face of it the guarantee takes effect as an obligation owed by the guarantor to B.

The only limiting factor is that the goods supplied must be 'offered with a consumer guarantee'. It is not at all clear what this means. One interpretation would be that it is sufficient that the goods were initially offered with a consumer guarantee—i.e. when A (in the example above) bought the goods. On this reading provided that the goods were initially offered with a guarantee, the guarantor would become subject to a fresh contractual obligation on each subsequent disposition of the goods. 'Otherwise supplied' in regulation 15 is wide enough to encompass a gift.

An alternative reading would be that regulation 15 requires the goods to be offered with a guarantee at the time of the sale or supply in question. On the face of it there is nothing in regulation 15 to require the guarantee to be offered by the prospective guarantor but it clearly cannot be the case that a seller of goods, whether a retailer or consumer reselling the goods, could offer a guarantee which would impose a guarantee obligation on another person, such as the manufacturer, without their authority. It is therefore submitted that regulation 15 must be read as requiring the guarantee to be offered, directly or indirectly, by the prospective guarantor. If, therefore, regulation 15 is read as requiring the guarantee to be offered at the same time the goods are supplied, it is submitted that the second-hand purchaser or donee can only take the benefit of the guarantee if its terms provide for it to be transmissible.

Even if it is not necessary that the guarantee is offered at the time of the relevant sale or supply, the guarantee only becomes binding on the guarantor 'under the conditions set out in the guarantee statement and the associated advertising'. A term in the guarantee document limiting the benefit of the guarantee to the first purchaser (A) would therefore prevent any subsequent owners (such as B) from being able to enforce the guarantee. It is therefore clear that where a guarantee is expressly stated to be restricted to the original consumer buyer it is not enforceable by any third party under regulation 15(1).

There are, however, two other potential routes by which the benefit of a guarantee might be transmissible to subsequent owners of the relevant goods. First, it may be possible to effect an assignment of the rights under the guarantee in accordance with section 136(1) of the Law of Property Act 1925. Such an assignment would have to be in writing, and notice of the assignment would have to be given to the guarantor. These requirements may make it impractical for most consumers to consider assigning the benefit of a guarantee. Moreover, assignment would be ineffective if prohibited by the terms of the guarantee. It might be possible to argue that such a restriction on assignment is unfair under the Unfair Terms in Consumer Contracts Regulations 1999, although this may depend on the type of guarantee and the nature of the corresponding goods. The OFT has taken this approach in the context of long-term guarantees on double-glazing and car engines, but not (yet) in the context of domestic appliances, (for example *East Yorkshire Aluminium*, OFT Bulletin 4 (1997), p 37; *Rimacroft Ltd*, OFT Bulletin 10 (2000), p 28).

Finally, it may be possible to apply the provisions of the Contracts (Rights of Third Parties) Act 1999. The main provisions of the 1999 Act have been described elsewhere (see 6.2.1). As we have noted, it allows a 'third party' beneficiary in certain circumstances to enforce a term of a contract to which he is not a party if either (a) the contract expressly states that he may do so or (b) the contract purports to confer a benefit on him and it does not appear that the parties did not intend the term to be enforceable by him (section 1). In either case the third party beneficiary must be identified in the contract by 'name, as a member of a class or as answering a particular description, but need not be in existence at the time the contract is entered into' (section 1(3)). A statement in a guarantee that it is intended to benefit third parties, identified by a generic description such as 'subsequent owners' or 'sub-buyers' would therefore sufficiently identify the members of the class for this purpose. Section 1(1) allows a third party to enforce a term in the contract either if the contract provides for this expressly, or if the term in question purports to confer a benefit on the third party.

The application of the Act therefore depends on the parties' intentions as expressed in the guarantee which, in the present context, means, effectively, the intentions of the guarantor, who will have drafted all the terms of the guarantee. If the guarantee expressly states that it is intended to be enforceable by, or that the benefit of it is to be transmissible to, an identified class of third parties, such as donees or subsequent owners, they will be entitled to enforce it. Conversely, a term in the guarantee expressly stating that it is *not* to be enforceable by third parties will mean that the Act has no application and will also, subject to what has been said above, prevent their enforcing the guarantee on any of the bases discussed above. Similarly, if there is no mention of any third party, either individually or as a member of a class, the Act's identification requirement will be unsatisfied and third parties will not be able to enforce the guarantee on this basis.

Finally, it should be noted that although the 1999 Act only allows the third party to take the benefit of the contract, it provides that if he does so he can only enforce the contract 'subject to and in accordance with any other relevant terms of the contract' (section 1(4)). As we have noted, at common law a guarantee will typically be a unilateral contract and will therefore impose no contractual duties on the consumer, and this approach is reflected in the Regulations which make the guarantee contractually binding on the guarantor. However, the guarantee will normally impose conditions on the guarantor's liability such as a requirement to maintain the goods in a particular way or to notify claims within a stated period and, although not promissory (so that the consumer cannot be held liable for their non-performance) the consumer will generally only be able to enforce the guarantee if he complies with the relevant conditions.

It may therefore be concluded that the 1999 Act will be, at best, of limited assistance in enabling third parties to enforce guarantees. The best that can be said is that a guarantee which expressly states that it is intended to be enforceable by third parties probably will be on one basis or another. Absent such a statement there is no general rule that guarantees are transferable.

7.4.2.2 *Enforceability*

Since a guarantee takes effect as a contractual obligation owed by the guarantor, in the event of the guarantor's failing to fulfil his obligations under the guarantee the consumer's remedy is an action for damages to put him in the same position as if the contract had been fulfilled. Thus if, say, the guarantee provides that goods which break down within two years of purchase will be repaired free of charge and the guarantor fails to repair the goods as promised, the consumer will be entitled to damages to cover the cost of having the goods repaired elsewhere. It is however not entirely clear that this is sufficient to satisfy the Directive's requirement that 'a guarantee shall be legally binding'. It would be possible to read this as requiring that the guarantor shall be bound to perform his guarantee obligations. As noted elsewhere, the principal remedies under the Directive are forms of specific performance, and that is entirely consistent with the civilian tradition from which the guarantee is drawn. However, this may be a relatively insignificant point. As noted earlier, guarantors tend to honour their undertakings as much out of concern for their commercial reputation as legal obligation.

7.4.2.3 *Liability in respect of the guarantee service*

Another consequence follows from the guarantee undertaking being contractual. Where the guarantee contains an undertaking to repair or replace goods the guarantor is now treated as having contracted to provide repair or replacement of the goods. Such an undertaking seems therefore to be an undertaking to supply either services, or goods, or both and, as a contract for the supply of goods and/or services will be subject to the Supply of Goods and Services Act 1982. Any goods supplied must therefore correspond with any description applied to them, be of satisfactory quality and reasonably fit for the buyer's purpose, and comply with any sample by reference to which they are supplied (SGSA sections 3–5), whilst any work performed, such as repair of the original goods, must be performed with reasonable skill and care (SGSA section 13). A further consequence of this and the amendments made to the SGSA is therefore that if goods are replaced pursuant to a guarantee, the replacement goods are supplied under a contract for the transfer of goods and the consumer will be entitled to the rights derived from the Directive, and now contained in Part 1B of the SGSA. Their application in this context may, however, raise difficulties. If the replacement goods are not in conformity with the contract of supply, the consumer will be entitled to have them repaired or replaced, but it is difficult to see how the remedies of price reduction and rescission can be applied where goods have been supplied pursuant to a guarantee.

Where goods are repaired under a guarantee, if defective parts are supplied the contract will arguably be one for supply and installation of goods (the replacement parts) for the purposes of the Directive, so that, again, the consumer will be entitled to rights derived from the Directive in respect of the repair.

This result seems to have been unintended. It certainly could have some curious consequences. For instance, suppose that a manufacturer offers a 12-month guarantee of his products. The goods break down after ten months and the consumer chooses to claim under the guarantee rather than pursuing the retailer under the contract of sale—perhaps because on these facts in a claim against the retailer he would bear the burden of proving that the lack of conformity existed at the time of delivery of the goods. The manufacturer supplies a replacement. The manufacturer is now potentially liable to repair or replace the replacement for a period of a further six years in accordance with the UK implementation of the Directive.

Now suppose that the manufacturer repairs the goods rather than replacing them. The manufacturer will be subject to the terms implied by sections 3–5 and 13 SGSA which require that any spare parts provided must comply with their description, be of satisfactory quality and fit for their purpose, and that the repair is carried out with reasonable skill and care. This will again lead to the result that the manufacturer will be potentially liable for six years for the standard of repair, as well as for the performance of the spare parts.

The result is that as soon as a remedy is provided in response to a consumer's claim under a manufacturer's guarantee, the guarantor's obligations are extended beyond the duration of the original guarantee. Moreover, any attempt to contract out of these liabilities will be subject to the UCTA 1977. Liability under the implied terms in respect of goods supplied, whether as a replacement for the original goods or as a spare part, cannot be excluded or restricted (UCTA section 7), whilst liability in respect of the duty to perform the repair with reasonable skill and care will be subject to UCTA section 2 (see 7.3.3.3).

7.4.3 Relationship with legal rights

The first paragraph of Article 6(2) requiring a clear reference to consumers' legal rights has no equivalent in the SSGCR. However, as noted at 7.3.3 above, the requirements of Article 6(2) are satisfied by existing English provisions in the Consumer Transactions (Restrictions on Statements) Order 1976, regulations 4 and 5, which remain in force. There was therefore no need for any further action by way of implementation of Article 6(2).

A problem not addressed in the Regulations, which may give rise to practical difficulties, is the relationship between guarantees and the new Part 5A of SOGA 1979 (see chapter 4). Potential problems may arise in the context of guarantees under which the seller assumes the obligation of repairing or replacing defective goods. A consumer may return a faulty item to a seller asking him to repair it, but it may not be clear if this is done pursuant to the guarantee or the seller's obligation under Part 5A. This may, for example, be significant if the seller takes a long time to repair the fault. Under Part 5A, if the seller takes longer than a reasonable time, the consumer may be entitled to price reduction or rescission of the contract of sale, but the same will not apply if the seller is acting under a guarantee.

7.4.4 Disclosure requirements

Regulation 15(2) requires that the guarantee sets out in plain and intelligible language:

The contents of the guarantee and the essential particulars necessary for making claims under the guarantee, notably the duration and territorial scope of the guarantee as well as the name and address of the guarantor.

This reproduces the provision in Article 6(2) of the Consumer Guarantees Directive. The same points made in relation to Article 6(2) also apply here. It would have been helpful if some clarification had been given of what the two key terms, 'contents' and 'essential particulars' might encompass, in addition to the rather limited list of aspects given in this Regulation.

7.4.5 Written availability

Regulations 15(3) and (4) state that a guarantor and any other person offering to consumers the goods which are the subject of the guarantee for sale or supply must, on request, make the guarantee available in writing or in another durable medium available and accessible to the consumer. This has to be done within a reasonable time. The difficulties with defining 'durable medium' were considered above at 7.2.5.1. In the absence of a definition in the SSGCR, the observations made in the context of Article 6(3) are therefore equally applicable here.

The language of regulation 15(3) closely follows that of Article 6(3) of the Directive. However, the SSGCR deviate in one respect from Article 6(3) of the Directive in that they specify the persons who are required to make available the guarantee when a consumer so requests. There does not appear to be a significant difference in scope between the two provisions, and regulation 15(3) merely clarifies that this obligation does not rest merely on the seller, but also extends to the guarantor. Some concern was expressed during the pre-implementation consultation that this would require retailers to hold stocks of guarantees. However, this requirement can easily be satisfied by the retailer holding the guarantee on computer so that it can be printed out to meet any requests from consumers. However, regulation 15(4) provides that the obligation to provide the guarantee 'applies to the guarantor and any other person who offers to consumers the goods which are the subject of the guarantee for sale or supply'. We repeat our earlier comments about the meaning of 'consumer' in regulation 15. The last part of regulation 15(4), ' any person who . . . sale or supply', seems to be wide enough to apply to a private sale as, for instance, where goods covered by a guarantee are sold second-hand.

The Regulations take up the option offered in the Directive (above 7.2.4) and require that where goods with a consumer guarantee are offered (presumably, although the Regulations do not say, for sale or supply) in the UK the guarantor must ensure that the guarantee is written in English.

The practical application of these provisions may be limited, because few consumers ask to see a guarantee before making a purchase, and the number of consumers who will take note of a guarantee in the absence of a defect is similarly small. Still, as noted at 7.2.5, there are several circumstances both before and after purchase where this provision may be relevant.

7.4.5.1 *Written availability and distance selling*

In the context of distance selling contracts, the obligation in regulation 15(3) overlaps with regulation 8 of the Consumer Protection (Distance Selling) Regulations 2002. This requires *inter alia* that a consumer is given information about any aftersales service and guarantees given on goods bought at a distance, in writing or in another durable medium available and accessible to him, either before the contract has been concluded or, at the latest, at the time of delivery of the goods. Presumably, a guarantee supplied to a consumer in response to a request under regulation 15(3) SSGCR will also satisfy the requirement in regulation 8 of the Distance Selling Regulations. However, even where no request is made under regulation 15(3) SSGCR, there is still an obligation under regulation 8 to provide the consumer with this information anyway. It may be that a guarantee card enclosed with the goods suffices, but the difficulty with this would be that the obligation under regulation 8 is on the *supplier* of the goods, whereas the guarantee card will usually have been prepared by the manufacturer. In that case, a supplier may have to provide additional information to a consumer, although this would almost certainly merely duplicate the information already provided by the manufacturer in the guarantee card itself. In addition, where details of a guarantee have been supplied in accordance with regulation 8 there seems to be nothing to prevent the consumer requesting a further copy of the guarantee under regulation 15 SSGCR 2002. There is indeed nothing in the latter provision to prevent the consumer demanding multiple copies of the guarantee. This overlap between the two measures is unfortunate, in particular because it is doubtful that information provided on a web site would fulfil either requirement (see the discussion at 7.2.5.1).

7.4.6 Enforcement

A failure to comply with the requirements of regulation 15 will be subject to regulatory enforcement under Part 8 of the Enterprise Act 2002, provided that it causes harm to the collective interests of consumers.

Regulations 15(6) and 15(7) of the SSGCR provide a further basis for regulatory enforcement of the implementing provisions. Regulation 15(6) specifies that an enforcement authority (defined in regulation 2 as the DGFT (now OFT) and every weights and measures authority) may apply for an injunction. Under regulation 15(7), a court may grant an injunction on terms it thinks fit. This provision would allow regulatory enforcement authorities to apply for an injunction without having to satisfy the requirement that the collective interests of consumers are harmed or that the guarantor has persisted in conduct which amounts to a failure to comply with regulation 15. At this stage, it is not possible to say how this provision will operate in practice. This enforcement mechanism seems to be more readily available than that under the Enterprise Act. It is not clear if in practice, the enforcement authorities will only intervene if there are several complaints about a particular guarantor, and even then it seems probable that attempts will be made to persuade the guarantor to amend his guarantee or to give undertakings to the enforcement authority to do so.

7.5 COMMENTARY AND CONCLUSIONS

Guarantees clearly provide a useful route for dealing with faulty goods, but they are capable of abuse. The Directive seeks to balance consumer protection with competition. On the one hand, guarantors are given a deal of freedom to determine the scope of the guarantees they offer, subject only to a requirement that the legal rights of consumers under sales law are not restricted in any way. On the other hand, if guarantees are to be a vehicle for competition, consumers must be able to make an informed choice between them. They must therefore be given as much information as possible about what a particular guarantee has to offer, and should be enabled to compare different guarantees. Article 6 of the Directive seems to achieve these balancing objectives. However, Article 6 is phrased in rather vague and general terms, and there are several questions about the correct interpretation of its provisions. Its implementation in regulation 15 has not served to clarify any of these matters. Moreover, it is important to appreciate that the provisions on guarantees in the Directive/SSGCR do not constitute the full extent of the legal rules applicable to guarantees. In particular the Unfair Terms in Consumer Contracts Regulations 1999 play an important role in regulating the substance of guarantees and to some extent curtail the freedom of guarantors to determine the scope of the guarantees they offer.

8

MANUFACTURERS' LIABILITY

8.1 INTRODUCTION

As will be clear from the preceding chapters, the Directive places primary responsibility for product quality on the contractual supplier—in effect in most consumer contexts, the retailer. The Commission's original *Green Paper* actually proposed a much more radical scheme under which manufacturers would have been jointly and severally liable with retailers for goods' conformity with the contract, so that in the event of goods not being in conformity the consumer would have had a choice of potential defendants from whom to seek redress. Ultimately, as we have seen, that radical proposal was not pursued in the Directive which adopted a traditional contractual liability scheme.

Nevertheless, although most of the provisions in the Directive are of primary relevance to retailers (final sellers), some of its provisions impact directly on manufacturers. Principal among them are the provisions on guarantees, examined in the preceding chapter.

At present therefore the manufacturer has no direct liability under the Directive for product quality unless he chooses to give a guarantee. However, that is not the whole picture. First, a retailer or other supplier who is held liable to a consumer may be able to seek redress, in turn, from his contractual supplier who, similarly may seek redress from *his* supplier and so on, and thus, by a series of contractual claims, liability may be passed back up the distribution chain ultimately to the manufacturer and the Directive seems to require that such a right of recourse be available to the seller. Second, although there is no direct liability on manufacturers under the Directive, a manufacturer may be held liable for defects in goods on other legal bases in either domestic or EC law, and the Directive expressly states that its provisions are without prejudice to any other rights the consumer may invoke under national law governing contractual or non-contractual liability (Article 8(1)). Finally, the Commission is required to prepare a report on the Directive by July 2006, which should, in particular, consider the case for introducing direct manufacturer liability. Manufacturers may therefore eventually be exposed to claims from two directions:

(a) from a seller who has had to provide a remedy to a consumer and now seeks to recover the cost of doing so; and

(b) from the consumer who has bought non-conforming goods.

8.2 PROVISIONS IN THE DIRECTIVE OF RELEVANCE TO MANUFACTURERS

As noted above, the provisions of the Directive of most relevance to manufacturers are probably those in Article 6 on guarantees. If the manufacturer chooses to give a guarantee of the goods within the terms of the Directive, the guarantee will be binding on him in accordance with Article 6 of the Directive, as discussed in chapter 7, above. The Directive does not however require the manufacturer to give a guarantee at all. Thus although the Directive does not impose liability for product quality on the manufacturer it does not prohibit his voluntarily assuming such liability. There are, however, other provisions of the Directive which have some impact on manufacturers.

8.2.1 Article 2—Conformity with the contract

Although a manufacturer is not directly liable for a lack of conformity, his actions may be relevant in establishing whether goods are in conformity. Not only is the manufacturer likely to be responsible for defects in the goods, whether originating in their design or the manufacture of the particular item, but in addition the manufacturer is likely to be primarily responsible for the promotion of the goods through advertising and so on which will often be the main factors shaping the consumer's expectations of the goods. The role of the manufacturer's promotion of the goods in shaping the consumer's expectations is recognised in Article 2(2)(d) of the Directive which provides that one aspect of the goods' conformity with the contract is that they

Show the quality and performance which are normal in goods of the same type and which the consumer can reasonably expect, given the nature of the goods and taking into account *any public statements on the specific characteristics of the goods made about them by the seller, the producer or his representative, particularly in advertising or on labelling* [emphasis added].

Article 2 thus recognises that the manufacturer's actions may play a crucial role in defining the consumer's expectations. Nevertheless liability for the goods' failure to satisfy those expectations is imposed not on the manufacturer but on the retail seller. Perhaps in recognition of the potential iniquity of this the Directive permits the seller to avoid liability for the goods' failure to conform to the manufacturer's statements if he shows that

(a) he was not, and could not reasonably have been, aware of the statement in question; or

(b) by the time of conclusion of the contract the statement had been corrected; or

(c) the consumer's decision to buy the goods could not have been influenced by the statement. (Article 3)

However, although primary responsibility for the goods' failure to match up to expectations created by the manufacturer's statements falls on the seller, manufacturers should bear in mind that their public statements about goods can give rise to liability, not least because where a seller is held liable on this basis he is likely to seek to pass that liability back to the manufacturer.

8.2.2 Article 4—'Pass Back' liability

As we have noted above, in the modern marketing context the retail seller's role will often be little more than that of an intermediary between consumer and manufacturer. The goods will be delivered to the retailer in sealed packaging and resold without being opened or tested. The origins of most instances of non-conformity will be the actions the manufacturer, and, as we have noted above, in the modern marketing environment the same is true whether the non-conformity consists of a defect in the particular item or a failure to live up to the consumer's expectations, shaped largely by mass-media advertising. However, although the retailer is the person primarily liable to the consumer under the Directive, the Directive recognises the manufacturer's responsibility for most cases of non-conformity. Article 4 provides that:

Where the final seller is liable to the consumer because of a lack of conformity resulting from an act or omission by the producer, a previous seller in the same chain of contracts or any other intermediary, the final seller shall be entitled to pursue remedies against the person or persons liable in the contractual chain. The person or persons liable against whom the final seller may pursue remedies, together with the relevant actions and conditions of exercise, shall be determined by national law.

This provision seems to recognise the iniquity of imposing front-line liability on the seller. A final seller who is liable to a consumer for a lack of conformity resulting from an act by somebody higher up in the distribution chain is, in principle, entitled to bring a claim against that person. As noted above, in most cases, that person will be the manufacturer himself. Unfortunately, however, the scope of Article 4 is the subject of some controversy. The problem lies in the last sentence of Article 4 which states that the persons against whom the seller may claim and the conditions on which this may be done is for the Member States to determine. As a result it is not clear to what extent national law may restrict, or permit exclusion of, the retail seller's right of redress. We return to this question in chapter 9. For present purposes it is sufficient to note that one of the ways in which a manufacturer may be held ultimately responsible for goods' lack of conformity is by liability thus being passed back up the distribution chain by a retail seller seeking indemnity against his liability to the consumer.

8.2.3 Article 12—Consideration of direct producer liability

Article 12 of the Directive requires that the Commission review the application of the Directive by 7 July 2006 and submit a report on its operation to the Council and Parliament. Crucially, this report should examine 'the case for introducing the producer's direct liability'. Although it is difficult to second-guess the Commission's position on this (after all, the proposals in the *Green Paper* were significantly watered down by the time the first draft directive appeared), the main arguments for and against manufacturer liability are briefly considered below (see 8.4).

8.3 THE POSITION IN DOMESTIC LAW

There are several bases on which a manufacturer may be held directly liable to the ultimate consumer of his products under existing domestic law. We have considered the manufacturer's liability on any guarantee he provides in the preceding chapter. In particular, we noted that once a manufacturer has dealt with a claim by a consumer under a guarantee, he may be liable for the repair or replacement provided in accordance with the SGSA 1982 (see 7.4.2.3).

However, even in the absence of such a guarantee a manufacturer or other producer may be held liable to a consumer for losses caused by defective goods either under the product liability regime of the Consumer Protection Act 1987 or in the tort of negligence according to the principle of *Donoghue v Stevenson*. In addition, although a manufacturer who does not sell direct to consumers is not normally in a direct contractual relationship with the ultimate purchasers of his products unless he chooses to give a guarantee, a manufacturer's statements about his goods, including statements in advertising, may in certain circumstances be construed as giving rise to a direct contractual relationship between manufacturer and ultimate purchaser.

As noted above, the Directive is expressed to be without prejudice to any other contractual or non-contractual rights available to the consumer under domestic law (Article 8(1)) so that these heads of liability continue to be relevant.

8.3.1 Tortious liability

It has been established since the landmark decision in *Donoghue v Stevenson* [1932] AC 562 that a manufacturer of a defective product which causes injury or damage to the end user can be held liable for that injury or damage in the tort of negligence notwithstanding the lack of privity between them. However, in order to establish a claim on this basis the claimant must prove that the defendant was negligent. Since 1987, however, manufacturers have been subject to a system of strict liability for injury or damage caused by defective products under the Consumer Protection Act 1987.

8.3.1.1 *Liability under the Consumer Protection Act 1987, Part I*
The 1987 Act was passed to implement EC Directive 85/374/EEC on liability for defective products, which introduced a system of strict producer liability for injury and damage caused by defective products. In essence the Act enables a person who suffers loss or injury as a result of a defective product to hold the producer of that product strictly liable for the loss or injury. The claimant is therefore able to recover damages from the producer without proving negligence. A product is defective for this purpose if its safety is 'not such as persons generally are entitled to expect', safety for this purpose including the risk of damage to other property as well as the risk of personal injury (CPA 1987 section 3). In assessing what persons generally are entitled to expect the court is required to take into account 'all the circumstances' including:

(a) the manner in which and purposes for which the product has been marketed; its get up, the use of any mark in relation to the product and any instructions for, or warnings with respect to, doing or refraining from doing anything with or in relation to the product;

(b) what might reasonably be expected to be done with or in relation to the product;

(c) the time when the product was supplied by its producer to another. (section 3(2))

Liability for defects is imposed not only on manufacturers but on 'producers', as defined, including

• the manufacturer of a finished product or, in certain circumstances, of a component part of a finished product;

• in the case of a non-manufactured product, the person who 'won or abstracted' it;

• in the case of a product which was neither manufactured nor abstracted but 'essential characteristics of which are attributable to an industrial or other process having been carried out', any person responsible for that process;

• any person who, 'by putting his name on the product or using a trade mark or other distinguishing mark in relation to the product, has held himself out to be the producer';

• any person who imported the product into the European Community.

In addition, in certain circumstances, any person who supplied the product—at any stage in the supply chain—may be held liable, unless when requested by a person who suffers damage caused by the product he is able to identify the producer, importer, 'own-brander' or his own supplier.

A claim under the Act can only be brought for (a) death or personal injury or (b) damage to personal property—that is, property of a description 'ordinarily intended for private use, occupation or consumption' and actually so intended by the person making the claim, and no claim can be brought for damage to property unless the total claim exceeds £275 (section 5). Most importantly of all, a claim cannot be made for damage to or diminution in the value of the defective product itself (or for an item of which the defective product is a component). A claim cannot therefore be made simply on the basis that the consumer has purchased goods of substandard quality unless they cause injury or damage to other property. Moreover, the exclusion of claims for property damage where the total claim is below £275 means that many small consumer claims about damage done by defective products will fall outside the Act. For instance, if a defective washing machine damages a load of clothes the claim may fall below the threshold leaving the consumer unable to invoke the 1987 Act.

Liability under the Act is strict. It is not absolute. Section 4 of the Act makes a number of defences available. In particular it is a defence for a defendant to show that he did not supply the product in question, or to show that the defect did not exist in the product at the time he supplied it (section 4). In addition the Act creates a so-called 'development risks' defence (section 4(1)(e)), according to which it is a defence to show that at the time the defendant supplied the product to any other person

the state of scientific and technical knowledge . . . was not such that a producer of products of the same description as the product in question might be expected to have discovered it if it had existed in his products while they were under his control. (section 4(1)(e))

Liability arising under the Act cannot be excluded or limited by any contract term or notice.

It took almost a decade before the first case under the Act was reported. Since then, however, there have been several reported decisions, including one of the Court of Appeal. In *Abouzaid v Mothercare (UK) Ltd.* [2000] All ER (D) 2436 a twelve-year-old boy was helping his mother attach a child's sleeping bag to a pushchair when an elastic strap slipped and injured his eye. His vision in the eye was permanently impaired. The defendant argued that as there was no record of any similar accident in professional literature or DTI accident records at the time of the accident—

(a)   the product was not defective within the meaning of the Act at the time it was marketed, or, if it was

(b) that the development risks defence should be available.

The Court of Appeal held that the product was defective, primarily because of the lack of adequate warnings about the propensity of an elastic strap to recoil under tension. A strap which created a risk of serious injury was not as safe as consumers generally were entitled to expect. Importantly, the Court emphasised that the reasonableness of the defendant's action in preventing a defect could not be relevant to the question whether the product was defective. The Court also held that, notwithstanding the absence of any record of a similar incident at the time the product was marketed, the defendant could not rely on the development risks defence. The absence of any reported accident did not make the defect undiscoverable. The development risks defence depends on the level of 'scientific and technical knowledge' and the absence of accident records was not 'scientific and technical knowledge'. The risk was technically discoverable by a manufacturer of similar products when the product was marketed and it clearly would have been possible to carry out appropriate tests. Otherwise producers would be encouraged not to test their products but to rely on the development risks defence. It is submitted that this approach is correct. In particular it should be noted that the 'development risks' defence as provided for in the CPA differs from that in the Directive, which is stricter. It provides that the defence is available where 'the state of scientific and technical knowledge at the time when [the producer] put the product into circulation was not such as to enable the defect to be discovered'. The emphasis is therefore on discoverability in absolute terms, rather than discoverability by the producer. The domestic legislation must therefore be construed so as to be consistent with the Directive.

The most detailed analysis of the Act to date was given in *A and others v The National Blood Authority* [2001] 3 All ER 289 where the court again considered the meaning of 'defect' and the development risks defence. Over 100 claimants had received blood transfusions with blood contaminated with the Hepatitis-C virus. The Authority argued that although at the time of supply the risk of contamination was known there was at that time no effective test to discover whether a particular batch was contaminated, and that therefore either (a) the blood was not defective because the risk of contamination was unavoidable and the blood was therefore as safe as consumers were entitled to expect, or (b) the development risks defence should apply because the state of scientific and technical knowledge was not such as to allow the defect to be discovered. Burton J rejected both arguments. In holding that the blood was defective the court drew a distinction between 'standard' and 'non-standard' products. A 'standard' product is one which meets the design and safety requirements intended by the producer. A 'non-standard' product is a particular unit of the product which does not meet that standard. Contaminated blood was a non-standard product. In passing we may note that if it is possible to draw such a distinction, it becomes significantly easier to establish that a particular unit is defective, and the claimant's task of proving defectiveness is less daunting. The claimant's task is more difficult where it is alleged that the 'standard' product is defective, because it is then impossible to compare a particular unit with the product generally to consider whether the unit which the consumer complaints about is 'non-standard' and therefore defective.

Burton J accepted that in assessing whether a product is defective the list of factors in section 3 is not exhaustive and that other factors may be relevant, but held that 'avoidability' of the defect is not a relevant factor, because to take it into account would undermine the purpose of the Directive, which is to allow the consumer to recover without proof of fault or negligence. The crucial question is whether the product is as safe as consumers generally are entitled to expect. Here the public was not aware of the risk of hepatitis contamination. The public therefore had a legitimate expectation that blood products would be free of the risk of contamination. (With the possibility of an appeal in mind Burton J did consider the alternative, that 'avoidability' could be relevant, and concluded that, even if that were the case, further steps could have been taken to avoid contaminated blood being used. Even if avoidability had been relevant, the product would therefore still have been defective.)

In relation to the development risks defence the defendant argued that since at the time the products in question were put into circulation there was no satisfactory test to discover viral infection, 'the state of scientific and technical knowledge' at the relevant time was 'not such that a producer of products of the same description as the product in question might be expected to have discovered it if it had existed in his products while they were under his control'. Burton J rejected this argument. Basing himself on the Directive he took the view that the development risks defence was concerned with the discoverability of a defect in a particular class of products, rather than in any one particular product. He accepted that information will only be relevant to the assessment of the state of 'scientific and technical knowledge' if it is accessible. Unpublished research or research retained within a particular company or group of companies was not accessible. Research published in little-known publications in remote countries might also not be regarded as accessible, although the availability of information via the Internet had made this an unlikely basis for a successful defence. However, in the present case, testing for Hepatitis-C had been possible, although not adopted by the defendant until some time after it had become available, and the defence therefore failed. The consequence of this approach is to restrict the availability of the development risks defence, especially where the claim relates to a 'non-standard' product. Once the potential existence of a defect in a particular class of product is known the defence is no longer available. The producer must then take steps to eliminate the defect or continue to supply the product at its own risk.

Finally, in *Sam Bogle and others v McDonald's Restaurants Ltd* ([2002] EWHC 490 (QB), 25 March 2002) the claimant sought damages for injuries caused by spillage of a hot drink served in a polystyrene cup. The court held that the product was not defective, because consumers could be expected to know that hot drinks would cause a serious injury if spilled on someone. It had been argued that the cups could have been designed to minimise the risk of tipping over, but this was rejected. The cups were supplied with lids. Although some precautions could be taken against the risk of spillage, the only real means of prevention would be not to sell hot drinks at all, or to sell them at a lower temperature, but this would be unacceptable to most customers. (The Court did not consider the potential liability under the Trade Descriptions Act 1968 for selling a lukewarm drink as a hot drink.)

What emerges from these cases is that the courts are adopting a common sense approach to application of the 1987 Act. In applying the test of 'defectiveness' much emphasis is placed on the reasonable, or legitimate, expectations of consumers. This is readily apparent in *Abouzaid* and *A v National Blood Authority*. At the same time the courts are adopting a strict approach to the development risks defence. Partly as a result there seems to be a degree of convergence between the test of defectiveness under the 1987 Act and the test of satisfactory quality and fitness for purpose under the SoGA 1979 where, as we have suggested earlier, the core test is the consumer's reasonable expectations. The factors listed in section 3 CPA as being relevant to the assessment of 'defectiveness' are also relevant to any assessment whether a product is of 'satisfactory quality' for the purposes of the 1979 Act. Clearly the two concepts are not entirely coterminous. In particular, although safety is relevant to the assessment of quality and fitness under the 1979 Act, that assessment is concerned with a much wider range of factors than merely safety. However, it is submitted that a product which is defective for the purposes of the 1987 Act will generally also be not of satisfactory quality and/or not reasonably fit for its purpose under the 1979 Act. And, conversely, a product which is judged unsatisfactory or unfit on the grounds of safety is likely to be considered defective for the purposes of the 1987 Act. A parallel can perhaps be drawn between *A v National Blood Authority* and the Court of Appeal's decision on satisfactory quality in *Britvic Soft Drinks v Messer UK Ltd* [2002] 1 Lloyd's Rep 20 (HC); [2002] EWCA Civ 548; [2002] 2 All ER Comm 321 (CA) in which the court held that an attempt to exclude the statutory implied terms relating to quality and fitness for purpose in relation to a consignment of carbon dioxide contaminated with benzene, a known carcinogen, was unreasonable because such exclusion would be contrary to a 'fundamental assumption' on the basis of which the parties would have contracted—viz., that the gas would be free of benzene contamination and would be suitable for use in the manufacture of carbonated drinks. In short, the defendants in both cases were liable because the claimants reasonably expected that they were being supplied with products—blood in *National Blood Authority*, carbon dioxide in *Britvic*—which were free of contamination. The most important distinction between the two heads of liability, however, is the categories of loss they cover. As noted above, no liability arises under the 1987 Act on the basis simply that the product delivered is defective. It must cause loss in the form of personal injury or damage to private property. A consumer who buys a defective product which causes injury can therefore proceed under the 1987 Act against the manufacturer. If on the other hand the consumer discovers the defect before it causes injury or damage, his only recourse will be against the seller on the grounds that the product was not of satisfactory quality.

8.3.1.2 Negligence liability

A manufacturer may also incur liability for loss or damage caused by defective products at common law in the tort of negligence. The principle was established in *Donoghue v Stevenson* [1932] AC 562 that:

a manufacturer of products, which he sells in such a form as to show that he intends them to reach the ultimate consumer in the form in which they left him with no reasonable possibility of intermediate examination, and with the knowledge that the absence of reasonable care in the preparation or putting up of the products will result in an injury to the consumer's life or property, owes a duty to that consumer to take reasonable care' [1932] AC 562 at 599.

If breach of that duty results in loss or damage to the consumer—or to any other person—the manufacturer is liable. Such liability does not depend on there being privity of contract between claimant and defendant. The breach of duty may consist of negligence in the manufacture of a particular item, as in *Donoghue v Stevenson* itself, or of negligent design, or failure to provide adequate warnings of dangers or instructions for product use. Although we are here concerned with manufacturers, other parties in the distribution chain may also owe a duty of care to the consumer so that they will be held liable if their failure to take reasonable care results in loss or damage to the consumer. (See, e.g. *Fisher v Harrods Ltd* [1966] 1 Lloyd's Rep 500 (retail distributors); *Goodchild v Vaclight* [1965] CLY 2669 (importers).) The essence of liability is that the defendant negligently put the product into circulation in a defective condition, in circumstances in which there was no probability of their being inspected and the defect discovered before their reaching the ultimate consumer. It is therefore entirely apposite to modern marketing conditions.

Liability under *Donoghue v Stevenson* is however limited by two important restrictions. First, liability is negligence based. The onus is therefore on the claimant to prove that the defendant failed to take reasonable care *and* that that failure caused the claimant's loss. The claimant may sometimes be able to rely on the maxim *res ipsa loquitur* and, effectively, say to the defendant: 'I was injured by this product. Common sense says that wouldn't happen unless you were negligent. Prove that you weren't', and thus transfer the burden of proof to the manufacturer to disprove negligence. In many cases, however, this presumption of negligence may not be available and, especially in cases of allegedly negligent design, the claimant may face an uphill battle to prove negligence.

Second, and most important in the present context, damages will only be awarded on this basis to compensate the claimant for personal injury or for damage to property. The scope of recovery is wider than under the 1987 Act in that damages can be awarded for damage to property other than private property, and with no lower limit. It is, however, now clear that damages will not normally be awarded in negligence for pure economic loss, and therefore no damages will be awarded to compensate for the diminution in value of the defective product itself (see *Murphy v Brentwood DC* [1991] AC 398, [1990] 2 All ER 908, HL).

A claim under the principle of *Donoghue v Stevenson* may therefore provide an alternative to a claim under the CPA 1987, but will generally add little and, because of the need to prove negligence, will generally be a less attractive option. It may be advantageous when it is sought to impose liability on an intermediary in the distribution chain who would not be liable under the CPA, but since importers and own-branders are liable under that Act, it will be relatively rare that a claim is available at common law but not under the Act. A common law claim may be the only option where the claimant wishes to claim for damage to business property but in the consumer context the main relevance of negligence liability now is likely to be where the consumer wishes to make a claim for damage to private property below the Act's £275 threshold.

8.3.2 Contractual liability

The main weakness of tortious claims under the CPA 1987 and the principle of *Donoghue v Stevenson* is that they do not permit recovery for pure economic loss, including for diminution in value of the defective product itself. Such claims are generally regarded as being the province of contract, involving a claim that the consumer did not receive what he expected. In general where goods are supplied through the typical retail distribution system, the consumer does not contract directly with the manufacturer and is thus unable to bring a contractual claim against the manufacturer where the goods are defective or of lower than expected quality and thus lower in value than expected. There is no necessary logic to this system. Had the law developed differently it might have been possible to infer a contract between manufacturer and ultimate consumer consisting of the consumer's agreement to purchase the goods on the strength of an implied under-taking by the former relating to the quality of the goods (see Bradgate and Twigg-Flesner, 2002) but at this stage of the law's development the contractual analysis of the retail distribution system is too well established to be easily disturbed. However, where the manufacturer gives an express undertaking to the consumer it may be possible to construe that undertaking as contractual and thus to bring the parties into privity. In such a case the manufacturer may incur contractual liability for the quality etc. of the goods.

8.3.2.1 *Manufacturers' guarantees*
Although manufacturers are not, at present, generally liable to consumers for quality defects etc. in their products, many manufacturers voluntarily assume a

limited degree of liability by giving a guarantee that, for instance, their goods are free from defects in workmanship and material. As noted in chapter 7, although there were doubts about the enforceability of guarantees at common law, it is now settled that any guarantee given takes effect as a contractual undertaking by the guarantor.

Such guarantees are usually restricted to a limited period after purchase, typically of one year, and cover a more limited range of defects than do the retailer's statutory implied undertakings under the SoGA. Moreover the manufacturer's liability is limited to honouring his undertaking and is generally enforceable only by an award of damages. Thus if, say, the manufacturer guarantees goods free of defects for one year after purchase and undertakes to repair free of charge any defects which appear in that period, the manufacturer will be contractually liable to the consumer if a defect appears in that period and he fails to repair it in accordance with the guarantee. The guarantee will be enforced by an award of damages to the consumer which will cover the costs of having the goods repaired elsewhere.

However, as soon as the manufacturer has provided a remedy under the guarantee to a consumer, he will be subject to the Supply of Goods and Services Act 1982 (see chapter 7). The guarantee will be a contract for services (repair) or the supply of goods (replacement; spare parts), or both, and will therefore be covered by the 1982 Act. So although the manufacturer's initial liability is limited to the duration of the guarantee, once a claim by a consumer has been honoured, liability will extend beyond the guarantee period, at least in respect of the service provided and/or the goods supplied. If goods are replaced in their entirety under the guarantee, the effect of the SGSA is that the manufacturer will then be in the same position as any other supplier under the 1982 Act, and, crucially, will be unable to restrict or exclude his liability for the quality etc. of the goods supplied. (See 7.4.2.3.)

8.3.2.2 *Liability under collateral contracts*
There is no obligation on a manufacturer to give a formal guarantee. A manufacturer who chooses not to do so may nevertheless incur contractual liability if he makes a statement to the ultimate consumer, either directly or, possibly through advertising. If such a statement is construed as involving a contractual undertaking it may be enforced against the manufacturer on its terms as a contractual warranty, and the consumer be awarded damages for its breach. Typically the consumer provides consideration for such an undertaking by buying goods on the strength of it.

Such 'collateral contracts' will not lightly be inferred. They must be proved to a high standard. As Lord Moulton observed in *Heilbut, Symons & Co. v Buckleton* ([1913] AC 30 at p 47) 'Collateral contracts . . . must be proved strictly. Not only the terms of such contracts but the existence of an *animus contrahendi* on the part of all the parties to them must be clearly shown.' Nevertheless in appropriate circumstances it may be possible to establish such a contract. A number of cases have involved undertakings given to consumers contemplating entering into hire-purchase contracts. In the typical hire-purchase situation the consumer negotiates with a dealer but the goods are contractually supplied to the consumer by a finance company to whom the dealer sells the goods. The dealer is therefore not party to the contract of hire-purchase itself. Nevertheless in a number of cases it has been held that the dealer may be held contractually liable on the basis of statements made to the consumer during negotiations on which the consumer relies in entering into the hire-purchase agreement. The consumer provides consideration for the dealer's undertaking by entering into the hire-purchase contract, thereby conferring a benefit on the dealer. In *Brown v Sheens and Richmond Car Sales* ([1950] 1 All ER 1102), motor car dealers assured the claimant that a car was in perfect condition and 'good for thousands of trouble-free miles'. Relying on that statement the consumer entered into a hire-purchase agreement for the car. The car was in anything but perfect condition and required substantial repairs. It was held that the dealers had given an express contractual warranty as to the condition of the car which had induced the consumer to enter into the hire-purchase agreement, which took effect as a contract between the dealer and the consumer. A similar case is *Andrews v Hopkinson* ([1957] 1 QB 229) where the consumer was told that a particular second-hand car was 'a good little bus'. This was also a collateral warranty to the hire-purchase agreement, because the consumer would not have contracted for the car without the warranty.

It is clear that a manufacturer's statements can give rise to liability on the same basis. In *Shanklin Pier v Detel Products Ltd* ([1951] 2 KB 854), Detel made representations to the owners of Shanklin Pier about the quality of their paint. Relying on those representations the pier owners instructed contractors to use Detel's paint to re-paint the pier. The paint failed to live up to Detel's claims. It was held that Detel's representations were a collateral warranty in favour of the owners. The owners supplied consideration for that undertaking by instructing the contractors to use Detel's paint, and Detel were therefore liable in damages for breach of that warranty. Similarly in *Wells (Merstham) Ltd v Buckland Sand and Silica Ltd* ([1965] 2 QB 170) the defendants stated that a particular type of sand was suitable for the claimant's business. The claimants then placed an order for that type of sand with another supplier. Nevertheless, the defendants' statement constituted an express warranty.

These cases concerned statements targeted at a particular customer. More typically a consumer's purchasing decision will be based on manufacturers' general promotional statements made through advertising and the like. The normal rule is that an advertisement that goods are for sale is not an offer to sell those goods, it being presumed that the advertiser does not intend to enter into a contractual commitment to sell to anyone who responds to the advertisement (*Partridge v Crittenden* ([1968] 2 All ER 421). However, there is no reason why a promotional statement in advertising should not be contractual if its language is sufficiently clear to indicate an intention, on an objective analysis, to enter into a contractual obligation. The classic example of such a contract is of course the decision in *Carlill v Carbolic Smoke Ball Company* ([1893] 1 QB 256), where it was held that an advertisement in which the manufacturers of the smoke ball promised users of the smoke ball a reward of £100 if they contracted influenza gave rise to a contract between the manufacturer and a purchaser of the ball. Objectively read, the advertisement constituted an offer. As Bowen LJ put it:

[The advertisement] was intended to be issued to the public and to be read by the public. How would an ordinary person reading this document construe it?

The consumer accepted and provided consideration for that offer by purchasing the smoke ball. A similar analysis was adopted in *Wood v Letrik* ((1932) (The Times LR, 12 January 1932)), where an advertisement promised that the defendant's electric comb would cure grey hair after 10 days' use and guaranteed that £500 would be paid if it failed to do so. The judge rejected claims that reliance had been unreasonable and that the plaintiff did not use the comb properly and held the defendant's undertaking enforceable. In *Esso Petroleum Co. Ltd v Customs and Excise Commissioners* ([1976] 1 WLR 1), a sales promotion promised that any customer purchasing four gallons of the defendant's petrol would receive a 'coin' bearing the image of one of the members of the England 1970 World Cup Squad. A majority of the House of Lords held that this could give rise to a collateral contract. The advertisement was clearly promissory and would be considered by a reasonable consumer to be intended to be legally binding. The consumer provided consideration for the undertaking by entering into the main contract to purchase the petrol.

   These cases suggest that in an appropriate case promotional statements could give rise to a collateral contract between manufacturer and ultimate consumer. However, in *Lambert v Lewis* ([1982] AC 225), the manufacturer of towing hitches had claimed in advertising leaflets that its towing hitches were fool-proof and required no maintenance. A claim was made against the manufacturer when one of the towing hitches failed in use. The Court of Appeal held that the manufacturer's statement was not intended to be legally binding. *Shanklin Pier* and *Wells v Buckland* were distinguished, because in each of those cases the relevant statement was given to a particular person to enter into a particular contract. In both cases there had been an express (oral) statement to the subsequent purchaser, in a situation in which both parties were clearly contemplating the conclusion of a specific contract. This was not the case where a manufacturer used general advertising, because no specific contract would be in his contemplation.

   Nevertheless, this does not mean that advertising statements can never be contractual. More recently, in *Bowerman v Association of British Travel Agents (ABTA)* ([1996] CLC 451) the Court of Appeal held that publicity material could give rise to a legally enforceable obligation. ABTA travel agents displayed a notice in their offices describing ABTA's scheme of protection against financial failure of ABTA members. Ms Bowerman claimed that this notice constituted a contractual offer by ABTA to those who booked their holidays through an ABTA agent to protect them financially should the agent go out of business. The Court of Appeal by a majority accepted Ms Bowerman's arguments. The majority, applying *Carlill*, found that the wording of the notice was sufficiently precise to form the basis of a contract and evidenced sufficient intention to create legal relations. Consideration was provided by the consumer by entering into a contract with an ABTA member.

It is clear therefore that in an appropriate case a manufacturer's statements about goods could give rise to a 'collateral contract' between advertiser and ultimate consumer, whereby the manufacturer would be contractually bound by the advertising claim. It will be relatively easy to find consideration to support such a contract in the consumer's entering into a contract to purchase the relevant product. The decisive factor will be whether or not the manufacturer's statement was intended to be legally binding. Many modern advertising claims will fail to satisfy this requirement, being either insufficiently precise, or of such a nature that a reasonable consumer would not think them intended to be legally binding (for instance because obviously intended to be humorous). Nevertheless should a manufacturer make claims for his products of sufficiently precise nature, the conceptual framework exists to hold the manufacturer contractually bound by such claims. Where the manufacturer's statement consists of an undertaking to replace or repair the goods, or to refund the price or otherwise to handle the goods in a particular way the statement will qualify as a guarantee for the purposes of the SSGCR and will therefore be binding on the basis of regulation 15 without the need to satisfy the common law requirements for contract formation. It is submitted, however, that this will only be the case where the statement in question consists of an 'undertaking' and where it is sufficiently certain that a reasonable person would take it seriously and think it intended to create a legal obligation. In other words, an (objectively assessed) intention to undertake a legal obligation is likely to be crucial under the Regulations as well as at common law. There will still however be a role for the common law. Undertakings such as those in *Carlill*, *Detel* and *Wells* would all fall outside the scope of the SSGCR definition of 'guarantee' and would therefore be binding, if at all, as 'collateral' contracts.

8.4 ARTICLE 12—CONSIDERATION OF DIRECT PRODUCER LIABILITY

There are then already several bases on which a manufacturer of a defective product may incur liability to the ultimate end-user of it. Nevertheless, in the normal run of cases the manufacturer will not be directly liable to the consumer simply for product *quality* (except, probably, for goods replaced under a voluntary guarantee—see 8.3.2.1 above, and 7.4.2.3) so that where the consumer's only claim is that the product itself is sub-standard or defective primary liability will fall on the retailer with whom the consumer is in privity. Although the retailer may be able to pass that liability back to his supplier, who may in turn pass liability back to *his* supplier and so on, so that ultimately liability may pass back along the contractual chain to the manufacturer, that process is circuitous and may break down.

As we have noted, although the Directive ultimately did not pursue the proposal in the Green Paper to impose on manufacturers liability for product quality, it requires the Commission by 2006 to review the operation of the Directive and to produce a report considering, in particular, the case for introduction of a system of manufacturer liability (Article 12; see also Recital 23). Clearly the Commission's recommendation is likely to be influenced by a range of political and economic factors, but we propose here to consider some of the arguments for and against the introduction of a system of manufacturer liability. (See generally Bradgate and Twigg-Flesner, 2002.)

8.4.1 The case for seller liability

It will be useful first briefly to highlight the arguments in favour of the system of seller liability. The arguments below would apply with equal force whether the seller be liable solely or jointly with the manufacturer.

First, the system is familiar and well established. It is, as the Directive observes (Recital 9) 'the traditional system enshrined in the legal orders of the Member States'. Many consumers are aware that if they are sold goods which do not conform to the contract of sale they have a right of redress against the seller.

Second, the system will often provide the consumer with the most practical means to obtain redress. The seller will often be geographically more accessible to the consumer than is the manufacturer. The majority of consumer purchases are still made in face-to-face transactions, often relatively close to the consumer's home. There is, of course, a growing trend towards Internet shopping, and 'shopping abroad', but such distance transactions are unlikely to replace the more traditional forms of shopping. That being so, it will often be more convenient for the consumer to return to the shop where he bought the goods, rather than to have to deal with a remote manufacturer. This may be especially important in the context of the Directive with its emphasis on the remedies of repair and replacement. Moreover, it will often be easier to resolve a dispute by face-to-face negotiation with the local seller than over the telephone. It may also be argued that sellers already deal with consumers on a day-to-day basis and therefore have staff trained in advising consumers. It will be easier for such staff to deal with consumer complaints about faulty goods and to suggest how to deal with such a problem than for a manufacturer to train specialist staff to do so. This argument must not however be overstated. Although manufacturers might incur some initial cost setting up complaints departments, that would be a one-off expense. In so far as there would be a continuing expense it can be argued that it would be economically wasteful to have two sets of staff trained to deal with the same complaints. It must however be borne in mind that that is already the case. A manufacturer who gives a guarantee must have complaints and claims handling procedures and staff, and even if the manufacturer chooses not to give a guarantee it will normally be necessary to have staff trained to deal with consumer complaints. Regardless of the legal position many consumers faced with defective goods will tend to approach the manufacturer with complaints.

The justification normally given for seller liability is that the seller thus acts as a conduit through which liability can be channelled back up the distribution chain to the manufacturer. Thus it is said that although the retailer may not be responsible for the defect in the goods or the consumer's expectation, he provides a convenient route for the consumer to obtain redress and suffers no real injustice since he is able to recoup his losses by means of a claim against his seller.

8.4.2 Arguments against exclusive seller liability

The 'seller as conduit' argument has some force as long as the seller *is* able to pass back liability along the distribution chain. However, the chain may break down for a number of reasons. One or more of the prior parties in the chain may exclude or limit his liability for breach of contract, possibly preventing the seller passing back liability, or preventing liability reaching the manufacturer ultimately responsible. The chain may break for other reasons. Even if a claim is not excluded by contract, it may be barred by limitation, or the retailer may find that his claim for indemnity is subject to different conditions from the consumer's claim against him. Or the chain may break because one or more of the parties in the chain is insolvent.

The best argument for imposing some liability on the manufacturer is the obvious one. The manufacturer will generally be the person ultimately responsible for the consumer's complaint. That will obviously be the case where the consumer complains that the goods are defective, due to defective manufacture or design. The retailer, who receives goods in sealed packages and sells them on in the same condition, is not only not responsible for any defect but will generally have no realistic opportunity of discovering that defect. Recognition of the reality of the roles of manufacturer and retailer—often no more than a conduit through whom the goods reach the consumer—in modern commerce underpins the imposition on manufacturers of liability for damage caused by defective products at common law in *Donoghue v Stevenson* and by statute in the Consumer Protection Act 1987. Even when the consumer's complaint is not that the product is defective but simply that it fails to live up to expectation—as where it is unfit for his intended purpose, does not correspond with description or simply fails to perform as expected—it will often be the manufacturer who, through his advertising and promotion, has created the consumer's expectation. The role of the manufacturer's promotional statements in shaping the consumer's expectation is explicitly recognised in the Directive in Article 2(2)(d), albeit for the purpose of imposing liability on the seller. It seems anomalous to recognise the role such statements play and yet to deny the consumer a right of action against the party responsible.

From the consumer perspective there may be circumstances where it is easier to pursue a claim against the manufacturer than against the retailer. In the worst-case scenario the retailer may be insolvent or have gone out of business. Or the retailer may simply be inaccessible. Although face-to-face transactions may remain the norm, distance transactions are growing in significance. Consumers are increasingly encouraged to shop abroad. Indeed, one of the objectives of the Directive is to encourage consumers to make use of the Single Market. In that context the manufacturer may be no less accessible, and often be more readily accessible, than the retailer. (Significantly in this regard Recital 13 states that, 'in order to enable consumers to take advantage of the internal market and to buy consumer goods in another Member State' it should be recommended that producers of consumer goods attach to the product a list with at least one contact address in every Member State where the product is marketed.) Or, quite simply, the consumer may have forgotten where a particular item was purchased. After all, the decision to purchase a particular brand or model may be based on a range of factors, including manufacturer's reputation or advertising. Thereafter the consumer may shop around different retailers in search of the best terms but have no real preference where he buys so long as the price is right (see Beale (1996), p 141). In this context it is worth bearing in mind that a claim may be brought under the Directive for a lack of conformity which becomes apparent in the period of up to two years from the date of delivery.

Nor would a system of manufacturer liability impose huge extra liabilities on manufacturers. They are already liable on several bases, as we have outlined above. In particular, they are already strictly liable for damages for injuries and property damage caused by defective products, claims for which will far exceed in value, if not in number, product quality claims. We have observed above that goods which are defective will often also not be of satisfactory quality or in conformity with the contract of sale. They will often voluntarily undertake liability for product quality by providing a guarantee. And, of course, in many cases even though not directly liable to the consumer, liability will be passed back to them via the distribution chain.

These are powerful arguments for a system of manufacturer liability for product quality. In addition, it has been suggested (see e.g. NCC, 1989; and *cf.* Bradgate and Twigg-Flesner, 2002) that imposing such liability on manufacturers could have the long-term benefit of raising overall quality standards. The exposure to product quality liability could provide an incentive for manufacturers to invest in quality improvements and reduce instances of liability.

That said, seller liability is probably too well known and too well established to be abolished. In addition where goods are imported from outside the EU it will generally be easier for the consumer to pursue a claim against the seller present within the EU than to have to claim against a distant manufacturer. If, then, there is a case for manufacturer liability for product quality, we would suggest that in the interests of consumer protection it should be a system of joint and several liability, allowing the consumer to choose against which of the parties to pursue remedies.

8.4.3 What should be the extent of manufacturer liability?

The arguments presented above are in themselves strong reasons for imposing at least some direct liability for product quality on manufacturers. In particular, such a system would avoid many of the problems consumers encounter as a result of the changing nature of consumer transactions. But what should be the extent of such liability? As discussed in the preceding chapters, the seller's liability under the Directive consists of delivering goods which are not in conformity with the contract. In domestic law it covers failure of the goods to correspond with their description, to be of satisfactory quality and to be fit for any particular purpose for which the consumer requires the goods.

There may appear to be some conceptual difficulty in holding the manufacturer liable for goods failing to be in conformity with the contract. After all, *ex hypothesi* there is no contract between manufacturer and consumer. But this is a purely technical quibble. The essence of the conformity test is that the goods fail to satisfy the consumer's reasonable, or legitimate, expectations—the same test which underpins the domestic implied terms and the concept of 'defectiveness' under the CPA. There is no conceptual difficulty in holding the manufacturer liable for such a failure.

What, then, should be the extent of the manufacturer's liability? There could be no objection to holding the manufacturer liable for defects in the goods which result either from their design or manufacture. However, some defects in goods may be the result of actions (such as inadequate storage or careless handling) of persons other than the manufacturer, such as a carrier or even the seller. It is arguable that the manufacturer should not be liable in such circumstances. If this view is accepted there are two possible solutions. The first would allow the manufacturer a defence to the consumer's claim where he can show that the defect in question did not exist when the goods left his control. This is effectively the model of the product liability system under the Consumer Protection Act and product liability directive (see 8.3.1.1). If, as we have suggested, the manufacturer's liability were to be supplemental to rather than substituted for that of the contractual seller, the consumer in such a case would still have a remedy against the seller and would therefore be no worse off than at present. The alternative approach would be to hold the manufacturer strictly liable to the consumer, but allow him a right of indemnity against the person responsible for the defect. One difficulty with this approach however might be that the person responsible for the defect might not be in a contractual relationship with the manufacturer. That need not be a bar to giving the manufacturer a statutory right of recourse, but it might therefore be preferable to adopt the former approach.

It is slightly less obvious that the manufacturer should be liable for the goods' non-correspondence with description or unfitness for the buyer's purpose. As we have noted, in many cases the manufacturer's public statements in advertising and in promotional literature will be the main source of the buyer's expectations with regard to the goods. However, should the manufacturer be liable for statements about the goods made by the retailer, over whom the manufacturer may have no control? To some extent the manufacturer's position here is weaker than that of the retailer who is held liable on the basis of the manufacturer's statements, for the manufacturer's statements must be 'public' and are reasonably likely to be known to the retailer, who may therefore correct or disassociate himself from them. The manufacturer will generally be wholly ignorant of statements made by the retailer to the consumer or by the consumer to the retailer. If this is seen as a problem, one solution would be that suggested above to allow the manufacturer a defence where the consumer's claim arises solely from the consumer's dealings with the seller, of which the manufacturer has no knowledge. This would effectively be an analogue of the retailer's defence in Article 2(2) of the Directive (see 3.4.6.4). This would seem preferable to the alternative of holding the manufacturer liable subject to a right of indemnity against the retailer.

Even, however, if it is accepted that a manufacturer should be liable for a breach of the implied terms in much the same way as a seller (subject to the defences suggested here), it may be questioned whether the manufacturer should have to provide the full range of remedies the seller has to make available. Generally, there can be no objection to the manufacturer's having to provide repair or replacement of the defective item. Nor does there seem to be any reason to exempt the manufacturer from claims for price reduction or damages, including consequential losses (for which liability already exists under the product liability regime). It is less clear however that the manufacturer should be liable for 'special' damages suffered by the consumer. Such damages are normally recoverable in contract only when they were reasonably foreseeable by the other contracting party, otherwise they are too remote. On this basis the lack of direct contact between manufacturer and consumer would mean that the manufacturer would generally not be liable for such losses. However, the test of remoteness of damage is more favourable to the claimant in tort. Where, therefore, the consumer's special damages are consequential on personal injury or damage to property so that they would be recoverable from the manufacturer by means of a statutory or common law product liability claim, there would be no reason to limit the manufacturer's liability.

Finally, should the manufacturer be liable to provide a full refund of the price? It may be objected that the manufacturer will normally have received only part of the price paid to the retail seller. However, where under the present scheme the seller provides a full refund, his claim against his supplier will be for the price paid plus his lost profit on the resale. In effect therefore the retailer's claim against his supplier will be for the full amount of the price refunded (plus costs and expenses handling the claim). That liability will be passed back up the contractual chain to the manufacturer. The objection to requiring the manufacturer to give a full refund therefore loses much of its force.

The preceding discussion suggests that the liability of a manufacturer would in principle be identical to that of the seller, albeit subject to two important defences. If the Commission decides to put forward proposals for the introduction of direct producer liability when it reports on the Directive in 2006, the analysis in this section (and see Bradgate and Twigg-Flesner, 2002) shows that there is a strong case to support such proposals.

8.5 CONCLUSIONS

The position of manufacturers is somewhat unusual. As a general rule, there is no liability under the Sale of Goods Act 1979 and related legislation at present. However, under the Consumer Protection Act 1987, manufacturers are liable for some of the consequences of supplying defective goods. Moreover, most manufacturers of consumer goods assume some liability on a voluntary basis by giving a guarantee (or warranty) on their goods, and providing a remedy under a guarantee may significantly expand their liability. There may also be liability based on particular public statements, but no clear principle can be identified.

The question of direct manufacturer liability, although currently suspended, will become topical by 2006 when the Commission has to consider the case for introducing this in reviewing the operation of the Directive. The arguments in favour of introducing direct liability are persuasive, but there may not be the political will to take this important step.

9

THE POSITION OF RETAILERS AND RIGHTS OF REDRESS

9.1 INTRODUCTION

As will be apparent from the discussion in the preceding chapters, primary responsibility for the conformity of goods supplied to the consumer under both the Directive and domestic law falls on the final contractual supplier to the consumer. In most cases the final supplier will be a retailer, and for simplicity we use the term 'retailer' in this chapter to refer to the final contractual supplier. Nevertheless, as we have noted in an earlier chapter, the party primarily responsible for any lack of conformity will, in most cases, be not the retailer but the original manufacturer of the goods, who will not only be responsible for any actual manufacturing or design defects in the goods themselves but who also, through advertising and promotion, is principally responsible for shaping the consumer's expectations of the goods. This last fact is implicitly recognised in Article 2(2)(d) of the Directive which provides that the assessment of the goods' conformity with the contract shall take account of 'any public statements on the specific characteristics of the goods made about them by the seller, the producer or his representative, particularly in advertising or on labelling'. However, although the Directive recognises the manufacturer's responsibility for shaping the consumer's expectations it places liability for fulfilling those expectations on the retailer—albeit subject to some qualifications which allow the retailer to escape liability for the manufacturer's public statements in a limited range of circumstances (see 3.4.6.4). The retailer cannot exclude or limit his liability to the consumer for the goods' conformity with the contract. If the goods are not in conformity with the contract the retailer must provide the appropriate remedy. Under the Directive he must, in the first instance, replace or repair the goods. We might immediately question whether it is appropriate to require a retail seller, rather than a manufacturer, to repair non-conforming goods. However, insofar as remedies such as repair, replacement and price reduction in effect simply require the seller to perform his contract, they are perhaps unobjectionable, but the retailer's liability does not end there, for if defective goods cause additional loss to the consumer the retailer is, in domestic law, liable to compensate the consumer for that loss by payment of damages. Nor is the retailer's liability limited to the requirement that goods be in conformity with the contract. If the manufacturer chooses to offer a guarantee of the goods the retailer is not liable to honour the guarantee but is responsible for ensuring that the consumer receives a copy of the manufacturer's guarantee (Article 6(3), SSGCR 2002 Regulation 15; see 7.2.5).

The Commission's original *Green Paper* proposed a very different scheme of liability under which, recognising the role of manufacturers in shaping consumer expectations, the manufacturer and retailer would have been jointly and severally liable to the consumer for the goods' conformity with the contract. That scheme was not pursued in the final version of the Directive which preferred a system of retailer liability as 'the traditional solution enshrined in the legal orders of the Member States' (Recital 9).

In holding the retailer liable for matters for which he is not responsible the system of retailer liability may be said to be unfair to the retailer. More to the point it is probably contrary to the intuitive expectation of the average consumer. We have briefly outlined some of the arguments in favour of a system of manufacturer liability in a previous chapter (see 8.4). Other arguments can be advanced. In particular it may be argued that ensuring that liability for product quality falls on the manufacturer gives the manufacturer an incentive to maintain product quality standards.

The traditional justification for the system of retailer liability is that it provides a ready and accessible source of redress for the consumer whilst at the same time providing a conduit by which liability for non-conforming goods can be passed back to the party ultimately responsible for the lack of conformity—in most cases, the manufacturer. On this analysis just as the retailer is, in many cases, effectively no more than a channel by which goods are distributed to consumers, as the final link in a distribution chain, the retailer is also the first link in a chain of liability via which liability for the supply of non-conforming goods can be returned to the manufacturer. However, this rationale breaks down unless the retailer is able to pass back any liability he incurs to the ultimate consumer. Goods normally reach the consumer via a chain of contracts. In the case of a simple distribution chain goods may be sold by the manufacturer to a wholesaler, by wholesaler to retailer and by retailer to consumer. In practice the chain may be longer and more complicated. The distribution chain as a mechanism for passing back liability may fail if either the retailer is unable to pass back the liability he incurs to the ultimate consumer, or if for any reason that liability cannot be passed back to the manufacturer so that it falls instead on an intermediate party in the chain.

9.2 ARTICLE 4 OF THE DIRECTIVE

The Directive seeks to compensate for its adoption of a system of retailer liability by the inclusion of Article 4. Headed 'Right of redress' Article 4 is one of the most difficult and controversial provisions in the Directive. It provides that:

Where the final seller is liable to the consumer because of a lack of conformity resulting from an act or omission by the producer, a previous seller in the same chain of contracts or any other intermediary, the final seller shall be entitled to pursue remedies against the person or persons liable in the contractual chain. The person or persons liable against whom the final seller may pursue remedies, together with the relevant actions and conditions of exercise, shall be determined by national law.

The inclusion of this provision in a Directive primarily concerned with consumer protection is in itself curious (see Bridge, 2002). It appears to be intended as a sop to compensate retailers for the imposition on them of liability for product quality and for abandoning the proposed scheme of joint liability. On its face Article 4 seems to recognise the iniquity of imposing front-line liability on the retail seller. The opening sentence is expressed in clear and mandatory terms: a final seller who is liable to a consumer for a lack of conformity resulting from an act by somebody higher up in the distribution chain '*shall* be entitled to pursue remedies against the person or persons liable in the contractual chain'. However, the language even of the first sentence is curious. The final seller is entitled to pursue remedies against— not to obtain a remedy from—the person or persons 'liable' in the contractual chain. The right of recourse is not against the person *responsible* for the act or omission giving rise to the final seller's liability. Liability is normally the legal consequence of responsibility, but the Directive contains no guidance on how to determine who is 'liable' in this sense. It is tempting to read 'liable' as 'responsible' but the choice of language seems to have been deliberate: an earlier draft text used the word 'responsible'.

However, the core problem in determining the ambit of Article 4 lies in the last sentence which states that 'The person or persons liable against whom the final seller may pursue remedies, together with the relevant actions and conditions of exercise, shall be determined by national law.' This seems to go some considerable way to undermining the mandatory nature of the first sentence. The problem is compounded by the statement in Recital 9 that 'the seller should be free, *as provided for by national law*, to pursue remedies against the producer, a previous seller in the same chain of contract or any other intermediary, *unless he has renounced that entitlement*' (emphasis added), and further that 'this Directive does not affect the principle of freedom of contract between the seller, the producer, a previous seller or any other intermediary'. As a result, the requirements of Article 4 are anything but clear. Two questions arise. First, against whom should the seller have a remedy? Second, to what extent may national law restrict the seller's right of redress?

Broadly speaking, two interpretations are possible (*cf.* Schmidt-Kessel, 2000; Micklitz, 1999). Essentially they differ on the extent of the discretion given to Member States in the implementation of Article 4. According to the narrow interpretation, Article 4 permits the retention of existing restrictions on liability, such as rules permitting the use of exclusion and limitation clauses in the seller's contract with his immediate supplier. According to this interpretation, the inclusion in the contract of an exclusion or limitation clause amounts to the seller 'renouncing' his entitlement to pursue remedies against his supplier, as apparently permitted by Recital 9. On this view, therefore, Article 4 gives Member States a wide discretion, not only as to the remedy available to the seller, the person from whom a remedy may be sought and the procedure for claiming a remedy, but also, in effect, whether to allow the remedy to be excluded. According to the wide view of Article 4, it permits Member States discretion as to the parties from whom the retailer can seek redress, the nature of the remedy, and the procedure for pursuing a claim. Member States would have a discretion whether to require the retailer to pursue his claim via the contract chain, or permit him to claim directly against the person responsible for the lack of conformity. However, it would not be open to Member States to allow the retailer's right of redress to be excluded. Recital 9 implicitly recognises that the retailer may renounce his right to redress, so to construe Article 4 as requiring Member States to provide a non-renounceable right of redress would conflict with Recital 9. However, commentators have suggested two possible interpretations of Recital 9. According to the first, the right of redress is renounceable but renunciation requires the retailer's explicit consent. According to the alternative interpretation the right of redress can be 'renounced' by inclusion of an appropriate term, such as a clause excluding liability, in a standard term contract. However, this approach would make it very easy to undermine Article 4, and it may be significant that Recital 9 speaks of the seller 'renouncing' his entitlement, rather than of his entitlement being excluded (and to this extent Recital 9 can be contrasted with the language of Article 7 which invalidates terms which 'directly or indirectly waive or restrict' the consumer's rights, language which seems more apt to describe exclusion by standard terms).

The first interpretation is therefore perhaps the more attractive and convincing reading of Recital 9. However, the issue is finely balanced. Either reading can be defended on the basis of the language of the Directive, and it will probably require an authoritative interpretation by the ECJ on this matter before the scope of Article 4 is determined. Alternatively, the Commission may put forward proposals to amend Article 4 following its 2006 report. If, however, we adopt the position that as a matter of policy liability should be imposed on the person *responsible* for the lack of conformity, then it seems that the wide view would be preferable.

9.3 THE POSITION OF RETAILERS IN ENGLISH LAW

The view of the DTI is that the existing rules of domestic law are sufficient to satisfy the requirements of Article 4 and that therefore no further action is required by way of implementation. In domestic law the Directive's conformity requirement is given effect by the statutory implied terms in sections 13–15 of the Sale of Goods Act and corresponding provisions in the legislation applicable to other forms of supply contract. Those terms are implied into a contract of sale regardless of the status of the buyer. They therefore apply not only on a sale by a retailer to a consumer but also on a sale by a business seller to a business buyer, and therefore, in principle, to each of the contracts which make up the distribution chain between manufacturer and retailer. On the face of it therefore the implied terms provide a perfect mechanism for the retailer's liability to the consumer to be passed back up the distribution chain to the manufacturer by a series of contractual claims for breach of the implied terms.

It is however far from clear that existing domestic law is sufficient to satisfy the Directive, and if the wide view of Article 4 described above is correct it will not do so. It seems clear that the determination of the parties against whom the retailer may seek redress is a matter within the scope of Member State discretion, so that it is acceptable to require the retailer to seek redress via the contract chain rather than direct from the manufacturer. Nevertheless, the retailer's rights against his supplier are far from a mirror image of his liabilities to his consumer customer, and the differences between them may result in his being unable to pass liability back even to his supplier, let alone back all the way up the chain to the person ultimately responsible. Although the statutory implied terms may be implied into both contracts, they may operate differently in each so that it does not follow that an event which constitutes a breach of contract as between retailer and consumer will constitute a breach as between (say) distributor and retailer or manufacturer and distributor. Moreover, even if there is *prima facie* a breach of contract, the remedies available to the retailer against his supplier may differ from those available to the consumer against the retailer. Finally, whereas a retailer can never exclude or limit his liability for breach of contract to a consumer buyer, it is possible for the retailer's supplier to exclude or limit his liability for breach, including (as is often the case) by an appropriate term in a standard form contract. As a result there may be situations in which a retailer held liable to a consumer for a lack of conformity is unable to pass back liability to his supplier and in view of the discussion above it is open to question whether this is sufficient to comply with Article 4.

9.3.1 Claims limited by privity

In general the only claim available to a retailer held liable to a consumer for a lack of conformity in the goods will be a contractual claim against his immediate supplier. In many cases the retailer's supplier may be no more responsible for the lack of conformity than the retailer himself. For instance, where a manufacturer's goods are distributed to retailers by a network of wholesale distributors, if the retailer is held liable to a consumer because of a manufacturing defect in the goods, the person 'responsible' is the manufacturer. However, the retailer must seek redress from the distributor leaving the distributor to claim against the manufacturer. The retailer is not in privity of contract with the manufacturer and a tort claim based on negligence will not be available as the retailer's loss (consisting of lost profits, compensation paid to the consumer and so on) would be classified as pure economic loss, which is not recoverable in negligence (see *Murphy v Brentwood DC* ([1990] 2 All ER 908, above 8.3.1.2).

Article 4 requires that 'where the final seller is liable to the consumer because of a lack of conformity resulting from an act or omission by the producer, a previous seller in the same chain of contracts of any other intermediary, the final seller shall be entitled to pursue remedies *against the person or persons liable in the contractual chain*' [emphasis added]. If there were no more Article 4 could be read as requiring the retailer to be given a direct right of action against the person ultimately responsible for the lack of conformity in the goods—in the example just discussed the manufacturer, reading 'liable' as 'responsible'. This reading is perhaps supported by the fact that, curiously, Article 4 only requires a right of redress to be available to the final seller so that, seemingly, if liability is passed back via the contractual chain, say by the retailer claiming against the wholesaler, there is no requirement to provide a similar right of redress to the wholesaler. However, as noted above, Article 4 continues 'The person or persons liable against whom the final seller may pursue remedies . . . shall be determined by national law' which seems to suggest that Member States have freedom to determine against whom the retailer can seek redress, and this view is supported by Recital 9 which states that 'the rules governing against whom and how the seller may pursue such remedies are to be determined by national law'. It is therefore not contrary to the Directive to require the retailer to seek redress from his contractual supplier. On the other hand it would be permissible for national law to determine that the 'persons liable' for the purposes of Article 4 are those 'responsible' for the lack of conformity and therefore to provide a direct right of redress against that person.

9.3.2 Implied terms operate differently

The retailer is therefore limited to his contractual claim against his immediate supplier. As noted, the terms implied by SoGA sections 13–15 are, in principle, implied into all sales, regardless of the buyer's status as consumer or otherwise. However, it does not follow that an event which amounts to a breach of the implied terms in a contract between consumer and seller would similarly give rise to a breach in the contract between seller and manufacturer. In some cases the consumer's claim may have nothing to do with the manufacturer, as where the goods fail to correspond with the retailer's description of them, or where the consumer complains that the goods are not fit for his purpose as notified to the retailer. Or the goods may not be of satisfactory quality because of the way they have been stored or handled by the retailer. Even where the consumer's claim does originate in some act or omission of the manufacturer, as will often be the case where the claim is that the goods are not of satisfactory quality, the retailer may be unable to claim against his supplier. As explained in chapter 3, it is one of the hallmarks of the satisfactory quality and fitness for purpose tests that they take account of all the relevant circumstances in respect of the particular contract. As a result goods which are of satisfactory quality under one contract may not be under another.

9.3.2.1 *Public statements about the goods*
In one important respect the satisfactory quality test may apply differently in consumer and non-consumer sales as a result of the SSGCR 2002. Where the buyer of goods deals as consumer, new section 14(2D) of SoGA provides that the relevant circumstances to be considered in assessing whether goods are of satisfactory quality include 'any public statements on the specific characteristics of the goods' made by the seller, the producer or his representative, including statements in advertising and on labelling. This provision does not apply in a non-consumer sale. It is not clear however that this will make any significant difference. It was suggested in chapter 3 that it would have been open to a court to consider such public statements as part of the relevant circumstances without the introduction of the new section 14(2D), and section 14(2F) seems to confirm this, providing that section 14(2D) does 'not prevent any public statement from being a relevant circumstance for the purposes of section 14(2A)' if the statement would otherwise have been such a circumstance. It would be surprising if in a case where the retailer were held liable to the consumer on the basis of such statements it were to be held that those statements were not relevant in relation to the retailer's claim. That would however be possible if, say, the manufacturer's promotional statements were made after the retailer bought the goods or it could otherwise be shown that they had no influence on the retailer's decision to purchase the goods.

9.3.2.2 *Evidential presumptions*
Another obstacle facing the retailer is that he cannot rely on the evidential presumptions available to the consumer. In particular where a lack of conformity manifests itself within the first six months after the sale to the consumer it is irrebuttably presumed in favour of the consumer that the lack of conformity was present at the time the goods were delivered to him (SoGA section 48A(3); see 4.4.1.2). If the retailer now seeks to recover in respect of that lack of conformity against *his* supplier he will have to prove that the lack of conformity was present at the time when risk of loss or damage to the goods passed to him under his contract. Whilst in some cases it may readily be inferred from the nature of the lack of

conformity that that must have been the case it will often be possible for the retailer's supplier to argue that (for instance) the lack of conformity is due to the retailer's handling of the goods.

9.3.3 Remedies

Even if the facts which give rise to a claim by the consumer also allow the retailer to claim against his supplier, he will not be entitled to the same range of remedies as the consumer. The new remedies in Part 5A of SoGA and derived from the Directive—repair, replacement, rescission and price reduction—are only available where the buyer deals as consumer. If therefore the consumer is entitled to repair or replacement of the goods, the retailer must provide it. He cannot, for instance, insist on the goods being repaired or replaced by his supplier, unless that is expressly provided for in the contract of supply.

9.3.3.1 *Rejection*

The only remedies available to the retailer will therefore be rejection of the goods and termination of the contract and/or damages, as provided for by the SoGA. In practice however the right to reject will often be unavailable. As explained in chapter 4, the right to reject is available where there is a breach of a condition relating to the goods, including the implied conditions in sections 13–15. However, the right of a non-consumer buyer to reject goods is generally more restricted than that of a consumer. First, the non-consumer, such as the retailer, cannot reject where the breach is so slight that rejection would be unreasonable (SoGA section 15A). In contrast the consumer has an absolute right to reject for breach of condition, regardless of its seriousness. There may therefore be cases where goods are rejected by the consumer but the breach is so slight that the retailer is not entitled to reject them to his supplier. Second, the rules on acceptance may mean that where goods are rejected by the consumer the retailer is deemed to have accepted them and therefore lost his right to reject them. It may be recalled that the right to reject is lost where the buyer has accepted the goods, and the buyer is taken to have accepted the goods where

(a) he expressly so intimates;

(b) he does any act inconsistent with the seller's ownership; or

(c) after the lapse of a reasonable time he retains the goods without rejecting them (SoGA section 35; see 4.3.1.2).

The Act expressly provides that a buyer is not to be taken as having accepted on either of the first two grounds until he has first had a reasonable opportunity of examining the goods to ascertain whether they are in conformity with the contract (section 35(2)) and that in determining what is a reasonable time for the purposes of the third ground, a material factor is whether the buyer has had a reasonable opportunity of examining the goods to ascertain whether they are in conformity with the contract (section 35(5)). However, whereas a consumer cannot be deprived of his right to examine the goods under these provisions by agreement, waiver or estoppel, a non-consumer buyer may be held to have waived, or be estopped from asserting, his right of examination; and although a contractual provision excluding the right to examine will be subject to control under the UCTA 1977, section 6, it will be valid if reasonable. The upshot is that a retailer to whom goods are rejected after sale to a consumer may find that he is deemed to have accepted them and therefore have lost the right to reject them to his buyer. For instance, he may be required to sign a delivery note acknowledging that he has examined the goods and accepts them as being in conformity with the contract; or stating that he accepts them and waives his right to examine them. Such a delivery note could be construed as an express intimation of acceptance which waives the right of examination. Alternatively the retailer may find that the resale prevents his rejecting the goods. The act of reselling the goods will not of itself amount to acceptance. A resale is capable of being an act inconsistent with the seller's ownership, but section 35(6) states that the buyer is not to be taken to have accepted the goods merely because he delivers them to another under a sub-sale or other disposition and if the goods are available for return to the retailer's supplier, rejection should be possible. But the right to reject is also lost by lapse of time. There will often be a delay between the goods being delivered to the retailer and their being resold to the consumer. There will then be a further delay before the consumer discovers the defect and rejects the goods. The effect of these combined delays will often be that by the time the consumer rejects the goods the time elapsed since sale to the retailer is too long to permit rejection by him.

It must be borne in mind that in assessing what is a reasonable time account must be taken of whether the buyer has had a reasonable opportunity of examining the goods. It might be possible to argue that where goods are supplied to a retailer knowing that they are for resale, since it will be anticipated that the retailer will not examine the goods and defects will only become apparent after resale, a reasonable time should include a reasonable time for the goods to be resold and then for the consumer purchaser to try them out to see if they are in conformity with the contract. This was the line taken in *Truk (UK) Ltd v Tokmakidis GmbH* [2000] 1 Lloyd's Rep 543 in which it was held that a delay of six months between delivery of goods to a retail supplier and his rejection of them was not too long to permit rejection. The seller knew that the goods were bought for resale and that any defect would only be discovered by the ultimate end-user after resale. However, on the facts of *Truk* it was reasonably foreseeable that resale might take six months. Where goods remain in stock longer than might reasonably be expected before resale the additional delay may preclude rejection.

The introduction of the SSGCR introduce a further possibility. The consumer is now entitled to demand replacement of the goods or, in extreme cases, rescission of the contract for up to six years after the date of delivery of the goods to him.

Even if the approach suggested above is adopted, a retailer to whom goods are rejected for replacement or refund under SoGA Part 5A more than a few months after resale is likely to be taken to have lost the right to reject. It must be remembered that 'reasonable time' for the purposes of SoGA section 35(5) means a reasonable time for examining the goods, not a reasonable time for discovering the particular defect—a point re-emphasised in *Truk*. A retailer may be allowed a reasonable time to resell the goods and a further period equivalent to a reasonable time for the consumer to examine/try out the goods and, if a defect is discovered, decide what to do (especially important given the range of remedies now available to the consumer); but if a latent defect only becomes manifest some time after sale it is likely to be too late for the retailer to reject.

9.3.3.2 *Damages*

We must conclude that there are therefore likely to be cases where goods are returned to the retailer following resale but the retailer is unable to reject them to his supplier and is left with goods on his hands. The retailer's only option in such a case will be to claim damages for breach of contract. Such damages will be awarded under SoGA sections 53 and 54. Damages are awarded under section 53 for 'breach of warranty', including cases where there is a breach of condition but the buyer accepts, or is deemed to have accepted, the goods and therefore treats the breach as a breach of warranty. The basic measure of damages is 'the estimated loss directly and naturally resulting, in the ordinary course of events, from the breach of warranty' (section 53(2)). Section 53(3) then provides that such loss is *prima facie* 'the difference between the value of the goods at the time of delivery to the buyer and the value they would have had if they had fulfilled the warranty'. Section 53(3) is stated to apply to cases of breach of warranty of quality but it is assumed that the same measure applies to breach of any of the statutory implied terms or any other term relating to quality, fitness for purpose, description and so on.

A seller claiming damages under section 53 is therefore not entitled to a full refund of the price. Even rejected goods will generally have some value. It may be possible to repair them and sell them as re-conditioned second-hand goods. Alternatively goods may be resaleable as 'seconds'. The retailer will be under a duty to take reasonable steps to mitigate his loss by taking such steps as are appropriate to dispose of the goods. (If this includes repairing the goods the costs of such repair will be included in his claim for damages.)

The retailer's claim will not necessarily be limited to difference in value damages under section 53. Section 54 SoGA expressly states that nothing in the Act affects the right of the buyer to recover 'special damages' where they would be available under the general law, and whilst the meaning of this provision is not entirely clear, it is apparent that where the buyer suffers losses over and above those compensated by difference in value damages under section 53, they will generally be recoverable, either as special damages under section 54, or under the general principle in section 53(2) (above) provided that they are not too remote. Thus a retailer may recover damages to compensate for loss of profit on a lost resale, an indemnity to cover any damages paid to his customer (see *Godley v Perry* [1960] 1 WLR 9, [1960] 1 All ER 36) and even damages to compensate for damage to his commercial reputation or goodwill (*GKN Centrax Gears Ltd v Matbro Ltd* [1976] 2 Lloyd's Rep 555).

Even where the retailer can pass liability back up the contractual chain the range of remedies available to him will be smaller than that available to the consumer. In most cases the only remedy available will be damages. Whilst in many cases an award of damages will adequately compensate the retailer's losses, it should be borne in mind that in pursuing a claim for damages the retailer will be under a duty to take reasonable steps to mitigate his loss. He cannot simply throw the whole loss back onto his seller by rejecting the goods.

9.3.4 Exclusion of liability

In many cases, however, the most important restriction on the retailer's ability to pass back liability to his supplier will be the inclusion in the contract with his supplier of clauses limiting or even excluding the supplier's liability. Whereas a clause excluding or limiting the statutory implied terms or liability or remedies for their breach is wholly ineffective in a contract with a consumer buyer, where the buyer does not deal as a consumer such clauses are subject to a test of reasonableness and therefore valid if reasonable (UCTA 1977, section 6(3)). In short, whereas the retailer cannot exclude his liability to the consumer, the retailer's supplier can exclude his liability to the retailer. In practice the contract between the retailer and his supplier will often be on the supplier's standard terms, in which case it will almost certainly, as a matter of course, seek to exclude or at least limit the supplier's liability for breach of the implied terms. It may even seek to exclude the implied terms altogether, or substitute for them a more limited warranty; or it may impose financial limits on the supplier's liability or time limits within which claims must be brought. The same rules apply to exclusion and limitation clauses in contracts between other parties in the distribution chain, such as between manufacturer and distributor, or distributor and wholesaler. The provisions of UCTA can therefore trap the retail supplier who may not exclude his liability to his consumer customer but who may find any attempt to pass back liability to his contractual supplier blocked by an exclusion or limitation clause.

9.3.4.1 *Incorporation of exclusion clauses*
Such a clause will only be effective if it is judged reasonable under the UCTA 1977. However, the 1977 Act is not the only restriction on the effectiveness of an exclusion. The supplier seeking to rely on an exclusion or limitation clause must first establish that the clause in question was effectively incorporated into the relevant contract. The supplier must show that he took reasonable steps to draw the clause

to the attention of the retailer before the contract was concluded. No new terms can be introduced after the contract is concluded unless the parties agree to vary the contract. It must be established that the clause was introduced before the contract was concluded, so that terms sent after the contract is made, on an invoice, will be too late to be incorporated. As noted above, generally an exclusion clause in a contract between a retailer and his supplier will appear in the supplier's standard terms. Generally it will be enough for the supplier to show that the terms were supplied to the retailer in a document which the retailer was aware, or ought to have been aware, contained contract terms. However, where the particular term is unusual in nature or particularly onerous it will not be incorporated unless special steps are taken to draw attention to it, for instance by highlighting it in some way (the so-called 'red-hand' test). This requirement of special notice which was developed in the context of exclusions in consumer contracts has been extended and applied to all types of terms, including in business to business contracts. It was applied to a term excluding the SoGA statutory implied terms in *AEG (UK) Ltd v Logic Resource Ltd* [1996] CLC 265, where a clause in a contract between a manufacturer and a retail supplier (albeit one not selling to consumers) purported to exclude the statutory implied terms in favour of a limited warranty against defects under which the buyer was required to return the goods to the manufacturer for repair and to bear the carriage costs incurred in so doing. The majority of the Court of Appeal held the clause ineffective on the grounds that it was unusual or particularly onerous and as such could only be incorporated if special steps were taken to draw attention to it.

9.3.4.2 *Construction of exclusion clauses*

Even if effectively incorporated into the contract, an exclusion clause will only be effective if, on its proper construction, it covers the breach in question. In the past the courts have tended to construe exclusions strictly, *contra proferentem*, so that any ambiguity in the clause is resolved contrary to the interests of the party seeking to rely on it, and this approach could therefore be used to cut back attempts to exclude a supplier's liability to his customer. On this basis it was held, for instance, that a clause excluding liability for breach of warranty did not cover a breach of condition (*Wallis Son & Wells v Pratt & Haynes* [1911] AC 394) and a clause excluding liability for breach of implied term did not cover liability for breach of express term (*Andrews Brothers (Bournemouth) Ltd v Singer and Co Ltd* [1934] 1 KB 17). Although in recent years the courts have advocated that a more purposive, 'common sense' approach should be taken to the interpretation of contracts generally there are no signs as yet that the courts are prepared to abandon this approach, which may provide a useful control on exclusions and similar clauses.

9.3.4.3 *Reasonableness*

Nevertheless, the most important control on a clause by which a supplier seeks to exclude or limit his liability to a retailer for supplying non-conforming goods will be the requirement in UCTA section 6 that any such exclusion is valid only insofar as it satisfies the requirement of reasonableness. It will be for the supplier to prove that the clause is reasonable, by establishing that the clause was a 'fair and reasonable one to be included in the contract, having regard to the circumstances which were, or ought reasonably to have been, known to the parties at the time the contract was made' (section 11(1)) UCTA).

The reasonableness test is unpredictable, although the Act does provide some guidelines on its application. For instance, section 11(2) provides that in determining the reasonableness of any particular clause under section 6 'regard shall be had' to the following factors, listed in Schedule 2:

(a) the relative strength of the parties' bargaining positions, taking into account alternative means by which the customer's requirements might be met;

(b) whether the customer received any inducement to agree to the term, or in accepting it, had an opportunity of entering into a similar contract with any other person without accepting a similar term;

(c) whether the customer knew or ought reasonably to have known of the existence and extent of the term;

(d) where the term excludes or restricts liability unless some condition is complied with, whether it was reasonable at the time of contract to expect that compliance with that condition would be practicable;

(e) whether the goods were manufactured, processed or adapted to the special order of the customer.

In addition, where the term in question restricts liability to a particular sum of money, the reasonableness of this restriction is considered with reference to (a) the resources available to the person relying on the term for the purposes of meeting the potential liability and (b) whether it was open to him to protect himself by insurance. Section 6 does not as such invalidate exclusion or limitation clauses in standard terms but it is clear that the degree of notice given of a term and the reality of the consent to it are relevant factors in assessing reasonableness, as is the degree of the defendant's responsibility for the breach. Nevertheless, since the test is whether the term was a fair and reasonable one to be included in the particular contract, application of the test will depend on the particular circumstances of each particular contract. A term could be reasonable in one contract and the identical term be unreasonable in another. It is therefore difficult to extrapolate general principles from reported cases. However, some examples may illustrate the operation of the test.

In the *AEG* case (above) the Court of Appeal held that the clause failed the reasonableness test. The supplier had given the customer insufficient notice of the exclusion. Moreover, it purported wholly to exclude the statutory implied terms and the warranty offered in their place was too limited to save the exclusion. In *Britvic Soft Drinks v Messer UK Ltd* ([2002] EWCA Civ 548, [2002] 2 All ER (Comm) 321 CA), B had bought from M carbon dioxide for use in the manufacture of soft drinks; M had, in turn, purchased it from T, the producer. As a result of a breakdown in manufacturing practice at T, some of the carbon dioxide had been contaminated with benzene, a carcinogen. Consequently, drinks which had been carbonated with that particular consignment of gas contained a higher than normal concentration of benzene. Although there was no immediate danger to human health B recalled all affected drinks from trade purchasers (although no consumer recall was undertaken) and brought a claim against M for the losses caused by the recall. It should be noted in the present context that M were therefore intermediaries in the supply chain rather than manufacturers. (M in turn pursued a claim against T.) M denied liability, *inter alia* on the grounds that its contract with B contained a clause which purported to exclude 'all other implied warranties and conditions as to quality or description . . . except to the extent that such exclusion is prevented by law'. The Court of Appeal held that that exclusion was unreasonable. The Court construed BS 4105 as not extending to a warranty of freedom from benzene contamination. On that basis, and rather as in *AEG*, the limited warranty offered was insufficient to validate the attempted total exclusion of the statutory implied terms since that would, as the court put it, have contradicted a 'fundamental assumption that all parties would have made in this respect'. No-one would have expected the manufacturing process to result in the introduction of benzene and it is unlikely that they would have appreciated the full extent of the exclusion clause.

It would be dangerous to generalise from this decision. As noted above, the reasonableness test is context sensitive and each case will depend on its own facts. Nevertheless it seems unlikely that a total exclusion of liability will be held reasonable in normal circumstances. (See also *AT Bright & Sons v PHR (Rayne)* [2003] All ER (D) 117, HC, 20 January 2003. A clause excluding liability for 'any claims for indirect or consequential losses arising from negligence or otherwise' was held reasonable in *Watford Electronics Ltd v Sanderson CFL Ltd* [2001] All ER 696, CA, but the contract was for the supply of computer software; both parties were in the information technology industry and should have known that it is difficult for a supplier to guarantee software to be defect free; the customer was found to have been fully aware of the term; and the term was of a type standard in the industry; indeed the buyer had a similar term in its own standard terms of business.)

It is submitted that two other factors which may be relevant to the assessment of reasonableness are whether the claim arises from a matter within the control of one of the parties and whether it is open to the party making the claim to exclude or limit his own liability. It is probably less likely to be reasonable for a manufacturer to exclude or limit liability for manufacturing defects in its goods (see *George Mitchell (Chesterhall) Ltd v Finney Lock Seeds Ltd* [1983] 2 AC 803, [1983] 2 All ER 737 where a seed supplier's exclusion of liability for seed supplied was held unreasonable partly because the breach of contract arose from the supplier's negligence). In *Britvic Soft Drinks* the defendants, M, accepted that it would have been unreasonable for the manufacturer of the carbon dioxide to exclude its liability but argued that it was reasonable for it, as a supplier, to do so. The Court of Appeal rejected that argument and it is submitted that it was correct to do so. If it is unreasonable for the manufacturer to exclude liability it should be unreasonable for a purchaser from the manufacturer to do so if it can pass back its liability to the manufacturer, and the Court's decision facilitated the use of the contractual chain to pass back liability for losses caused by the defect to the party responsible for the defect.

Conversely, it may be unreasonable to exclude liability as against a party who cannot exclude or limit his own liability. Thus where S supplies goods to R for resale to consumers, it may be arguable that it is unreasonable for S to exclude its liability for breach of the SoGA terms to R on the grounds that R cannot exclude or limit its liability to its consumer customers.

If this reasoning were to be accepted it might be that an attempt to exclude liability as against a retail seller would generally be unreasonable, at least where the retailer's customers are consumers. It must be conceded however that there is no authority in point, and it is possible to envisage cases where such an exclusion might be reasonable—for instance where the retailer is a larger business than the manufacturer and is better able to protect itself by insurance, or where the parties are of equal bargaining power and the contract was freely negotiated.

9.4 CONCLUSIONS

Retailers are exclusively liable to consumers for the quality and conformity with the contract of the goods they sell. It remains the case, however, that it cannot be guaranteed that in English law a retailer held liable to a consumer for a lack of conformity will necessarily be able to pass that liability back up the contractual supply chain, even where the lack of conformity resulted from the act or omission of some prior party in the chain. The best that we can say is that he may be able to do so. Even where such a claim is available the retailer's rights will differ significantly from those available to the consumer. It is not clear that this is sufficient to satisfy Article 4 of the Directive. It is submitted that the difference between the remedies available to the consumer and the retailer is permitted within the terms of Article 4, which provides that the retailer's 'actions and conditions of exercise shall be determined by national law'. If we adopt the narrow interpretation of Article 4 described earlier in this chapter, English law is therefore consistent with the Directive. On the other hand it is at least arguable that Article 4 requires that the retailer should have some right of recourse in all cases and that the possibility of its exclusion other than by the explicit consent of the retailer is not permitted. It is of course true that Recital 9 expressly recognises 'the principle of freedom of contract' and that the retailer may 'renounce' his entitlement to pursue a claim back up the supply chain, but the language of Article 4 is mandatory ('the final seller *shall* be entitled to pursue remedies . . .' and, as we have noted previously, it is open to serious doubt whether the inclusion of an exclusion clause in a set of standard terms can be construed as a renunciation of liability. If then we adopt this, wider, view of Article 4 it is strongly arguable that English law does not satisfy the Directive. There is undoubtedly sufficient flexibility in the controls on exclusion and limitation clauses, especially the common law 'red hand' test and the statutory reasonableness test to enable it to be applied in a way which accords with the Directive, but as we have noted in an earlier chapter that is not sufficient to satisfy the requirements of EC law.

Appendix 1

DIRECTIVE 1999/44/EC OF THE EUROPEAN PARLIAMENT AND OF THE COUNCIL

of 25 May 1999
on certain aspects of the sale of consumer goods and associated guarantees

THE EUROPEAN PARLIAMENT AND THE COUNCIL OF THE EUROPEAN UNION

Having regard to the Treaty establishing the European Community, and in particular Article 95 thereof,

Having regard to the proposal from the Commission,

Having regard to the opinion of the Economic and Social Committee,

Acting in accordance with the procedure laid down in Article 251 of the Treaty in the light of the joint text approved by the Conciliation Committee on 18 March 1999.

(1)   Whereas Article 153(1) and (3) of the Treaty provides that the Community should contribute to the achievement of a high level of consumer protection by the measures it adopts pursuant to Article 95 thereof;

(2)   Whereas the internal market comprises an area without internal frontiers in which the free movement of goods, persons, services and capital is guaranteed; whereas free movement of goods concerns not only transactions by persons acting in the course of a business but also transactions by private individuals; whereas it implies that consumers resident in one Member State should be free to purchase goods in the territory of another Member State on the basis of a uniform minimum set of fair rules governing the sale of consumer goods;

(3)   Whereas the laws of the Member States concerning the sale of consumer goods are somewhat disparate, with the result that national consumer goods markets differ from one another and that competition between sellers may be distorted;

(4)   Whereas consumers who are keen to benefit from the large market by purchasing goods in Member States other than their State of residence play a fundamental role in the completion of the internal market; whereas the artificial reconstruction of frontiers and the compartmentalisation of markets should be prevented; whereas the opportunities available to consumers have been greatly broadened by new communication technologies which allow ready access to distribution systems in other Member States or in third countries;

whereas, in the absence of minimum harmonisation of the rules governing the sale of consumer goods, the development of the sale of goods through the medium of new distance communication technologies risks being impeded;

(5) Whereas the creation of a common set of minimum rules of consumer law, valid no matter where goods are purchased within the Community, will strengthen consumer confidence and enable consumers to make the most of the internal market;

(6) Whereas the main difficulties encountered by consumers and the main source of disputes with sellers concern the non-conformity of goods with the contract; whereas it is therefore appropriate to approximate national legislation governing the sale of consumer goods in this respect, without however impinging on provisions and principles of national law relating to contractual and non-contractual liability;

(7) Whereas the goods must, above all, conform with the contractual specifications; whereas the principle of conformity with the contract may be considered as common to the different national legal traditions; whereas in certain national legal traditions it may not be possible to rely solely on this principle to ensure a minimum level of protection for the consumer; whereas under such legal traditions, in particular, additional national provisions may be useful to ensure that the consumer is protected in cases where the parties have agreed no specific contractual terms or where the parties have concluded contractual terms or agreements which directly or indirectly waive or restrict the rights of the consumer and which, to the extent that these rights result from this Directive, are not binding on the consumer;

(8) Whereas, in order to facilitate the application of the principle of conformity with the contract, it is useful to introduce a rebuttable presumption of conformity with the contract covering the most common situations; whereas that presumption does not restrict the principle of freedom of contract; whereas, furthermore, in the absence of specific contractual terms, as well as where the minimum protection clause is applied, the elements mentioned in this presumption may be used to determine the lack of conformity of the goods with the contract; whereas the quality and performance which consumers can reasonably expect will depend inter alia on whether the goods are new or second-hand; whereas the elements mentioned in the presumption are cumulative; whereas, if the circumstances of the case render any particular element manifestly inappropriate, the remaining elements of the presumption nevertheless still apply;

(9) Whereas the seller should be directly liable to the consumer for the conformity of the goods with the contract; whereas this is the traditional solution enshrined in the legal orders of the Member States; whereas nevertheless the seller should be free, as provided for by national law, to pursue remedies against the producer, a previous seller in the same chain of contracts or any other intermediary, unless he has renounced that entitlement; whereas this Directive does not affect the principle of freedom of contract between the seller, the producer, a previous seller or any other intermediary; whereas the rules governing against whom and how the seller may pursue such remedies are to be determined by national law;

(10) Whereas, in the case of non-conformity of the goods with the contract, consumers should be entitled to have the goods restored to conformity with the contract free of charge, choosing either repair or replacement, or, failing this, to have the price reduced or the contract rescinded;

(11) Whereas the consumer in the first place may require the seller to repair the goods or to replace them unless those remedies are impossible or disproportionate; whereas whether a remedy is disproportionate should be determined objectively; whereas a remedy would be

disproportionate if it imposed, in comparison with the other remedy, unreasonable costs; whereas, in order to determine whether the costs are unreasonable, the costs of one remedy should be significantly higher than the costs of the other remedy;

(12) Whereas in cases of a lack of conformity, the seller may always offer the consumer, by way of settlement, any available remedy; whereas it is for the consumer to decide whether to accept or reject this proposal;

(13) Whereas, in order to enable consumers to take advantage of the internal market and to buy consumer goods in another Member State, it should be recommended that, in the interests of consumers, the producers of consumer goods that are marketed in several Member States attach to the product a list with at least one contact address in every Member State where the product is marketed;

(14) Whereas the references to the time of delivery do not imply that Member States have to change their rules on the passing of the risk;

(15) Whereas Member States may provide that any reimbursement to the consumer may be reduced to take account of the use the consumer has had of the goods since they were delivered to him; whereas the detailed arrangements whereby rescission of the contract is effected may be laid down in national law;

(16) Whereas the specific nature of second-hand goods makes it generally impossible to replace them; whereas therefore the consumer's right of replacement is generally not available for these goods; whereas for such goods, Member States may enable the parties to agree a shortened period of liability;

(17) Whereas it is appropriate to limit in time the period during which the seller is liable for any lack of conformity which exists at the time of delivery of the goods; whereas Member States may also provide for a limitation on the period during which consumers can exercise their rights, provided such a period does not expire within two years from the time of delivery; whereas where, under national legislation, the time when a limitation period starts is not the time of delivery of the goods, the total duration of the limitation period provided for by national law may not be shorter than two years from the time of delivery;

(18) Whereas Member States may provide for suspension or interruption of the period during which any lack of conformity must become apparent and of the limitation period, where applicable and in accordance with their national law, in the event of repair, replacement or negotiations between seller and consumer with a view to an amicable settlement;

(19) Whereas Member States should be allowed to set a period within which the consumer must inform the seller of any lack of conformity; whereas Member States may ensure a higher level of protection for the consumer by not introducing such an obligation; whereas in any case consumers throughout the Community should have at least two months in which to inform the seller that a lack of conformity exists;

(20) Whereas Member States should guard against such a period placing at a disadvantage consumers shopping across borders; whereas all Member States should inform the Commission of their use of this provision; whereas the Commission should monitor the effect of the varied application of this provision on consumers and on the internal market; whereas information on the use made of this provision by a Member State should be available to the other Member States and to consumers and consumer organisations throughout the Community; whereas a summary of the situation in all Member States should therefore be published in the Official Journal of the European Communities;

(21) Whereas, for certain categories of goods, it is current practice for sellers and producers to offer guarantees on goods against any defect which becomes apparent within a

certain period; whereas this practice can stimulate competition; whereas, while such guarantees are legitimate marketing tools, they should not mislead the consumer; whereas, to ensure that consumers are not misled, guarantees should contain certain information, including a statement that the guarantee does not affect the consumer's legal rights;

(22) Whereas the parties may not, by common consent, restrict or waive the rights granted to consumers, since otherwise the legal protection afforded would be thwarted; whereas this principle should apply also to clauses which imply that the consumer was aware of any lack of conformity of the consumer goods existing at the time the contract was concluded; whereas the protection granted to consumers under this Directive should not be reduced on the grounds that the law of a non-Member State has been chosen as being applicable to the contract;

(23) Whereas legislation and case-law in this area in the various Member States show that there is growing concern to ensure a high level of consumer protection; whereas, in the light of this trend and the experience acquired in implementing this Directive, it may be necessary to envisage more far-reaching harmonisation, notably by providing for the producer's direct liability for defects for which he is responsible;

(24) Whereas Member States should be allowed to adopt or maintain in force more stringent provisions in the field covered by this Directive to ensure an even higher level of consumer protection;

(25) Whereas, according to the Commission recommendation of 30 March 1998 on the principles applicable to the bodies responsible for out-of-court settlement of consumer disputes, Member States can create bodies that ensure impartial and efficient handling of complaints in a national and cross-border context and which consumers can use as mediators;

(26) Whereas it is appropriate, in order to protect the collective interests of consumers, to add this Directive to the list of Directives contained in the Annex to Directive 98/27/EC of the European Parliament and of the Council of 19 May 1998 on injunctions for the protection of consumers' interests,

HAVE ADOPTED THIS DIRECTIVE:

Article 1

Scope and definitions
1.   The purpose of this Directive is the approximation of the laws, regulations and administrative provisions of the Member States on certain aspects of the sale of consumer goods and associated guarantees in order to ensure a uniform minimum level of consumer protection in the context of the internal market.

2.   For the purposes of this Directive:
   (a)   *consumer*: shall mean any natural person who, in the contracts covered by this Directive, is acting for purposes which are not related to his trade, business or profession;
   (b)   *consumer goods*: shall mean any tangible movable item, with the exception of:
— goods sold by way of execution or otherwise by authority of law,
— water and
— gas where they are not put up for sale in a limited volume or set quantity,
— electricity;

(c) *seller*: shall mean any natural or legal person who, under a contract, sells consumer goods in the course of his trade, business or profession;

(d) *producer*: shall mean the manufacturer of consumer goods, the importer of consumer goods into the territory of the Community or any person purporting to be a producer by placing his name, trade mark or other distinctive sign on the consumer goods;

(e) *guarantee*: shall mean any undertaking by a seller or producer to the consumer, given without extra charge, to reimburse the price paid or to replace, repair or handle consumer goods in any way if they do not meet the specifications set out in the guarantee statement or in the relevant advertising;

(f) *repair*: shall mean, in the event of lack of conformity, bringing consumer goods into conformity with the contract of sale.

3.   Member States may provide that the expression "consumer goods" does not cover second-hand goods sold at public auction where consumers have the opportunity of attending the sale in person.

4.   Contracts for the supply of consumer goods to be manufactured or produced shall also be deemed contracts of sale for the purpose of this Directive.

Article 2

Conformity with the contract

1.   The seller must deliver goods to the consumer which are in conformity with the contract of sale.

2.   Consumer goods are presumed to be in conformity with the contract if they:

(a) comply with the description given by the seller and possess the qualities of the goods which the seller has held out to the consumer as a sample or model;

(b) are fit for any particular purpose for which the consumer requires them and which he made known to the seller at the time of conclusion of the contract and which the seller has accepted;

(c) are fit for the purposes for which goods of the same type are normally used;

(d) show the quality and performance which are normal in goods of the same type and which the consumer can reasonably expect, given the nature of the goods and taking into account any public statements on the specific characteristics of the goods made about them by the seller, the producer or his representative, particularly in advertising or on labelling.

3.   There shall be deemed not to be a lack of conformity for the purposes of this Article if, at the time the contract was concluded, the consumer was aware, or could not reasonably be unaware of, the lack of conformity, or if the lack of conformity has its origin in materials supplied by the consumer.

4.   The seller shall not be bound by public statements, as referred to in paragraph 2(d) if he:

— shows that he was not, and could not reasonably have been, aware of the statement in question,

— shows that by the time of conclusion of the contract the statement had been corrected, or

— shows that the decision to buy the consumer goods could not have been influenced by the statement.

5.   Any lack of conformity resulting from incorrect installation of the consumer goods shall be deemed to be equivalent to lack of conformity of the goods if installation forms part of the contract of sale of the goods and the goods were installed by the seller or under his responsibility. This shall apply equally if the product, intended to be installed by the consumer, is installed by the consumer and the incorrect installation is due to a shortcoming in the installation instructions.

Article 3

Rights of the consumer
1.   The seller shall be liable to the consumer for any lack of conformity which exists at the time the goods were delivered.

2.   In the case of a lack of conformity, the consumer shall be entitled to have the goods brought into conformity free of charge by repair or replacement, in accordance with paragraph 3, or to have an appropriate reduction made in the price or the contract rescinded with regard to those goods, in accordance with paragraphs 5 and 6.

3.   In the first place, the consumer may require the seller to repair the goods or he may require the seller to replace them, in either case free of charge, unless this is impossible or disproportionate.
   A remedy shall be deemed to be disproportionate if it imposes costs on the seller which, in comparison with the alternative remedy, are unreasonable, taking into account:
— the value the goods would have if there were no lack of conformity,
— the significance of the lack of conformity, and
— whether the alternative remedy could be completed without significant inconvenience to the consumer.
   Any repair or replacement shall be completed within a reasonable time and without any significant inconvenience to the consumer, taking account of the nature of the goods and the purpose for which the consumer required the goods.

4.   The terms 'free of charge' in paragraphs 2 and 3 refer to the necessary costs incurred to bring the goods into conformity, particularly the cost of postage, labour and materials.

5.   The consumer may require an appropriate reduction of the price or have the contract rescinded:
— if the consumer is entitled to neither repair nor replacement, or
— if the seller has not completed the remedy within a reasonable time, or
— if the seller has not completed the remedy without significant inconvenience to the consumer.

6.   The consumer is not entitled to have the contract rescinded if the lack of conformity is minor.

Article 4

Right of redress
Where the final seller is liable to the consumer because of a lack of conformity resulting from an act or omission by the producer, a previous seller in the same chain of contracts or any other intermediary, the final seller shall be entitled to pursue remedies against the person or persons liable in the contractual chain. The person or persons liable against whom

the final seller may pursue remedies, together with the relevant actions and conditions of exercise, shall be determined by national law.

Article 5

Time limits
1.   The seller shall be held liable under Article 3 where the lack of conformity becomes apparent within two years as from delivery of the goods. If, under national legislation, the rights laid down in Article 3(2) are subject to a limitation period, that period shall not expire within a period of two years from the time of delivery.

2.   Member States may provide that, in order to benefit from his rights, the consumer must inform the seller of the lack of conformity within a period of two months from the date on which he detected such lack of conformity. Member States shall inform the Commission of their use of this paragraph. The Commission shall monitor the effect of the existence of this option for the Member States on consumers and on the internal market. Not later than 7 January 2003, the Commission shall prepare a report on the use made by Member States of this paragraph. This report shall be published in the *Official Journal of the European Communities.*

3.   Unless proved otherwise, any lack of conformity which becomes apparent within six months of delivery of the goods shall be presumed to have existed at the time of delivery unless this presumption is incompatible with the nature of the goods or the nature of the lack of conformity.

Article 6

Guarantees
1.   A guarantee shall be legally binding on the offerer under the conditions laid down in the guarantee statement and the associated advertising.

2.   The guarantee shall:
— state that the consumer has legal rights under applicable national legislation governing the sale of consumer goods and make clear that those rights are not affected by the guarantee,
— set out in plain intelligible language the contents of the guarantee and the essential particulars necessary for making claims under the guarantee, notably the duration and territorial scope of the guarantee as well as the name and address of the guarantor.

3.   On request by the consumer, the guarantee shall be made available in writing or feature in another durable medium available and accessible to him.

4.   Within its own territory, the Member State in which the consumer goods are marketed may, in accordance with the rules of the Treaty, provide that the guarantee be drafted in one or more languages which it shall determine from among the official languages of the Community.

5.   Should a guarantee infringe the requirements of paragraphs 2, 3 or 4, the validity of this guarantee shall in no way be affected, and the consumer can still rely on the guarantee and require that it be honoured.

Article 7

Binding nature
1.   Any contractual terms or agreements concluded with the seller before the lack of conformity is brought to the seller's attention which directly or indirectly waive or restrict the rights resulting from this Directive shall, as provided for by national law, not be binding on the consumer. Member States may provide that, in the case of second-hand goods, the seller and consumer may agree contractual terms or agreements which have a shorter time period for the liability of the seller than that set down in Article 5(1). Such period may not be less than one year.

2. Member States shall take the necessary measures to ensure that consumers are not deprived of the protection afforded by this Directive as a result of opting for the law of a non-Member State as the law applicable to the contract where the contract has a close connection with the territory of the Member States.

Article 8

National law and minimum protection
1.   The rights resulting from this Directive shall be exercised without prejudice to other rights which the consumer may invoke under the national rules governing contractual or non-contractual liability.

2.   Member States may adopt or maintain in force more stringent provisions, compatible with the Treaty in the field covered by this Directive, to ensure a higher level of consumer protection.

Article 9

Member States shall take appropriate measures to inform the consumer of the national law transposing this Directive and shall encourage, where appropriate, professional organisations to inform consumers of their rights.

Article 10

The Annex to Directive 98/27/EC shall be completed as follows:
'10. Directive 1999/44/EC of the European Parliament and of the Council of 25 May 1999 on certain aspects of the sale of consumer goods and associated guarantees (OJ L 171, 7.7.1999, p. 12).'

Article 11

Transposition
1.   Member States shall bring into force the laws, regulations and administrative provisions necessary to comply with this Directive not later than 1 January 2002. They shall forthwith inform the Commission thereof. When Member States adopt these measures, they shall contain a reference to this Directive, or shall be accompanied by such reference at the time of their official publication. The procedure for such reference shall be adopted by Member States.

2.   Member States shall communicate to the Commission the provisions of national law which they adopt in the field covered by this Directive.

Article 12

Review

The Commission shall, not later than 7 July 2006, review the application of this Directive and submit to the European Parliament and the Council a report. The report shall examine, inter alia, the case for introducing the producer's direct liability and, if appropriate, shall be accompanied by proposals.

Article 13

Entry into force

This Directive shall enter into force on the day of its publication in the *Official Journal of the European Communities*.

Article 14

This Directive is addressed to the Member States.

Appendix 2

The Sale and Supply of Goods to Consumers Regulations 2002

(operative provisions only)

The Secretary of State, being a Minister designated[a] for the purposes of section 2(2) of the European Communities Act 1972[b] in relation to measures relating to consumer protection, in exercise of the powers conferred on her by that subsection, makes the following Regulations:—

1. Title, commencement and extent

(1) These Regulations may be cited as the Sale and Supply of Goods to Consumers Regulations 2002 and shall come into force on 31/03/03.

(2) These Regulations extend to Northern Ireland.

2. Interpretation

In these Regulations—

'consumer' means any natural person who, in the contracts covered by these Regulations, is acting for purposes which are outside his trade, business or profession;

'consumer guarantee' means any undertaking to a consumer by a person acting in the course of his business, given without extra charge, to reimburse the price paid or to replace, repair or handle consumer goods in any way if they do not meet the specifications set out in the guarantee statement or in the relevant advertising;

'court' in relation to England and Wales and Northern Ireland means a county court or the High Court, and in relation to Scotland, the sheriff or the Court of Session;

'enforcement authority' means the Director General of Fair Trading, every local weights and measures authority in Great Britain and the Department of Enterprise, Trade and Investment for Northern Ireland;

'goods' has the same meaning as in section 61 of the Sale of Goods Act 1979[c];

'guarantor' means a person who offers a consumer guarantee to a consumer; and

'supply' includes supply by way of sale, lease, hire or hire-purchase.

---

[a] SI 1993/2661.

[b] 1972 c.68.

[c] 1979 c.54.

AMENDMENTS TO THE SALE OF GOODS ACT 1979

3. Additional implied terms in consumer cases
[...]

4. Amendments to rules on passing of risk and acceptance of goods in consumer cases
[...]

5. Buyer's additional remedies in consumer cases
[...]

6. Other amendments to the 1979 Act
[...]

AMENDMENTS TO THE SUPPLY OF GOODS AND SERVICES ACT 1982

7. Additional implied terms in cases where goods are transferred to consumers—England, Wales and Northern Ireland
[...]

8. Additional implied terms in cases where goods are transferred to consumers—Scotland
[...]

9. Transferee's additional remedies in consumer cases
[...]

10. Additional implied terms where goods are hired to consumers—England, Wales and Northern Ireland
[...]

11. Additional implied terms where goods are hired to consumers—Scotland
[...]

12. Other Amendments to 1982 Act
[...]

AMENDMENTS TO THE SUPPLY OF GOODS (IMPLIED TERMS) ACT 1973

13. Additional implied terms in consumer cases.
[...]

14. Amendments to the Unfair Contract Terms Act 1977
[...]

15. Consumer guarantees
(1)   Where goods are sold or otherwise supplied to a consumer which are offered with a consumer guarantee, the consumer guarantee takes effect at the time the goods are delivered as a contractual obligation owed by the guarantor under the conditions set out in the guarantee statement and the associated advertising.
(2)   The guarantor shall ensure that the guarantee sets out in plain intelligible language the contents of the guarantee and the essential particulars necessary for making claims

under the guarantee, notably the duration and territorial scope of the guarantee as well as the name and address of the guarantor.

(3) On request by the consumer to a person to whom paragraph (4) applies, the guarantee shall within a reasonable time be made available in writing or in another durable medium available and accessible to him.

(4) This paragraph applies to the guarantor and any other person who offers to consumers the goods which are the subject of the guarantee for sale or supply.

(5) Where consumer goods are offered with a consumer guarantee, and where those goods are offered within the territory of the United Kingdom, then the guarantor shall ensure that the consumer guarantee is written in English.

(6) If the guarantor fails to comply with the provisions of paragraphs (2) or (5) above, or a person to whom paragraph (4) applies fails to comply with paragraph (3) then the enforcement authority may apply for an injunction or (in Scotland) an order of specific implement against that person requiring him to comply.

(7) The court on an application under this Regulation may grant an injunction or (in Scotland) an order of specific implement on such terms as it thinks fit.

Appendix 3

Sale of Goods Act 1979

(as amended by SSGCR 2002; changes in italics)

PART I
CONTRACTS TO WHICH ACT APPLIES

1. Contracts to which Act applies

(1)   This Act applies to contracts of sale of goods made on or after (but not to those made before) 1 January 1894.

(2)   In relation to contracts made on certain dates, this Act applies subject to the modification of certain of its sections as mentioned in Schedule 1 below.

(3)   Any such modification is indicated in the section concerned by a reference to Schedule 1 below.

(4)   Accordingly, where a section does not contain such a reference, this Act applies in relation to the contract concerned without such modification of the section.

PART II
FORMATION OF THE CONTRACT

Contract of sale

2. Contract of sale

(1)   A contract of sale of goods is a contract by which the seller transfers or agrees to transfer the property in goods to the buyer for a money consideration, called the price.

(2)   There may be a contract of sale between one part owner and another.

(3)   A contract of sale may be absolute or conditional.

(4)   Where under a contract of sale the property in the goods is transferred from the seller to the buyer the contract is called a sale.

(5)   Where under a contract of sale the transfer of the property in the goods is to take place at a future time or subject to some condition later to be fulfilled the contract is called an agreement to sell.

(6)   An agreement to sell becomes a sale when the time elapses or the conditions are fulfilled subject to which the property in the goods is to be transferred.

3. Capacity to buy and sell

(1)   Capacity to buy and sell is regulated by the general law concerning capacity to contract and to transfer and acquire property.

(2)   Where necessaries are sold and delivered to a minor or to a person who by reason of mental incapacity or drunkenness is incompetent to contract, he must pay a reasonable price for them.
(3)   In subsection (2) above "necessaries" means goods suitable to the condition in life of the minor or other person concerned and to his actual requirements at the time of the sale and delivery.

Formalities of contract

4. How contract of sale is made
(1)   Subject to this and any other Act, a contract of sale may be made in writing (either with or without seal), or by word of mouth, or partly in writing and partly by word of mouth, or may be implied from the conduct of the parties.
(2)   Nothing in this section affects the law relating to corporations.

Subject matter of contract

5. Existing or future goods
(1)   The goods which form the subject of a contract of sale may be either existing goods, owned or possessed by the seller, or goods to be manufactured or acquired by him after the making of the contract of sale, in this Act called future goods.
(2)   There may be a contract for the sale of goods the acquisition of which by the seller depends on a contingency which may or may not happen.
(3)   Where by a contract of sale the seller purports to effect a present sale of future goods, the contract operates as an agreement to sell the goods.

6. Goods which have perished
Where there is a contract for the sale of specific goods, and the goods without the knowledge of the seller have perished at the time when the contract is made, the contract is void.

7. Goods perishing before sale but after agreement to sell
Where there is an agreement to sell specific goods and subsequently the goods, without any fault on the part of the seller or buyer, perish before the risk passes to the buyer, the agreement is avoided.

The price

8. Ascertainment of price
(1)   The price in a contract of sale may be fixed by the contract, or may be left to be fixed in a manner agreed by the contract, or may be determined by the course of dealing between the parties.
(2)   Where the price is not determined as mentioned in subsection (1) above the buyer must pay a reasonable price.
(3)   What is a reasonable price is a question of fact dependent on the circumstances of each particular case.

9. Agreement to sell at valuation
(1)   Where there is an agreement to sell goods on the terms that the price is to be fixed by the valuation of a third party, and he cannot or does not make the valuation, the agreement is avoided; but if the goods or any part of them have been delivered to and appropriated by the buyer he must pay a reasonable price for them.

(2)   Where the third party is prevented from making the valuation by the fault of the seller or buyer, the party not at fault may maintain an action for damages against the party at fault.

10. Stipulations about time
(1)   Unless a different intention appears from the terms of the contract, stipulations as to time of payment are not of the essence of a contract of sale.
(2)   Whether any other stipulation as to time is or is not of the essence of the contract depends on the terms of the contract.
(3)   In a contract of sale 'month' prima facie means calendar month.

11. When condition to be treated as warranty
(1)   This section does not apply to Scotland.
(2)   Where a contract of sale is subject to a condition to be fulfilled by the seller, the buyer may waive the condition, or may elect to treat the breach of the condition as a breach of warranty and not as a ground for treating the contract as repudiated.
(3)   Whether a stipulation in a contract of sale is a condition, the breach of which may give rise to a right to treat the contract as repudiated, or a warranty, the breach of which may give rise to a claim for damages but not to a right to reject the goods and treat the contract as repudiated, depends in each case on the construction of the contract; and a stipulation may be a condition, though called a warranty in the contract.
(4)   Subject to section 35A below where a contract of sale is not severable and the buyer has accepted the goods or part of them, the breach of a condition to be fulfilled by the seller can only be treated as a breach of warranty, and not as a ground for rejecting the goods and treating the contract as repudiated, unless there is an express or implied term of the contract to that effect.
(5)   . . .
(6)   Nothing in this section affects a condition or warranty whose fulfilment is excused by law by reason of impossibility or otherwise.
(7)   Paragraph 2 of Schedule 1 below applies in relation to a contract made before 22 April 1967 or (in the application of this Act to Northern Ireland) 28 July 1967.

12. Implied terms about title, etc
(1)   In a contract of sale, other than one to which subsection (3) below applies, there is an implied term on the part of the seller that in the case of a sale he has a right to sell the goods, and in the case of an agreement to sell he will have such a right at the time when the property is to pass.
(2)   In a contract of sale, other than one to which subsection (3) below applies, there is also an implied term that—
    (a)   the goods are free, and will remain free until the time when the property is to pass, from any charge or encumbrance not disclosed or known to the buyer before the contract is made, and
    (b)   the buyer will enjoy quiet possession of the goods except so far as it may be disturbed by the owner or other person entitled to the benefit of any charge or encumbrance so disclosed or known.
(3)   This subsection applies to a contract of sale in the case of which there appears from the contract or is to be inferred from its circumstances an intention that the seller should transfer only such title as he or a third person may have.

(4)   In a contract to which subsection (3) above applies there is an implied term that all charges or encumbrances known to the seller and not known to the buyer have been disclosed to the buyer before the contract is made.

(5)   In a contract to which subsection (3) above applies there is also an implied term that none of the following will disturb the buyer's quiet possession of the goods, namely—

    (a)   the seller;

    (b)   in a case where the parties to the contract intend that the seller should transfer only such title as a third person may have, that person;

    (c)   anyone claiming through or under the seller or that third person otherwise than under a charge or encumbrance disclosed or known to the buyer before the contract is made.

(5A) As regards England and Wales and Northern Ireland, the term implied by subsection (1) above is a condition and the terms implied by subsections (2),(4) and (5) above are warranties.

(6)   Paragraph 3 of Schedule 1 below applies in relation to a contract made before 18 May 1973.

13. Sale by description

(1)   Where there is a contract for the sale of goods by description, there is an implied term that the goods will correspond with the description.

(1A) As regards England and Wales and Northern Ireland, the term implied by subsection (1) above is a condition.

(2)   If the sale is by sample as well as by description it is not sufficient that the bulk of the goods corresponds with the sample if the goods do not also correspond with the description.

(3)   A sale of goods is not prevented from being a sale by description by reason only that, being exposed for sale or hire, they are selected by the buyer.

(4)   Paragraph 4 of Schedule 1 below applies in relation to a contract made before 18th May 1973.

14. Implied terms about quality or fitness

(1)   Except as provided by this section and section 15 below and subject to any other enactment, there is no implied term about the quality or fitness for any particular purpose of goods supplied under a contract of sale.

(2)   Where the seller sells goods in the course of a business, there is an implied term that the goods supplied under the contract are of satisfactory quality.

(2A) For the purposes of this Act, goods are of satisfactory quality if they meet the standard that a reasonable person would regard as satisfactory, taking account of any description of the goods, the price (if relevant) and all the other relevant circumstances.

(2B) For the purposes of this Act, the quality of goods includes their state and condition and the following (among others) are in appropriate cases aspects of the quality of goods—

    (a)   fitness for all the purposes for which goods of the kind in question are commonly supplied,

    (b)   appearance and finish,

    (c)   freedom from minor defects,

    (d)   safety, and

    (e)   durability.

(2C) The term implied by subsection (2) above does not extend to any matter making the quality of goods unsatisfactory—

    (a)   which is specifically drawn to the buyer's attention before the contract is made,

    (b)   where the buyer examines the goods before the contract is made, which that examination ought to reveal, or

    (c)   in the case of a contract for sale by sample, which would have been apparent on a reasonable examination of the sample.

(2D) If the buyer deals as consumer or, in Scotland, if a contract of sale is a consumer contract, the relevant circumstances mentioned in subsection (2A) above include any public statements on the specific characteristics of the goods made about them by the seller, the producer or his representative, particularly in advertising or on labelling.

(2E) A public statement is not by virtue of subsection (2D) above a relevant circumstance for the purposes of subsection (2A) above in the case of a contract of sale, if the seller shows that—

    (a)   at the time the contract was made, he was not, and could not reasonably have been, aware of the statement,

    (b)   before the contract was made, the statement had been withdrawn in public or, to the extent that it contained anything which was incorrect or misleading, it had been corrected in public, or

    (c)   the decision to buy the goods could not have been influenced by the statement.

(2F) Subsections (2D) and (2E) above do not prevent any public statement from being a relevant circumstance for the purposes of subsection (2A) above (whether or not the buyer deals as consumer or, in Scotland, whether or not the contract of sale is a consumer contract) if the statement would have been such a circumstance apart from those subsections.

(3)   Where the seller sells goods in the course of a business and the buyer, expressly or by implication, makes known—

    (a)   to the seller, or

    (b)   where the purchase price or part of it is payable by instalments and the goods were previously sold by a credit-broker to the seller, to that credit-broker, any particular purpose for which the goods are being bought, there is an implied [term] that the goods supplied under the contract are reasonably fit for that purpose, whether or not that is a purpose for which such goods are commonly supplied, except where the circumstances show that the buyer does not rely, or that it is unreasonable for him to rely, on the skill or judgment of the seller or credit-broker.

(4)   An implied term about quality or fitness for a particular purpose may be annexed to a contract of sale by usage.

(5)   The preceding provisions of this section apply to a sale by a person who in the course of a business is acting as agent for another as they apply to a sale by a principal in the course of a business, except where that other is not selling in the course of a business and either the buyer knows that fact or reasonable steps are taken to bring it to the notice of the buyer before the contract is made.

(6)   As regards England and Wales and Northern Ireland, the terms implied by subsections (2) and (3) above are conditions.

(7)   Paragraph 5 of Schedule 1 below applies in relation to a contract made on or after 18 May 1973 and before the appointed day, and paragraph 6 in relation to one made before 18th May 1973.

(8)   In subsection (7) above and paragraph 5 of Schedule 1 below references to the appointed day are to the day appointed for the purposes of those provisions by an order of the Secretary of State made by statutory instrument.

Sale by sample

15. Sale by sample

(1)   A contract of sale is a contract for sale by sample where there is an express or implied term to that effect in the contract.
(2)   In the case of a contract for sale by sample there is an implied term—
    (a)   that the bulk will correspond with the sample in quality;
    (b)   . . .
    (c)   that the goods will be free from any defect, making their quality unsatisfactory, which would not be apparent on reasonable examination of the sample.
(3)   As regards England and Wales and Northern Ireland, the term implied by subsection (2) above is a condition.
(4)   Paragraph 7 of Schedule 1 below applies in relation to a contract made before 18 May 1973.

15A.   Modification of remedies for breach of condition in non-consumer cases

(1)   Where in the case of a contract of sale—
    (a)   the buyer would, apart from this subsection, have the right to reject goods by reason of a breach on the part of the seller of a term implied by section 13, 14 or 15 above, but
    (b)   the breach is so slight that it would be unreasonable for him to reject them, then, if the buyer does not deal as consumer, the breach is not to be treated as a breach of condition but may be treated as a breach of warranty.
(2)   This section applies unless a contrary intention appears in, or is to be implied from, the contract.
(3)   It is for the seller to show that a breach fell within subsection (1)(b) above.
(4)   This section does not apply to Scotland.

15B.   Remedies for breach of contract as respects Scotland

(1)   Where in a contract of sale the seller is in breach of any term of the contract (express or implied), the buyer shall be entitled—
    (a)   to claim damages, and
    (b)   if the breach is material, to reject any goods delivered under the contract and treat it as repudiated.
(2)   Where a contract of sale is a consumer contract, then, for the purposes of subsection (1)(b) above, breach by the seller of any term (express or implied)—
    (a)   as to the quality of the goods or their fitness for a purpose,
    (b)   if the goods are, or are to be, sold by description, that the goods will correspond with the description,
    (c)   if the goods are, or are to be, sold by reference to a sample, that the bulk will correspond with the sample in quality,
shall be deemed to be a material breach.
(3)   This section applies to Scotland only.

PART III
EFFECTS OF THE CONTRACT

Transfer of property as between seller and buyer

16. Goods must be ascertained
Subject to section 20A below, where there is a contract for the sale of unascertained goods no property in the goods is transferred to the buyer unless and until the goods are ascertained.

17. Property passes when intended to pass
(1)   Where there is a contract for the sale of specific or ascertained goods the property in them is transferred to the buyer at such time as the parties to the contract intend it to be transferred.
(2)   For the purpose of ascertaining the intention of the parties regard shall be had to the terms of the contract, the conduct of the parties and the circumstances of the case.

18. Rules for ascertaining intention
Unless a different intention appears, the following are rules for ascertaining the intention of the parties as to the time at which the property in the goods is to pass to the buyer.
   Rule 1—
   Where there is an unconditional contract for the sale of specific goods in a deliverable state the property in the goods passes to the buyer when the contract is made, and it is immaterial whether the time of payment or the time of delivery, or both, be postponed.
   Rule 2—
   Where there is a contract for the sale of specific goods and the seller is bound to do something to the goods for the purpose of putting them into a deliverable state, the property does not pass until the thing is done and the buyer has notice that it has been done.
   Rule 3—
   Where there is a contract for the sale of specific goods in a deliverable state but the seller is bound to weigh, measure, test, or do some other act or thing with reference to the goods for the purpose of ascertaining the price, the property does not pass until the act or thing is done and the buyer has notice that it has been done.
   Rule 4—
   When goods are delivered to the buyer on approval or on sale or return or other similar terms the property in the goods passes to the buyer—
      (a)   when he signifies his approval or acceptance to the seller or does any other act adopting the transaction;
      (b)   if he does not signify his approval or acceptance to the seller but retains the goods without giving notice of rejection, then, if a time has been fixed for the return of the goods, on the expiration of that time, and, if no time has been fixed, on the expiration of a reasonable time.
   Rule 5—
   (1)   Where there is a contract for the sale of unascertained or future goods by description, and goods of that description and in a deliverable state are unconditionally appropriated to the contract, either by the seller with the assent of the buyer or by the buyer with the assent of the seller, the property in the goods then passes to the buyer; and the assent may be express or implied, and may be given either before or after the appropriation is made.

(2)   Where, in pursuance of the contract, the seller delivers the goods to the buyer or to a carrier or other bailee or custodier (whether named by the buyer or not) for the purpose of transmission to the buyer, and does not reserve the right of disposal, he is to be taken to have unconditionally appropriated the goods to the contract.

(3)   Where there is a contract for the sale of a specified quantity of unascertained goods in a deliverable state forming part of a bulk which is identified either in the contract or by subsequent agreement between the parties and the bulk is reduced to (or to less than) that quantity, then, if the buyer under that contract is the only buyer to whom goods are then due out of the bulk—

(a)   the remaining goods are to be taken as appropriated to that contract at the time when the bulk is so reduced; and

(b)   the property in those goods then passes to that buyer.

(4)   Paragraph (3) above applies also (with the necessary modifications) where a bulk is reduced to (or to less than) the aggregate of the quantities due to a single buyer under separate contracts relating to that bulk and he is the only buyer to whom goods are then due out of that bulk.

19. Reservation of right of disposal

(1)   Where there is a contract for the sale of specific goods or where goods are subsequently appropriated to the contract, the seller may, by the terms of the contract or appropriation, reserve the right of disposal of the goods until certain conditions are fulfilled; and in such a case, notwithstanding the delivery of the goods to the buyer, or to a carrier or other bailee or custodier for the purpose of transmission to the buyer, the property in the goods does not pass to the buyer until the conditions imposed by the seller are fulfilled.

(2)   Where goods are shipped, and by the bill of lading the goods are deliverable to the order of the seller or his agent, the seller is prima facie to be taken to reserve the right of disposal.

(3)   Where the seller of goods draws on the buyer for the price, and transmits the bill of exchange and bill of lading to the buyer together to secure acceptance or payment of the bill of exchange, the buyer is bound to return the bill of lading if he does not honour the bill of exchange, and if he wrongfully retains the bill of lading the property in the goods does not pass to him.

20. Passing of risk

(1)   Unless otherwise agreed, the goods remain at the seller's risk until the property in them is transferred to the buyer, but when the property in them is transferred to the buyer the goods are at the buyer's risk whether delivery has been made or not.

(2)   But where delivery has been delayed through the fault of either buyer or seller the goods are at the risk of the party at fault as regards any loss which might not have occurred but for such fault.

(3)   Nothing in this section affects the duties or liabilities of either seller or buyer as a bailee or custodier of the goods of the other party.

(4)   In a case where the buyer deals as consumer or, in Scotland, where there is a consumer contract in which the buyer is a consumer, subsections (1) to (3) above must be ignored and the goods remain at the seller's risk until they are delivered to the consumer.

20A. Undivided shares in goods forming part of a bulk

(1)   This section applies to a contract for the sale of a specified quantity of unascertained goods if the following conditions are met—

(a)   the goods or some of them form part of a bulk which is identified either in the contract or by subsequent agreement between the parties; and

(b)   the buyer has paid the price for some or all of the goods which are the subject of the contract and which form part of the bulk.

(2)   Where this section applies, then (unless the parties agree otherwise), as soon as the conditions specified in paragraphs (a) and (b) of subsection (1) above are met or at such later time as the parties may agree—

(a)   property in an undivided share in the bulk is transferred to the buyer, and

(b)   the buyer becomes an owner in common of the bulk.

(3)   Subject to subsection (4) below, for the purposes of this section, the undivided share of a buyer in a bulk at any time shall be such share as the quantity of goods paid for and due to the buyer out of the bulk bears to the quantity of goods in the bulk at that time.

(4)   Where the aggregate of the undivided shares of buyers in a bulk determined under subsection (3) above would at any time exceed the whole of the bulk at that time, the undivided share in the bulk of each buyer shall be reduced proportionately so that the aggregate of the undivided shares is equal to the whole bulk.

(5)   Where a buyer has paid the price for only some of the goods due to him out of a bulk, any delivery to the buyer out of the bulk shall, for the purposes of this section, be ascribed in the first place to the goods in respect of which payment has been made.

(6)   For the purposes of this section payment of part of the price for any goods shall be treated as payment for a corresponding part of the goods.

20B. Deemed consent by co-owner to dealings in bulk goods

(1)   A person who has become an owner in common of a bulk by virtue of section 20A above shall be deemed to have consented to—

(a)   any delivery of goods out of the bulk to any other owner in common of the bulk, being goods which are due to him under his contract;

(b)   any dealing with or removal, delivery or disposal of goods in the bulk by any other person who is an owner in common of the bulk in so far as the goods fall within that co-owner's undivided share in the bulk at the time of the dealing, removal, delivery or disposal.

(2)   No cause of action shall accrue to anyone against a person by reason of that person having acted in accordance with paragraph (a) or (b) of subsection (1) above in reliance on any consent deemed to have been given under that subsection.

(3)   Nothing in this section or section 20A above shall—

(a)   impose an obligation on a buyer of goods out of a bulk to compensate any other buyer of goods out of that bulk for any shortfall in the goods received by that other buyer;

(b)   affect any contractual arrangement between buyers of goods out of a bulk for adjustments between themselves; or

(c)   affect the rights of any buyer under his contract.

Transfer of title

21. Sale by person not the owner
(1)   Subject to this Act, where goods are sold by a person who is not their owner, and who does not sell them under the authority or with the consent of the owner, the buyer acquires no better title to the goods than the seller had, unless the owner of the goods is by his conduct precluded from denying the seller's authority to sell.
(2)   Nothing in this Act affects—
    (a)   the provisions of the Factors Acts or any enactment enabling the apparent owner of goods to dispose of them as if he were their true owner;
    (b)   the validity of any contract of sale under any special common law or statutory power of sale or under the order of a court of competent jurisdiction.

22. Market overt
(1)   ...
(2)   This section does not apply to Scotland.
(3)   Paragraph 8 of Schedule 1 below applies in relation to a contract under which goods were sold before 1st January 1968 or (in the application of this Act to Northern Ireland) 29th August 1967.

23. Sale under voidable title
When the seller of goods has a voidable title to them, but his title has not been avoided at the time of the sale, the buyer acquires a good title to the goods, provided he buys them in good faith and without notice of the seller's defect of title.

24. Seller in possession after sale
Where a person having sold goods continues or is in possession of the goods, or of the documents of title to the goods, the delivery or transfer by that person, or by a mercantile agent acting for him, of the goods or documents of title under any sale, pledge, or other disposition thereof, to any person receiving the same in good faith and without notice of the previous sale, has the same effect as if the person making the delivery or transfer were expressly authorised by the owner of the goods to make the same.

25. Buyer in possession after sale
(1)   Where a person having bought or agreed to buy goods obtains, with the consent of the seller, possession of the goods or the documents of title to the goods, the delivery or transfer by that person, or by a mercantile agent acting for him, of the goods or documents of title, under any sale, pledge, or other disposition thereof, to any person receiving the same in good faith and without notice of any lien or other right of the original seller in respect of the goods, has the same effect as if the person making the delivery or transfer were a mercantile agent in possession of the goods or documents of title with the consent of the owner.
(2)   For the purposes of subsection (1) above—
    (a)   the buyer under a conditional sale agreement is to be taken not to be a person who has bought or agreed to buy goods, and
    (b)   'conditional sale agreement' means an agreement for the sale of goods which is a consumer credit agreement within the meaning of the Consumer Credit Act 1974 under which the purchase price or part of it is payable by instalments, and the property in the goods is to remain in the seller (notwithstanding that the buyer is to be in possession of the

goods) until such conditions as to the payment of instalments or otherwise as may be specified in the agreement are fulfilled.

(3)   Paragraph 9 of Schedule 1 below applies in relation to a contract under which a person buys or agrees to buy goods and which is made before the appointed day.

(4)   In subsection (3) above and paragraph 9 of Schedule 1 below references to the appointed day are to the day appointed for the purposes of those provisions by an order of the Secretary of State made by statutory instrument.

26. Supplementary to sections 24 and 25

In sections 24 and 25 above 'mercantile agent' means a mercantile agent having in the customary course of his business as such agent authority either—

    (a)   to sell goods, or

    (b)   to consign goods for the purpose of sale, or

    (c)   to buy goods, or

    (d)   to raise money on the security of goods.

PART IV

PERFORMANCE OF THE CONTRACT

27. Duties of seller and buyer

It is the duty of the seller to deliver the goods, and of the buyer to accept and pay for them, in accordance with the terms of the contract of sale.

28. Payment and delivery are concurrent conditions

Unless otherwise agreed, delivery of the goods and payment of the price are concurrent conditions, that is to say, the seller must be ready and willing to give possession of the goods to the buyer in exchange for the price and the buyer must be ready and willing to pay the price in exchange for possession of the goods.

29. Rules about delivery

(1)   Whether it is for the buyer to take possession of the goods or for the seller to send them to the buyer is a question depending in each case on the contract, express or implied, between the parties.

(2)   Apart from any such contract, express or implied, the place of delivery is the seller's place of business if he has one, and if not, his residence; except that, if the contract is for the sale of specific goods, which to the knowledge of the parties when the contract is made are in some other place, then that place is the place of delivery.

(3)   Where under the contract of sale the seller is bound to send the goods to the buyer, but no time for sending them is fixed, the seller is bound to send them within a reasonable time.

(4)   Where the goods at the time of sale are in the possession of a third person, there is no delivery by seller to buyer unless and until the third person acknowledges to the buyer that he holds the goods on his behalf; but nothing in this section affects the operation of the issue or transfer of any document of title to goods.

(5)   Demand or tender of delivery may be treated as ineffectual unless made at a reasonable hour; and what is a reasonable hour is a question of fact.

(6)   Unless otherwise agreed, the expenses of and incidental to putting the goods into a deliverable state must be borne by the seller.

30. Delivery of wrong quantity

(1)   Where the seller delivers to the buyer a quantity of goods less than he contracted to sell, the buyer may reject them, but if the buyer accepts the goods so delivered he must pay for them at the contract rate.

(2)   Where the seller delivers to the buyer a quantity of goods larger than he contracted to sell, the buyer may accept the goods included in the contract and reject the rest, or he may reject the whole.

(2A) A buyer who does not deal as consumer may not—

(a)   where the seller delivers a quantity of goods less than he contracted to sell, reject the goods under subsection (1) above, or

(b)   where the seller delivers a quantity of goods larger than he contracted to sell, reject the whole under subsection (2) above,

if the shortfall or, as the case may be, excess is so slight that it would be unreasonable for him to do so.

(2B) It is for the seller to show that a shortfall or excess fell within subsection (2A) above.

(2C) Subsections (2A) and (2B) above do not apply to Scotland.

(3)   Where the seller delivers to the buyer a quantity of goods larger than he contracted to sell and the buyer accepts the whole of the goods so delivered he must pay for them at the contract rate.

(4)   . . .

(5)   This section is subject to any usage of trade, special agreement, or course of dealing between the parties.

31. Instalment deliveries

(1)   Unless otherwise agreed, the buyer of goods is not bound to accept delivery of them by instalments.

(2)   Where there is a contract for the sale of goods to be delivered by stated instalments, which are to be separately paid for, and the seller makes defective deliveries in respect of one or more instalments, or the buyer neglects or refuses to take delivery of or pay for one or more instalments, it is a question in each case depending on the terms of the contract and the circumstances of the case whether the breach of contract is a repudiation of the whole contract or whether it is a severable breach giving rise to a claim for compensation but not to a right to treat the whole contract as repudiated.

32. Delivery to carrier

(1)   Where, in pursuance of a contract of sale, the seller is authorised or required to send the goods to the buyer, delivery of the goods to a carrier (whether named by the buyer or not) for the purpose of transmission to the buyer is prima facie deemed to be a delivery of the goods to the buyer.

(2)   Unless otherwise authorised by the buyer, the seller must make such contract with the carrier on behalf of the buyer as may be reasonable having regard to the nature of the goods and the other circumstances of the case; and if the seller omits to do so, and the goods are lost or damaged in course of transit, the buyer may decline to treat the delivery to the carrier as a delivery to himself or may hold the seller responsible in damages.

(3)   Unless otherwise agreed, where goods are sent by the seller to the buyer by a route involving sea transit, under circumstances in which it is usual to insure, the seller must give

such notice to the buyer as may enable him to insure them during their sea transit; and if the seller fails to do so, the goods are at his risk during such sea transit.

(4) In a case where the buyer deals as consumer or, in Scotland, where there is a consumer contract in which the buyer is a consumer, subsections (1) to (3) above must be ignored, but if in pursuance of a contract of sale the seller is authorised or required to send the goods to the buyer, delivery of the goods to the carrier is not delivery of the goods to the buyer.

33. Risk where goods are delivered at distant place
Where the seller of goods agrees to deliver them at his own risk at a place other than that where they are when sold, the buyer must nevertheless (unless otherwise agreed) take any risk of deterioration in the goods necessarily incident to the course of transit.

34. Buyer's right of examining the goods
. . . Unless otherwise agreed, when the seller tenders delivery of goods to the buyer, he is bound on request to afford the buyer a reasonable opportunity of examining the goods for the purpose of ascertaining whether they are in conformity with the contract and, in the case of a contract for sale by sample, of comparing the bulk with the sample.

35. Acceptance
(1)   The buyer is deemed to have accepted the goods subject to subsection (2) below—

(a)   when he intimates to the seller that he has accepted them, or

(b)   when the goods have been delivered to him and he does any act in relation to them which is inconsistent with the ownership of the seller.

(2)   Where goods are delivered to the buyer, and he has not previously examined them, he is not deemed to have accepted them under subsection (1) above until he has had a reasonable opportunity of examining them for the purpose—

(a)   of ascertaining whether they are in conformity with the contract, and

(b)   in the case of a contract for sale by sample, of comparing the bulk with the sample.

(3)   Where the buyer deals as consumer or (in Scotland) the contract of sale is a consumer contract, the buyer cannot lose his right to rely on subsection (2) above by agreement, waiver or otherwise.

(4)   The buyer is also deemed to have accepted the goods when after the lapse of a reasonable time he retains the goods without intimating to the seller that he has rejected them.

(5)   The questions that are material in determining for the purposes of subsection (4) above whether a reasonable time has elapsed include whether the buyer has had a reasonable opportunity of examining the goods for the purpose mentioned in subsection (2) above.

(6)   The buyer is not by virtue of this section deemed to have accepted the goods merely because—

(a)   he asks for, or agrees to, their repair by or under an arrangement with the seller, or

(b)   the goods are delivered to another under a sub-sale or other disposition.

(7)   Where the contract is for the sale of goods making one or more commercial units, a buyer accepting any goods included in a unit is deemed to have accepted all the goods making the unit; and in this subsection 'commercial unit' means a unit division of which would materially impair the value of the goods or the character of the unit.

(8) Paragraph 10 of Schedule 1 below applies in relation to a contract made before 22nd April 1967 or (in the application of this Act to Northern Ireland) 28th July 1967.

35A. Right of partial rejection

(1)   If the buyer—

(a)   has the right to reject the goods by reason of a breach on the part of the seller that affects some or all of them, but

(b)   accepts some of the goods, including, where there are any goods unaffected by the breach, all such goods,

he does not by accepting them lose his right to reject the rest.

(2)   In the case of a buyer having the right to reject an instalment of goods, subsection (1) above applies as if references to the goods were references to the goods comprised in the instalment.

(3)   For the purposes of subsection (1) above, goods are affected by a breach if by reason of the breach they are not in conformity with the contract.

(4)   This section applies unless a contrary intention appears in, or is to be implied from, the contract.

36. Buyer not bound to return rejected goods

Unless otherwise agreed, where goods are delivered to the buyer, and he refuses to accept them, having the right to do so, he is not bound to return them to the seller, but it is sufficient if he intimates to the seller that he refuses to accept them.

37. Buyer's liability for not taking delivery of goods

(1)   When the seller is ready and willing to deliver the goods, and requests the buyer to take delivery, and the buyer does not within a reasonable time after such request take delivery of the goods, he is liable to the seller for any loss occasioned by his neglect or refusal to take delivery, and also for a reasonable charge for the care and custody of the goods.

(2)   Nothing in this section affects the rights of the seller where the neglect or refusal of the buyer to take delivery amounts to a repudiation of the contract.

PART V

RIGHTS OF UNPAID SELLER AGAINST THE GOODS

Preliminary

38. Unpaid seller defined

(1)   The seller of goods is an unpaid seller within the meaning of this Act—

(a)   when the whole of the price has not been paid or tendered;

(b)   when a bill of exchange or other negotiable instrument has been received as conditional payment, and the condition on which it was received has not been fulfilled by reason of the dishonour of the instrument or otherwise.

(2)   In this Part of this Act 'seller' includes any person who is in the position of a seller, as, for instance, an agent of the seller to whom the bill of lading has been indorsed, or a con-signor or agent who has himself paid (or is directly responsible for) the price.

39. Unpaid seller's rights

(1)   Subject to this and any other Act, notwithstanding that the property in the goods may have passed to the buyer, the unpaid seller of goods, as such, has by implication of law—

(a)   a lien on the goods or right to retain them for the price while he is in possession of them;

(b)   in case of the insolvency of the buyer, a right of stopping the goods in transit after he has parted with the possession of them;

(c)   a right of re-sale as limited by this Act.

(2)   Where the property in goods has not passed to the buyer, the unpaid seller has (in addition to his other remedies) a right of withholding delivery similar to and co-extensive with his rights of lien or retention and stoppage in transit where the property has passed to the buyer.

40. ...

Unpaid seller's lien

41. Seller's lien

(1)   Subject to this Act, the unpaid seller of goods who is in possession of them is entitled to retain possession of them until payment or tender of the price in the following cases—

(a)   where the goods have been sold without any stipulation as to credit;

(b)   where the goods have been sold on credit but the term of credit has expired;

(c)   where the buyer becomes insolvent.

(2)   The seller may exercise his lien or right of retention notwithstanding that he is in possession of the goods as agent

42. Part delivery

Where an unpaid seller has made part delivery of the goods, he may exercise his lien or right of retention on the remainder, unless such part delivery has been made under such circumstances as to show an agreement to waive the lien or right of retention.

43. Termination of lien

(1)   The unpaid seller of goods loses his lien or right of retention in respect of them—

(a)   when he delivers the goods to a carrier or other bailee or custodier for the purpose of transmission to the buyer without reserving the right of disposal of the goods;

(b)   when the buyer or his agent lawfully obtains possession of the goods;

(c)   by waiver of the lien or right of retention.

(2)   An unpaid seller of goods who has a lien or right of retention in respect of them does not lose his lien or right of retention by reason only that he has obtained judgment or decree for the price of the goods.

Stoppage in transit

44. Right of stoppage in transit

Subject to this Act, when the buyer of goods becomes insolvent the unpaid seller who has parted with the possession of the goods has the right of stopping them in transit, that is to say, he may resume possession of the goods as long as they are in course of transit, and may retain them until payment or tender of the price.

45. Duration of transit

(1)   Goods are deemed to be in course of transit from the time when they are delivered to a carrier or other bailee or custodier for the purpose of transmission to the buyer, until the buyer or his agent in that behalf takes delivery of them from the carrier or other bailee or custodier.

(2)   If the buyer or his agent in that behalf obtains delivery of the goods before their arrival at the appointed destination, the transit is at an end.

(3)   If, after the arrival of the goods at the appointed destination, the carrier or other bailee or custodier acknowledges to the buyer or his agent that he holds the goods on his behalf and continues in possession of them as bailee or custodier for the buyer or his agent, the transit is at an end, and it is immaterial that a further destination for the goods may have been indicated by the buyer.

(4)   If the goods are rejected by the buyer, and the carrier or other bailee or custodier continues in possession of them, the transit is not deemed to be at an end, even if the seller has refused to receive them back.

(5)   When goods are delivered to a ship chartered by the buyer it is a question depending on the circumstances of the particular case whether they are in the possession of the master as a carrier or as agent to the buyer.

(6)   Where the carrier or other bailee or custodier wrongfully refuses to deliver the goods to the buyer or his agent in that behalf, the transit is deemed to be at an end.

(7)   Where part delivery of the goods has been made to the buyer or his agent in that behalf, the remainder of the goods may be stopped in transit, unless such part delivery has been made under such circumstances as to show an agreement to give up possession of the whole of the goods.

46. How stoppage in transit is effected

(1)   The unpaid seller may exercise his right of stoppage in transit either by taking actual possession of the goods or by giving notice of his claim to the carrier or other bailee or custodier in whose possession the goods are.

(2)   The notice may be given either to the person in actual possession of the goods or to his principal.

(3)   If given to the principal, the notice is ineffective unless given at such time and under such circumstances that the principal, by the exercise of reasonable diligence, may communicate it to his servant or agent in time to prevent a delivery to the buyer.

(4)   When notice of stoppage in transit is given by the seller to the carrier or other bailee or custodier in possession of the goods, he must re-deliver the goods to, or according to the directions of, the seller; and the expenses of the re-delivery must be borne by the seller.

Re-sale etc by buyer

47. Effect of sub-sale etc by buyer

(1)   Subject to this Act, the unpaid seller's right of lien or retention or stoppage in transit is not affected by any sale or other disposition of the goods which the buyer may have made, unless the seller has assented to it.

(2)   Where a document of title to goods has been lawfully transferred to any person as buyer or owner of the goods, and that person transfers the document to a person who takes it in good faith and for valuable consideration, then—

(a)   if the last-mentioned transfer was by way of sale the unpaid seller's right of lien or retention or stoppage in transit is defeated; and

(b)   if the last-mentioned transfer was made by way of pledge or other disposition for value, the unpaid seller's right of lien or retention or stoppage in transit can only be exercised subject to the rights of the transferee.

Rescission: and re-sale by seller

48. Rescission: and re-sale by seller

(1)   Subject to this section, a contract of sale is not rescinded by the mere exercise by an unpaid seller of his right of lien or retention or stoppage in transit.

(2)   Where an unpaid seller who has exercised his right of lien or retention or stoppage in transit re-sells the goods, the buyer acquires a good title to them as against the original buyer.

(3)   Where the goods are of a perishable nature, or where the unpaid seller gives notice to the buyer of his intention to re-sell, and the buyer does not within a reasonable time pay or tender the price, the unpaid seller may re-sell the goods and recover from the original buyer damages for any loss occasioned by his breach of contract.

(4)   Where the seller expressly reserves the right of re-sale in case the buyer should make default, and on the buyer making default re-sells the goods, the original contract of sale is rescinded but without prejudice to any claim the seller may have for damages.

PART 5A ADDITIONAL RIGHTS OF BUYER IN CONSUMER CASES

48A.   Introductory

(1)   This section applies if—

(a)   the buyer deals as consumer or, in Scotland, there is a consumer contract in which the buyer is a consumer, and

(b)   the goods do not conform to the contract of sale at the time of delivery.

(2)   If this section applies, the buyer has the right—

(a)   under and in accordance with section 48B below, to require the seller to repair or replace the goods, or

(b)   under and in accordance with section 48C below—

(i)   to require the seller to reduce the purchase price of the goods to the buyer by an appropriate amount, or

(ii)   to rescind the contract with regard to the goods in question.

(3)   For the purposes of subsection (1)(b) above goods which do not conform to the contract of sale at any time within the period of six months starting with the date on which the goods were delivered to the buyer must be taken not to have so conformed at that date.

(4)   Subsection (3) above does not apply if—

(a)   *it is established that the goods did so conform at that date;*

(b)   *its application is incompatible with the nature of the goods or the nature of the lack of conformity.*

48B.   Repair or replacement of the goods

(1)   If section 48A above applies, the buyer may require the seller—

(a)   to repair the goods, or

(b)   to replace the goods.

(2)   If the buyer requires the seller to repair or replace the goods, the seller must—

(a)   repair or, as the case may be, replace the goods within a reasonable time but without causing significant inconvenience to the buyer;

(b)   bear any necessary costs incurred in doing so (including in particular the cost of any labour, materials or postage).

(3)   The buyer must not require the seller to repair or, as the case may be, replace the goods if that remedy is—

  (a)   impossible, or

  (b)   disproportionate in comparison to the other of those remedies, or

  (c)   disproportionate in comparison to an appropriate reduction in the purchase price under paragraph (a), or rescission under paragraph (b), of section 48C(1) below.

(4)   One remedy is disproportionate in comparison to the other if the one imposes costs on the seller which, in comparison to those imposed on him by the other, are unreasonable, taking into account—

  (a)   the value which the goods would have if they conformed to the contract of sale,

  (b)   the significance of the lack of conformity, and

  (c)   whether the other remedy could be effected without significant inconvenience to the buyer.

(5)   Any question as to what is a reasonable time or significant inconvenience is to be determined by reference to—

  (a)   the nature of the goods, and

  (b)   the purpose for which the goods were acquired.

48C. Reduction of purchase price or rescission of contract

(1)   If section 48A above applies, the buyer may—

  (a)   require the seller to reduce the purchase price of the goods in question to the buyer by an appropriate amount, or

  (b)   rescind the contract with regard to those goods,

if the condition in subsection (2) below is satisfied.

(2)   The condition is that—

  (a)   by virtue of section 48B(3) above the buyer may require neither repair nor replacement of the goods; or

  (b)   the buyer has required the seller to repair or replace the goods, but the seller is in breach of the requirement of section 48B(2)(a) above to do so within a reasonable time and without significant inconvenience to the buyer.

(3)   For the purposes of this Part, if the buyer rescinds the contract, any reimbursement to the buyer may be reduced to take account of the use he has had of the goods since they were delivered to him.

48D. Relation to other remedies etc.

(1)   If the buyer requires the seller to repair or replace the goods the buyer must not act under subsection (2) until he has given the seller a reasonable time in which to repair or replace (as the case may be) the goods.

(2)   The buyer acts under this subsection if—

  (a)   in England and Wales or Northern Ireland he rejects the goods and terminates the contract for breach of condition;

  (b)   in Scotland he rejects any goods delivered under the contract and treats it as repudiated;

  (c)   he requires the goods to be replaced or repaired (as the case may be).

48E. Powers of the court

(1)   In any proceedings in which a remedy is sought by virtue of this Part the court, in addition to any other power it has, may act under this section.

(2)   On the application of the buyer the court may make an order requiring specific per-formance or, in Scotland, specific implement by the seller of any obligation imposed on him by virtue of section 48B above.

(3)   Subsection (4) applies if—

(a)   the buyer requires the seller to give effect to a remedy under section 48B or 48C above or has claims to rescind under section 48C, but

(b)   the court decides that another remedy under section 48B or 48C is appropriate.

(4)   The court may proceed—

(a)   as if the buyer had required the seller to give effect to the other remedy, or if the other remedy is rescission under section 48C

(b)   as if the buyer had claimed to rescind the contract under that section.

(5)   If the buyer has claimed to rescind the contract the court may order that any reimburse-ment to the buyer is reduced to take account of the use he has had of the goods since they were delivered to him.

(6)   The court may make an order under this section unconditionally or on such terms and conditions as to damages, payment of the price and otherwise as it thinks just.

48F. Conformity with the contract

For the purposes of this Part, goods do not conform to a contract of sale if there is, in relation to the goods, a breach of an express term of the contract or a term implied by section 13, 14 or 15 above.

PART VI
ACTIONS FOR BREACH OF THE CONTRACT

Seller's remedies

49. Action for price

(1)   Where, under a contract of sale, the property in the goods has passed to the buyer and he wrongfully neglects or refuses to pay for the goods according to the terms of the contract, the seller may maintain an action against him for the price of the goods.

(2)   Where, under a contract of sale, the price is payable on a day certain irrespective of delivery and the buyer wrongfully neglects or refuses to pay such price, the seller may maintain an action for the price, although the property in the goods has not passed and the goods have not been appropriated to the contract.

(3)   Nothing in this section prejudices the right of the seller in Scotland to recover interest on the price from the date of tender of the goods, or from the date on which the price was payable, as the case may be.

50. Damages for non-acceptance

(1)   Where the buyer wrongfully neglects or refuses to accept and pay for the goods, the seller may maintain an action against him for damages for non-acceptance.

(2)   The measure of damages is the estimated loss directly and naturally resulting, in the ordinary course of events, from the buyer's breach of contract.

(3)   Where there is an available market for the goods in question the measure of damages is prima facie to be ascertained by the difference between the contract price and the market or current price at the time or times when the goods ought to have been accepted or (if no time was fixed for acceptance) at the time of the refusal to accept.

Buyer's remedies

51. Damages for non-delivery

(1)   Where the seller wrongfully neglects or refuses to deliver the goods to the buyer, the buyer may maintain an action against the seller for damages for non-delivery.

(2)   The measure of damages is the estimated loss directly and naturally resulting, in the ordinary course of events, from the seller's breach of contract.

(3)   Where there is an available market for the goods in question the measure of damages is prima facie to be ascertained by the difference between the contract price and the market or current price of the goods at the time or times when they ought to have been delivered or (if no time was fixed) at the time of the refusal to deliver.

52. Specific performance

(1)   In any action for breach of contract to deliver specific or ascertained goods the court may, if it thinks fit, on the plaintiff's application, by its judgment or decree direct that the contract shall be performed specifically, without giving the defendant the option of retaining the goods on payment of damages.

(2)   The plaintiff's application may be made at any time before judgment or decree.

(3)   The judgment or decree may be unconditional, or on such terms and conditions as to damages, payment of the price and otherwise as seem just to the court.

(4)   The provisions of this section shall be deemed to be supplementary to, and not in derogation of, the right of specific implement in Scotland.

53. Remedy for breach of warranty

(1)   Where there is a breach of warranty by the seller, or where the buyer elects (or is compelled) to treat any breach of a condition on the part of the seller as a breach of warranty, the buyer is not by reason only of such breach of warranty entitled to reject the goods; but he may—

     (a)   set up against the seller the breach of warranty in diminution or extinction of the price, or

     (b)   maintain an action against the seller for damages for the breach of warranty.

(2)   The measure of damages for breach of warranty is the estimated loss directly and naturally resulting, in the ordinary course of events, from the breach of warranty.

(3)   In the case of breach of warranty of quality such loss is prima facie the difference between the value of the goods at the time of delivery to the buyer and the value they would have had if they had fulfilled the warranty.

(4)   The fact that the buyer has set up the breach of warranty in diminution or extinction of the price does not prevent him from maintaining an action for the same breach of warranty if he has suffered further damage.

(5)   This section does not apply to Scotland.

53A. Measure of damages—Scotland

(1)   The measure of damages for the seller's breach of contract is the estimated loss directly and naturally resulting, in the ordinary course of events, from the breach.

(2)   Where the seller's breach consists of the delivery of goods which are not of the quality required by the contract and the buyer retains the goods, such loss as aforesaid is prima facie the difference between the value of the goods at the time of the delivery to the buyer and the value they would have had if they had fulfilled the contract.

(3)   This section applies to Scotland only.

Interest, etc

54. Interest
Nothing in this Act affects the right of the buyer or the seller to recover interest or special damages in any case where by law interest or special damages may be recoverable, or to recover money paid where the consideration for the payment of it has failed.

PART VII
SUPPLEMENTARY

55. Exclusion of implied terms
(1)   Where a right, duty or liability would arise under a contract of sale of goods by implication of law, it may (subject to the Unfair Contract Terms Act 1977) be negatived or varied by express agreement, or by the course of dealing between the parties, or by such usage as binds both parties to the contract.

(2)   An express term does not negative a term implied by this Act unless inconsistent with it.

(3)   Paragraph 11 of Schedule 1 below applies in relation to a contract made on or after 18th May 1973 and before 1st February 1978, and paragraph 12 in relation to one made before 18th May 1973.

56. Conflict of laws
Paragraph 13 of Schedule 1 below applies in relation to a contract made on or after 18th May 1973 and before 1st February 1978, so as to make provision about conflict of laws in relation to such a contract.

57. Auction sales
(1)   Where goods are put up for sale by auction in lots, each lot is prima facie deemed to be the subject of a separate contract of sale.

(2)   A sale by auction is complete when the auctioneer announces its completion by the fall of the hammer, or in other customary manner; and until the announcement is made any bidder may retract his bid.

(3)   A sale by auction may be notified to be subject to a reserve or upset price, and a right to bid may also be reserved expressly by or on behalf of the seller.

(4)   Where a sale by auction is not notified to be subject to a right to bid by or on behalf of the seller, it is not lawful for the seller to bid himself or to employ any person to bid at the sale, or for the auctioneer knowingly to take any bid from the seller or any such person.

(5)   A sale contravening subsection (4) above may be treated as fraudulent by the buyer.

(6)   Where, in respect of a sale by auction, a right to bid is expressly reserved (but not otherwise) the seller or any one person on his behalf may bid at the auction.

58. Payment into court in Scotland
In Scotland where a buyer has elected to accept goods which he might have rejected, and to treat a breach of contract as only giving rise to a claim for damages, he may, in an action by the seller for the price, be required, in the discretion of the court before which the action depends, to consign or pay into court the price of the goods, or part of the price, or to give other reasonable security for its due payment.

59. Reasonable time a question of fact
Where a reference is made in this Act to a reasonable time the question what is a reasonable
time is a question of fact.

60. Rights etc enforceable by action
Where a right, duty or liability is declared by this Act, it may (unless otherwise provided by
this Act) be enforced by action.

61. Interpretation
(1)   In this Act, unless the context or subject matter otherwise requires—
      'action' includes counterclaim and set-off, and in Scotland condescendence and claim
and compensation;
      'bulk' means a mass or collection of goods of the same kind which—
            (a)   is contained in a defined space or area; and
            (b)   is such that any goods in the bulk are interchangeable with any other goods
therein of the same number or quantity;
      'business' includes a profession and the activities of any government department
(including a Northern Ireland department) or local or public authority;
      'buyer' means a person who buys or agrees to buy goods;
      'consumer contract' has the same meaning as in section 25(1) of the Unfair Contract
Terms Act 1977; and for the purposes of this Act the onus of proving that a contract is not
to be regarded as a consumer contract shall lie on the seller;
      'contract of sale' includes an agreement to sell as well as a sale;
      'credit-broker' means a person acting in the course of a business of credit brokerage car-
ried on by him, that is a business of effecting introductions of individuals desiring to obtain
credit—
            (a)   to persons carrying on any business so far as it relates to the provision of credit,
or
            (b)   to other persons engaged in credit brokerage;
      'defendant' includes in Scotland defender, respondent, and claimant in a multiplepoind-
ing;
      'delivery' means voluntary transfer of possession from one person to another except that
in relation to sections 20A and 20B above it includes such appropriation of goods to the
contract as results in property in the goods being transferred to the buyer;
      'document of title to goods' has the same meaning as it has in the Factors Acts;
      'Factors Acts' means the Factors Act 1889, the Factors (Scotland) Act 1890, and any
enactment amending or substituted for the same;
      'fault' means wrongful act or default;
      'future goods' means goods to be manufactured or acquired by the seller after the mak-
ing of the contract of sale;
      'goods' includes all personal chattels other than things in action and money, and in
Scotland all corporeal moveables except money; and in particular 'goods' includes emblements, industrial growing crops, and things attached to or forming part of the land which
are agreed to be severed before sale or under the contract of sale and includes an undivided
share in goods;
      'plaintiff' includes pursuer, complainer, claimant in a multiplepoinding and defendant
or defender counter-claiming;
      'producer' means the manufacturer of goods, the importer of goods into the European

Economic Area or any person purporting to be a producer by placing his name, trade mark or other distinctive sign on the goods;

'property' means the general property in goods, and not merely a special property;

'repair' means, in cases where there is a lack of conformity in goods for the purposes of section 48F of this Act, to bring the goods into conformity with the contract;

. . .

'sale' includes a bargain and sale as well as a sale and delivery;

'seller' means a person who sells or agrees to sell goods;

'specific goods' means goods identified and agreed on at the time a contract of sale is made and includes an undivided share, specified as a fraction or percentage, of goods identified and agreed on as aforesaid;

'warranty' (as regards England and Wales and Northern Ireland) means an agreement with reference to goods which are the subject of a contract of sale, but collateral to the main purpose of such contract, the breach of which gives rise to a claim for damages, but not to a right to reject the goods and treat the contract as repudiated.

(2) . . .

(3) A thing is deemed to be done in good faith within the meaning of this Act when it is in fact done honestly, whether it is done negligently or not.

(4) A person is deemed to be insolvent within the meaning of this Act if he has either ceased to pay his debts in the ordinary course of business or he cannot pay his debts as they become due, . . .

(5) Goods are in a deliverable state within the meaning of this Act when they are in such a state that the buyer would under the contract be bound to take delivery of them.

(5A) References in this Act to dealing as consumer are to be construed in accordance with Part I of the Unfair Contract Terms Act 1977; and, for the purposes of this Act, it is for a seller claiming that the buyer does not deal as consumer to show that he does not.

(6) As regards the definition of "business" in subsection (1) above, paragraph 14 of Schedule 1 below applies in relation to a contract made on or after 18th May 1973 and before 1st February 1978, and paragraph 15 in relation to one made before 18th May 1973.

62. Savings: rules of law etc

(1) The rules in bankruptcy relating to contracts of sale apply to those contracts, notwithstanding anything in this Act.

(2) The rules of the common law, including the law merchant, except in so far as they are inconsistent with the provisions of this Act, and in particular the rules relating to the law of principal and agent and the effect of fraud, misrepresentation, duress or coercion, mistake, or other invalidating cause, apply to contracts for the sale of goods.

(3) Nothing in this Act or the Sale of Goods Act 1893 affects the enactments relating to bills of sale, or any enactment relating to the sale of goods which is not expressly repealed or amended by this Act or that.

(4) The provisions of this Act about contracts of sale do not apply to a transaction in the form of a contract of sale which is intended to operate by way of mortgage, pledge, charge, or other security.

(5) Nothing in this Act prejudices or affects the landlord's right of hypothec or sequestration for rent in Scotland.

63. Consequential amendments, repeals and savings

(1)   Without prejudice to section 17 of the Interpretation Act 1978 (repeal and re-enactment), the enactments mentioned in Schedule 2 below have effect subject to the amendments there specified (being amendments consequential on this Act).

(2)   The enactments mentioned in Schedule 3 below are repealed to the extent specified in column 3, but subject to the savings in Schedule 4 below.

(3)   The savings in Schedule 4 below have effect.

64. Short title and commencement

(1)   This Act may be cited as the Sale of Goods Act 1979.

(2)   This Act comes into force on 1st January 1980.

(Schedules omitted)

Appendix 4

Supply of Goods and Services Act 1982

(as amended by SSGCR 2002; changes in italics)

PART I
SUPPLY OF GOODS

Contracts for the transfer of property in goods

1. The contracts concerned

(1) In this Act in its application to England and Wales and Northern Ireland a 'contract for the transfer of goods' means a contract under which one person transfers or agrees to transfer to another the property in goods, other than an excepted contract.

(2) For the purposes of this section an excepted contract means any of the following:—

    (a) a contract of sale of goods;

    (b) a hire-purchase agreement;

    (c) a contract under which the property in goods is (or is to be) transferred in exchange for trading stamps on their redemption;

    (d) a transfer or agreement to transfer which is made by deed and for which there is no consideration other than the presumed consideration imported by the deed;

    (e) a contract intended to operate by way of mortgage, pledge, charge or other security.

(3) For the purposes of this Act in its application to England and Wales and Northern Ireland a contract is a contract for the transfer of goods whether or not services are also provided or to be provided under the contract, and (subject to subsection (2) above) whatever is the nature of the consideration for the transfer or agreement to transfer.

2. Implied terms about title, etc

(1) In a contract for the transfer of goods, other than one to which subsection (3) below applies, there is an implied condition on the part of the transferor that in the case of a transfer of the property in the goods he has a right to transfer the property and in the case of an agreement to transfer the property in the goods he will have such a right at the time when the property is to be transferred.

(2) In a contract for the transfer of goods, other than one to which subsection (3) below applies, there is also an implied warranty that—

(a)   the goods are free, and will remain free until the time when the property is to be transferred, from any charge or encumbrance not disclosed or known to the transferee before the contract is made, and

(b)   the transferee will enjoy quiet possession of the goods except so far as it may be disturbed by the owner or other person entitled to the benefit of any charge or encumbrance so disclosed or known.

(3)   This subsection applies to a contract for the transfer of goods in the case of which there appears from the contract or is to be inferred from its circumstances an intention that the transferor should transfer only such title as he or a third person may have.

(4)   In a contract to which subsection (3) above applies there is an implied warranty that all charges or encumbrances known to the transferor and not known to the transferee have been disclosed to the transferee before the contract is made.

(5)   In a contract to which subsection (3) above applies there is also an implied warranty that none of the following will disturb the transferee's quiet possession of the goods, namely—

(a)   the transferor;

(b)   in a case where the parties to the contract intend that the transferor should transfer only such title as a third person may have, that person;

(c)   anyone claiming through or under the transferor or that third person otherwise than under a charge or encumbrance disclosed or known to the transferee before the contract is made.

3. Implied terms where transfer is by description

(1)   This section applies where, under a contract for the transfer of goods, the transferor transfers or agrees to transfer the property in the goods by description.

(2)   In such a case there is an implied condition that the goods will correspond with the description.

(3)   If the transferor transfers or agrees to transfer the property in the goods by sample as well as by description it is not sufficient that the bulk of the goods corresponds with the sample if the goods do not also correspond with the description.

(4)   A contract is not prevented from falling within subsection (1) above by reason only that, being exposed for supply, the goods are selected by the transferee.

4. Implied terms about quality or fitness

(1)   Except as provided by this section and section 5 below and subject to the provisions of any other enactment, there is no implied condition or warranty about the quality or fitness for any particular purpose of goods supplied under a contract for the transfer of goods.

(2)   Where, under such a contract, the transferor transfers the property in goods in the course of a business, there is an implied condition that the goods supplied under the contract are of satisfactory quality.

(2A) For the purposes of this section and section 5 below, goods are of satisfactory quality if they meet the standard that a reasonable person would regard as satisfactory, taking account of any description of the goods, the price (if relevant) and all the other relevant circumstances.

(2B) If the transferee deals as consumer, the relevant circumstances mentioned in subsection (2A) above include any public statements on the specific characteristics of the goods made about them by the transferor, the producer or his representative, particularly in advertising or on labelling.

(2C) A public statement is not by virtue of subsection (2B) above a relevant circumstance for the purposes of subsection (2A) above in the case of a contract for the transfer of goods, if the transferor shows that—

(a)   at the time the contract was made, he was not, and could not reasonably have been, aware of the statement,

(b)   before the contract was made, the statement had been withdrawn in public or, to the extent that it contained anything which was incorrect or misleading, it had been corrected in public, or

(c)   the decision to acquire the goods could not have been influenced by the statement.

(2D) Subsections (2B) and (2C) above do not prevent any public statement from being a relevant circumstance for the purposes of subsection (2A) above (whether or not the transferee deals as consumer) if the statement would have been such a circumstance apart from those subsections.

(3)   The condition implied by subsection (2) above does not extend to any matter making the quality of goods unsatisfactory—

(a)   which is specifically drawn to the transferee's attention before the contract is made,

(b)   where the transferee examines the goods before the contract is made, which that examination ought to reveal, or

(c)   where the property in the goods is transferred by reference to a sample, which would have been apparent on a reasonable examination of the sample.

(4)   Subsection (5) below applies where, under a contract for the transfer of goods, the transferor transfers the property in goods in the course of a business and the transferee, expressly or by implication, makes known—

(a)   to the transferor, or

(b)   where the consideration or part of the consideration for the transfer is a sum payable by instalments and the goods were previously sold by a credit-broker to the transferor, to that credit-broker, any particular purpose for which the goods are being acquired.

(5)   In that case there is (subject to subsection (6) below) an implied condition that the goods supplied under the contract are reasonably fit for that purpose, whether or not that is a purpose for which such goods are commonly supplied.

(6)   Subsection (5) above does not apply where the circumstances show that the transferee does not rely, or that it is unreasonable for him to rely, on the skill or judgment of the transferor or credit-broker.

(7)   An implied condition or warranty about quality or fitness for a particular purpose may be annexed by usage to a contract for the transfer of goods.

(8)   The preceding provisions of this section apply to a transfer by a person who in the course of a business is acting as agent for another as they apply to a transfer by a principal in the course of a business, except where that other is not transferring in the course of a business and either the transferee knows that fact or reasonable steps are taken to bring it to the transferee's notice before the contract concerned is made.

(9)   . . .

5. Implied terms where transfer is by sample

(1)   This section applies where, under a contract for the transfer of goods, the transferor transfers or agrees to transfer the property in the goods by reference to a sample.

(2)   In such a case there is an implied condition—

(a)   that the bulk will correspond with the sample in quality; and

(b)   that the transferee will have a reasonable opportunity of comparing the bulk with the sample; and

(c)   that the goods will be free from any defect, making their quality unsatisfactory, which would not be apparent on reasonable examination of the sample.

(3)   . . .

(4)   For the purposes of this section a transferor transfers or agrees to transfer the property in goods by reference to a sample where there is an express or implied term to that effect in the contract concerned.

5A.   Modification of remedies for breach of statutory condition in non-consumer cases

(1)   Where in the case of a contract for the transfer of goods—

(a)   the transferee would, apart from this subsection, have the right to treat the contract as repudiated by reason of a breach on the part of the transferor of a term implied by section 3, 4 or 5(2)(a) or (c) above, but

(b)   the breach is so slight that it would be unreasonable for him to do so, then, if the transferee does not deal as consumer, the breach is not to be treated as a breach of condition but may be treated as a breach of warranty.

(2)   This section applies unless a contrary intention appears in, or is to be implied from, the contract.

(3)   It is for the transferor to show that a breach fell within subsection (1)(b) above.

Contracts for the hire of goods

6.   The contracts concerned

(1)   In this Act in its application to England and Wales and Northern Ireland a 'contract for the hire of goods' means a contract under which one person bails or agrees to bail goods to another by way of hire, other than an excepted contract.

(2)   For the purposes of this section an excepted contract means any of the following—

(a)   a hire-purchase agreement;

(b)   a contract under which goods are (or are to be) bailed in exchange for trading stamps on their redemption.

(3)   For the purposes of this Act in its application to England and Wales and Northern Ireland a contract is a contract for the hire of goods whether or not services are also provided or to be provided under the contract, and (subject to subsection (2) above) whatever is the nature of the consideration for the bailment or agreement to bail by way of hire.

7.   Implied terms about right to transfer possession, etc

(1)   In a contract for the hire of goods there is an implied condition on the part of the bailor that in the case of a bailment he has a right to transfer possession of the goods by way of hire for the period of the bailment and in the case of an agreement to bail he will have such a right at the time of the bailment.

(2)   In a contract for the hire of goods there is also an implied warranty that the bailee will enjoy quiet possession of the goods for the period of the bailment except so far as the possession may be disturbed by the owner or other person entitled to the benefit of any charge or encumbrance disclosed or known to the bailee before the contract is made.

(3)   The preceding provisions of this section do not affect the right of the bailor to repossess the goods under an express or implied term of the contract.

8. Implied terms where hire is by description

(1)   This section applies where, under a contract for the hire of goods, the bailor bails or agrees to bail the goods by description.

(2)   In such a case there is an implied condition that the goods will correspond with the description.

(3)   If under the contract the bailor bails or agrees to bail the goods by reference to a sample as well as a description it is not sufficient that the bulk of the goods corresponds with the sample if the goods do not also correspond with the description.

(4)   A contract is not prevented from falling within subsection (1) above by reason only that, being exposed for supply, the goods are selected by the bailee.

9. Implied terms about quality or fitness

(1)   Except as provided by this section and section 10 below and subject to the provisions of any other enactment, there is no implied condition or warranty about the quality or fitness for any particular purpose of goods bailed under a contract for the hire of goods.

(2)   Where, under such a contract, the bailor bails goods in the course of a business, there is an implied condition that the goods supplied under the contract are of satisfactory quality.

(2A) For the purposes of this section and section 10 below, goods are of satisfactory quality if they meet the standard that a reasonable person would regard as satisfactory, taking account of any description of the goods, the consideration for the bailment (if relevant) and all the other relevant circumstances.

(2B) If the bailee deals as consumer, the relevant circumstances mentioned in subsection (2A) above include any public statements on the specific characteristics of the goods made about them by the bailor, the producer or his representative, particularly in advertising or on labelling.

(2C) A public statement is not by virtue of subsection (2B) above a relevant circumstance for the purposes of subsection (2A) above in the case of a contract for the hire of goods, if the bailor shows that—

(a)   at the time the contract was made, he was not, and could not reasonably have been, aware of the statement,

(b)   before the contract was made, the statement had been withdrawn in public or, to the extent that it contained anything which was incorrect or misleading, it had been corrected in public, or

(c)   the decision to acquire the goods could not have been influenced by the statement.

(2D) Subsections (2B) and (2C) above do not prevent any public statement from being a relevant circumstance for the purposes of subsection (2A) above (whether or not the bailee deals as consumer) if the statement would have been such a circumstance apart from those subsections.

(3)   The condition implied by subsection (2) above does not extend to any matter making the quality of goods unsatisfactory—

(a)   which is specifically drawn to the bailee's attention before the contract is made,

(b)   where the bailee examines the goods before the contract is made, which that examination ought to reveal, or

(c)   where the goods are bailed by reference to a sample, which would have been apparent on a reasonable examination of the sample.

(4)   Subsection (5) below applies where, under a contract for the hire of goods, the bailor bails goods in the course of a business and the bailee, expressly or by implication, makes known—
   (a)   to the bailor in the course of negotiations conducted by him in relation to the making of the contract, or
   (b)   to a credit-broker in the course of negotiations conducted by that broker in relation to goods sold by him to the bailor before forming the subject matter of the contract, any particular purpose for which the goods are being bailed.
(5)   In that case there is (subject to subsection (6) below) an implied condition that the goods supplied under the contract are reasonably fit for that purpose, whether or not that is a purpose for which such goods are commonly supplied.
(6)   Subsection (5) above does not apply where the circumstances show that the bailee does not rely, or that it is unreasonable for him to rely, on the skill or judgment of the bailor or credit-broker.
(7)   An implied condition or warranty about quality or fitness for a particular purpose may be annexed by usage to a contract for the hire of goods.
(8)   The preceding provisions of this section apply to a bailment by a person who in the course of a business is acting as agent for another as they apply to a bailment by a principal in the course of a business, except where that other is not bailing in the course of a business and either the bailee knows that fact or reasonable steps are taken to bring it to the bailee's notice before the contract concerned is made.
(9)   . . .

10. Implied terms where hire is by sample
(1)   This section applies where, under a contract for the hire of goods, the bailor bails or agrees to bail the goods by reference to a sample.
(2)   In such a case there is an implied condition—
   (a)   that the bulk will correspond with the sample in quality; and
   (b)   that the bailee will have a reasonable opportunity of comparing the bulk with the sample; and
   (c)   that the goods will be free from any defect, making their quality unsatisfactory, which would not be apparent on reasonable examination of the sample.
(3)   . . .
(4)   For the purposes of this section a bailor bails or agrees to bail goods by reference to a sample where there is an express or implied term to that effect in the contract concerned.

10A. Modification of remedies for breach of statutory condition in non-consumer cases
(1)   Where in the case of a contract for the hire of goods—
   (a)   the bailee would, apart from this subsection, have the right to treat the contract as repudiated by reason of a breach on the part of the bailor of a term implied by section 8, 9 or 10(2)(a) or (c) above, but
   (b)   the breach is so slight that it would be unreasonable for him to do so,
then, if the bailee does not deal as consumer, the breach is not to be treated as a breach of condition but may be treated as a breach of warranty.
(2)   This section applies unless a contrary intention appears in, or is to be implied from, the contract.
(3)   It is for the bailor to show that a breach fell within subsection (1)(b) above.

Exclusion of implied terms, etc

11. Exclusion of implied terms, etc

(1)   Where a right, duty or liability would arise under a contract for the transfer of goods or a contract for the hire of goods by implication of law, it may (subject to subsection (2) below and the 1977 Act) be negatived or varied by express agreement, or by the course of dealing between the parties, or by such usage as binds both parties to the contract.

(2)   An express condition or warranty does not negative a condition or warranty implied by the preceding provisions of this Act unless inconsistent with it.

(3)   Nothing in the preceding provisions of this Act prejudices the operation of any other enactment or any rule of law whereby any condition or warranty (other than one relating to quality or fitness) is to be implied in a contract for the transfer of goods or a contract for the hire of goods.

PART IA

SUPPLY OF GOODS AS RESPECTS SCOTLAND

11A. The contracts concerned

(1)   In this Act in its application to Scotland a 'contract for the transfer of goods' means a contract under which one person transfers or agrees to transfer to another the property in goods, other than an excepted contract.

(2)   For the purposes of this section an excepted contract means any of the following—

    (a)   a contract of sale of goods;

    (b)   a hire-purchase agreement;

    (c)   a contract under which the property in goods is (or is to be) transferred in exchange for trading stamps on their redemption;

    (d)   a transfer or agreement to transfer for which there is no consideration;

    (e)   a contract intended to operate by way of mortgage, pledge, charge or other security.

(3)   For the purposes of this Act in its application to Scotland a contract is a contract for the transfer of goods whether or not services are also provided or to be provided under the contract, and (subject to subsection (2) above) whatever is the nature of the consideration for the transfer or agreement to transfer.

11B. Implied terms about title, etc

(1)   In a contract for the transfer of goods, other than one to which subsection (3) below applies, there is an implied term on the part of the transferor that in the case of a transfer of the property in the goods he has a right to transfer the property and in the case of an agreement to transfer the property in the goods he will have such a right at the time when the property is to be transferred.

(2)   In a contract for the transfer of goods, other than one to which subsection (3) below applies, there is also an implied term that—

    (a)   the goods are free, and will remain free until the time when the property is to be transferred, from any charge or encumbrance not disclosed or known to the transferee before the contract is made, and

    (b)   the transferee will enjoy quiet possession of the goods except so far as it may be disturbed by the owner or other person entitled to the benefit of any charge or encumbrance so disclosed or known.

(3)   This subsection applies to a contract for the transfer of goods in the case of which there appears from the contract or is to be inferred from its circumstances an intention that the transferor should transfer only such title as he or a third person may have.

(4)   In a contract to which subsection (3) above applies there is an implied term that all charges or encumbrances known to the transferor and not known to the transferee have been disclosed to the transferee before the contract is made.

(5)   In a contract to which subsection (3) above applies there is also an implied term that none of the following will disturb the transferee's quiet possession of the goods, namely—

   (a)   the transferor;

   (b)   in a case where the parties to the contract intend that the transferor should transfer only such title as a third person may have, that person;

   (c)   anyone claiming through or under the transferor or that third person otherwise than under a charge or encumbrance disclosed or known to the transferee before the contract is made.

(6)   . . .

11C. Implied terms where transfer is by description

(1)   This section applies where, under a contract for the transfer of goods, the transferor transfers or agrees to transfer the property in the goods by description.

(2)   In such a case there is an implied term that the goods will correspond with the description.

(3)   If the transferor transfers or agrees to transfer the property in the goods by reference to a sample as well as by description it is not sufficient that the bulk of the goods corresponds with the sample if the goods do not also correspond with the description.

(4)   A contract is not prevented from falling within subsection (1) above by reason only that, being exposed for supply, the goods are selected by the transferee.

11D. Implied terms about quality or fitness

(1)   Except as provided by this section and section 11E below and subject to the provisions of any other enactment, there is no implied term about the quality or fitness for any particular purpose of goods supplied under a contract for the transfer of goods.

(2)   Where, under such a contract, the transferor transfers the property in goods in the course of a business, there is an implied term that the goods supplied under the contract are of satisfactory quality.

(3)   For the purposes of this section and section 11E below, goods are of satisfactory quality if they meet the standard that a reasonable person would regard as satisfactory, taking account of any description of the goods, the price (if relevant) and all the other relevant circumstances.

(3A)   If the contract for the transfer of goods is a consumer contract, the relevant circumstances mentioned in subsection (3) above include any public statements on the specific characteristics of the goods made about them by the transferor, the producer or his representative, particularly in advertising or on labelling.

(3B)   A public statement is not by virtue of subsection (3A) above a relevant circumstance for the purposes of subsection (3) above in the case of a contract for the transfer of goods, if the transferor shows that—

   (a)   at the time the contract was made, he was not, and could not reasonably have been, aware of the statement,

   (b)   before the contract was made, the statement had been withdrawn in public or, to

the extent that it contained anything which was incorrect or misleading, it had been corrected in public, or

(c)   the decision to acquire the goods could not have been influenced by the statement.

(3C) Subsections (3A) and (3B) above do not prevent any public statement from being a relevant circumstance for the purposes of subsection (3) above (whether or not the contract for the transfer of goods is a consumer contract) if the statement would have been such a circumstance apart from those subsections.

(4)   The term implied by subsection (2) above does not extend to any matter making the quality of goods unsatisfactory—

(a)   which is specifically drawn to the transferee's attention before the contract is made,

(b)   where the transferee examines the goods before the contract is made, which that examination ought to reveal, or

(c)   where the property in the goods is, or is to be, transferred by reference to a sample, which would have been apparent on a reasonable examination of the sample.

(5)   Subsection (6) below applies where, under a contract for the transfer of goods, the transferor transfers the property in goods in the course of a business and the transferee, expressly or by implication, makes known—

(a)   to the transferor, or

(b)   where the consideration or part of the consideration for the transfer is a sum payable by instalments and the goods were previously sold by a credit-broker to the transferor, to that credit-broker, any particular purpose for which the goods are being acquired.

(6)   In that case there is (subject to subsection (7) below) an implied term that the goods supplied under the contract are reasonably fit for the purpose, whether or not that is a purpose for which such goods are commonly supplied.

(7)   Subsection (6) above does not apply where the circumstances show that the transferee does not rely, or that it is unreasonable for him to rely, on the skill or judgment of the transferor or credit-broker.

(8)   An implied term about quality or fitness for a particular purpose may be annexed by usage to a contract for the transfer of goods.

(9)   The preceding provisions of this section apply to a transfer by a person who in the course of a business is acting as agent for another as they apply to a transfer by a principal in the course of a business, except where that other is not transferring in the course of a business and either the transferee knows that fact or reasonable steps are taken to bring it to the transferee's notice before the contract concerned is made.

(10)   For the purposes of this section, 'consumer contract' has the same meaning as in section 11F(3) below.

11E. Implied terms where transfer is by sample

(1)   This section applies where, under a contract for the transfer of goods, the transferor transfers or agrees to transfer the property in the goods by reference to a sample.

(2)   In such a case there is an implied term—

(a)   that the bulk will correspond with the sample in quality;

(b)   that the transferee will have a reasonable opportunity of comparing the bulk with the sample; and

(c)   that the goods will be free from any defect, making their quality unsatisfactory, which would not be apparent on reasonable examination of the sample.

(3)   For the purposes of this section a transferor transfers or agrees to transfer the property in goods by reference to a sample where there is an express or implied term to that effect in the contract concerned.

11F.   Remedies for breach of contract
(1)   Where in a contract for the transfer of goods a transferor is in breach of any term of the contract (express or implied), the other party to the contract (in this section referred to as 'the transferee') shall be entitled—
    (a)   to claim damages; and
    (b)   if the breach is material, to reject any goods delivered under the contract and treat it as repudiated.
(2)   Where a contract for the transfer of goods is a consumer contract and the transferee is the consumer, then, for the purposes of subsection (1)(b) above, breach by the transferor of any term (express or implied)—
    (a)   as to the quality of the goods or their fitness for a purpose;
    (b)   if the goods are, or are to be, transferred by description, that the goods will correspond with the description;
    (c)   if the goods are, or are to be, transferred by reference to a sample, that the bulk will correspond with the sample in quality, shall be deemed to be a material breach.
(3)   In subsection (2) above, 'consumer contract' has the same meaning as in section 25(1) of the 1977 Act; and for the purposes of that subsection the onus of proving that a contract is not to be regarded as a consumer contract shall lie on the transferor.

Contracts for the hire of goods

11G.   The contracts concerned
(1)   In this Act in its application to Scotland a 'contract for the hire of goods' means a contract under which one person ('the supplier') hires or agrees to hire goods to another, other than an excepted contract.
(2)   For the purposes of this section, an excepted contract means any of the following—
    (a)   a hire-purchase agreement;
    (b)   a contract under which goods are (or are to be) hired in exchange for trading stamps on their redemption.
(3)   For the purposes of this Act in its application to Scotland a contract is a contract for the hire of goods whether or not services are also provided or to be provided under the contract, and (subject to subsection (2) above) whatever is the nature of the consideration for the hire or agreement to hire.

11H.   Implied terms about right to transfer possession etc
(1)   In a contract for the hire of goods there is an implied term on the part of the supplier that—
    (a)   in the case of a hire, he has a right to transfer possession of the goods by way of hire for the period of the hire; and
    (b)   in the case of an agreement to hire, he will have such a right at the time of commencement of the period of the hire.
(2)   In a contract for the hire of goods there is also an implied term that the person to whom the goods are hired will enjoy quiet possession of the goods for the period of the hire except so far as the possession may be disturbed by the owner or other person entitled to the

benefit of any charge or encumbrance disclosed or known to the person to whom the goods are hired before the contract is made.

(3)   The preceding provisions of this section do not affect the right of the supplier to repossess the goods under an express or implied term of the contract.

11I. Implied terms where hire is by description

(1)   This section applies where, under a contract for the hire of goods, the supplier hires or agrees to hire the goods by description.

(2)   In such a case there is an implied term that the goods will correspond with the description.

(3)   If under the contract the supplier hires or agrees to hire the goods by reference to a sample as well as by description it is not sufficient that the bulk of the goods corresponds with the sample if the goods do not also correspond with the description.

(4)   A contract is not prevented from falling within subsection (1) above by reason only that, being exposed for supply, the goods are selected by the person to whom the goods are hired.

11J. Implied terms about quality or fitness

(1)   Except as provided by this section and section 11K below and subject to the provisions of any other enactment, there is no implied term about the quality or fitness for any particular purpose of goods hired under a contract for the hire of goods.

(2)   Where, under such a contract, the supplier hires goods in the course of a business, there is an implied term that the goods supplied under the contract are of satisfactory quality.

(3)   For the purposes of this section and section 11K below, goods are of satisfactory quality if they meet the standard that a reasonable person would regard as satisfactory, taking account of any description of the goods, the consideration for the hire (if relevant) and all the other relevant circumstances.

(3A) If the contract for the hire of goods is a consumer contract, the relevant circumstances mentioned in subsection (3) above include any public statements on the specific characteristics of the goods made about them by the hirer, the producer or his representative, particularly in advertising or on labelling.

(3B) A public statement is not by virtue of subsection (3A) above a relevant circumstance for the purposes of subsection (3) above in the case of a contract for the hire of goods, if the hirer shows that—

(a)   at the time the contract was made, he was not, and could not reasonably have been, aware of the statement,

(b)   by the time the contract was made, the statement had been withdrawn in public or, to the extent that it contained anything which was incorrect or misleading, it had been corrected in public, or

(c)   the decision to acquire the goods could not have been influenced by the statement.

(3C) Subsections (3A) and (3B) above do not prevent any public statement from being a relevant circumstance for the purposes of subsection (3) above (whether or not the contract for the hire of goods is a consumer contract) if the statement would have been such a circumstance apart from those subsections.

(4)   The term implied by subsection (2) above does not extend to any matter making the quality of goods unsatisfactory—

(a) which is specifically drawn to the attention of the person to whom the goods are hired before the contract is made; or

(b) where that person examines the goods before the contract is made, which that examination ought to reveal; or

(c) where the goods are hired by reference to a sample, which would have been apparent on reasonable examination of the sample.

(5) Subsection (6) below applies where, under a contract for the hire of goods, the supplier hires goods in the course of a business and the person to whom the goods are hired, expressly or by implication, makes known—

(a) to the supplier in the course of negotiations conducted by him in relation to the making of the contract; or

(b) to a credit-broker in the course of negotiations conducted by that broker in relation to goods sold by him to the supplier before forming the subject matter of the contract, any particular purpose for which the goods are being hired.

(6) In that case there is (subject to subsection (7) below) an implied term that the goods supplied under the contract are reasonably fit for that purpose, whether or not that is a purpose for which such goods are commonly supplied.

(7) Subsection (6) above does not apply where the circumstances show that the person to whom the goods are hired does not rely, or that it is unreasonable for him to rely, on the skill or judgment of the hirer or credit-broker.

(8) An implied term about quality or fitness for a particular purpose may be annexed by usage to a contract for the hire of goods.

(9) The preceding provisions of this section apply to a hire by a person who in the course of a business is acting as agent for another as they apply to a hire by a principal in the course of a business, except where that other is not hiring in the course of a business and either the person to whom the goods are hired knows that fact or reasonable steps are taken to bring it to that person's notice before the contract concerned is made.

(10) For the purposes of this section, 'consumer contract' has the same meaning as in section 11F(3) above.

11K. Implied terms where hire is by sample

(1) This section applies where, under a contract for the hire of goods, the supplier hires or agrees to hire the goods by reference to a sample.

(2) In such a case there is an implied term—

(a) that the bulk will correspond with the sample in quality; and

(b) that the person to whom the goods are hired will have a reasonable opportunity of comparing the bulk with the sample; and

(c) that the goods will be free from any defect, making their quality unsatisfactory, which would not be apparent on reasonable examination of the sample.

(3) For the purposes of this section a supplier hires or agrees to hire goods by reference to a sample where there is an express or implied term to that effect in the contract concerned.

Exclusion of implied terms, etc

11L. Exclusion of implied terms etc

(1) Where a right, duty or liability would arise under a contract for the transfer of goods or a contract for the hire of goods by implication of law, it may (subject to subsection (2)

below and the 1977 Act) be negatived or varied by express agreement, or by the course of dealing between the parties, or by such usage as binds both parties to the contract.

(2)   An express term does not negative a term implied by the preceding provisions of this Part of this Act unless inconsistent with it.

(3)   Nothing in the preceding provisions of this Part of this Act prejudices the operation of any other enactment or any rule of law whereby any term (other than one relating to quality or fitness) is to be implied in a contract for the transfer of goods or a contract for the hire of goods.

PART 1B

ADDITIONAL RIGHTS OF TRANSFEREE IN CONSUMER CASES

11M. Introductory

(1)   This section applies if—

(a)   the transferee deals as consumer or, in Scotland, there is a consumer contract in which the transferee is a consumer, and

(b)   the goods do not conform to the contract for the transfer of goods at the time of delivery.

(2)   If this section applies, the transferee has the right—

(a)   under and in accordance with section 11N below, to require the transferor to repair or replace the goods, or

(b)   under and in accordance with section 11P below—

(i)   to require the transferor to reduce the amount to be paid for the transfer by the transferee by an appropriate amount, or

(ii)   to rescind the contract with regard to the goods in question.

(3)   For the purposes of subsection (1)(b) above, goods which do not conform to the contract for the transfer of goods at any time within the period of six months starting with the date on which the goods were delivered to the transferee must be taken not to have so conformed at that date.

(4)   Subsection (3) above does not apply if—

(a)   it is established that the goods did so conform at that date;

(b)   its application is incompatible with the nature of the goods or the nature of the lack of conformity.

(5)   For the purposes of this section, 'consumer contract' has the same meaning as in section 11F(3) above.

11N. Repair or replacement of the goods

(1)   If section 11M above applies, the transferee may require the transferor—

(a)   to repair the goods, or

(b)   to replace the goods.

(2)   If the transferee requires the transferor to repair or replace the goods, the transferor must—

(a)   repair or, as the case may be, replace the goods within a reasonable time but without causing significant inconvenience to the transferee;

(b)   bear any necessary costs incurred in doing so (including in particular the cost of any labour, materials or postage).

(3)   The transferee must not require the transferor to repair or, as the case may be, replace the goods if that remedy is—

(a)   impossible,

(b)   disproportionate in comparison to the other of those remedies, or

(c)   disproportionate in comparison to an appropriate reduction in the purchase price under paragraph (a), or rescission under paragraph (b), of section 11P(1) below.

(4)   One remedy is disproportionate in comparison to the other if the one imposes costs on the transferor which, in comparison to those imposed on him by the other, are unreasonable, taking into account—

(a)   the value which the goods would have if they conformed to the contract for the transfer of goods,

(b)   the significance of the lack of conformity to the contract for the transfer of goods, and

(c)   whether the other remedy could be effected without significant inconvenience to the transferee.

(5)   Any question as to what is a reasonable time or significant inconvenience is to be determined by reference to—

(a)   the nature of the goods, and

(b)   the purpose for which the goods were acquired.

11P. Reduction of purchase price or rescission of contract

(1)   If section 11M above applies, the transferee may—

(a)   require the transferor to reduce the purchase price of the goods in question to the transferee by an appropriate amount, or

(b)   rescind the contract with regard to those goods,

if the condition in subsection (2) below is satisfied.

(2)   The condition is that—

(a)   by virtue of section 11N(3) above the transferee may require neither repair nor replacement of the goods, or

(b)   the transferee has required the transferor to repair or replace the goods, but the transferor is in breach of the requirement of section 11N(2)(a) above to do so within a reasonable time and without significant inconvenience to the transferee.

(3)   If the transferee rescinds the contract, any reimbursement to the transferee may be reduced to take account of the use he has had of the goods since they were delivered to him.

11Q. Relation to other remedies etc.

(1)   If the transferee requires the transferor to repair or replace the goods the transferee must not act under subsection (2) until he has given the transferor a reasonable time in which to repair or replace (as the case may be) the goods.

(2)   The transferee acts under this subsection if—

(a)   in England and Wales or Northern Ireland he rejects the goods and terminates the contract for breach of condition;

(b)   in Scotland he rejects any goods delivered under the contract and treats it as repudiated; or

(c)   he requires the goods to be replaced or repaired (as the case may be).

11R. Powers of the court

(1)   In any proceedings in which a remedy is sought by virtue of this Part the court, in addition to any other power it has, may act under this section.

(2)   On the application of the transferee the court may make an order requiring specific performance or, in Scotland, specific implement by the transferor of any obligation imposed on him by virtue of section 11N above.

(3)   Subsection (4) applies if—

    (a)   the transferee requires the transferor to give effect to a remedy under section 11N or 11P above or has claims to rescind under section 11P, but

    (b)   the court decides that another remedy under section 11N or 11P is appropriate.

(4)   The court may proceed—

    (a)   as if the transferee had required the transferor to give effect to the other remedy, or if the other remedy is rescission under section 11P,

    (b)   as if the transferee had claimed to rescind the contract under that section.

(5)   If the transferee has claimed to rescind the contract the court may order that any reimbursement to the transferee is reduced to take account of the use he has had of the goods since they were delivered to him.

(6)   The court may make an order under this section unconditionally or on such terms and conditions as to damages, payment of the price and otherwise as it thinks just.

11S.   Conformity with the contract

(1)   Goods do not conform to a contract for the supply or transfer of goods if—

    (a)   there is, in relation to the goods, a breach of an express term of the contract or a term implied by section 3, 4 or 5 above or, in Scotland, by section 11C, 11D or 11E above, or

    (b)   installation of the goods forms part of the contract for the transfer of goods, and the goods were installed by the transferor, or under his responsibility, in breach of the term implied by section 13 below or (in Scotland) in breach of any term implied by any rule of law as to the manner in which the installation is carried out.

PART II
SUPPLY OF SERVICES

12.   The contracts concerned

(1)   In this Act a 'contract for the supply of a service' means, subject to subsection (2) below, a contract under which a person ('the supplier') agrees to carry out a service.

(2)   For the purposes of this Act, a contract of service or apprenticeship is not a contract for the supply of a service.

(3)   Subject to subsection (2) above, a contract is a contract for the supply of a service for the purposes of this Act whether or not goods are also—

    (a)   transferred or to be transferred, or

    (b)   bailed or to be bailed by way of hire, under the contract, and whatever is the nature of the consideration for which the service is to be carried out.

(4)   The Secretary of State may by order provide that one or more of sections 13 to 15 below shall not apply to services of a description specified in the order, and such an order may make different provision for different circumstances.

(5)   The power to make an order under subsection (4) above shall be exercisable by statutory instrument subject to annulment in pursuance of a resolution of either House of Parliament.

13.   Implied term about care and skill

In a contract for the supply of a service where the supplier is acting in the course of a business, there is an implied term that the supplier will carry out the service with reasonable care and skill.

14. Implied term about time for performance

(1) Where, under a contract for the supply of a service by a supplier acting in the course of a business, the time for the service to be carried out is not fixed by the contract, left to be fixed in a manner agreed by the contract or determined by the course of dealing between the parties, there is an implied term that the supplier will carry out the service within a reasonable time.

(2) What is a reasonable time is a question of fact.

15. Implied term about consideration

(1) Where, under a contract for the supply of a service, the consideration for the service is not determined by the contract, left to be determined in a manner agreed by the contract or determined by the course of dealing between the parties, there is an implied term that the party contracting with the supplier will pay a reasonable charge.

(2) What is a reasonable charge is a question of fact.

16. Exclusion of implied terms, etc

(1) Where a right, duty or liability would arise under a contract for the supply of a service by virtue of this Part of this Act, it may (subject to subsection (2) below and the 1977 Act) be negatived or varied by express agreement, or by the course of dealing between the parties, or by such usage as binds both parties to the contract.

(2) An express term does not negative a term implied by this Part of this Act unless inconsistent with it.

(3) Nothing in this Part of this Act prejudices—

(a) any rule of law which imposes on the supplier a duty stricter than that imposed by section 13 or 14 above; or

(b) subject to paragraph (a) above, any rule of law whereby any term not inconsistent with this Part of this Act is to be implied in a contract for the supply of a service.

(4) This Part of this Act has effect subject to any other enactment which defines or restricts the rights, duties or liabilities arising in connection with a service of any description.

PART III
SUPPLEMENTARY

17. Minor and consequential amendments

(1)–(3)   ...

18. Interpretation: general

(1) In the preceding provisions of this Act and this section—

'bailee', in relation to a contract for the hire of goods means (depending on the context) a person to whom the goods are bailed under the contract, or a person to whom they are to be so bailed, or a person to whom the rights under the contract of either of those persons have passed;

'bailor', in relation to a contract for the hire of goods, means (depending on the context) a person who bails the goods under the contract, or a person who agrees to do so, or a person to whom the duties under the contract of either of those persons have passed;

'business' includes a profession and the activities of any government department or local or public authority;

'credit-broker' means a person acting in the course of a business of credit brokerage carried on by him;

'credit brokerage' means the effecting of introductions—

(a)   of individuals desiring to obtain credit to persons carrying on any business so far as it relates to the provision of credit; or

(b)   of individuals desiring to obtain goods on hire to persons carrying on a business which comprises or relates to the bailment or as regards Scotland the hire of goods under a contract for the hire of goods; or

(c)   of individuals desiring to obtain credit, or to obtain goods on hire, to other credit-brokers;

'enactment' means any legislation (including subordinate legislation) of the United Kingdom or Northern Ireland;

'goods' includes all personal chattels, other than things in action and money, and as regards Scotland all corporeal moveables; and in particular 'goods' includes emblements, industrial growing crops, and things attached to or forming part of the land which are agreed to be severed before the transfer, bailment or hire concerned or under the contract concerned . . .;

'hire-purchase agreement' has the same meaning as in the 1974 Act;

'producer' means the manufacturer of goods, the importer of goods into the European Economic Area or any person purporting to be a producer by placing his name, trade mark or other distinctive sign on the goods;

'property', in relation to goods, means the general property in them and not merely a special property;

'redemption', in relation to trading stamps, has the same meaning as in the Trading Stamps Act 1964 or, as respects Northern Ireland, the Trading Stamps Act (Northern Ireland) 1965;

'repair' means, in cases where there is a lack of conformity in goods for the purposes of this Act, to bring the goods into conformity with the contract;

'trading stamps' has the same meaning as in the said Act of 1964 or, as respects Northern Ireland, the said Act of 1965;

'transferee', in relation to a contract for the transfer of goods, means (depending on the context) a person to whom the property in the goods is transferred under the contract, or a person to whom the property is to be so transferred, or a person to whom the rights under the contract of either of those persons have passed;

'transferor', in relation to a contract for the transfer of goods, means (depending on the context) a person who transfers the property in the goods under the contract, or a person who agrees to do so, or a person to whom the duties under the contract of either of those persons have passed.

(2)   In subsection (1) above, in the definitions of bailee, bailor, transferee and transferor, a reference to rights or duties passing is to their passing by assignment [assignation], operation of law or otherwise.

(3)   For the purposes of this Act, the quality of goods includes their state and condition and the following (among others) are in appropriate cases aspects of the quality of goods—

(a)   fitness for all the purposes for which goods of the kind in question are commonly supplied,

(b)   appearance and finish,

(c)   freedom from minor defects,

(d)   safety, and

(e)   durability.

(4)   References in this Act to dealing as consumer are to be construed in accordance with Part I of the Unfair Contract Terms Act 1977; and, for the purposes of this Act, it is for the transferor or bailor claiming that the transferee or bailee does not deal as consumer to show that he does not.

19. Interpretation: references to Acts
In this Act—
    'the 1973 Act' means the Supply of Goods (Implied Terms) Act 1973;
    'the 1974 Act' means the Consumer Credit Act 1974;
    'the 1977 Act' means the Unfair Contract Terms Act 1977; and
    'the 1979 Act' means the Sale of Goods Act 1979.

20. Citation, transitional provisions, commencement and extent
(1)   This Act may be cited as the Supply of Goods and Services Act 1982.
(2)   The transitional provisions in the Schedule to this Act shall have effect.
(3)   Part I of this Act together with section 17 and so much of sections 18 and 19 above as relates to that Part shall not come into operation until 4th January 1983; and Part II of this Act together with so much of sections 18 and 19 above as relates to that Part shall not come into operation until such day as may be appointed by an order made by the Secretary of State.
(4)   The power to make an order under subsection (3) above shall be exercisable by statutory instrument.
(5)   No provision of this Act applies to a contract made before the provision comes into operation.
(6)   This Act, except Part IA, which extends only to Scotland, extends to Northern Ireland and Parts I and II do not extend to Scotland.

Appendix 5

Supply of Goods (Implied Terms) Act 1973

(as amended by SSGCR 2002; changes in italics)

SECTIONS 1–7 REPEALED BY THE SALE OF GOODS ACT 1979

Hire-purchase agreements

8. Implied terms as to title

(1) In every hire-purchase agreement, other than one to which subsection (2) below applies, there is—

(a) an implied term on the part of the creditor that he will have a right to sell the goods at the time when the property is to pass; and

(b) an implied term that—

(i) the goods are free, and will remain free until the time when the property is to pass, from any charge or encumbrance not disclosed or known to the person to whom the goods are bailed or (in Scotland) hired before the agreement is made, and

(ii) that person will enjoy quiet possession of the goods except so far as it may be disturbed by any person entitled to the benefit of any charge or encumbrance so disclosed or known.

(2) In a hire-purchase agreement, in the case of which there appears from the agreement or is to be inferred from the circumstances of the agreement an intention that the creditor should transfer only such title as he or a third person may have, there is—

(a) an implied term that all charges or encumbrances known to the creditor and not known to the person to whom the goods are bailed or hired have been disclosed to that person before the agreement is made; and

(b) an implied term that neither—

(i) the creditor; nor

(ii) in a case where the parties to the agreement intend that any title which may be transferred shall be only such title as a third person may have, that person; nor

(iii) anyone claiming through or under the creditor or that third person otherwise than under a charge or encumbrance disclosed or known to the person to whom the goods are bailed or hired, before the agreement is made;

will disturb the quiet possession of the person to whom the goods are bailed or hired.

(3) As regards England and Wales and Northern Ireland, the term implied by subsection (1)(a) above is a condition and the terms implied by subsections (1)(b),(2)(a) and (2)(b) above are warranties.

9. Bailing or hiring by description

(1)   Where under a hire-purchase agreement goods are bailed or (in Scotland) hired by description, there is an implied term that the goods will correspond with the description, and if under the agreement the goods are bailed or hired by reference to a sample as well as a description, it is not sufficient that the bulk of the goods corresponds with the sample if the goods do not also correspond with the description.

(1A) As regards England and Wales and Northern Ireland, the term implied by subsection (1) above is a condition.

(2)   Goods shall not be prevented from being bailed or hired by description by reason only that, being exposed for sale, bailment or hire, they are selected by the person to whom they are bailed or hired.

10. Implied undertakings as to quality or fitness

(1)   Except as provided by this section and section 11 below and subject to the provisions of any other enactment, including any enactment of the Parliament of Northern Ireland, or the Northern Ireland Assembly, there is no implied term as to the quality or fitness for any particular purpose of goods bailed or (in Scotland) hired under a hire-purchase agreement.

(2)   Where the creditor bails or hires goods under a hire purchase agreement in the course of a business, there is an implied term that the goods supplied under the agreement are of satisfactory quality.

(2A) For the purposes of this Act, goods are of satisfactory quality if they meet the standard that a reasonable person would regard as satisfactory, taking account of any description of the goods, the price (if relevant) and all the other relevant circumstances.

(2B) For the purposes of this Act, the quality of goods includes their state and condition and the following (among others) are in appropriate cases aspects of the quality of goods—

    (a)   fitness for all the purposes for which goods of the kind in question are commonly supplied,

    (b)   appearance and finish,

    (c)   freedom from minor defects,

    (d)   safety, and

    (e)   durability.

(2C) The term implied by subsection (2) above does not extend to any matter making the quality of goods unsatisfactory—

    (a)   which is specifically drawn to the attention of the person to whom the goods are bailed or hired before the agreement is made,

    (b)   where that person examines the goods before the agreement is made, which that examination ought to reveal, or

    (c)   where the goods are bailed or hired by reference to a sample, which would have been apparent on a reasonable examination of the sample.

(2D) If the person to whom the goods are bailed or hired deals as consumer or, in Scotland, if the goods are hired to a person under a consumer contract, the relevant circumstances mentioned in subsection (2A) above include any public statements on the specific characteristics of the goods made about them by the creditor, the producer or his representative, particularly in advertising or on labelling.

(2E) A public statement is not by virtue of subsection (2D) above a relevant circumstance for the purposes of subsection (2A) above in the case of a contract of hire-purchase, if the creditor shows that—

(a)   at the time the contract was made, he was not, and could not reasonably have been, aware of the statement,

(b)   before the contract was made, the statement had been withdrawn in public or, to the extent that it contained anything which was incorrect or misleading, it had been corrected in public, or

(c)   the decision to acquire the goods could not have been influenced by the statement.

(2F) Subsections (2D) and (2E) above do not prevent any public statement from being a relevant circumstance for the purposes of subsection (2A) above (whether or not the person to whom the goods are bailed or hired deals as consumer or, in Scotland, whether or not the goods are hired to a person under a consumer contract) if the statement would have been such a circumstance apart from those subsections.

(3)   Where the creditor bails or hires goods under a hire-purchase agreement in the course of a business and the person to whom the goods are bailed or hired, expressly or by implication, makes known—

(a)   to the creditor in the course of negotiations conducted by the creditor in relation to the making of the hire-purchase agreement, or

(b)   to a credit-broker in the course of negotiations conducted by that broker in relation to goods sold by him to the creditor before forming the subject matter of the hire-purchase agreement, any particular purpose for which the goods are being bailed or hired, there is an implied term that the goods supplied under the agreement are reasonably fit for that purpose, whether or not that is a purpose for which such goods are commonly supplied, except where the circumstances show that the person to whom the goods are bailed or hired does not rely, or that it is unreasonable for him to rely, on the skill or judgment of the creditor or credit-broker.

(4)   An implied term as to quality or fitness for a particular purpose may be annexed to a hire-purchase agreement by usage.

(5)   The preceding provisions of this section apply to a hire-purchase agreement made by a person who in the course of a business is acting as agent for the creditor as they apply to an agreement made by the creditor in the course of a business, except where the creditor is not bailing or hiring in the course of a business and either the person to whom the goods are bailed or hired knows that fact or reasonable steps are taken to bring it to the notice of that person before the agreement is made.

(6)   In subsection (3) above and this subsection—

(a)   'credit-broker' means a person acting in the course of a business of credit brokerage;

(b)   'credit brokerage' means the effecting of introductions of individuals desiring to obtain credit—

(i)   to persons carrying on any business so far as it relates to the provision of credit, or

(ii)   to other persons engaged in credit brokerage.

(7)   As regards England and Wales and Northern Ireland, the terms implied by subsections (2) and (3) above are conditions.

(8)   In Scotland, 'consumer contract' in this section has the same meaning as in section 12A(3) below.

11. Samples

(1)   Where under a hire-purchase agreement goods are bailed or (in Scotland) hired by reference to a sample, there is an implied term—

    (a)   that the bulk will correspond with the sample in quality; and

    (b)   that the person to whom the goods are bailed or hired will have a reasonable opportunity of comparing the bulk with the sample; and

    (c)   that the goods will be free from any defect, making their quality unsatisfactory, which would not be apparent on reasonable examination of the sample.

(2)   As regards England and Wales and Northern Ireland, the term implied by subsection (1) above is a condition.

11A.   Modification of remedies for breach of statutory condition in non-consumer cases

(1)   Where in the case of a hire purchase agreement—

    (a)   the person to whom goods are bailed would, apart from this subsection, have the right to reject them by reason of a breach on the part of the creditor of a term implied by section 9, 10 or 11(1)(a) or (c) above, but

    (b)   the breach is so slight that it would be unreasonable for him to reject them, then, if the person to whom the goods are bailed does not deal as consumer, the breach is not to be treated as a breach of condition but may be treated as a breach of warranty.

(2)   This section applies unless a contrary intention appears in, or is to be implied from, the agreement.

(3)   It is for the creditor to show—

    (a)   that a breach fell within subsection (1)(b) above, and

    (b)   that the person to whom the goods were bailed did not deal as consumer.

(4)   The references in this section to dealing as consumer are to be construed in accordance with Part I of the Unfair Contract Terms Act 1977.

(5)   This section does not apply to Scotland.

12.   Exclusion of implied terms

An express term does not negative a term implied by this Act unless inconsistent with it.

12A.   Remedies for breach of hire-purchase agreement as respects Scotland

(1)   Where in a hire-purchase agreement the creditor is in breach of any term of the agreement (express or implied), the person to whom the goods are hired shall be entitled—

    (a)   to claim damages, and

    (b)   if the breach is material, to reject any goods delivered under the agreement and treat it as repudiated.

(2)   Where a hire-purchase agreement is a consumer contract, then, for the purposes of subsection (1) above, breach by the creditor of any term (express or implied)—

    (a)   as to the quality of the goods or their fitness for a purpose,

    (b)   if the goods are, or are to be, hired by description, that the goods will correspond with the description,

    (c)   if the goods are, or are to be, hired by reference to a sample, that the bulk will correspond with the sample in quality, shall be deemed to be a material breach.

(3)   In subsection (2) above 'consumer contract' has the same meaning as in section 25(1) of the Unfair Contract Terms Act 1977, and for the purposes of that subsection the onus of proving that a hire-purchase agreement is not to be regarded as a consumer contract shall lie on the creditor.

(4)   This section applies to Scotland only.

13.   ...

14. Special provisions as to conditional sale agreements
(1)   Section 11(4) of the Sale of Goods Act 1979 (whereby in certain circumstances a breach of a condition in a contract of sale is treated only as a breach of warranty) shall not apply to a conditional sale agreement where the buyer deals as consumer within Part I of the Unfair Contract Terms Act 1977.
(2)   In England and Wales and Northern Ireland a breach of a condition (whether express or implied) to be fulfilled by the seller under any such agreement shall be treated as a breach of warranty, and not as grounds for rejecting the goods and treating the agreement as repudiated, if (but only if) it would have fallen to be so treated had the condition been contained or implied in a corresponding hire-purchase agreement as a condition to be fulfilled by the creditor.

15. Supplementary
(1)   In sections 8 to 14 above and this section—
      'business' includes a profession and the activities of any government department (including a Northern Ireland department),or local or public authority;
      'buyer' and 'seller' includes a person to whom rights and duties under a conditional sale agreement have passed by assignment or operation of law;
      'conditional sale agreement' means an agreement for the sale of goods under which the purchase price or part of it is payable by instalments, and the property in the goods is to remain in the seller (notwithstanding that the buyer is to be in possession of the goods) until such conditions as to the payment of instalments or otherwise as may be specified in the agreement are fulfilled;
      'creditor' means the person by whom the goods are bailed or (in Scotland) hired under a hire-purchase agreement or the person to whom his rights and duties under the agreement have passed by assignment or operation of law; and
      'hire-purchase agreement' means an agreement, other than a conditional sale agreement, under which—
      (a)   goods are bailed or (in Scotland) hired in return for periodical payments by the person to whom they are bailed or hired, and
      (b)   the property in the goods will pass to that person if the terms of the agreements are complied with and one or more of the following occurs—
            (i)   the exercise of an option to purchase by that person,
            (ii)   the doing of any other specified act by any party to the agreement,
            (iii) the happening of any other specified event.
      'producer' means the manufacturer of goods, the importer of goods into the European Economic Area or any person purporting to be a producer by placing his name, trade mark or other distinctive sign on the goods;
(2)   ...
(3)   In section 14(2) above 'corresponding hire-purchase agreement' means, in relation to a conditional sale agreement, a hire-purchase agreement relating to the same goods as the conditional sale agreement and made between the same parties and at the same time and in the same circumstances and, as nearly as may be, in the same terms as the conditional sale agreement.

(4)   Nothing in sections 8 to 13 above shall prejudice the operation of any other enactment including any enactment of the Parliament of Northern Ireland or the Northern Ireland Assembly or any rule of law whereby any [term], other than one relating to quality or fitness, is to be implied in any hire-purchase agreement.

Trading Stamps

16. Terms to be implied on redemption of trading stamps for goods

. . .

17. Miscellaneous

Northern Ireland

(1)   It is hereby declared that this Act extends to Northern Ireland.

(2)   . . .

18. Short title, citation, interpretation, commencement, repeal and saving

(1)   This Act may be cited as the Supply of Goods (Implied Terms) Act 1973.

(2)   . . .

(3)   This Act shall come into operation at the expiration of a period of one month beginning with the date on which it is passed.

(4)   . . .

(5)   This Act does not apply to contracts of sale or hire-purchase agreements made before its commencement.

Appendix 6

Unfair Contract Terms Act 1977, s. 12 and s. 25

(as amended by SSGCR 2002; changes in italics)

12. 'Dealing as consumer'

(1) A party to a contract 'deals as consumer' in relation to another party if—

　(a) he neither makes the contract in the course of a business nor holds himself out as doing so; and

　(b) the other party does make the contract in the course of a business; and

　(c) in the case of a contract governed by the law of sale of goods or hire-purchase, or by section 7 of this Act, the goods passing under or in pursuance of the contract are of a type ordinarily supplied for private use or consumption.

(1A) But if the first party mentioned in subsection (1) is an individual paragraph (c) of that subsection must be ignored.

(2) But the buyer is not in any circumstances to be regarded as dealing as consumer—

　(a) if he is an individual and the goods are second hand goods sold at public auction at which individuals have the opportunity of attending the sale in person;

　(b) if he is not an individual and the goods are sold by auction or by competitive tender.

(3) Subject to this, it is for those claiming that a party does not deal as consumer to show that he does not.

25. Interpretation of Part II

(1) In this Part of this Act—

　'breach of duty' means the breach—

　(a) of any obligation, arising from the express or implied terms of a contract, to take reasonable care or exercise reasonable skill in the performance of the contract;

　(b) of any common law duty to take reasonable care or exercise reasonable skill;

　(c) of the duty of reasonable care imposed by section 2(1) of the Occupiers' Liability (Scotland) Act 1960;

　'business' includes a profession and the activities of any government department or local or public authority;

　'consumer' has the meaning assigned to that expression in the definition in this section of 'consumer contract';

　'consumer contract' means, *subject to subsections (1A) and (1B) below,* a contract in which—

(a)   one party to the contract deals, and the other party to the contract ('the consumer') does not deal or hold himself out as dealing, in the course of a business, and

(b)   in the case of a contract such as is mentioned in section 15(2)(a) of this Act, the goods are of a type ordinarily supplied for private use or consumption;

and for the purposes of this Part of this Act the onus of proving that a contract is not to be regarded as a consumer contract shall lie on the party so contending;

'goods' has the same meaning as in [the Sale of Goods Act 1979];

'hire-purchase agreement' has the same meaning as in section 189(1) of the Consumer Credit Act 1974;

'notice' includes an announcement, whether or not in writing, and any other communication or pretended communication;

'personal injury' includes any disease and any impairment of physical or mental condition.

(1A) Where the consumer is an individual, paragraph (b) in the definition of 'consumer contract' in subsection (1) must be disregarded.

(1B) The expression of 'consumer contract' does not include a contract in which—

the buyer is an individual and the goods are second hand goods sold by public auction at which individuals have the opportunity of attending in person; or

the buyer is not an individual and the goods are sold by auction or competitive tender.

(2)   In relation to any breach of duty or obligation, it is immaterial for any purpose of this Part of this Act whether the act or omission giving rise to that breach was inadvertent or intentional, or whether liability for it arises directly or vicariously.

(3)   In this Part of this Act, any reference to excluding or restricting any liability includes—

(a)   making the liability or its enforcement subject to any restrictive or onerous conditions;

(b)   excluding or restricting any right or remedy in respect of the liability, or subjecting a person to any prejudice in consequence of his pursuing any such right or remedy;

(c)   excluding or restricting any rule of evidence or procedure;

(d)   . . .

but does not include an agreement to submit any question to arbitration.

(4)   . . .

(5)   In sections 15 and 16 and 19 to 21 of this Act, any reference to excluding or restricting liability for breach of an obligation or duty shall include a reference to excluding or restricting the obligation or duty itself.

Bibliography

Adams, J.N., Beyleveld, D. and Brownsword, R. (1997). 'Privity of Contract—the Benefits and the Burdens of Law Reform', 60 *Modern Law Review* 238.

Beale, H. (1996). 'Customers, Chains and Networks', in Willett, C. (ed.), *Aspects of Fairness in Contract* (London: Blackstone Press).

Bianca, M.C. (2002), 'Article 3', in Grundmann, S. and Bianca, M.C. (eds.), *EU Sales Directive—Commentary* (Oxford: Intersentia).

Bradgate, R. (1991). 'Misrepresentation And Product Liability In English Law' *in* Howells, G. and Phillips, J. (eds.) *Product Liability—Anglo-American Law Review Special Edition* (Chichester: Rose).

—— (1995). 'Harmonisation of Legal Guarantees: A Common Law Perspective', *Consumer Law Journal*, 94.

—— (1997) 'Consumer Guarantees: the EC's draft Directive', *Web Journal of Current Legal Issues*, <http://webjcli.ncl.ac.uk/1997/issue1/bradgate1.html> [last accessed 27 January 1998].

—— (2000). *Commercial Law*, 3rd edition (London: Butterworths).

—— and Twigg-Flesner, C. (2002). 'Expanding the Boundaries of Liability For Quality Defects', 25 *Journal of Consumer Policy* 345–377.

—— and White, F. (1995). 'Rejection and Termination in Contracts for the Sale of Goods' in Birds, J., Bradgate, R. and Villiers, C. (eds.) *Termination of Contracts* (Chichester: Wiley Chancery).

Bridge, M. (2002), 'Article 4', in Grundmann, S. and Bianca, M.C. (eds.), *EU Sales Directive—Commentary* (Oxford: Intersentia).

Collins, H. (1999). *Regulating Contracts* (Oxford: Oxford University Press).

Cusine, D. (1980) 'Manufacturers' Guarantees and the Unfair Contract Terms Act', 25 *Juridical Review* 185

Department of Trade and Industry (DTI, 1992), *Consumer Guarantees* (London: Department of Trade and Industry).

—— (DTI, 2001a), *Consumer Knowledge Survey* (London: Department of Trade and Industry).

—— (DTI, 2001b), *Consumer Knowledge Performance Monitor* (London: Department of Trade and Industry)

Genn, H. (1999). *Paths to Justice* (Oxford: Hart Publishing).

Law Commission (1987). *Report 160—Sale and Supply of Goods* (London: Her Majesty's Stationery Office).

—— (2002), *Consultation Paper No 166—Unfair Terms in Contracts* (London: TSO).

Malinvaud, P. (2002), 'Article 6', in Grundmann, S. and Bianca, M.C. (eds.), *EU Sales Directive—Commentary* (Oxford: Intersentia).

Micklitz, H.W. (1999). 'Die Verbrauchsgüterkauf-Richtlinie', 10 *Europäische Zeitschrift für Wirtschaftsrecht* 485.

——, (2002). 'The New German Sales Law: Changing Patterns in the Regulation of Product Quality', 25 *Journal of Consumer Policy* 379–402.

Mitchell, P. (2001), 'The development of quality obligations in the sale of goods', 117 *Law Quarterly Review* 645.

National Consumer Council (NCC, 1989), *Competing in Quality* (London: NCC).

Office of Fair Trading (OFT, 1996). *Unfair Contract Terms Bulletin* 2 (London: OFT).

—— (OFT, 2000), *Consumer Detriment* (London: OFT).

—— (OFT, 2001), *OFT 311—Unfair Contract Terms Guidance* (London: OFT)

Schmidt-Kessel, M. (2000). 'Der Rückgriff des Letztverkäufers', 55 *Österreichische Juristen-Zeitung* 668–673.

Serrano, L. (2002), 'Article 1', in Grundmann, S. and Bianca, M.C. (eds.), *EU Sales Directive—Commentary* (Oxford: Intersentia).

Staudenmeyer, D. (2000), 'The Directive on the Sale of Consumer Goods and Associated Guarantees—a Milestone in the European Consumer and Private Law', 4 *European Review of Private Law* 547–564.

Twigg-Flesner, C. (1999a). 'The E.C. Directive On Certain Aspects Of The Sale Of Consumer Goods And Associated Guarantees', 7 *Consumer Law Journal* 177–192.

—— (1999b). 'Network Liability for Manufacturers' Guarantees—Remedying Legislative Shortcomings With A Legal Jigsaw', *Journal of Business Law*, 568–580.

—— (2002), 'Dissatisfaction Guaranteed? The Legal Issues of Extended Warranties Explored', *Web Journal of Current Legal Issues* <http://webjcli.ncl.ac.uk/2002/issue4/twigg-flesner4.html>.

—— (2003a), 'New Remedies for Consumer Sales Transactions: A Change for the Worse?', *Journal of Obligations and Remedies*, 5–24.

—— (2003b) *Consumer Product Guarantees* (Aldershot: Ashgate).

—— and Bradgate, R. (2000). 'The E.C. Directive On Certain Aspects of the Sale of Consumer Goods and Associated Guarantees—All Talk and No Do?', *Web Journal of Current Legal Issues* No.2 <http://webjcli.ncl.ac.uk/2000/issue2/flesner2.html> .

Watterson, S. (2001), 'Consumer Sales Directive 1999/44/EC—The impact on English law', 9 *European Review of Private Law* 197–221.

Williams, J. and Hamilton, J. (2000), 'The Impact in the UK of the EU Directive on the Sale of Consumer Goods and Associated Guarantees: Part One', *International Company and Commercial Law Review* 318.

—— and —— (2001), 'The Impact in the UK of the EU Directive on the Sale of Consumer Goods and Associated Guarantees: Part Two', *International Company and Commercial Law Review* 31.

Index